Targeting Investments in Children

A National Bureau
of Economic Research
Conference Report

Targeting Investments in Children
Fighting Poverty When Resources Are Limited

Edited by **Phillip B. Levine and David J. Zimmerman**

The University of Chicago Press

Chicago and London

PHILLIP B. LEVINE is the Class of 1919 Professor and chair of
the Department of Economics at Wellesley College, and a research
associate of the National Bureau of Economic Research. DAVID J.
ZIMMERMAN is a professor of economics and the Orrin Sage Professor
of Political Economy at Williams College, and a research associate of
the National Bureau of Economic Research.

The University of Chicago Press, Chicago 60637
The University of Chicago Press, Ltd., London
© 2010 by the National Bureau of Economic Research
All rights reserved. Published 2010
Printed in the United States of America

19 18 17 16 15 14 13 12 11 10   1 2 3 4 5
ISBN-13: 978-0-226-47581-3   (cloth)
ISBN-10: 0-226-47581-6   (cloth)

Library of Congress Cataloging-in-Publication Data

Targeting investments in children : fighting poverty when resources are
    limited / edited by Phillip B. Levine and David J. Zimmerman.
        p. cm. — (National Bureau of Economic Research conference
    report)
    Includes bibliographical references and index.
    ISBN-13: 978-0-226-47581-3 (cloth : alk. paper)
    ISBN-10: 0-226-47581-6 (cloth : alk. paper) 1. Poor children—
Services for—United States—Evaluation. 2. Child welfare—
Government policy—United States—Evaluation. 3. Federal aid to
child welfare—United States—Evaluation. 4. Economic assistance,
Domestic—United States—Evaluation. I. Levine, Phillip B. II.
Zimmerman, David J. (David John) III. Series: National Bureau of
Economic Research conference report.
    HV741.T327 2010
    362.7—dc22   2009054453

Relation of the Directors to the
Work and Publications of the
National Bureau of Economic Research

1. The object of the NBER is to ascertain and present to the economics profession, and to the public more generally, important economic facts and their interpretation in a scientific manner without policy recommendations. The Board of Directors is charged with the responsibility of ensuring that the work of the NBER is carried on in strict conformity with this object.

2. The President shall establish an internal review process to ensure that book manuscripts proposed for publication DO NOT contain policy recommendations. This shall apply both to the proceedings of conferences and to manuscripts by a single author or by one or more co-authors but shall not apply to authors of comments at NBER conferences who are not NBER affiliates.

3. No book manuscript reporting research shall be published by the NBER until the President has sent to each member of the Board a notice that a manuscript is recommended for publication and that in the President's opinion it is suitable for publication in accordance with the above principles of the NBER. Such notification will include a table of contents and an abstract or summary of the manuscript's content, a list of contributors if applicable, and a response form for use by Directors who desire a copy of the manuscript for review. Each manuscript shall contain a summary drawing attention to the nature and treatment of the problem studied and the main conclusions reached.

4. No volume shall be published until forty-five days have elapsed from the above notification of intention to publish it. During this period a copy shall be sent to any Director requesting it, and if any Director objects to publication on the grounds that the manuscript contains policy recommendations, the objection will be presented to the author(s) or editor(s). In case of dispute, all members of the Board shall be notified, and the President shall appoint an ad hoc committee of the Board to decide the matter; thirty days additional shall be granted for this purpose.

5. The President shall present annually to the Board a report describing the internal manuscript review process, any objections made by Directors before publication or by anyone after publication, any disputes about such matters, and how they were handled.

6. Publications of the NBER issued for informational purposes concerning the work of the Bureau, or issued to inform the public of the activities at the Bureau, including but not limited to the NBER Digest and Reporter, shall be consistent with the object stated in paragraph 1. They shall contain a specific disclaimer noting that they have not passed through the review procedures required in this resolution. The Executive Committee of the Board is charged with the review of all such publications from time to time.

7. NBER working papers and manuscripts distributed on the Bureau's web site are not deemed to be publications for the purpose of this resolution, but they shall be consistent with the object stated in paragraph 1. Working papers shall contain a specific disclaimer noting that they have not passed through the review procedures required in this resolution. The NBER's web site shall contain a similar disclaimer. The President shall establish an internal review process to ensure that the working papers and the web site do not contain policy recommendations, and shall report annually to the Board on this process and any concerns raised in connection with it.

8. Unless otherwise determined by the Board or exempted by the terms of paragraphs 6 and 7, a copy of this resolution shall be printed in each NBER publication as described in paragraph 2 above.

Contents

IV. ADOLESCENT INTERVENTIONS

V. EPILOGUE

Preface

Unlike many academic exercises, this project did not start out primarily as an intellectual inquiry, but rather as a practical one. We were first approached by the Robin Hood Foundation in 2003,and asked to provide input regarding their spending decisions. The charity, based in New York City, spends $100 million or more each year in the city to promote the goal of fighting poverty. A hallmark of Robin Hood's pioneering approach is to evaluate potential antipoverty strategies in much the same way that a financial manager would choose investments with an eye to maximizing profits. The objectives differ, but the need to carefully assess benefits and costs is the same. Robin Hood reached out to us at the time seeking additional input into the procedures that formed the backbone of its "Metrics Project."[1] That initial contact led to a relationship that is still ongoing and was the genesis of this volume.

Throughout our relationship, we have shared a common vision that money should be spent in a manner that delivers the most return on the investment made. In this instance, if the only policy objective is poverty reduction, then money spent attempting to reduce poverty should generate the most poverty reduction possible. If not, it can be spent more efficiently. If resources dedicated to one program can be reallocated to another program and reduce poverty by more, it should be done.

The question then becomes how one does that. The contents of this volume provide an indication of our thoughts on this. Clearly, we favor a strongly evidence-based approach. Promise is one thing, but results are another. This does not mean that we should never experiment with new programs, but that is a different goal. That said, all evidence is not created

---

1. This approach is well-formulated in their publication, *Measuring Success: How Robin Hood Estimates the Impact of Grants,* which was written in 2009 by Michael M. Weinstein with the assistance of Cynthia Esposito Lamy.

equal; the approach we describe in this book emphasizes our preference to rely on the strongest evidence possible.

After a number of years of working with Robin Hood, we felt the desire to broaden the reach of our work. We proposed that we organize a conference, bringing some of the leading scholars on each topical area together. We proposed that this conference would lead to this edited volume, summarizing all of the thinking and synthesizing the results. Robin Hood strongly supported our vision, and we are extremely grateful for its support, both financial and otherwise, in seeing this project through to fruition.

We are particularly grateful to Michael Weinstein, the senior vice president at Robin Hood. We have worked effectively with Michael throughout our relationship with Robin Hood. He has always challenged us to go that one additional step in thinking through the issues, both in our work for the charity and in the execution of this project. This work would not have been possible without his contributions. Cindy Esposito Lamy is a member of Robin Hood's staff of experts who also contributed to the effort; we would like to express our thanks to her.

No project of this nature can be undertaken without the help and support of many other people. Marty Feldstein and Jim Poterba, the former and current presidents of the National Bureau of Economic Research (NBER), were big supporters of this project from its inception. The NBER conference department did an outstanding job organizing both a preconference in Cambridge and the final conference in New York City. David Pervin at the University of Chicago Press helped guide the book through their review and production processes, and Helena Fitz-Patrick helped coordinate the production of the book at the NBER. Finally, we recognize the contributions that our families have made in providing the supportive environment that enabled us to complete this work. Our thanks to all.

I

Prologue

Introduction

Phillip B. Levine and David J. Zimmerman

It is not difficult to motivate attempts to reduce childhood poverty. Living in poverty is a distressing outcome for any individual, but our compassion is that much greater when that individual is a child. Children living in poverty are more likely to experience developmental problems, attend inferior schools, and suffer from poor health. The difficulties they face as children may carry into their adult years, resulting in poor educational, labor market, and physical and mental health outcomes. They are subject to all of those risks through no fault of their own.

An alarming number of American children experience poverty. Although defining poverty is a difficult task, formal government statistics indicate that almost 13 million children lived in poverty in 2006, comprising about 17 percent of the population of those under the age of 18.[1] Although that rate ebbs and flows over time, the extent of childhood poverty is about the same today as it was thirty years ago. Moreover, children in particular demographic groups experience even higher poverty rates. Fully one-third of black, non-Hispanic children and over one-quarter of Hispanic children lived in poverty in 2006. As extreme as these figures are, they have fallen from close to half of black, non-Hispanic children and 40 percent of Hispanic children as recently as the early 1990s.

Among economically developed countries, the United States stands as an outlier with child poverty rates that are considerably higher than elsewhere.

Phillip B. Levine is the Class of 1919 Professor and chair of the department of economics at Wellesley College, and a research associate of the National Bureau of Economic Research. David J. Zimmerman is a professor of economics and Orrin Sage Professor of Political Economy at Williams College, and a research associate of the National Bureau of Economic Research.

1. Statistics regarding child poverty in the United States were obtained from the U.S. Census Bureau (2007) and from the historical statistics on their Web page at http://www.census.gov/hhes/www/poverty/histpov/hstpov3.html.

Using a somewhat different measure to that reported earlier, one recent study found child poverty rates of 21.9 percent in the United States. The next highest set of countries, including Australia, Canada, Ireland, Italy, Spain, and the United Kingdom had rates that were in the vicinity of 15 to 16 percent.[2] Levels of child poverty in a number of countries, including Denmark, France, Germany, and Switzerland, are less than 10 percent. Childhood poverty is particularly an American problem. If children "outgrew" the problem, then perhaps the high rates of childhood poverty in the United States would be less of a concern. We have many legends of prominent Americans who started out with nothing and rose to great levels of success, both economically and otherwise, despite the obstacles they faced.[3] Although these success stories certainly exist, they are not so common as to alleviate our concern that those who start out with very little do not have the same chance of success as others.

In fact, research on the question of intergenerational income mobility suggests that those who begin life on the bottom of the economic ladder have a very difficult time climbing up it over their lives. Recent research has found that the correlation in income between parents and their children is on the order of 0.6 (c.f. Bowles and Gintis 2002; and Mazumder 2005). Mazumder (2005) provides a useful way to describe the implications of this statistic: "Consider a family of four with two children whose income is right at the poverty threshold . . . It will take the descendants of the family five to six generations (125 to 150 years) before their income would be within 5 percent of the national average" (235). Needless to say, typical children who grow up in poverty are likely to experience economic difficulties throughout their lives.

Is it possible to jumpstart this process? Can we identify ways to help poor children that will enable them to overcome the obstacles they face at the beginning of their lives so that they will be more successful later in their lives? The idea of doing so is an old one. A well-known proverb states: "Give a man a fish; you have fed him for today. Teach a man to fish, and you have fed him for a lifetime." One way to "solve" the problem of childhood poverty is to give money to their families. Another way is to make the investments necessary that would enable the children to succeed—teach them to fish. If we choose the latter approach, the question then becomes what investments should we make?

The policy world is full of ideas to help children overcome the obstacles they face in life. Advocacy groups routinely form around a particular type

2. International statistics on child poverty were obtained from Mishel, Bernstein, and Allegretto (2006).

3. In fact, one can read about many of them at the Web site of the Horatio Alger Association of Distinguished Americans (www.horatioalger.com). This organization is "dedicated to the simple but powerful belief that hard work, honesty and determination can conquer all obstacles."

of activity and devote a tremendous amount of effort in fundraising to support that activity and to lobby for governmental support to fund it as well. A Google search for children's advocacy groups will quickly lead one to organizations like the Center on Education Policy, the National Institute on Out-of-School Time, the National Campaign to Prevent Teen Pregnancy, or the National Association for the Education of Young Children. These institutions and the many others out there like them are all dedicated to helping children overcome a particular obstacle. Whether the focus is early childhood education, child care, education policy, teen pregnancy prevention, or otherwise, the idea is that investing resources in that goal will help improve the lives of America's youth and, particularly, those who start out disadvantaged.

The problem with this is that resources are limited. If society had an unlimited capacity to support every policy that was directed at helping children with disadvantaged backgrounds, then spending money on all of them may make sense. Unfortunately, that is not the case. In reality, the funds available to be directed toward this purpose are scarce. Our real goal is not to promote the policy, but to help the kids. This behooves us to think about which types of intervention are the most effective and then to dedicate our resources in that direction to best accomplish our goal.[4]

This is not a simple task. Conceptually, the idea of devoting resources in the direction to which they are most effective makes perfect sense. In practice, it is not obvious how to identify the most effective interventions. A primary limitation is that it is not always easy to identify the effectiveness of any intervention. For instance, programs typically enroll children, provide them with services, and then see how they do sometime in the future. An important problem in evaluating the effectiveness of programs like this is that those children who choose to enroll are not randomly selected. If they (or their parents) are sufficiently motivated to identify programs that may help them, then they may have what it takes to do well on their own even without entering the program. The fact that participants may end up with greater success than others does not tell us anything about the program's effectiveness.

Even if we are able to circumvent this problem, we are still left with the difficult task of comparing the effectiveness across programs. The fundamental limitation in this regard is that program effectiveness is often measured in totally different ways across types of interventions. Education reforms may be considered successful if they improve test scores. Teen pregnancy prevention programs are designed to reduce teen pregnancies. Programs that provide college preparatory services are successful if they get more students

---

4. The goal and methods of this exercise is philosophically similar to that of the *Copenhagen Consensus* (Lomborg 2004), which focused on addressing pressing issues facing the world, including poverty, the environment, education, public health, and the like.

to enroll in college. How does one compare the relative effectiveness of these programs?

One of the (perhaps unenviable) tasks of this volume is to tackle these thorny issues. The bottom line is that there is no perfect way to do so. If we were constrained to only address questions that we felt we could answer with complete confidence, we would not be able to undertake this exercise. There is no doubt that the approach we adopt will be open to criticism. Nevertheless, we believe that the questions raised are too important and the stakes are too high to simply throw up our hands and ignore the fact that decisions need to be made and funds need to be spent to support the goal of helping children escape from poverty. Our goal is to implement methods that are the best we are able to generate to provide the best possible answers, recognizing that there are limitations to our analysis.

In fact, we begin our analysis in chapter 1 by detailing a number of the complicated issues and our approach to addressing them in the analysis to follow. Chapter 1 lays out a number of specific challenges that we face in structuring this analysis, broken down into two main categories. First, we discuss a set of issues about "targeting" because they define the target at which we are shooting. What is the subpopulation of poor people that we will focus on? What do we consider success? Who are we seeking to benefit, the individual or society more broadly? The second set of issues we address relate to how we will evaluate the evidence. What evidence "counts"? Does the scale of the program matter? What outcomes are considered?

The answers to each of these questions are not obvious. We have made specific decisions to address them, which we believe are necessary to define the project in such a way that it can be executed. In that discussion, we justify why we chose to make those decisions, but we also recognize that some may disagree with them. It is our hope that such disagreements will spur additional research activity that will help further the goal of identifying the most effective interventions.

Once we have addressed these issues of implementation, we then present a review of a number of different types of interventions. The interventions we chose to examine cover the most common types and, particularly, those for which solid empirical evidence exists regarding their effectiveness. The federal government expends substantial funds to provide some of them, including Head Start, Pell Grants, the State Children's Health Insurance Program (SCHIP), among others. Other interventions that we examine are provided by state and local governments along with the private, nonprofit sector.

We categorize these interventions by the age of the target population: early childhood, middle childhood, and adolescence. The early childhood interventions that we consider are early childhood education, child care, and child health. In middle childhood, we review interventions in after-school care and education reforms (like school choice and vouchers, class size, etc.) The biggest category is adolescent interventions, which spans the horizon from drug prevention, teen pregnancy prevention, dropout prevention and college preparatory services, college aid, neighborhood initiatives, and vocational training. This section of the book will occupy chapters 2 through 12.

We are fortunate to be able to draw from the expertise of individuals who have spent their careers studying these interventions. Each chapter is authored by an expert or team of experts who know the specific type of intervention and the literature examining its impact backward and forward. The structure of each of these chapters is identical. The authors will motivate why the intervention may help, provide some background regarding its implementation in practice, and then review the literature assessing its effectiveness. Where appropriate, they will also provide input regarding their thoughts on how programs of that type may be improved or how future evaluations should be conducted.

These chapters, taken as a whole, will be of tremendous value to the policy-making community simply by cataloging so many different types of interventions and evaluating the evidence of their effectiveness on their own terms. Most analyses focus on one intervention at a time and raise the victory flag if they are able to find that the program provided benefits, particularly if they are greater than their costs. The availability of the breadth of interventions reviewed, all in a similar format, greatly facilitates the review process.

The results of the analyses in each of these chapters will then be used as inputs into a methodology that will synthesize them and enable us to compare across interventions. Chapter 13 will provide the specifics of this approach and describe the results of our analysis. The trick here is to find a common metric so that the effects of these programs can be compared. Again, some programs will measure success using standardized test scores, others will focus on high school graduation, and still others by the number of pregnancies prevented. It will be our job in this chapter to introduce our approach for comparing across outcomes.

The basic idea is to convert each of these outcomes to their impact on the adult earnings of program participants. Consider, for instance, a school reform program that improves the reading and math test scores of its participants. We can use outside information regarding the relationship between reading and math test scores in school to subsequent earnings to convert the program's impact. We do that for every outcome to which we have access so that all interventions are judged on a single metric—impact on adult earnings. Clearly, there are a number of specific issues involved in implementing this approach: we will document those in chapter 13 as well before presenting the results of our analysis.

Besides the value in unifying measured outcomes, this approach also is useful because adult earnings may be a better metric for assessing program impacts anyway. We may value improved test scores, for instance, for their own ends because we believe there are benefits to having a better-educated society. But clearly another important goal, as we have described earlier, is the alleviation of poverty later in life among children who grow up facing economic disadvantage. It is the greater subsequent economic success that those higher test scores may generate that better reflects the accomplishment of that goal.

This is not to say that economic success later in life is the only goal that we believe is important. Although it is difficult to compare child health to test scores, for instance, child health is clearly an important outcome in its own right. As a society we certainly value it. Our goal in standardizing outcomes is not because of our failure to recognize other outcomes, but because it is so difficult to compare them. Indeed, the authors of each chapter focusing on specific types of interventions include discussions about the impact on earnings as well as other outcomes, where appropriate. It is only when we go to synthesize the results that our focus turns exclusively to earnings.

It is also important to recognize how this study compares to past analyses. Moffitt (2003) provides an extensive review of a number of means-tested transfer programs and evaluates their effects. Our work is different than that partly because not all interventions are part of large government programs and because a formal benefit-cost analysis is not a goal of that work. Currie (2006) also focuses on governmental programs exclusively and evaluates the role that they play in assessing contemporaneous child well-being. Our goal is to evaluate program effectiveness at reducing subsequent poverty in adulthood.

The work that is most closely related to ours is that of Heckman and co-authors, who have done some excellent work in this area (cf. Carneiro and Heckman 2003; Cunha et al. 2006; and Cunha and Heckman 2007). He and his coauthors usefully place an important emphasis on the dynamics of human capital accumulation—early human capital improvements foster later improvements—suggesting that early interventions usually trump later interventions. He also emphasizes the importance (and likely feasibility) of nurturing noncognitive traits.

Yet we believe that this volume will make important contributions beyond those of Heckman and coauthors' work. First, we plan to provide a review of a greater variety of program types and more extensive reviews of those programs. Heckman and coauthors' approach is to use the evidence from these programs to examine his broader focus on the dynamics of human capital accumulation and in evaluating the role of noncognitive skills. Their evaluation of program effects is more of an overview, spending less time delving into the details of the interventions and the existing literature related to their outcomes. Our objectives are much more pragmatic, attempting to identify programs that "work."

Second, our goal is much more narrowly targeted at finding the best ways to reduce poverty in adulthood among those who grow up disadvantaged, and this is captured in our benefit-cost analysis. We focus on program impacts on subsequent earnings, whereas Heckman and coauthors' approach is more broad-based in measuring benefits. It is this narrower focus on poverty reduction in adulthood that pushes the need to take greater empirical "risks" in our benefit-cost analysis.

The results of our analysis indicate that there are a number of different types of programs that have been found to improve children's outcomes in ways that would lead to subsequent poverty reduction. Chapter 13 describes the complete results of our analysis, but table I.1 summarizes our findings.

In table I.1, we distinguish programs into three distinct categories. In the first category, we identify those programs for which there is little conclusive evidence that these programs are able to alter children's outcomes in any dimension. This is not to say that they do not work, but rather that the evidence supporting their efficacy is limited. One particular example is school vouchers and school choice programs. In this case, evidence is available that shows that these programs do not alter children's educational outcomes much. Alternatively, after-school programs may be effective, but the evidence supporting this position is sufficiently weak that more work is needed before we would be able to conclude anything stronger. The details supporting our decisions for placing these programs into this category can be found in the relevant chapters later in this volume.

The second category includes those programs that have been found to be effective in changing outcomes for children and teens, but not in a way that is likely to alter their poverty status. Included in this category are child care, child health, and teen pregnancy prevention. The research reviewed in the relevant chapters of this volume indicates that they are all effective in certain dimensions. For instance, child care policies have been shown to effectively enable mothers to work, but the translation into benefits to the children in their poverty status down the road is limited. Some teen pregnancy prevention programs have been able to reduce the teen

Table I.1   **Summary of results**

Programs with limited evidence of effectiveness	Programs that are difficult to link to poverty reduction	Programs that can be linked to poverty reduction
Parenting programs	Child care	Early childhood education
Vouchers/school choice	Child health	Mentoring programs
After-school programs	Teen pregnancy prevention	Class size reduction
Dropout prevention programs	Housing voucher/mobility programs	Curriculum reforms
Substance abuse programs		Teacher training
General jobs programs		Increased teacher pay
Employment/training subsidies		College aid
		Intensive vocational training

pregnancy rate but do not appear to be likely to alter those teens' subsequent poverty status.

The final category includes those programs that have been found to alter children's outcomes in a way that can be linked to poverty reduction. These programs have been found effective using methods strong enough to support their link to poverty reduction. Again, the details that indicate this is the appropriate column for placing these programs are found in the relevant chapters later in the volume. Our discussion in chapter 13 takes the analysis of these programs one step further by comparing the impact on subsequent earnings per $1,000 invested in each program. Most of them generate between $2,000 and $5,000 in lifetime earnings (in present discounted value terms) for the $1,000 investment. We interpret the exact values of these returns later in this volume, but for now it is appropriate to conclude that they each pass a basic benefit-cost comparison test even when the benefits are narrowly defined to be lifetime earnings of the participants.

In looking at table I.1, one conclusion that comes to mind is that almost all the programs that seem to be effective are the ones that directly attack human capital attainment. Programs that are really designed to focus on a different problem that may then have a subsequent impact on human capital attainment do not appear to do that job. This makes sense to us. A teen pregnancy prevention program may reduce the likelihood that teens get pregnant. But that reduction is going to be relatively small as a share of the whole group. If we could prevent an additional 10 percent of teens from becoming pregnant, this would be a huge accomplishment. This means, though, that 90 percent of the population has no change in their circumstances. Of the 10 percent who remain child-free, the earnings impact would have to be huge in order for it to have much of an effect on group average outcomes. This is simply unlikely to occur. Teen pregnancy prevention programs and others targeted at other outcomes may be desirable for other reasons, but it is going to be very hard for them to have much of an impact on broader measures of poverty.

That is not to say that all direct human capital interventions will be successful either. Traditional jobs programs that find employment for underprivileged youth and employment and training subsidies that offer small increments to an individual's human capital have not been found to be effective for the population of individuals (and men, in particular) transitioning into adulthood. Only intensive interventions, like Job Corps and Career Academies seem to be able to make the difference. These programs have the potential to improve participants' human capital considerably, albeit at a relatively high cost.

Among those programs that are found to be effective, we see one other interesting pattern. Most are direct human capital interventions, but they are not necessarily tilted to younger children. The emphasis on human capital is consistent with Heckman and coauthors' work that we have described earlier. But it is not consistent with their implication that investing at younger ages works better. Their notion that "skill begets skill" would suggest that early childhood interventions should dominate the rest of the group because the improvements in human capital at early ages will compound as the child ages. As we show in chapter 13, we do not see such an age profile in the estimated earnings impact per $1,000 investment in each type of program. Interventions at older ages, including college aid, appear to be at least as effective as early childhood interventions.

The remainder of this volume provides the details regarding the methods we used to arrive at these conclusions, along with an extensive review of all of the programs. After completely presenting the evidence, we will return to these conclusions in chapter 14 and provide some further thoughts regarding interpretation. Overall, we view our contribution as a starting point rather than the final word for thinking about appropriate methods of allocating scarce resources to the goal of reducing poverty. This goal is important enough that spending the money wisely is worth the effort.

References

Bowles, Samuel, and Herbert Gintis. 2002. The Inheritance of inequality. *Journal of Economic Perspectives* 16 (3): 3–30.

Carneiro, P., and J. Heckman. 2003. Human capital policies. In *Inequality in America: What role for human capital policies?*, ed. J. J. Heckman, A. B. Kruger, and B. M. Friedman, 77–239. Cambridge, MA: MIT Press.

Cunha, F., and J. J. Heckman. 2007. The technology of skill formation. *American Economic Review* 97 (2): 31–47.

Cunha, F., J. J. Heckman, L. Lochner, and D. Masterov. 2006. Interpreting the evidence on life cycle skill formation. In *Handbook of the economics of education,* ed. E. Hanushek and F. Welch, 697–812. Amsterdam: North Holland.

Currie, Janet M. 2006. *The invisible safety net: Protecting the nation's poor children and families.* Princeton, NJ: Princeton University Press.

Lomborg, Bjørn. 2004. *Global crises, global solutions.* Cambridge, UK: Cambridge University Press.

Mazumder, Bhashkar. 2005. Fortunate sons: New estimates of intergenerational mobility in the United States using Social Security earnings data. *Review of Economics and Statistics* 87 (2): 235–55.

Mishel, Lawrence, Jared Bernstein, and Sylvia Allegretto. 2006. *The state of working America, 2006/2007.* Ithaca, NY: ILR Press.

Moffitt, Robert A., ed. 2003. *Means-tested transfer programs in the United States.* Chicago: University of Chicago Press.

U.S. Census Bureau. 2007. *Income, poverty, and health insurance coverage in the United States: 2006.* Washington, DC: U.S. Government Printing Office.

1

Issues in Implementation

Phillip B. Levine and David J. Zimmerman

1.1 Introduction

As we described in the introduction to this volume, the goal of this exercise is to identify the childhood interventions that are most successful at alleviating subsequent poverty. Although this goal is straightforward in theory, its implementation in practice raises a number of difficulties. It raises a number of conceptual issues that need to be resolved to better frame the scope of the exercise. It also raises a number of empirical issues regarding the specific approach we will use to be able to measure interventions along a scale of success. These specific empirical issues are addressed directly in chapter 13; this chapter focuses on those issues that are more conceptual in nature.

We begin by describing the specific questions we will be able to address and which ones we will leave for further, future analysis. We label these "targeting" issues because they define the target that we are shooting at. What is the subpopulation of poor people that we will focus on? What do we consider success? Who are we seeking to benefit, the individual or society more broadly? The first part of the chapter will more fully describe these issues and describe our approach to resolve them in the subsequent analysis.

This chapter will also address an additional set of conceptual issues that will affect the implementation of our analysis. Broadly speaking, we will consider the standards to be used in culling information from the broad array of program evaluations that have been conducted. We call these "empirical evaluation issues," and our resolution of them will define the way that we

Phillip B. Levine is the Class of 1919 Professor and chair of the department of economics at Wellesley College, and a research associate of the National Bureau of Economic Research. David J. Zimmerman is a professor of economics and Orrin Sage Professor of Political Economy at Williams College, and a research associate of the National Bureau of Economic Research.

plan to incorporate the results of previous research. What evidence counts? Does the scale of the evaluation matter? Which outcomes should we consider? The second part of the chapter will focus on these issues and resolve how we will address them subsequently.

Our approach in this chapter will be to specify individual, substantive challenges that we face that require specific decisions to be made in order to organize the remainder of the study. The decisions we have made are by no means the definitively correct ones. It is certainly possible to question any or all of them. We recognize that there are counterarguments to many of those that we make in supporting our decisions; in fact, we engaged in many of those arguments in the process of formulating this volume. But we also recognize that decisions need to be made to narrow the scope of the exercise sufficiently so that we can arrive at a useful and informative final product. We believe we have made the best ones to meet the needs of our particular analysis.

1.2   Targeting Issues

Targeting issues refer to the scope of the exercise that we seek to conduct. We need to limit its scope because addressing all of the potential issues would quickly overload any productive evaluation. This section will identify those challenges and describe the decisions we have made to resolve them in this volume.

1.2.1   Challenge 1: What Is the Relevant Subpopulation?

Our broad goal is to evaluate the effectiveness of policies designed to help improve the future economic success of the poor. The first challenge that we face in implementing that goal is deciding what we mean by "the poor." The poor is a multifarious group; different policy interventions focus on different subsets of that group. Do we focus on all poor people? Perhaps at a more basic level, we need to decide what we mean by poor. Who is poor?

This latter question turns out to be the one that is easier to answer. One way to address the problem of who is poor is to rely on national standards incorporated into the poverty line. If you are below the poverty line, you are poor, and if you are above it, you are not. Yet the poverty line is not necessarily a perfect indicator of who is poor; it has been widely criticized in the past.[1] If we jettison that definition, we are restricted to more ambiguous concepts. We could, for instance, focus on the most destitute (the homeless?) or perhaps the working poor.

In practice, we take a more pragmatic approach to addressing this challenge. The core of our analysis is an examination of policy interventions that have been conducted attempting to reduce poverty through alternative

poverty line (handwritten margin note)

1. See Blank (2008) for a useful discussion regarding the measurement of poverty.

mechanisms. Each of those interventions struggled with this issue of the target population. Because our analysis simply synthesizes the results of those analyses, we are bound by the earlier decisions made by past analysts. These decisions generally have not led to a focus on the working poor or the most destitute, but to a broader population of low-income households. Throughout the remainder of our discussion, we will use the term "poverty" as a synonym for low income and not according to its more formal definition.

Now that we have "defined" who is poor (where our definition will just rely on those incorporated into past policy interventions), we need to address whether we want to focus on particular subgroups of the poor. The issues and needs of different groups of poor individuals differ, and policy interventions attacking them take very different approaches. Addressing all of them would be quite an undertaking.

One way that we have chosen to cut down the scope of the exercise is to limit the set of policies we consider to those targeted at those who are young. We explore interventions that focus on the early childhood years, the primary school years, the secondary school years, and the very early adult years (into the early twenties). Our rationale for doing so is two-pronged. From a practical perspective, low-income children are the focus of a large number of policy interventions. This group appears to enjoy greater political support, which is needed to have funds moved in their direction. The willingness to spend resources to support low-income adults wanes in the face of their potential to support themselves. The sweeping welfare reform legislation in 1996 is an example of this. Interventions targeted at children may be more popular because it is "not their fault" that they are poor. For whatever reason, one reason to focus on low income children is that they are the target of more interventions. It just makes more sense to look where the light is shining.

We can justify the focus on interventions targeted at low-income children from a broader, conceptual framework as well, imbedding this decision within a human capital framework. From this viewpoint, investments in children make more sense because any persistent benefit from such an intervention will accrue for a longer time. In fact, James Heckman, along with different coauthors (Carneiro and Heckman 2003; Cunha et al. 2006; Cunha and Heckman 2007), has made this a cornerstone of one of his recent research agendas. He takes the human capital perspective to the extreme, arguing that interventions should target the youngest of the poor population. Skill begets skill, from his viewpoint, and early, effective interventions generate the equivalent of compound interest on the investment return. We are sympathetic to this message but prefer to take a less philosophical approach, letting the data tell us exactly where the greatest returns are found. We are willing, however, to use the human capital perspective to justify focusing our attention on interventions directed at the young.

Where is the focus? (handwritten margin note)

1.2.2   Challenge 2: What Do We Consider Success?

Policy interventions designed to help the poor often have different goals. Some target their health (mental or physical). Others attempt to improve their safety, making them more secure in their environment. Still others attempt to improve their economic conditions. Among those focusing on economic well-being, some interventions identify short-term improvements as the goal, whereas others emphasize long-term gains in economic standing.

All of these goals are important, tackling a different aspect of the ways in which we can improve the well-being of the poor. If the poor do not have access to adequate health care, their health may suffer and reduce their quality of life. Similar arguments can be made regarding personal safety. Quality of life surely suffers if one is victimized by a violent act or even if one is so worried about victimization that daily activities are modified to reduce its likelihood. Improving one's economic circumstances can help improve these aspects of quality of life as well as others. But policies directed at immediate economic remediation may require repeated interventions to alleviate the problem. Other policies that offer longer-term economic gains may do nothing to resolve current deficits but may reduce the need for subsequent interventions.

In our analysis, we focus our attention on the policy impact on longer-term economic success as the relevant outcome measure. In particular, we consider the adult earnings levels of the poor children who are the targets of the policy interventions considered. This is not to say that other outcome measures are not important; clearly, they are. Yet again, we make this decision because we believe that incorporating all forms of outcomes would quickly overwhelm the analysis.

Consider what would be needed to fully evaluate the totality of the impact of an early childhood education program, for example. Suppose that the program is successful in a number of dimensions. It improves educational performance of the students, enhances their "soft skills" through their ability to communicate and deal effectively with others. The students are more likely to go on to college and get better jobs. All of this shows up in the higher wages that the participants subsequently receive. Incorporating all of this into a measure of success has some pitfalls, but is something we hope to accomplish in this volume.

How do we measure? (handwritten margin note)

Now consider the other effects. Suppose the intervention enhances the child's nutritional status so that he or she is less likely to be overweight, which reduces the likelihood of juvenile diabetes and its health implications both today and, potentially, for the rest of the child's life. How do we measure that? The child may learn better coping mechanisms for the violence going on outside his or her home, or perhaps the child's success prompts the family to move to a safer neighborhood. The improved safety results in a lower likelihood of exposure to violence, which improves the child's emotional well-being. How do we measure that? We could continue by providing additional examples, but we believe the point is clear that these other relevant and important outcomes are a lot more difficult to incorporate into our analysis. It is very difficult, if not impossible, to find ways to measure these outcomes in a way that would enable us to compare across interventions.

Instead, we simply choose not to do so and focus on the long-term economic success that these programs may generate. This is not to diminish the value of studying these other outcomes. In fact, in each of the subsequent chapters focusing on specific interventions, authors have included discussions of these other outcomes, where appropriate, in their reviews of the evidence. We simply focus on earnings as an outcome when we move on to synthesize the results later in the volume.

It is important to recognize the implications of our decisions here for interpreting the results of our analysis. What we will be left with in the end is one or more interventions that would appear to provide a greater ability to improve children's economic standing when they become adults. We believe that this is a useful piece of information that should definitely be used in policy discussions.

On the other hand, it would be unwise to base policy judgments purely on this piece of information. Other factors may come into play that are useful as well. Consider two alternative programs. The first one reduces long-term poverty among children, and the second one has no such effect. The second one, however, will reduce the likelihood of asthma attacks and obesity for the remainder of the child's life relative to the first one. Which program should be supported? We believe that we are not even close to being in a position to answer a question like that, so we choose to avoid the question. The question that we are more confident we can answer is the narrow one regarding the impact on subsequent wages, that is, the question on which we focus.

1.2.3   Challenge 3: Whose Benefit Matters?

This challenge is related to the last one, but we believe that a full discussion of the issue would usefully inform the reader regarding the contribution of our analysis, despite some overlap. The issue at hand here is whether our measure of success is one that focuses exclusively on the target population or whether the real beneficiary is society more broadly. As we just discussed, policy interventions can benefit the target population in a number of ways (health, safety, current income, subsequent earnings, etc.). But each of these benefits to the target population bring along external benefits to society more broadly.

Consider, for example, an intervention that reduces the likelihood that a child will commit crime. That program may benefit the child because he or she is more likely to lead a productive life and less likely to endure the difficulties associated with incarceration. But the crimes that would be avoided as a result of the program would result in benefits to society more broadly. Others would be less likely to be victimized, and expenditures for the police and corrections department could be reduced. These are benefits that are received by society, but not by the individual.

Standard economic terminology uses the terms "private benefits" and "external benefits" to distinguish these concepts. Private benefits are those that are received by the individual participating in the program him- or herself. External benefits are those that are received by others beyond the program participant.

Benefit-cost analyses frequently rely on the external benefits, particularly when the government is attempting to determine whether a program is "working." Job training programs are designed to place workers into jobs that they would not have obtained otherwise. The private benefit is the higher earnings that the worker would receive relative to what they would have received had they not entered the program. The external benefit is the additional tax revenue that the incremental earnings would generate. From a societal perspective, the job training program is "worth it" if it can pay for itself—the tax revenue generated is greater than the cost of the spot in the training program. Any program that can substantially reduce the likelihood of crime is likely to be "worth it" because crime is so costly to society. This general approach is one that is exemplified by Karoly (1998). It makes sense from a government accounting standpoint where spending money on programs that generate more revenue or cost savings than the intervention costs is clearly desirable.

Our perspective is somewhat different. We want to know the most effective ways to help poor children pull themselves out of poverty by adulthood. The government is looking for a return on its investment based on its budget or on social welfare more broadly. But consider an alternative perspective where a certain amount of money is set aside to help poor children, and we want to get the most return on that investment in the form of subsequent poverty reduction. We would focus on the private return to the individual.

That does not mean that the external benefits to society more broadly are not important. They are, and they may play a role in the process of policy determination. Where appropriate, individual chapters will discuss the external benefits that are generated by specific interventions, but that will not be part of the broader comparison across interventions.

One justification for the approach that we are taking here is that it clarifies the issue of who is being helped by the policy. For instance, beneficiaries of interventions that reduce crime may be individuals who are not poor. Distributional issues like these are relevant but are typically not included in program evaluations. Our approach also helps narrow the scope of the exercise so that we are left with an "answerable" question. What types of policies targeted at poor children result in the greatest reduction in subsequent poverty? That is the question we will answer.

1.3   Empirical Evaluation Issues

The types of programs that we will explore in this book have been the subject of a tremendous amount of research. Reviewing the full body of evidence on any one intervention would be a substantial undertaking, let alone doing so for the array of interventions that we examine. In addition, any synthesis across interventions requires that common ground be established regarding their measured effectiveness. In this section of the chapter, we elaborate on the specific issues we face and the decisions we have made to resolve them.

1.3.1   Challenge 4: What Evidence "Counts"?

Previous research examining the types of interventions on which we focus in this analysis has adopted numerous methodologies in determining program impacts. The first type of study simply compares outcomes for program participants before and after the intervention. We call this approach "non-experimental." This technique is seriously flawed because it does nothing to hold constant the fact that participants who volunteer for the program are not necessarily representative of children from lower-income households. In particular, they are likely to be from households that are more motivated to overcome the obstacles they face. These children are likely to be the ones who would have done well anyway. If we see that outcomes improved for these children after they participated in the program, this does not necessarily tell us that the program had any impact.

What we really want to know is how a program would do with a typical child from a low-income household. It is the ability to properly answer this question that is the key to an effective evaluation. An effective methodology needs to be able to take a child who would have had one set of outcomes if he or she did not participate in the program and distinguish whether he or she experienced a different set of outcomes because of the intervention itself. This is what is needed to show that the program had a *causal* impact on the child. This is where a lot of previous research stumbles.

Another methodology that suffers from this problem is the use of comparison groups. This approach attempts to determine what would have happened to program participants had they not participated in the program by selecting a different group of children who do not participate in the program and comparing their outcomes. This is the right idea in that we need to know a counterfactual; this approach attempts to establish a counterfactual. The problem is that it is very difficult, if not impossible, to find perfect matches in a comparison group for those in the program. Outcomes for the two groups would need to have been similar in the absence of the intervention for this approach to work. But if program participation is voluntary, then we already know of one important difference between the two groups—one was willing to participate. If they are different in this important dimension, they are likely to be different in other important dimensions as well. This makes it very hard to attribute causality to differences in outcomes between program participants and members of a comparison group.

Multiple regression analysis is another approach that researchers sometimes use to compare children whose outcomes would have been otherwise similar. In a multiple regression, researchers specify a dependent variable, which reflects children's outcomes (like test scores). They also specify a relevant independent variable (like program participation), and they want to know whether that variable has an impact on the dependent variable. The key to a multiple regression is that the researcher can also specify any number of other independent variables (demographic factors, geography, etc.) that are held constant in estimating the impact of the relevant independent variable (program participation) on the dependent variable (test scores). In theory, this would be quite an effective technique for identifying a causal impact of an intervention on children's outcomes. If we can hold constant the things that matter other than program participation, then our estimated impact on outcomes would be causal.

The problem with this approach is that it is difficult to observe all of the things that matter. If we leave some of them out, then our estimate of the program effect may, in reality, capture some of the impact of those omitted factors (assuming those omitted factors are related to program participation). Things like differences in a family's motivation level to help their kids overcome obstacles and differences in internal family functioning are very hard to observe and easily could be related to the child's success. This weakness suggests that we are unlikely to obtain causal estimates using a multiple regression approach.

The gold standard in obtaining causal estimates is a controlled experiment. In this approach, children eligible for a particular program are randomized into control and treatment groups. Members of the treatment group are subject to the intervention, and members of the control group are not. The true strength of a controlled experiment is that randomization (if properly conducted) guarantees that the control group and the treatment group are statistically identical. There may be individual differences between members within the two groups, but, on average, the only differences between the two groups are attributable to random variation. As such, we have a metric for determining how members of the treatment group would have fared had they not experienced the intervention. The control group sets that standard. This approach is the strongest for identifying causal effects.

Practical limitations, however, make controlled experiments relatively less common. The difficulty in recruiting candidates for a program that they may not get to participate in, ethical questions of withholding services to the control group, and the administrative difficulty and expense of setting up the experiment and tracking both control and treatment group members are important roadblocks in their widespread use. Nevertheless, they are periodically conducted to evaluate interventions like those we study here, and we certainly rely on them wherever possible.

Sometimes circumstances in the world line up in such a way that something resembling a controlled experiment just happens to occur. For instance, subsidized child care programs for young children from low-income households may have too many applicants for the number of slots available. One way to allocate those slots is to randomly draw names of children to enter and others to sit on a waitlist. In this example, the children on the waitlist can act like a control group for the treatment group of students who happened to have been chosen to enroll. We call events like this "quasi-experiments."

Other forms of quasi-experiments occur when different geographic entities establish policies that differ from other places. If those policy differences can be plausibly attributed to factors unrelated to underlying differences in anticipated outcomes (like political factors—a newly elected governor implements components of his or her agenda), then we can similarly define treatment and control groups. An important limitation of this sort of analysis would occur if different geographic units adopted different policies in response to differences in outcomes (like passing school reforms because test scores were falling). Quasi-experimental approaches that rely on this sort of policy variation need to be acutely aware of this problem. Nevertheless, if implemented properly, quasi-experiments may provide an effective approach for identifying causal effects of program interventions.

In summary, despite the vast literatures that exist to examine different interventions directed at lower-income children, we discard large amounts of it because they rely on empirical methods that cannot plausibly provide causal estimates of their impact. Throughout the remainder of this volume, we will place heavy emphasis on evidence obtained from controlled experiments and well-designed quasi-experimental studies.

1.3.2   Challenge 5: Does the Scale of the Program Matter?

One of the disadvantages of relying so heavily on experimental evidence is that the logistical and financial constraints associated with large-scale experiments are formidable. This limits their frequency, and when they are conducted, the number of participants is sometimes reasonably small. This creates two potential difficulties. First, smaller sample sizes lead to estimated impacts that are less precise. If exactly the same intervention were conducted again, the results from the second attempt may be considerably different than that obtained the first time. This would reduce the confidence one would place in the estimate.

Our "solution" to this problem is simply to recognize its existence and interpret the results accordingly. Consider two interventions evaluated with experimental evidence where both interventions are estimated to have the same impact on the adult earnings of the children participating. If one intervention included more participants, we would place greater weight on the results from that experiment. Throughout our review of experimental evidence, we will be clear to state the number of participants in the evaluation to help accomplish this task.

The second potential problem associated with experimental evidence using smaller sample sizes is the ability to "scale-up" an intervention. Programs that are effective when they are introduced to a group of 100 children may not work as well with 10,000 child participants if there are diseconomies of scale. This is the sort of problem that might be experienced if, say, a state or the federal government tried to replicate a successful, small-scale program that was privately funded. One successful charter school may be hard to turn into 100 successful identical charter schools if, for instance, the availability of teachers able to succeed in the new environment were limited. These are the sorts of problems that economists label general equilibrium effects. The small-scale intervention may be too small to disturb the broader marketplace, but ramping up the intervention to a larger scale may do so.

Again, this is a problem that we "solve" simply by recognizing its existence and interpreting the results accordingly. If we see that certain types of interventions are found to have been successful when evaluated, but those evaluations were based on small-scale demonstrations, we need to take note of that fact. If, for instance, private foundations want to spend more money to replicate those interventions on a relatively small scale with a few more sites or in a different location, then it would be appropriate to base that decision on the existing evidence. If similar interventions are considered by, say, the federal government, then this limitation of the existing evidence needs to be taken very seriously. If there are other interventions that appear to be successful and based on evidence from larger experimental studies, then we should prefer those.

1.3.3   Challenge 6: What Outcomes Are Considered?

Interventions designed to improve the lives of children and youths from low-income households have the potential to affect a wide variety of outcomes. School-based interventions, for instance, may alter students' educational performance, but there are a number of ways to assess educational performance, including test scores, grades, attendance, high school graduation, and college attendance. But these interventions may alter less-concrete outcomes as well, including self-esteem, sense of safety, and ability to communicate. Teen drug prevention and pregnancy prevention programs focus on a different array of outcomes. Even within the same types of interventions, different assessments may focus on different outcomes.

The problem that we face is to determine what outcomes we consider. The first thing to keep in mind is that our goal is not the measurement of each of these individual outcomes, but to translate everything into their impact on subsequent earnings levels. We deal exclusively with the issue of how we accomplish this task in chapter 13. The question here is which outcomes from previous evaluations are we going to use as inputs into that translation?

Again, we will take a pragmatic approach and use whatever outcomes are available to us from the individual studies previously conducted that we have the ability to translate into earnings. Although school-based interventions may affect a large number of outcomes, assessments of their success tend to focus on a relatively narrow range of them. We will use whichever ones are available to us to convert to earnings affects. For the most part, the outcomes typically considered are things that we can convert to subsequent earnings. We describe in detail the process of taking an outcome like test scores and converting it to earnings effects in chapter 13. Outcomes that are more difficult to translate (self-esteem, ability to communicate, etc.) are typically not measured in these assessments anyway, so we have no inputs available to translate even if we had a method to do so. The contribution of "soft-skills" to subsequent economic well-being is something that we unavoidably will miss in our formal analysis. We will discuss the issue further in chapter 13, however, and offer some input as to its contribution.

References

Blank, Rebecca M. 2008. How to improve poverty measurement in the United States. *Journal of Policy Analysis and Management* 23 (2): 233–54.

Carneiro, Pedro, and James J. Heckman. 2003. Human capital policy. In *Inequality in America: What role for human capital policies?,* ed. James J. Heckman and Alan B. Krueger, 77–240. Cambridge, MA: MIT Press.

Cunha, Flavio, and James J. Heckman. 2007. The technology of skill formation. *American Economic Review* 97 (2): 31–47.

Cunha, Flavio, James J. Heckman, Lance Lochner, and Dimitriy V. Masterov. 2006. Interpreting the evidence on life cycle skill formation. In *Handbook of the economics of education,* ed. Eric Hanushek and Finis Welch, 697–812. Amsterdam: North Holland.

Karoly, Lynn A. 1998. *Investing in our children: What we know and don't know about the costs and benefits of early childhood interventions.* Santa Monica, CA: Rand Corp.

II

Early Childhood Interventions

2

Child Development

Greg J. Duncan, Jens Ludwig, and Katherine A. Magnuson

2.1 Introduction

The best way to reduce poverty in America is to make people more productive. In this chapter, we review the available evidence about the ability of early childhood interventions to improve children's lifetime earnings prospects and, in turn, reduce their poverty over the long term. Early childhood appears to represent a particularly promising period for human capital investments, based on accumulated evidence regarding the lifelong implications of early brain development as well as the efficacy of early childhood interventions (Nelson 2000; Shonkoff and Phillips 2000; Karoly 2002; Carniero and Heckman 2003; Knudsen et al. 2006).

Most early childhood interventions seek to improve the quality of the learning and social interactions that children experience. We first review programs that attempt to enhance the skills of *parents* in hopes that parents will better teach, nurture, or in other ways provide for their children and in

Greg J. Duncan is Distinguished Professor of Education at the University of California at Irvine, and an adjunct professor in the School of Education and Social Policy at Northwestern University. Jens Ludwig is the McCormick Foundation Professor of Social Service Administration, Law, and Public Policy at the University of Chicago, a nonresident senior fellow in Economic Studies at the Brookings Institution, and a research associate and codirector of the working group on the Economics of Crime at the National Bureau of Economic Research. Katherine A. Magnuson is an assistant professor of social work at the University of Wisconsin-Madison.

Thanks to Phil Levine, David Zimmerman, and participants in the National Bureau of Economic Research (NBER) preconference for helpful comments. We are grateful for additional support provided by the Buffett Early Childhood Fund and the McCormick Tribune Foundation to the National Forum on Early Childhood Program Evaluation, and thank Clive Belfield for additional results for the Perry Preschool program as well as David Olds for additional information about Nurse-Family Partnership (NFP) evaluations. Comments can be directed to any of the authors. All opinions and any errors are our own.

so doing enhance their children's well-being. We then discuss *child*-based interventions that seek to provide enriching experiences to children directly, as with intensive preschool education programs. Some early interventions target both the child and the parent at the same time, but most programs fit into either child- or parent-based categories.

Early childhood interventions also differ in the *types* of children's skills and behavior they ultimately seek to influence. Some programs aim to improve children's early cognitive, literacy, or numeracy skills. By building these skills and learning capacity more generally, these programs hope to promote later school success. Other programs focus on developing children's socioemotional behaviors by, for example, reducing antisocial and disruptive problem behaviors. If these behaviors develop in early childhood and persist into the later years, they may limit education and career prospects and result in costly delinquent and adult crime. Some programs attempt to promote both cognitive skills and positive behavior on the premise that they are interrelated and that improving multiple rather than single domains of development is most effective.

Our review of parenting intervention research suggests that it has proven difficult to change parenting practices in ways that lead to improvements in children's academic outcomes. A notable exception is the nurse home-visitation program developed by David Olds, in which high-risk, first-time mothers are visited repeatedly in their homes by nurses.

The evidence supporting the efficacy of high-quality, center-based early childhood education is stronger. Model demonstration programs such as Perry Preschool and Abecedarian have been shown to improve long-term school attainment and earnings; the Perry program appears to reduce crime and the risk of adult poverty as well.

An emerging body of rigorous research suggests that the larger-scale and less-expensive federal Head Start program may also generate long-term improvements in the life chances of participants, but the estimated effect sizes are smaller than those of the model programs. Rigorous evaluations of state pre-Kindergarten (pre-K) programs are also encouraging, although only very short-term program impacts are known at this point. Focusing solely on the magnitude of program effects, however, is misguided. For policy purposes, the goal is not to find the program that produces the biggest benefits but rather to find programs that generate the largest benefits relative to their costs. Programs that generate large benefits, but even larger costs, are unwise public expenditures. The corollary is also true—programs that produce only modest gains in children's outcomes can be worthwhile if their costs are sufficiently low.

All in all, we conclude that investing in selected early childhood interventions appears likely to be a very cost-effective way to reduce poverty over the long term and that current public investments in such programs appear to have helped in this regard. Prior research provides little guidance regarding what form *incremental* investments should take—for example, whether additional funding should be focused on expanding Head Start, pre-K programs, or intensive home visitation programs. But we are confident that additional investments in well-implemented and proven program designs are likely to do a great deal of good, and compare quite favorably on a cost-effectiveness basis with alternative strategies for reducing poverty in America.

The remainder of this essay is organized as follows. In section 2.2, we describe how socioeconomic disadvantages in early childhood outcomes can increase long-term risks of poverty in adulthood. Section 2.3 describes the existing major federal early childhood programs, Head Start, as well as the universal state pre-K programs that have developed in recent years. Evaluation evidence on parenting programs is reviewed in section 2.4. In section 2.5, we discuss what is known about the ability of early childhood interventions to improve children's cognitive outcomes. Section 2.6 reviews the literature linking early childhood cognitive (and, to a lesser extent, socioemotional skills and behavior) outcomes to long-term earnings and adult poverty rates. Section 2.7 discusses other benefits to society that may result from these kinds of interventions, while section 2.8 summarizes our thoughts about the cost-effectiveness of additional investments in early childhood interventions.

2.2   Description of the Problem

Children cannot choose their parents. Although people disagree about how social policy should treat adults who have been unlucky or unwise, most would agree that there is something fundamentally unfair about holding children's life chances hostage to the circumstances of their parents. The reality, though, is that family background has a powerful influence on how U.S. children develop, beginning very early in their lives. Much of the early disparities in children's development can be traced back to their family experiences before they enter school.

The human brain grows and changes at an astonishingly rapid rate during the first few years of life (Shonkoff and Phillips 2000; Knudsen et al. 2006). The brain's unusual "plasticity" appears to make young children unusually responsive to environmental influences. Psychologists often refer to these early years as "sensitive" or even "critical" periods for a child's cognitive and socioemotional development (Nelson 2000). Neuroscience research has documented how complex cognitive and socioemotional capacities are built on earlier foundational skills, and such development is strongly shaped by interactions with the environment (Knudsen et al. 2006; Nelson 2000; National Scientific Council on the Developing Child 2007). Moreover, cognitive skills and socioemotional behaviors are closely connected with brain development, as early experiences literally become embedded in the architecture of infants' brains (LeDoux 2000).

The environments that children experience during their early years differ dramatically across socioeconomic lines. More highly educated parents are more likely to provide their children home learning environments that support academic success, for example, by providing rich language and literacy environments and engaging children in learning activities (Davis-Kean 2005; Raviv, Kessenich, and Morrison 2004). They also tend to use teaching strategies with their children that mimic formal instructional techniques, such as asking questions and offering feedback rather than issuing directives (Laosa 1983). Parents with more money are able to buy a larger range of goods and services for their families, such as prenatal health care, nutrition, and learning opportunities, both in the home and outside the home (Duncan and Brooks-Gunn 1997).

The inability to meet household and other basic expenses may cause some poor parents to feel frustrated, helpless, and depressed (Conger et al. 2002; McLoyd 1998). This distress may, in turn, lead to less-responsive and more harsh and punitive parenting. Taken together, the multiple disadvantages poor children face are considerable (Evans 2004; Magnuson and Votruba-Drzal 2009). Compared with kindergarteners from families in the bottom fifth of the socioeconomic distribution (measured by a combination of parental education, occupation, and income), children from the most advantaged fifth of all families are four times more likely to have a computer in the home, have three times as many books, are read to more often, watch far less television, and are more likely to visit museums or libraries (Lee and Burkham 2002).

These differences in early environments contribute to large gaps in children's early academic skills. Numerous studies have compared the outcomes of young children from different socioeconomic backgrounds and find large differences in cognitive skills even as young as three or four years old (Duncan and Brooks-Gunn 1997; Lee and Burkham 2002). For example, one study found that three-year-olds in families of low socioeconomic status had half the vocabulary of their more affluent peers, which, in turn, could be linked to the lower quality and quantity of parental speech (Hart and Risley 1995). Research has also documented a number of differences in the socioemotional skills of poor and nonpoor children—as young as seventeen months in the case of physical aggression (Cunha et al. 2005; Tremblay et al. 2004).

These early gaps in cognitive skills and behaviors tend to persist through the school years and into later life, in part because of the possibility that "learning begets learning"—that mastery by young children of a range of cognitive and behavioral competencies may improve their ability to learn when they are older (Carniero and Heckman 2003; Cunha et al. 2005). Researchers have learned that rudimentary reading and, especially, mathematics skills at kindergarten entry strongly predict later school achievement (Duncan et al. 2007). Although the correspondence is far from perfect, children scoring poorly on academic assessments before entering kindergarten are more likely to become teen parents, engage in crime, and be unemployed as adults (Rouse, Brooks-Gunn, and McLanahan, forthcoming). Moreover, preschool problem behaviors like physical aggression are predictive of criminal behavior later in life (Reiss and Roth 2003).

2.3   Background on Existing Early Childhood Programs

Nationwide, about 57 percent of three- and four-year-old children attend some form of early education program. Rates of participation are higher among older children and more advantaged children. About 69 percent of four-year-olds are in such programs, compared with just 43 percent of three-year-olds. Preschool attendance is 13 percentage points lower among poor children than nonpoor children. Finally, preschool attendance also differs by racial and ethnic group. Preschool attendance is higher among black (66 percent) than among white (59 percent) or Hispanic children (43 percent) (U.S. Department of Education, National Center for Education Statistics 2007).

The importance of children's preschool years is not reflected well in federal government budget priorities. The United States currently spends around $7,900 on elementary and secondary public schooling for each school-aged child (five to seventeen) in the United States, around $588 billion in total (see U.S. Department of Education 2005).[1] Most of this funding is collected and disbursed by states and localities. (All dollar figures reported in the paper, unless otherwise noted, are in 2007 dollars.) But disparities in family background generate large differences in children's development well before school and even before children are old enough to participate in the federal government's preschool program for disadvantaged children, Head Start. Per-student spending by the federal government on Head Start is similar to that in public elementary and secondary schools, but the program's annual budget of nearly $8 billion is enough to serve only about 900,000 children, not even half of all income-eligible three- and four-year-olds (U.S. Department of Health and Human Services 2005). Although the federal and state government spending on child care subsidies exceeds its spending on Head Start, the subsidies are designed to support parental employment rather than improve children's development (Magnuson and Shager, forthcoming).

Head Start began in 1965, amidst the War on Poverty, as a summer program for children around age three to five; by 1970, a majority of participants attended year-round. Widely perceived as a schooling program, early childhood education is only one of Head Start's six service components

---

1. The U.S. Statistical Abstract (2007) reports average per-pupil spending for children in elementary and secondary schooling of around $8,200 in 2004. These data also suggest that around 89 percent of all school-aged children are enrolled in public schools. So public school spending per school-aged child equals (.89 × $8,200) ≈ $7,200. The figure reported in the text converts this from 2004 to 2007 dollars.

and accounts for less than half (about 40 percent) of the program's budget (Currie and Neidell 2007). Other program elements include parent involvement, social services, nutrition, and children's physical and mental health screening and services.

Head Start involves relatively low pupil-teacher ratios of around 6.5 to 1 (see table 2.1) although only around one-third of teachers hold a college degree, and average salaries for teachers in the program tend to be around one-half those found among teachers in the public K-12 system. This bundle of Head Start services might affect schooling outcomes in several ways. In addition to the direct effects on cognitive academic skills from early childhood education, nutrition, and health services, Head Start may indirectly affect children's schooling by influencing parents' life course or parenting practices.

More recently, states and local school districts have initiated their own pre-Kindergarten programs. Pre-K is usually (but not always) a part-day educational program located within public schools. Typically, some additional services are offered, including meals and transportation, but few programs provide a full array of comprehensive services such as health screenings (Ripple et al. 1999; Schulman, Blank, and Ewen 1999). States also directly fund, and school districts may subcontract with, other programs to provide early education services. In 2007, thirty-eight states funded prekindergarten programs, and spending reached $3.9 billion. Despite large increases in funding in recent years, these programs serve just a fraction of children—22 percent of four-year-olds in 2007.

Table 2.1 summarizes the characteristics of a selected set of prekindergarten programs operating in five states (Michigan, New Jersey, Oklahoma, South Carolina, and West Virginia) that have been subject to evaluation (described in further detail in the following). The average spending level per child across these five state programs is about $6,100. (All costs reported in table 2.1 and in the paper are in 2007 dollars and have been discounted back to age zero using a 3 percent discount rate to facilitate comparison of costs that target children of different ages.) It should be noted, however, that spending levels vary considerably across the states and are difficult to estimate precisely.[2]

2.4   Parenting Interventions

It is useful to distinguish two types of parenting programs—parenting education and parenting management training. Parenting education programs seek to boost parents' general knowledge about parenting and child

2. Because these state pre-K programs tend to operate within the public school system, there may be some question about whether the accounting of fixed costs is comparable with these state programs compared to either the model programs or Head Start.

Table 2.1   Alternative early childhood education programs—program characteristics

	Abecedarian	Perry Preschool	Head Start	State universal pre-K
Ages covered	0–5	3 and 4	3–4	4
Quantity (coverage) per year	7:30–5:30 each day, five days a week, fifty weeks a year	2.5 hours a day, five days a week, October–May	Half day or full day, academic year	Half day (MI, SC), full day (NJ), varied (OK, WV)
Teacher qualifications	Mostly high school for teachers of young children, mostly BA for teachers of 3- to five-year-olds[a]	≥BA plus education certificate	31% BA, 27% AA, 27% early-education teaching certificate	BA (MI), BA with training in early education (NJ, OK, SC), BA or AA with training in early education (WV)
Teacher salaries	Comparable to public schools	Comparable to public schools (plus 10%)	~1/2 public school	
Pupil–teacher ratios	3:1 infants and toddlers, 6:1 older children	5 or 6:1	6.5:1 (5.4:1 including volunteers)	8:1 (MI), 15:2 (NJ), 10:1 (OK, SC, WV)
Number of students served	112 in model program	45	905,000	24,729 (MI), 21,286 (NJ), 30,180 (OK), 17,821 (SC), 6,541 (WV)
Program population	Low-income African American (Chapel Hill, NC)	Low-income, low-IQ African American (Ypsilanti, MI)	Mostly low-income (national)	
Curricular emphasis	Communication skills plus other motor, social, cognitive skills	Logic, math, literacy, creativity, social	Varied	
Nonacademic services	Medical and nutrition	Weekly home visits with parents	Dental, other health, nutrition	
Total cost per year	$19,080	$8,700	$9,000[c]	$5,031 (MI), $10,361 (NJ), $6,167 (OK), $3,219 (SC), $6,829 (WV)
Total cost per student (present value at age 0, 3% discount rate)[b]	$90,000	$15,700	$8,000	$6,100

Notes: For Head Start, we assume one year of program participation per child as in Garces, Thomas, and Currie (2002). Abecedarian program description and impacts from Ramey and Campbell (1984), Campbell and Ramey (1994), and Campbell et al. (2002); test score impacts for reading and math achievement reported for ages four and five in our table were actually measured for Abecedarian at forty-two and fifty-four months. For Perry Preschool, the age-three results are actually for "end of first preschool year" and age-four test results are for "end of second preschool year," which should roughly correspond to ages three and four (Schweinhart et al. 2005). Results from Head Start from Hart and Schumacher (2005), Zill et al. (2003), and Puma et al. (2005). Results for the study of five state pre-K programs are from Wong et al. (2008), who report a cost of $6,300 per year, which we discount back to age 0 using a 3% discount rate.

[a]From personal communication September 16, 2005, between Stephen Robblee and Frances Campbell, based on her recollections rather than actual program records on teacher qualifications.

[b]Present value of total cost per student at age 0, calculated using a 3% discount rate.

[c]This figure includes federal, state, and local grants and subsidies, as calculated by Ludwig and Phillips (2007).

development. Often, information is provided in conjunction with instrumental and emotional support and can take a variety of formats including, but not limited to, short instructional workshops provided by educators or community centers, parent discussion groups, and home visitation programs. Home visitation programs for new mothers and parent-teacher programs are perhaps the most widespread and familiar.

Management training programs are designed for parents of children with problem behavior, usually conduct disorders. Clinical therapists teach parents concrete behavioral strategies designed to improve their children's behavior. Typically, parents are taught how to reinforce their child's positive behavior and punish negative behavior appropriately.

Two theoretical assertions undergird most parenting interventions. First, parental behavior has a strong influence on children's healthy development. Second, positive parenting can be learned. Both of these assertions are controversial. That parents influence children is beyond debate; however, the relative contribution of environmental influences (including parental) and genetic influences to development remains a point of contention (Collins et al. 2000; Scarr 1992).

Even if pathways of parental influence are identified correctly, and children benefit from changes in parent-child interaction patterns, or in the quality of their home learning environments, the success of parent-based interventions is premised on the ability of interventions to improve parents' behavior in cost-effective ways. The research reviewed here suggests that affecting change in parents through parenting programs is indeed possible although more difficult than often thought.

Parenting education and training programs make demands on the time and effort of parents—demands that, for some parents, appear too high. Work conflicts, stress, and lack of motivation result in nonparticipation rates as high as 50 percent in some programs (Prinz and Miller 1994; Webster-Stratton and Spitzer 1996). In addition, parental engagement appears to be a function of parents' perceptions of how well their needs are met by a particular program (Brooks-Gunn, Berlin, and Fuligni 2000). Furthermore, even when parents do participate in the program, they are not all equally engaged or capable of implementing and maintaining the strategies they are taught. Unfortunately, parents of children most at risk of academic or behavior problems—single and low-income parents—appear least able to participate in programs and maintain changes in parenting behavior (Prinz and Miller 1994; Webster-Stratton and Hammond 1990).

Parenting education for new parents is increasingly being provided through home visitation. Most families adapt successfully to the challenges of preparing for a newborn's birth and caring for a young baby. Nevertheless, this transition can be a difficult time, particularly for first-time parents who may be socially isolated or experiencing severe adversity. Under such circumstances, some home visiting has proven to be an effective way of providing families with support and education, resulting in positive impacts on a variety of outcomes.

The successes of a few intensive parenting intervention programs are noteworthy. Most famously, the experimental evaluation of an intensive nurse home visitation program by Olds et al. (1999) in Elmira, New York, found that the program had lasting effects on important indicators of disadvantaged children's well-being. In particular, a fifteen-year follow-up study found that unmarried mothers assigned to the program group had fewer verified reports of child abuse and neglect than mothers assigned to the control group (table 2.2). Furthermore, their children had fewer emergency health-related visits and reported arrests. It is worth noting that the program had early effects on children's cognitive development, but these effects faded over time (table 2.2).

Olds and colleagues have undertaken replication studies in two sites— Denver and Memphis. Results from the Denver trial indicated that nurse home visitors were more effective than paraprofessionals who did not have any postsecondary education in a helping profession. One explanation for this finding is that mothers are more likely to perceive nurses as having legitimacy and authority when it comes to issues related to their infants' health and development than visitors with other backgrounds (Olds, Sadler, and Kitzman 2007). Results from a nine-year follow-up study of the Memphis program indicate positive, but more limited, impacts on parenting and child outcomes (Olds, Sadler, and Kitzman 2007). Evidence from additional follow-up studies in Memphis and Denver will provide important information about the likelihood of replicating the success of the Elmira program.

Involving an average of nine visits by registered nurses during the pregnancy and twenty-three visits during the first two years of the child's life, and costing approximately $10,300, Olds's program was clearly at the intensive end of parenting programs.[3] Yet its benefits exceed its costs. Aos et al. (2004) estimate the total value of gross benefits to be nearly $30,000, most of which comes from reduced crime on the part of the child together with reductions in child abuse on the part of the parent.

It is crucial to ask whether the positive child impacts from intensive programs such as Olds's would carry over to more-practical, less-intensive programs. As suggested by Gomby, Culross, and Behrman (1999), the answer appears to be no. Evaluations of other home visiting models have shown less consistent positive impacts. One example is Healthy Families America (HFA), a program to prevent child maltreatment that was modeled after the Hawaii Healthy Start Program, which was developed in the early 1990s and implemented statewide in several states. The core of this program involved

3. This figure represents the cost of the Denver nurses program, as reported by Aos et al. (2004). The Elmira program, as reported by Olds and Kitzman (1993), reported somewhat lower costs of $8,200.

Table 2.2 Parenting intervention programs—program description and impacts

	Nurse family partnership, full sample (Elmira)	Nurse family partnership, at risk sample (Elmira)	Early Head Start home visiting	Incredible Years parent training
	Prenatal home visiting program	Prenatal home visiting program	Home visiting program	Parent management training
		Program description		
Year of enrollment in program	1978–1980	1978–1980	1996–1998	1995–1997
Child age	Prenatal to age two	Prenatal to age two	Prenatal to age three	Four–eight years old
Program length	Prenatal to age two	Prenatal to age two	Prenatal to age three	Twenty-two–twenty-four weeks
Average dosage	Eight prenatal visits, twenty-three postnatal visits	Eight prenatal visits, twenty-three postnatal visits	90% received one visit; 30% received weekly visits throughout the program	On average, twenty-one two-hour weekly sessions of ten–twelve parents and two therapists
Inclusion criteria	All mothers in Elmira, NY	Low SES, teen mothers	Low-income, poor, pregnant women and mothers	Clinical levels of behavior problems lasting for six months
Providers	Nurses	Nurses	58% had a college degree; 12% had a two-year degree; training was "extensive"	Trained therapists, masters or PhD, and at least five years of clinical experience
No. of families assigned to receive services[a]	116	38	448	31
Evaluation method	Experimental	Experimental	Experimental	Experimental
		Impacts at program completion		
IQ (Cattell Developmental Quotient)	0.19 SD	0.52 SD		
Avoidance of restriction and punishment	0.25 SD	0.58 SD		
CPS abuse	0.14 SD (ns)	0.35 SD		
No. of emergency room visits	0.29 SD	0.26 SD (ns)		
Parenting stress			0.14 SD	
Mother negative parenting			HOME hostility scale: 0.06 SD (ns)	0.81 SD

Mother positive parenting	HOME warmth scale: −0.01 SD (ns)	0.51 SD
Receptive vocabulary	PPVT: 0.09 SD (ns)	
Problem behavior, age three	Aggression: 0.08 sd	Conduct problems: 0.63 SD (father report), 0.66 SD (mother report), 0.35 SD (teacher report)

Long-term follow-up

Child IQ (Stanford Binet), age four	0.19 SD (ns)	0.21 SD (ns)
HOME Inventory Total Scale, age four	0.00 SD (ns)	0.33 SD (ns)
HOME Stimulation of Language Skills, age four	0.12 SD (ns)	0.65 SD
Avoidance of punishment, age four	−0.38 SD	−0.28 SD (ns)
Log incidence of the no. of emergency room visits, age twenty-five–fifty months	0.36 SD	0.43 SD
Log incidence of substantiated abuse and neglect, age fifteen	0.34 SD	0.54 SD
Log incidence of child arrest, age fifteen	0.37 SD	0.45 SD
Log incidence of alcohol and drug impairment, age fifteen (parent report)	0.05 SD (ns)	0.36 SD

Notes: ns = not statistically significant (results otherwise are all statistically significant at conventional 5% cutoff). SD = standard deviation. CPS = Child Protective Services; PPVT = Peabody Picture Vocabulary Test. All effects are presented so that positive effects represent better outcomes. All estimates reflect intent to treat calculations based on experimental data, with the exception of Early Head Start, in which estimates are provided for those who received at least one home visit (see footnote 4 for more details). Effect sizes for the nurse family partnership program for continuous variables have been calculated by dividing the program treatment impact by the control group standard deviation, which were generously provided by David Olds (see also Olds et al. 1986; Olds, Henderson, and Kitzman 1994). Effect sizes for log incidence variables are the authors' calculation of data provided in Olds et al. (1997) and Olds et al. (1998). These are calculated based on *p*-value for statistical significance of a covariated adjusted analysis, and are likely to be conservative. Effect sizes for Early Head Start are taken from Love et al. (2005); effect sizes for the Incredible Years parent training are taken from Webster-Stratton, Reid, and Hammond (2004).

[a]The number of families receiving services in Early Head Start is the number who received services and who participated in the follow-up parent interview.

identifying parents at high risk of abusing or neglecting their children through broad-based screening and then offering voluntary home visiting services delivered by paraprofessionals for a period of three to five years. Home visitors were expected to provide a range of services including service referrals, modeling problem-solving skills, and parent education.

Randomized trials have yielded mixed findings. One study conducted in Hawaii yielded disappointing results, with as many negative impacts as positive effects on key family process outcomes (Duggan et al. 2004). A study in New York showed some promising reductions in harsh parenting and maltreatment during the first year of the program, but these effects had faded by the second year of the program (DuMont et al. 2008).

The Early Head Start evaluation study also provides some recent evidence on the effectiveness of home-visiting programs for low-income families with children (Love et al. 2002; see table 2.2). Early Head Start is designed to provide educational and other health and social services to disadvantaged children between birth and age three. The program includes several modes of program delivery including both center-based early education programs as well as home visiting programs. Seven sites in the larger evaluation provided programming primarily through weekly home visits and biweekly parent-child socialization activities. The programs also provided case management and health screenings. The evaluation assessed the program's effects on several aspects of children's development and family life when the children were aged two and three. Of the families enrolled in home-visiting programs, 90 percent participated for at least one visit, and although most of these had more than one visit, only 30 percent of families participated in weekly home visits for all three years (table 2.2). Rates of home-visiting in the control group were significantly lower, but not insubstantial, with close to one-third reporting that they received a home visit during the first three years of their child's life.[4]

The evaluation study found a few small effects of the program on measures of participants' parenting. For example, mothers reported lower levels of parenting stress (table 2.2), with an effect size of around 0.14 of a standard deviation.[5] With a few exceptions, experimental-control differences in parents' mental health, children's home learning environments, and harsh parenting favored the experimental group, but almost none of these differences was statistically significant at conventional levels (table 2.2).

With so few detectable effects on parenting, one might not expect large

4. The evaluation study reports the effects of home-visiting programs for those families who participated in Early Head Start Services, rather than the effect of the program on those who were offered the services (Love et al. 2002). Assuming that the programs would not benefit or harm the nonparticipating families, with 10 percent of families not participating, the program's impacts are likely to be 10 percent lower than reported.

5. Standard deviation units are a common way of expressing effect sizes. For comparison, the standard deviation is 15 to 16 points for a typical IQ test and 100 points for the SAT.

positive effects on children. Indeed, the reported program impacts on children's cognitive development and socioemotional development at age three were positive but not statistically significant. The effect of the program on participating children's cognitive development translated into effect sizes of about 0.10. Effect sizes for program impacts on measures of children's socioemotional development ranged from 0.02 to 0.19 of a standard deviation, with most below 0.10 (table 2.2).

Taken together, evaluations of many forms of parenting education programs support the conclusion that most programs for parents of young children can result in modest improvements in some aspects of parenting; however, such modest changes yield few and usually insignificant changes in children's developmental outcomes. The failure of these programs to result in improvements in children's outcomes may be due either to their failure to produce large improvements in parenting, or to the lack of links between the types of parenting behaviors targeted and the types of outcomes considered. At the same time, the evidence suggests that a particular parenting program model—an intensive home visiting program staffed by nurses and serving vulnerable first-time mothers—can be effective at improving children's developmental outcomes in meaningful ways.

In contrast to the largely ineffective parent *education* programs, parent *management training* programs appear to be a more promising strategy, at least for improving the behavior of children with serious behavior problems. These programs were developed in response to research showing that maladaptive parenting and parent-child interaction patterns are common in families of severely conduct-disordered children (Kazdin 1997; Kazdin and Weisz 1998; Taylor and Biglan 1998). Often described as coercive, this type of parenting involves harsh but inconsistent punishment for children's problem behavior and a failure to reward positive child behavior (Dumas 1989; Patterson, DeBaryshe, and Ramsey 1989).

Parent management training programs teach parents to respond more appropriately to their children's behavior. Specifically, parents are taught to reward and attend to their children's positive behavior but to ignore or punish their child's problem behavior appropriately and consistently. Treatment sessions provide parents with the opportunity to observe appropriate parenting skills as well as practice and refine their own use of these skills. Families involved in these types of programs include, but are not limited to, low-income families.

A successful example of parenting management training is Webster-Stratton's group discussion videotape program, now known as the Incredible Years program (Webster-Stratton, Kolpacoff, and Hollinsworth 1988). The program has been replicated and evaluated in several settings and has also been adapted for teachers in school settings. A recent evaluation of the program randomly assigned families to one of five variations of the treatment (combinations of parent training, child training, and teacher training) or a waiting list control group. Of interest in our discussion is the comparison of families in which parents were engaged in training program to a control group that received no training. The parents met weekly in groups of ten to twelve parents and two therapists for two-hour sessions. Over the course of twenty-two to twenty-four weeks, parents watched seventeen videotaped programs on parenting and interpersonal skills. The parent training, as well as other treatment conditions, had large positive effects on measures of negative and positive parenting as well as parent and teacher reports of children's behavior (table 2, Webster-Stratton, Reid, and Hammond 2004). Studies have suggested that these effects are maintained at least a year after program completion (Webster-Stratton 1990). Foster, Olchowski, and Webster-Stratton (2008) provide estimates of program costs but not benefits.

One reason that parenting interventions may be more successful in reducing severe problem behavior than in promoting academic achievement is that parents of children with severe behavior problems may feel they are "under siege" and, thus, be more engaged in parenting programs than parents of children with less-severe problems (Webster-Stratton and Spitzer 1996). Most parents who participated in these studies were referred for treatment or were seeking help for their children's behavior. For example, to be admitted to Webster-Stratton's parenting program, parents had to be referred to the clinic for children's "excessive noncompliance, aggression, and oppositional behavior for more than six months" (Webster-Stratton 1990, 145).

More generally, reviews of evaluations of parent management training programs show that these programs can lead to meaningful reductions in children's problem behaviors. One review suggests that approximately two-thirds of the children exhibit clinically significant improvements in behavior at the completion of the program (Taylor and Biglan 1998). Another review suggests that the average effect size was 0.87 of a standard deviation—a large effect (Durlak, Fuhrman, and Lampman 1991). However it is important to caution that not all of the studies included in these reviews used random assignment, sample sizes were typically quite small, and attrition rates, if reported, were high. Perhaps most worrisome is that when families dropped out of treatment, they were not included in the follow-up study, suggesting that the evaluation findings reflect the effect of completing the program. Few studies have follow-up data beyond six months after program treatment, and, therefore, the long-term benefit of parenting programs is still questionable (Greenberg, Domitrovich, and Bumbarger 2000).

2.5   Early Education Programs

An alternative to attempting to change parents' behavior is to provide children with high-quality center-based early childhood educational programs. This approach seeks to compensate for disadvantaging family backgrounds or poor parenting with time spent in a developmentally appropriate enriching and stimulating classroom setting. A growing body of research shows that a variety of different early childhood educational programs, ranging from very intensive model programs like Perry Preschool and Abecedarian, to larger-scale programs like Head Start and pre-K programs, are capable of generating meaningful gains in learning and perhaps longer-term life outcomes for low-income children. Moreover, the benefits generated by these programs often seem large enough to eclipse program costs.

The ability of intensive model programs to improve the life chances of disadvantaged children can be illustrated by the well-known Perry Preschool intervention. Perry provided one or two years of part-day educational services and home visits to a sample of low-income, low-IQ African American children aged three and four in Ypsilanti, Michigan, during the 1960s. Perry Preschool hired highly educated teachers (at least a BA) and was implemented as a randomized experiment (table 2.1). The great advantage of random assignment to the Perry program or the control condition is that differences in outcomes for treatments and controls can be attributed to the effects of the program with a high degree of confidence.

When the children entered school, those who had participated in the Perry program scored higher on IQ tests than those who had not—as shown in table 2.3, an impressive nine-tenths of a standard deviation higher (Schweinhart et al. 2005). These IQ effects, however, disappeared by third grade. Nevertheless, the program produced lasting effects through age forty on employment rates (76 percent for the program participation group, compared with 62 percent among the control group) and earnings (median annual earnings of $25,000 compared with $18,000 in 2007 dollars, not discounted back to age zero) and substantially reduced the chances that participants had been arrested (29 percent of the participating children reached age forty without an arrest as compared with 17 percent of the control group).

The Abecedarian program, which began in 1972 and served a sample of low-income, mostly African American families from Chapel Hill, North Carolina, was even more intensive than Perry (see table 2.1). Mothers and children assigned to the Abecedarian "treatment" received year-round, full-time center-based care for five years, starting with the child's first year of life. The Abecedarian preschool program included transportation, individualized educational activities that changed as the children aged, and low child-teacher ratios (3:1 for the youngest children and up to 6:1 for older children). Abecedarian teachers followed a curriculum that focused on language development and explained to teachers the importance of each task as well as how to teach it. High-quality health care, additional social services, and nutritional supplements were also provided to participating families (Ramey and Campbell 1979; Campbell et al. 2002; Barnett and Masse 2007).

Abecedarian was a high-cost, high-quality program run by researchers. It cost about $19,080 a year for each of a child's first five years and produced dramatic effects on the future life outcomes of its participants (Currie 2001).

Table 2.3   Early childhood education programs—program impacts

	Abecedarian	Perry Preschool	Head Start	State pre-K
			Short-term impacts	
Evaluation method	Experimental	Experimental	Experimental	
IQ scores, age three	1.22 SD	0.88 SD		
Reading/verbal, age three	0.69 SD	0.74 SD	0.35 SD	
Math/quant, age three	0.71 SD		0.21 SD (ns)	
Aggressive behavior, age three			–.10 SD (ns)	
Behavior problems, age three			–0.19 SD	
IQ scores, age four	0.93 SD	0.87 SD		
Reading/verbal, age four	0.68 SD	0.91 SD	0.13 SD	PPVT: –.16 SD (MI, NS); .36 SD (NJ); .29 SD (OK); .05 SD (SC, NS); .14 SD (WV, NS). Print awareness: .96 SD (MI); .50 SD (NJ); .43 SD (OK, NS); .79 SD (SC); .83 SD (WV, NS)
Math/quantitative, age four	0.57 SD		0.16 SD (ns)	.47 SD (MI); .23 SD (NJ); .35 SD (OK, NS); .11 SD (WV, NS)
Aggressive behavior, age four			–.04 SD (ns)	
Behavior problems, age four			–.01 SD (ns)	
IQ scores				
Age five	–0.66 SD			
Age six		0.32 SD		
Age twelve	0.50 SD			

Evaluation method	Experimental	Experimental	*Long-term impacts* Non-experimental
Age outcomes measured	Twenty-one	Forty	Twenty-three
High school graduation (%)	70 vs. 67 (ns)	77 vs. 60	86 vs. 65 (whites)
College entry (%)	36 vs. 14		
Ever arrested (%)		71 vs. 83	
Arrested 5× or more (%)		36 vs. 55	
Employment rate (%)	26 vs. 45	76 vs. 62	
Teen parent (%)	18 vs. 39		
Marijuana use (%)		48 vs. 71 (males)	
IQ scores	0.38 SD		

Notes: ns = not statistically significant (results otherwise are all statistically significant at conventional 5 percent cutoff). SD = standard deviation. Results for Head Start short-term impacts are estimates from Ludwig and Phillips (2007) for the effects of Head Start participation per se, calculated based on data from the recent randomized Head Start experimental evaluation (U.S. Department of Health and Human Services 2005). The age-four reading effect is the average of the treatment on the treated (TOT) estimates for the Peabody Picture Vocabulary Test (PPVT) for three- and four-year-olds. The effects of Head Start participation in the table equal the effects of assignment to the Head Start experimental treatment group on children's outcomes divided by the effects of treatment-group assignment on the probability of participating in Head Start. Results for Head Start's long-term impacts come from Garces, Thomas, and Currie (2002), and show the mean high school completion rate among all Head Start children in their sample versus this mean added to the estimated Head Start effect for whites (the white mean is not reported separately in the paper). Note that Ludwig and Miller (2007) find complementary evidence suggesting that Head Start's impacts on schooling attainment is large for blacks as well as whites. See also Schweinhart, Barnes, and Weikart (1993).

Early IQ scores of Abecedarian and control-group children averaged about 1 standard deviation below the mean, as might be expected for children from very economically disadvantaged backgrounds. By the time the Abecedarian children reached age five, however, their IQ scores were close to the national average and higher than scores of children who did not participate (table 2.3). Similarly large effects were observed for achievement on verbal and quantitative tests (Ramey and Campbell 1984). Nearly fifteen years later, the program's effect on IQ scores at age twenty-one was smaller than at age five (around 0.38 standard deviation) but still impressive. This problem of partial "fade out" of the effects of early education, which has been widely documented for a variety of different programs, suggests that sustaining the effects of early interventions on the child's ability to learn may require high-quality follow-up learning environments. We return to this point in the following.

Although early IQ effects faded somewhat over time with Abecedarian, other long-term effects were dramatic and arguably just as important for reducing poverty. For example, children who received the Abecedarian program entered college at 2.5 times the rate of the control group. The Abecedarian intervention also reduced rates of teen parenthood and marijuana use by nearly half. Smoking rates of Abecedarian participants were about 30 percent lower than those of the control group (Campbell et al. 2002). Although employment rates were not statistically different between the Abecedarian and control groups (64 percent compared with 50 percent), children who had participated in the program were about two-thirds more likely to be working in a skilled job (67 percent compared with 41 percent).[6]

Abecedarian's impacts on criminal behavior were not statistically significant, although the point estimates suggest lower rates of offending among the treatment than control-group children. Given the small size of the program it is difficult to draw any confident conclusions about Abecedarian's impacts on crime, which is particularly unfortunate for comparing benefit-cost ratios across programs because crime effects account for up to 70 percent of the dollar value of the benefits from the Perry Preschool program (Belfield et al. 2006).

Encouraging evidence on existing publicly funded early education programs illustrate what can be achieved for large numbers of children in programs of more variable quality than Perry or Abecedarian. A recent random-assignment experimental evaluation of Head Start found positive short-term effects of program participation on elementary prereading and prewriting for three- and four-year olds equal to about 0.3 and 0.2

---

6. In addition, criminal involvement was less common for treatments than controls (14 percent vs. 18 percent for misdemeanor convictions, and 8 percent vs. 12 percent for felony convictions) although the absolute numbers of those arrested in the two Abecedarian groups were small enough that it is impossible to prove statistically that this particular difference did not result from chance.

of a standard deviation, respectively, but not on advanced skills in these two outcome domains (table 2.3).[7] Head Start participation also increased parent-reported literacy skills of children by around 0.45 of a standard deviation. Statistically significant effects on other outcome domains were typically concentrated among three-year-olds, with effect sizes of 0.15 for vocabulary and 0.20 for problem behaviors. Effects on math skills were positive but not statistically significant. However, if one calculates Head Start impacts pooling together the three- and four-year-olds in the experiment, rather than showing results only separately for each age group, the increased statistical power leads to statistically significant program impacts on math and almost all of the main cognitive skill outcomes in the report (Ludwig and Phillips 2007).

As for behavior and socioemotional outcomes, the Head Start experimental evaluation finds that three-year-olds assigned to the experimental rather than treatment group have lower scores on the total problem behavior scale and the hyperactive behavior scale (effect sizes from attending Head Start equal to .19 and .26, respectively), with most of the other measures in the direction of better socioemotional outcomes for treatment group children relative to controls, but not statistically significant. Among four-year-olds, none of the estimated Head Start effects on socioemotional outcomes was statistically significant.

For policy purposes, the crucial question is whether these early improvements from Head Start attendance translate into better adjustment in adolescence and a successful transition into adulthood. Nonexperimental studies of children who participated in Head Start several decades ago suggest lasting effects on schooling attainment and perhaps criminal activity, although test score effects appear to fade out over time (Currie and Thomas 1995; Garces, Thomas, and Currie 2002; Ludwig and Miller 2007; Deming 2009).

Of course, it is possible that the long-term effects of Head Start on more recent cohorts of children may differ from those for previous cohorts of

---

7. See Puma et al. (2005). Note that the point estimates we report in the text are larger than those in the Puma report, which presents the difference in average outcomes for all children assigned to the treatment group with all children assigned to the control group, known in the program evaluation literature as the "intent to treat" (ITT) effect. But not all of the four-year-old children assigned to the experimental group participated in Head Start (the figure is around 84 percent), while some four-year-olds (18 percent) assigned to the control group enrolled in the program. If we divide the ITT effect by the difference between the treatment and control groups in Head Start participation (66 percent), the implied effect of Head Start participation on participants is around 1.5 times as large as the ITT effects presented in Puma et al. For a discussion of this methodology, see Bloom (1984). If we define the "treatment" more broadly as participation in any center-based care, the effects of Head Start participation may be up to 2.5 times as large as the ITT impacts reported by Puma et al. because more than 96 percent of the treatment group receives some sort of center-based care in the experiment but so does about 55 percent of the control group (see exhibits 3.2 and 3.3 by Puma et al. 2005). For more on our calculations, see Ludwig and Phillips (2007).

program participants because of changes over time in program quality or the quality of the environments experienced by children who do not attend Head Start. But the short-term test score impacts that have been estimated for recent cohorts of Head Start participants in the randomized experiment described in the preceding appear to be similar to those found by researchers among earlier cohorts of children. So there is a reason for cautious optimism that Head Start might improve the long-term outcomes for recent waves of program participants, even though this cannot be directly tested for many years (see Ludwig and Phillips [2007] for additional discussion).

Wong et al. (2008) examined the effects of newer state-initiated pre-K programs on children's test scores. These studies typically find short-run effects on achievement test scores that are slightly larger than those estimated for Head Start (table 2.3), although the size of the impacts varies considerably across states and outcome domains. The average effect size of participation in pre-K across the states is equal to .14 standard deviations for the Peabody Picture Vocabulary Test (PPVT), .29 standard deviations for math, and .70 standard deviations for print awareness.[8] In a head-to-head regression-discontinuity-based comparison of Head Start and pre-K programs in Tulsa, Gormley, Phillips, and Gayer (2008) found that pre-K students outperformed Head Start students on early reading and writing but not early math skills. These recent pre-K studies have not considered children's behavior or socioemotional outcomes, but evidence from rigorous research is mixed (Magnuson, Ruhm, and Waldfogel 2007).

Why are the effects estimated for recent state pre-K programs somewhat larger than those for Head Start? One possible explanation is that pre-K programs hire more qualified teachers, pay them more, and offer a more academically oriented curriculum than do Head Start programs. Another explanation is that the Head Start comparison group received more center-based care than did children in the pre-K comparison group.[9] A third possible explanation is that the recent Head Start study relies on a rigorous randomized experimental design. Although the recent state pre-K studies are big improvements over past efforts to examine such programs, all are nonetheless derived using a research design that may be susceptible to bias that may overstate the benefits of pre-K participation.[10]

8. Studies of the Tulsa pre-K program find effects on prereading skills (letter-word identification) of around 0.8 of a standard deviation and for early math scores (applied problems) of around 0.38 of a standard deviation (Gormley et al. 2005; see also Gormley and Gayer 2005). We focus on the study by Wong et al. (2008) because of the more generalizable sample, which seems important given their evidence of variability across states in program impacts.

9. See http://www.northwestern.edu/ipr/events/briefingdec06-cook/slide16.html.

10. Specifically, these recent studies all use a regression discontinuity design that compares fall semester tests for kindergarten children who participated in pre-K the previous year and have birthdates close to the cutoff for having enrolled last year with fall tests of children who are just starting pre-K by virtue of having birthdates that just barely excluded them from participating the previous year. The key assumption behind these studies is that the selection process of children into pre-K does not change dramatically by child age around the birthday

While there remains some uncertainty about what is the "best" early childhood program model, it seems clear that early education interventions represent a promising way to improve the life chances of poor children. The importance of the early years is not well reflected in current federal government budget priorities, which allocate nearly seven times as much money per capita for K-12 schooling as for early education and child care subsidies for three- to five-year-olds.[11]

2.6   Link between Early Childhood Outcomes and Adult Poverty

We have good evidence that both small-scale model programs like Perry Preschool or Abecedarian and Head Start can generate long-term benefits for children in these programs when compared with children in no-treatment control groups, most of whom were in maternal care. Most relevant for current social policy is what can be accomplished by Head Start, pre-K programs, home visitation, or parent management intervention programs as they operate today in an environment in which higher levels of maternal employment has led to much larger fractions of children experiencing center-based child care. For recent cohorts of children, we can only assess the program's impacts in the short term, and so understanding implications for future poverty rates will necessarily require some extrapolation and educated guessing. In this section, we consider several different approaches for answering this question.

One way to think about the long-term consequences for poverty from children's short-term cognitive test score gains takes advantage of the fact that with the Perry experiment, we have extended longitudinal information for program participants from early childhood to age forty. At the end of the second year of services, Perry had increased PPVT vocabulary scores by around .91 standard deviations and scores on a test of nonverbal intellectual performance (the Leiter International Performance test) by around .77

enrollment cutoff (that is, changes "smoothly" with child age), but this need not be the case because there is a discrete change at the birthday threshold in terms of the choice set that families face in making this decision. Suppose, for instance, that among the children whose birthdays just barely excluded them from enrolling in pre-K during the previous year, those with the most motivated parents wound up being sent the previous year to private programs that are analogous to the public pre-K program and are then enrolled in private kindergarten programs in the fall semester that the pre-K study outcome measures are collected. This type of selection would reduce the share of more-motivated parents among the control group in the pre-K studies and lead them to overstate the benefits of pre-K participation.

11. According to U.S. Budget, Fiscal Year 2005, the United States now spends more than $530 billion a year on elementary and secondary schooling for children aged five and older, including $13 billion in extra federal funding through the Title I program for schools serving poor children. In contrast, the federal government spends only about $18 billion on the Head Start program and child care subsidies, most of which go to preschoolers (see testimony of Douglas J. Besharov before the Subcommittee on 21st Century Competitiveness of the Committee on Education and the Workforce, February 27, 2002, www.welfareacademy.org/pubs/testimony-022702.pdf [February 2007]).

standard deviations (Schweinhart et al. 2005, 61). By age nine, the impact on vocabulary scores had faded out entirely, while around half of the original impact on nonverbal performance had dissipated. By age fourteen, impacts on reading and math scores are just over .3 standard deviations, and the gap in high school completion was about 17 percentage points. In unpublished calculations that he generously shared with us, Clive Belfield found that Perry reduced adult poverty rates by about one-fifth at age twenty-seven and one-quarter at age forty. Put differently, for each $1,000 in program spending per child, Perry Preschool reduces long-term adult poverty rates among program participants by around (.25 / $15.71) = .016 (around 1.5 percent).

By way of comparison, the set of five state pre-K programs evaluated by Wong et al. (2008) cost around $6,100 on average, and achieved PPVT score gains at age four that were .14 standard deviations, on average. Put differently, the five state pre-K programs studied by Wong cost around 40 percent as much as Perry and increase PPVT scores at age four by around 15 percent as much so that the expected effect on long-term poverty from enrolling in one of these pre-K programs is (.15 × .25) = .0375. Thus, according to this method, each $1,000 in spending per child on the state pre-K programs is estimated to reduce long-term poverty among program participants by around (.0375 / 6.1) = .006, or six-tenths of a percent.

Head Start costs around 50 percent as much as Perry and increases PPVT scores by .12 standard deviations (this is the average treatment effect on enrollees—-the so-called treatment on the treated [TOT] effect for three- and four-year-olds together in the Head Start experiment), or about 13 percent of Perry's impacts. Enrollment in Head Start would under this procedure then be expected to reduce long-term poverty by (.13 × .25) = .0325, so for each $1,000 in spending per child on Head Start, long-term poverty rates among participating children when they reach adulthood would be reduced by (.0325 / 8) = .004, or four-tenths of a percent. (Head Start looks a bit more favorable compared to Perry if we focus on scores for other reading or vocabulary tests such as the Woodcock-Johnson-Revised tests for letter identification or spelling, although results for those tests are not available for the Perry Preschool sample.)

Of course it might be possible that long-term gains are not strictly proportional to short-term impacts. For example, it could be the case that some minimum short-term impact is necessary in order to generate lasting cognitive, socioemotional, or behavioral benefits. It could also be the case that the long-term behavioral consequences of achievement impacts on the low-IQ sample of Michigan children in Perry Preschool are different from those arising from similar-sized impacts on a more representative population of children in current Head Start or state pre-K programs.

A different sort of concern with these calculations is that they focus on the proportion of program participants for whom earnings and other sources of family income are pushed above some specific threshold, in this case the federal poverty line. But earnings increases for people who would still find themselves below the poverty line (or for those who are "nearly poor" above the poverty line) should also count in any social accounting of the value of these programs. So a potentially better measure of the value of early childhood programs would be to focus on earnings. Belfield et al. (2006) found Perry increased participants' lifetime earnings by about $61,000 (discounted by 3 percent, in 2007 dollars). If, as calculated in the preceding, pre-K effects are about 15 percent those of Perry, we would expect increases in lifetime earnings of (.15 × $61,000) = $9,150. Likewise, if Head Start effects amount to about 13 percent those of Perry, increases in earnings might amount to about (.13 × $61,000) = $7,930.

We can also estimate long-term earnings gains from these early childhood programs using associations from observational data. Because few studies have followed people from early childhood all the way through adulthood, this exercise is necessarily subject to some uncertainty. The British National Child Development Study (NCDS) is one of the few data sets available for this purpose and includes achievement test scores measured at age seven and earnings measured at age thirty-three for a sample of people born in the United Kingdom in 1958. Krueger (2003) argues that analyses of these data suggest that an increase in early childhood test scores in either reading or math of 1 standard deviation might plausibly be associated with higher lifetime earnings of about 8 percent (using a 3 percent discount rate and assuming no productivity growth in the economy over time), although we suspect this is likely to be an upper bound of the effect.[12] If the .08 estimate is correct, the implication is that a 1 standard deviation increase in test scores boosts lifetime present value earnings by around $75,870 in 1998 dollars, or around $97,000 in 2007 dollars, and assuming proportional effects based on PPVT scores this estimate could be used to provide rough estimates of Head Start and pre-K benefits ($12,610 for Head Start and $13,580 for pre-K).

There remains some debate about the relative importance of different early childhood cognitive or noncognitive skills in predicting subsequent outcomes, although the literature as a whole is consistent with the idea that there are multiple pathways to long-term success.[13] For example, Duncan

12. This estimate is derived from Currie and Thomas's (1999) analysis and is based on estimates from a regression model without any covariates and, as such, is likely to reflect an upper bound of the association. Yet this impact is smaller than what has been estimated for a 1 standard deviation increase in test scores measured during adolescence for more recent U.S. samples, which typically suggest earnings gains of around 10 to 20 percent. The difference is presumably due as Krueger notes to some combination of differences in the time period studied, the U.S. and U.K. labor markets, the fact that Currie and Thomas control for both reading and math scores simultaneously while most U.S. studies examine one type of test score at a time in their effects on earnings, and the different age at which the test scores are measured.

13. For example, Duncan et al. (2007) do not find much evidence that behavior outcomes measured during early childhood (aside from attention skills) predict later test scores although other correlational studies have found that socioemotional outcomes, notably aggressive behavior, do seem to contribute to children's achievement trajectories (Hinshaw 1992; Jimerson,

et al. (2007) find that early math skills are the strongest predictor of subsequent academic achievement; early reading and attention skills also predict later test scores but just not quite as strongly as do early math skills. The fact that early childhood programs like Head Start achieve long-term behavioral impacts despite "fade out" of initial achievement test score gains raises the question of whether lasting program impacts on socioemotional or behavior skills might be the key drivers of long-term program impacts on outcomes such as school completion or employment (see, for example, Carniero and Heckman 2003). Unfortunately, with most short-run research focusing on academic and cognitive outcomes, it is unclear what dimensions of early behavior might be affected by the program and whether such effects persist over time. A possible alternative explanation is that short-term boosts in academic skills are a key mechanism for reducing special education placement and improving socioemotional skills such as motivation and persistence by, for example, increasing children's confidence in school (Barnett, Young, and Schweinhart 1998; Deming 2009). Our calculations here assume that short-term test scores are serving as a proxy for the bundle of early skills that promote long-term outcomes, not only academic or cognitive skills.

One possible objection is that we are trying to use nonexperimental correlations between early test scores and adult earnings to extrapolate earnings gains from short-term experimental impacts, which fade over time. But as noted in the preceding, there is considerable fade out in nonexperimental achievement test advantage as well—that is, test scores measured in early childhood and adolescence are correlated, but imperfectly.[14] That said, estimating the long-run program impacts on earnings based on correlations observed in population data from the United Kingdom has many limitations and is, at best, a good guess based on available evidence.

2.7 Other Potential Benefits from Early Childhood Interventions

The previous section focuses on just part of the long-term benefits of early childhood interventions, specifically those that result from increased adult earnings and reductions in adult poverty rates. But as noted in the preceding, most of these programs generate other benefits to society that would also need to be accounted for in a systematic benefit-cost analysis for purposes of allocating scarce government resources across competing potential uses.

Despite this partial fade out of test score impacts, Perry Preschool shows

---

Egeland, and Teo 1999; Miles and Stipek 2006; Tremblay et al. 1992). Despite efforts to reduce omitted-variable biases, because the Duncan et al. (2007) study is nonexperimental, the estimates may not identify causal impacts.

14. Jencks and Phillips (1998, 28) think a plausible estimate is that the correlation between first and twelfth grade test scores is around .52. The implication is that a child starting at the sixteenth percentile of the test score distribution in first grade will on average be at the twenty-seventh percentile of the distribution in twelfth grade.

large long-term impacts on schooling, crime, and other behavioral outcomes measured through age forty (Schweinhart et al. 2005). For example, the study found that Perry Preschool reduced criminal activity (with 83 percent of the control group having been arrested by age forty, as against 71 percent of the treatment group).[15] The dollar value of Perry Preschool's long-term benefits (in 2007 dollars) range from around $102,000 using a 7 percent discount rate, to about $277,000 using a 3 percent discount rate (Belfield et al. 2006, 180–81). Reductions in crime account for fully two-thirds of the dollar-value benefits of Perry, and a large share of the dollar-value benefits of the Olds home visitation program as well. While there has to date been no long-term study of the effects of state pre-K programs, previous research on Head Start suggests that large-scale government program might reduce crime (Garces, Thomas, and Currie 2002; Deming 2009) and improve health outcomes (Ludwig and Miller 2007).

Finally, we note that early childhood interventions may reduce both future and current poverty. Early childhood development programs may effectively serve as subsidized child care that may result in increased employment and work effort and, thus, in turn, higher earnings for participating families. A good portion of the spending on subsidized care itself amounts to "near cash" income for the poor families and should figure into a poverty status calculation based on an expansive definition of family income.

2.8   Conclusion

Many antipoverty strategies confront society with some trade-off between equity and efficiency: policies or programs that transfer resources to the poor often run the risk of reducing work effort by program participants (the Earned Income Tax Credit being one noteworthy exception in that regard, at least with respect to labor force participation rates), and raising government revenue through taxation generates some deadweight loss to society as well. Put differently, poverty programs targeted at providing help to adults typically serve to redistribute resources but may make the overall "pie" smaller. On the other hand, human capital programs targeted at poor children can help reduce poverty while at the same time enhancing future economic growth and competitiveness and increasing the overall resources available to society. A growing body of research in a variety of fields ranging from neuroscience to economics suggests that investing in the earliest years of life for disadvantaged children may be a particularly promising strategy. Most social policies are devoted to playing catch-up against children's early disadvantages, but disparities are already apparent among young children, and many disadvantaged children never catch up. Programs that try

---

15. See Schweinhart et al. (2005), *Lifetime Effects* (see their note 17).

to improve young children's school readiness could be an effective way to combat poverty.

In the choice between child- and parent-based programs, in general, the former have a much better track record than the latter. There is a very strong body of research suggesting that a wide range of high-quality early childhood education centers are capable of enhancing the developmental outcomes of low-income children and produce benefits to society well in excess of program costs. Evidence from program evaluation research supports efforts to enroll children who are living in poverty in high-quality early care and education programs, beginning around age three.

Two types of parent-based programs show considerable promise. Intensive family support through home visiting by skilled personnel can produce benefits for children and parents, especially when it is targeted to families at high risk. The best studied and most effective example of this model provides nurse home visitation targeted to first-time parents who are living in poverty. Home visitation and parenting programs staffed by paraprofessionals of low intensity (for example, fewer than ten visits) or provided on a universal basis appear unlikely to produce significant lasting benefits for children (Olds, Sadler, and Kitzman 2007). Among children with identified behavior problems, some programs have proved effective at reducing children's problem behavior in the short term, particularly in the home setting. But there is no evidence that these behavior-focused programs have positive effects on children's academic outcomes.

For the purpose of increasing children's academic skills, the available evidence seems to point, at least tentatively, toward the relative cost-effectiveness of child-focused interventions like center-based early childhood education over even the most successful parent-focused programs. For example, the Olds nurse family visitation program generated gains in Stanford-Binet scores of around .2 standard deviations at age four, two years after program completion (among the high risk Elmira sample) at a cost of around $10,300 per child. In contrast, the federal Head Start program increases reading scores for three- and four-year-olds by around .12 standard deviations, with larger impacts on other cognitive outcomes, at a cost that is around 10 percent higher than the home visitation program. But newer state pre-K programs seem to generate even larger cognitive test score gains at even lower per-pupil costs, although nothing is known to date about their effects on key behavior and socioemotional outcomes that also predict adult poverty status, and the quality of the evaluation evidence for these state pre-K programs is not quite as strong as what is available for Head Start.

So while there remains some uncertainty about what form new investments early childhood programs should take—for example, whether we should expand Head Start program, or increase pre-K programs—there are reasons to be confident that additional spending on quality programs may reduce poverty in America over the long term. These early childhood programs also generate a number of other important benefits to both program participants and society at large, including improved health and reductions in criminal offending rates. If we adopt an appropriately broad view of what benefits should count in any program evaluation, then there would seem to be very few other antipoverty strategies that are capable of generating benefits on the order of what have been estimated for early childhood educational programs.

References

Aos, S., R. Lieb, J. Mayfield, M. Miller, and A. Pennucci. 2004. Benefits and costs of prevention and early intervention programs for youth. Olympia, WA: Washington State Institute for Public Policy.

Barnett, W. S., and L. N. Masse. 2007. Comparative cost-benefit analysis of the Abecedarian program and its policy implications. *Economics of Education Review* 26 (1): 113–25.

Barnett, W. S., J. W. Young, and L. J. Schweinhart. 1998. How preschool education influences long-term cognitive development and school success. In Early care and education for children in poverty: Promises, programs, and long-term results, ed. W. S. Barnett and S. S. Boocock, 167–84. Albany, NY: State University of New York Press.

Belfield, C. R., M. Nores, W. S. Barnett, and L. J. Schweinhart. 2006. The High/Scope Perry Preschool Program: Cost-benefit analysis using data from the age-40 followup. *Journal of Human Resources* 41 (1): 162–90.

Bloom, H. S. 1984. Accounting for no-shows in experimental evaluation designs. *Evaluation Review* 8 (2): 225–46.

Brooks-Gunn, J., L. J. Berlin, and A. Fuligni. 2000. Early childhood intervention programs: What about the family? In *The handbook of early intervention.* 2nd ed. Ed. S. Meisels and J. Shonkoff, 549–88. New York: Cambridge University Press.

Campbell, F. A., and C. T. Ramey. 1994. Effects of early intervention on intellectual and academic achievements: A follow-up study of children from low-income families. *Child Development* 65:684–98.

Campbell, F. A., C. T. Ramey, E. Pungello, J. Sparkling, and S. Miller-Johnson. 2002. Early childhood education: Young adult outcomes from the Abecedarian Project. *Applied Developmental Science* 6 (1): 42–57.

Carneiro, P., and J. Heckman. 2003. Human capital policy. In *Inequality in America: What role for human capital policies?,* ed. J. Heckman and A. Krueger, 77–240. Cambridge, MA: MIT Press.

Collins, W. A., E. E. Maccoby, L. Steinberg, E. M. Hetherington, and M. H. Bornstein. 2000. Contemporary research on parenting: The case for nurture and nature. *American Psychologist* 55:218–32.

Conger, R. D., L. E. Wallace, Y. Sun, R. L. Simons, V. C. McLoyd, and G. H. Brody. 2002. Economic pressure in African American families: A replication and extension of the family stress model. *Developmental Psychology* 38 (2): 179–93.

Cunha, F., J. Heckman, L. Lochner, and D. V. Masterov. 2005. Interpreting the evidence of life-cycle skill formation. In *Handbook of the economics of education,* ed. F. Hanushek and F. Welch, 697–812. Amsterdam: North Holland.

Currie, J. 2001. Early childhood education programs. *Journal of Economic Perspectives* 15 (2): 213–38.

Currie, J., and M. Neidell. 2007. Getting inside the "black box" of Head Start quality: What matters and what doesn't? *Economics of Education Review* 26 (1): 83–99.

Currie, J., and D. Thomas. 1995. Does Head Start make a difference? *American Economic Review* 85 (3): 341–64.

———. 1999. Early test scores, socioeconomic status, and future outcomes. NBER Working Paper no. 6943. Cambridge, MA: National Bureau of Economic Research. http://papers.nber.org/papers/w6943.pdf.

Davis-Kean, P. E. 2005. The influence of parent education and family income on child achievement: The indirect role of parental expectations and the home environment. *Journal of Family Psychology* 19:294–304.

Deming, David. 2009. Early childhood intervention and life-cycle skill development: Evidence from Head Start. *American Economic Journal: Applied Economics* 1 (3): 111–34.

Duggan, A., E. McFarlane, L. Fuddy, L. Burrell, S. M. Higman, A. Windham, and C. Sia. 2004. Randomized trial of a statewide home visiting program: Impact in preventing child abuse and neglect. *Child Abuse and Neglect* 28:597–622.

Dumas, J. E. 1989. Treating anti-social behavior in children: Child and family approaches. *Clinical Psychology Review* 9:197–222.

DuMont, K. S. Mitchell-Herzfeld, R. Greene, E. Lee, A. Lowenfels, M. Rodriguez, and V. Dorabawila. 2008. Healthy Families New York (HFNY) randomized trial: Effects on early child abuse and neglect. *Child Abuse and Neglect* 32:295–315.

Duncan, G., and J. Brooks-Gunn, eds. 1997. *Consequences of growing up poor.* New York: Russell Sage.

Duncan, G., C. Dowsett, A. Classens, K. Magnuson, A. Huston, P. Klebanov, L. Pagani, L. Feinstein, M. Engel, J. Brooks-Gunn, H. Sexton, et al. 2007. School readiness and later achievement. *Developmental Psychology* 43:1428–46.

Durlak, J. A., T. Fuhrman, and C. Lampman. 1991. Effectiveness of cognitive-behavioral therapy for maladapting children: A meta-analysis. *Psychological Bulletin* 2:204–14.

Evans, G. 2004. The environment of childhood poverty. *American Psychologist* 59:77–92.

Foster, M., A. Olchowski, and C. Webster-Stratton. 2008. Is stacking program components cost-effective? An analysis of the Incredible Years Program. *Journal of the American Academy of Child and Adolescent Psychiatry* 46:1414–24.

Garces, E., D. Thomas, and J. Currie. 2002. Longer-term effects of Head Start. *American Economic Review* 92 (4): 999–1012.

Gomby, D. S., P. L. Culross, and R. E. Behrman. 1999. Home visiting: Recent program evaluations: Analysis and recommendations. *The Future of Children* 9 (1): 4–26.

Gormley, W., and T. Gayer. 2005. Promoting school readiness in Oklahoma: An evaluation of Tulsa's pre-K program. *Journal of Human Resources* 40 (3): 533–58.

Gormley, W. T., T. Gayer, D. Phillips, and B. Dawson. 2005. The effects of universal pre-K on cognitive development. *Developmental Psychology* 41 (6): 872–84.

Gormley, W. T., D. Phillips, and T. Gayer. 2008. Preschool programs can boost school readiness. *Science* 320:1723–24.

Greenberg, M., C. Domitrovich, and B. Bumbarger. 2000. *Preventing mental disorders in school-age children: A review of the effectiveness of prevention programs.* Prevention Research Center for the Promotion of Human Development College of Health and Human Development, Pennsylvania State University. http://www.prevention.psu.edu/CMHS.PDF.

Hart, B., and T. Risley. 1995. *Meaningful differences in the everyday experiences of young American children.* Baltimore: Brookes.

Hart, K., and R. Schumacher. 2005. Making the case: Improving Head Start teacher qualifications requires increased investment. CLASP Head Start Series, Policy Paper no. 1. Washington, DC: Center for Law and Social Policy.

Hinshaw, S. P. 1992. Externalizing behavior problems and academic underachievement in childhood and adolescence: Causal relationships and underlying mechanisms. *Psychological Bulletin* 111:127–54.

Jencks, C., and M. Phillips. 1998. *Introduction.* In *The black-white test score gap,* ed. C. Jencks and M. Phillips, 1–54. Washington, DC: Brookings Institution.

Jimerson, S., B. Egeland, and A. Teo. 1999. A longitudinal study of achievement trajectories: Factors associated with change. *Journal of Educational Psychology* 91 (1): 116–26.

Karoly, L. 2002. Investing in the future: Reducing poverty through human capital programs. In *Understanding poverty in America: Progress and problems,* ed. S. Danziger and R. Haveman, 314–46. Cambridge, MA: Harvard University Press.

Kazdin, A. E. 1997. Parent management training: Evidence, outcomes, and issues. *Journal of the American Academy of Child and Adolescent Psychiatry* 36:1349–56.

Kazdin, A., and J. R. Weisz. 1998. Identifying and developing empirically supported child and adolescent treatments. *Journal of Consulting and Clinical Psychology* 66:19–36.

Knudsen, E., J. Heckman, J. Cameron, and J. Shonkoff. 2006. Economic, neurobiological and behavioral perspectives on building America's future workforce. *Proceedings of the National Academy of Sciences of the United States of America* 103 (27): 10155–62.

Krueger, A. B. 2003. Economic considerations and class size. *Economic Journal* 113:F34–F63.

Laosa, L. 1983. School, occupation, culture and family. In *Changing families,* ed. E. Sigel and L. Laosa, 79–135.

LeDoux, J. 2000. Emotion circuits in the brain. *Annual Review of Neuroscience* 133:155–84.

Lee, V., and D. Burkham. 2002. *Inequality at the starting gate.* Washington, DC: Economic Policy Institute.

Love, J. M., E. E. Kisker, C. Ross, J. Constantine, K. Boller, J. Brooks-Gunn, R. Chazan-Cohen, L. B. Tarullo, C. Brady-Smith, A. S. Fuligni, et al. 2005. The effectiveness of Early Head Start for 3-year-old children and their parents: Lessons for policy and programs. *Developmental Psychology* 41 (6): 885–901.

Love, J. M., E. E. Kisker, C. M. Ross, P. Z. Schochet, J. Brooks-Dunn, D. Paulsell, K. Boller, J. Constantine, C. Vogel, A. S. Fuligni, and C. Brady-Smith. 2002. *Making a difference in the lives of infants and toddlers and their families: The impacts of Early Head Start. Volume 1: Final technical report.* Princeton, NJ: Mathematica Policy Research.

Ludwig, J., and D. L. Miller. 2007. Does Head Start improve children's life chances? Evidence from a regression discontinuity design. *Quarterly Journal of Economics* 122 (1): 159–208.

Ludwig, J., and D. Phillips. 2007. The benefits and costs of Head Start. *Society for Research in Child Development Social Policy Report* 21 (3): 3–18.

Magnuson, K., C. Ruhm, and J. Waldfogel. 2007. Does prekindergarten improve school preparation and performance? *Economics of Education Review* 26:33–51.

Magnuson, K., and H. Shager. Forthcoming. Early education: Progress and promise for low-income children. *Children and Youth Services Review.*

Magnuson, K., and E. Votruba-Drzal. 2009. Enduring influences of poverty. In

Changing poverty, changing policies, ed. S. Danziger and M. Cancian, 153–79. New York: Russell Sage Foundation.

McLoyd, V. 1998. Socioeconomic disadvantage and child development. *American Psychologist* 53:185–204.

Miles, S. B., and D. Stipek. 2006. Contemporaneous and longitudinal associations between social behavior and literacy achievement in a sample of low-income elementary school children. *Child Development* 77 (1): 103–17.

National Scientific Council on the Developing Child. 2007. The timing and quality of early experiences combine to shape brain architecture. Harvard University, Center for the Developing Children, Working Paper no. 5. http://www.developingchild.net/pubs/wp/Timing_Quality_Early_Experiences.pdf.

Nelson, C. 2000. Neural plasticity and human development: The role of early experience in sculpting memory systems. *Developmental Science* 3 (2): 115–36.

Olds, D. L., J. Eckenrode, C. R. Henderson, H. Kitzman, J. Powers, R. Cole, et al. 1997. Long-term effects of home visitation on maternal life course and child abuse and neglect. Fifteen-year follow-up of a randomized trial. *Journal of the American Medical Association* 278:637–43.

Olds, D. L., C. R. Henderson, R. Chamberlin, and R. Tatelbaum. 1986. Preventing child abuse and neglect: a randomized trial of nurse home visitation. *Pediatrics* 78:65–78.

Olds, D. L., C. R. Henderson, R. Cole, J. Eckenrode, H. Kitzman, D. Luckey, et al. 1998. Long-term effects of nurse home visitation on children's criminal and antisocial behavior: 15-year follow-up of a randomized trial. *Journal of the American Medical Association* 280:1238–44.

Olds, D., C. R. Henderson, and H. J. Kitzman. 1994. Does prenatal and infancy nurse home visitation have enduring effects on qualities of parental caregiving and child health at 25 to 50 months of life? *Pediatrics* 93:89–98.

Olds, D., C. R. Henderson, H. J. Kitzman, J. J. Eckenrode, R. E. Cole, and R. C. Tatelbaum. 1999. Prenatal and infancy home visitation by nurses: Recent findings. *The Future of Children* 9:44–65.

Olds, D. L., and H. Kitzman. 1993. Review of research on home visiting for pregnant women and parents of young children. *Future of Children* 3:53–92.

Olds, D. L., L. Sadler, and H. Kitzman. 2007. Programs for infants and toddlers: Recent evidence from randomized trials. *Journal of Child Psychology and Psychiatry* 48:355–91.

Patterson, G. R., B. D. DeBaryshe, and E. Ramsey. 1989. A developmental perspective on anti-social behavior. *American Psychologist* 44:329–35.

Prinz, R. J., and G. E. Miller. 1994. Family-based treatment for childhood anti-social behavior: Experimental influences on dropout and engagement. *Journal of Consulting and Clinical Psychology* 62:645–50.

Puma, M., S. Bell, R. Cook, C. Heid, and M. Lopez. 2005. *Head Start impact study: First year findings.* Washington, DC: U.S. Department of Health and Human Services, Administration for Children and Families.

Ramey, C. T., and F. A. Campbell. 1979. Compensatory education for disadvantaged children. *School Review* 87 (2): 171–89.

———. 1984. Preventive education for high-risk children: Cognitive consequences of the Carolina Abecedarian Project. *American Journal of Mental Deficiency* 88 (5): 515–23.

Raviv, T., M. Kessenich, and F. J. Morrison. 2004. A mediational model of the association between socioeconomic status and three-year-old language abilities: The role of parenting factors. *Early Childhood Research Quarterly* 19 (4): 528–47.

Reiss, A. J., and J. A. Roth. 2003. *Understanding and preventing violence.* Washington, DC: National Academies Press.

Ripple, C. H., W. S. Gilliam, N. Chanana, and E. Zigler. 1999. Will fifty cooks spoil the broth? *American Psychologist* 54:327–43.

Rouse, C., J. Brooks-Gunn, and S. McLanahan. Forthcoming. Introducing the issue. *Future of Children* 15 (1): 5–13.

Scarr, S. 1992. Developmental theories for the 1990s: Development and individual differences. *Child Development* 63:1–19.

Schulman, H., H. Blank, and D. Ewen. 1999. *Seeds of success: State prekindergarten initiatives 1998–1999.* Washington, DC: Children's Defense Fund.

Schweinhart, L., H. Barnes, and D. Weikart. 1993. *Significant benefits: The High/Score Perry Preschool study through age 27.* Ypsilanti, MI: High Scope Press.

Schweinhart, L. J., J. Montie, Z. Xiang, W. S. Barnett, C. R. Belfield, and M. Nores. 2005. *The High/Scope Perry Preschool study through age 40.* Ypsilanti, MI: High/Scope Press.

Shonkoff, J. P., and D. A., Phillips, eds. 2000. *From neurons to neighborhoods: The science of early childhood development.* Washington, DC: National Academies Press.

Taylor, T. K., and A. Biglan. 1998. Behavioral family interventions for improving child-rearing: A review of the literature for clinicians and policy makers. *Clinical Child & Family Psychology Review* 1:41–60.

Tremblay, R. E., B. Masse, D. Perron, M. Leblanc, A. E. Schwartzman, and J. E. Ledingham. 1992. Early disruptive behavior, poor school achievement, delinquent behavior, and delinquent personality: Longitudinal analyses. *Journal of Consulting and Clinical Psychology* 60 (1): 64–72.

Tremblay, R. E., D. S. Nagin, J. R. Séguin, M. Zoccolillo, P. D. Zelazo, M. Boivin, D. Pérusse, and C. Japal. 2004. Physical aggression during early childhood: Trajectories and predictors. *Pediatrics* 114:43–50.

U.S. Department of Education. 2005. 10 facts about K-12 education funding. Washington, DC: U.S. Department of Education. http://www.ed.gov/about/overview/fed/10facts/10facts.pdf.

U.S. Department of Education, National Center for Education Statistics. 2007. *The condition of education 2007.* NCES 2007-064. Washington, DC: U.S. Government Printing Office.

U.S. Department of Health and Human Services. 2005. Head Start impact study: First-year findings. Washington, DC: Administration for Children and Families, Department of Health and Human Services. http://www.acf.hhs.gov/programs/opre/hs/impact_study/reports/first_yr_finds/first_yr_finds.pdf.

U.S. Statistical Abstract. 2007. *Statistical abstract of the United States.* Washington, DC: U.S. Census Bureau.

Webster-Stratton, C. 1990. Long-term follow-up with young conduct problem children: From preschool to grade school. *Journal of Clinical Child Psychology* 19:144–49.

Webster-Stratton, C., and M. Hammond. 1990. Predictors of treatment outcomes in parenting training with conduct problem children. *Behavior Therapy* 21:319–37.

Webster-Stratton, C., M. Kolpacoff, and T. Hollinsworth. 1988. Self-administered videotape therapy for families with conduct problem children: Comparison with two cost-effective treatments and a control group. *Journal of Consulting and Clinical Psychology* 56:558–66.

Webster-Stratton, C., M. J. Reid, and M. Hammond. 2004. Treating children with early-onset conduct problems: Intervention outcomes for parent, child, and teacher training. *Journal of Clinical Child and Adolescent Psychology* 33 (1): 105–24.

Webster-Stratton, C., and A. Spitzer. 1996. Parenting a young child with conduct problems. New insights using qualitative methods. In *Advances in clinical child psychology,* ed. T. H. Ollendick and R. J. Prinz, 1–62. New York: Plenum Press.

Wong, V. C., T. D. Cook, S. W. Barnett, and K. Jung. 2008. An effectiveness-based evaluation of five state pre-kindergarten programs. *Journal of Policy Analysis and Management* 27:122–54.

Zill, N., G. Resnick, K. Kim, K. O'Donnell, A. Sorongon, R. H. McKey, S. Pai-Samant, C. Clark, R. O'Brien, and M. A. D'Elio. 2008. Head Start FACES 2000: A whole-child perspective on program performance. Washington, DC: U.S. Administration for Children and Families, Child Outcomes Research and Evaluation.

3

Child Care

Patricia M. Anderson

3.1 Introduction

Child care is a necessity for the many dual career and single parent families in the United States. The percentage of currently married women with a child under six years of age who are labor force participants nearly doubled between 1970 and 2005, from 30.3 percent to 59.8 percent. Participation rates for never-married mothers and widowed, divorced, or separated mothers were even higher in 2005, at 68.4 and 73.6 percent, respectively (U.S. Census Bureau 2008). One obvious way that child care might contribute to the future success of a child is by making it less likely that he or she grows up in poverty or on public assistance because the mother can be a full labor market participant. In fact, as discussed more in the following, child care provision has been an important component of welfare reform. More directly, though, time spent in child care may have immediate effects on the child and, hence, ultimately on his or her adult outcomes. Whether these effects are likely to be positive or negative is the main topic of this chapter.

It is important to note that the focus here is not on early childhood education programs (such as Head Start or Early Head Start), or even on child development programs more broadly defined. These types of programs are covered in another chapter. Rather, the focus here is simply on basic child care, which exists to care for children while their parents participate in the labor force. That said, there will be a focus on the evidence regarding different types of child care, which necessitates a discussion of what "quality child care" means in this context.

Patricia M. Anderson is a professor of economics at Dartmouth College, and a research associate of the National Bureau of Economic Research.

A minimum indicator of child care quality is meeting state licensing requirements. While each state sets its own requirements, they typically will cover a range of issues such as staff training and qualification levels, child-to-caregiver ratios, safety and sanitation procedures, and so on. Child care providers wishing to signal a higher level of quality can apply to one of several professional organizations (e.g., National Association for Family Care, National Association of Child Care Professionals) for accreditation. In order to become an accredited child care provider, one needs to follow a series of steps, typically including a period of self-study and observational visits by an outside team of evaluators. Finally, note that being unlicensed is not necessarily the same thing as being illegal or unregulated. As an example, consider Virginia, where there are a range of options beyond a licensed provider. First, there are unlicensed day care centers (e.g., one that is religiously exempt) that, while not required to be licensed, do meet certain guidelines and are monitored by the state. Similarly, family day care can be voluntarily registered with the state, while not formally licensed. Finally, there is unregulated family day care, which is not inspected or monitored but which is not illegal unless more than five children beyond those resident in the home are cared for (or more than four total under the age of two).[1]

Overall, then, while we may see evidence of beneficial effects of "quality" child care, it is clear that not all children are in such high quality care. Additionally, some aspects of high quality, especially in center-based care, are functions of the center providing extensive early education services. Any positive outcomes that are due to these types of services will be covered more fully in the child development chapter. This chapter proceeds by first reviewing the data on current child care utilization. It then reviews the observational literature on the effects of child care and discusses the drawbacks before moving on to the few nonobservational studies available. While experimental studies focused purely on child care are rare, there were many random assignment welfare-to-work demonstrations that had an important child care component. We are likely to be able to learn something about the effect of child care investments in poor families from these studies, so they are discussed next. Implications and extensions are then presented before concluding.

3.2   Background

The high labor force participation rate among mothers of preschool-aged children implies large numbers of children are spending time in child care. According to data from the Survey of Income and Program Participation

---

1. See "A Guide for Choosing Quality Child Care," Virginia Department of Social Services, available at http://www.dss.virginia.gov/files/division/cc/publications/choosing_quality_childcare/guidelines_one_document/brochure-eng.pdf.

(SIPP), for children of employed mothers, we see 19 percent spending time in center-based care, 8 percent in family day care, and another 9 percent in some other type of nonrelative care.[2] Almost 21 percent are cared for by a grandparent, and another 7 percent are cared for by a sibling or other relative. It is worth pointing out that the type of care used varies tremendously by the education level of the mother, with center-based care being more common among the more educated and relative care more common among the less educated.

Another source of information on children's care arrangements is the 2005 Early Childhood Program Participation Survey (ECPP).[3] For weekly care arrangements for children through age five who are not in kindergarten, this survey reports that 20 percent were in only one type of relative care, 14 percent were in one type of nonrelative care, 45 percent were in one type of center-based care, and 22 percent were in combinations of types of care. Note that center-based care here again includes Head Start and other early childhood education programs. Overall, children in the ECPP spend about twenty-nine hours weekly in nonparental care, with average out-of-pocket costs ranging from about $60 to $105, and 19% receiving assistance in paying child care costs. The SIPP data provides similar information on child care costs, reporting average weekly child care costs of $128, implying that families spend about 9 percent of monthly income on child care. Note that this figure is only for those making child care payments—about half of families with children under age five and an employed mother have no child care payments. Making no payments can be due to either a relative (or possibly a close friend) volunteering their time or to receiving a child care subsidy that covers 100 percent of child care costs.

Overall, then, it is clear that child care is an important part of many children's lives, with the SIPP showing that about 15 million children under age five spend time in nonparental care that is not explicitly an early education facility. This number includes about 6.3 million in relative care, 4.5 million in nonrelative care outside their home, and another 700,000 in nonrelative care in their own home. Additionally, over 3 million children are in multiple care arrangements. In addition to any effect having a gainfully employed mother might have on a child's future outcomes, investments in quality child care may help set the child on the path to adult success.

In evaluating whether increased investments in child care can be an efficient strategy for ameliorating later adult poverty, it is important to consider the counterfactual. Often, the child will typically be at home with a

2. All statistics based on SIPP come from the detailed tables of "Who's Minding the Kids? Child Care Arrangements: Spring 2005" available from the U.S. Census Bureau at http://www.census.gov/population/www/socdemo/child/ppl-2005.html.

3. All statistics based on ECPP come from the tables in "Initial Results from the 2005 NHES Early Childhood Program Participation Survey" available from the U.S. Department of Education at http://nces.ed.gov/pubs2006/earlychild/02.asp.

mother who is now not a participant in the labor market. This indirect effect of maternal labor market participation will be considered more fully in the following. Taking as given that the child will be in nonparental care while the mother works, though, for preschool-aged children, a lack of day care options will very rarely imply that the child is in self-care. Rather, the child is likely to be cared for by a patchwork of providers, including relatives and friends, but rarely an accredited day care center. Thus, we really should think of investments in day care as insuring that children will incur stability and quality of care throughout their preschool years.

3.3   Nonexperimental Studies on the Effects of Day Care

The majority of studies analyzing the impact of child care on preschool-aged children are observational. Table 3.1 summarizes the nonexperimental studies. One common approach is to use an existing data set, such as the National Longitudinal Survey of Youth (NLSY) 1979 Mother-Child Matched file. Waldfogel (2002) reviews a range of these studies, which generally tend to find a negative relationship between early child care and later cognitive outcomes. Interestingly, these negative effects are not always found for minority children, perhaps due to differences in the non-child care environments. It is important to realize, though, that because the NLSY data are observational, there is likely to be selection into child care. While a large amount of background information is available that allows researchers to control for many observable differences across children, unobservable differences are not controlled for, and, thus, the results may be biased. Therefore, none of these relationships can be considered causal. More importantly, the data on child care in the NLSY is relatively weak, in that one cannot really differentiate high-quality care from low-quality care. Thus, these studies tend to simply focus on the presence of any nonparental care in the early years of life.

In the early 1990s, a new data collection effort began to explicitly study children's experiences in day care and to allow for the type, quality, and quantity of care to be determined. The National Institute of Child Health and Development (NICHD) Study of Early Child Care and Youth Development (SECCYD) began in 1991 when mothers were approached in hospitals based on having given birth in a selected time interval. Families have since been followed longitudinally, with a voluminous literature produced that analyzes the data collected. Again, because the data is observational, there is still likely to be a problem of selection, not only in terms of being in any child care, but also in terms of the type, quality, and quantity of care. Additionally, the NICHD study is not nationally representative. Nonetheless, it remains the "state of the art" in terms of observing correlations between children's day care experiences and their outcomes, having followed the children now past their primary schooling.

Results on the impact of child care from the NICHD have been somewhat mixed, depending on the outcome studied and the age of the child.[4] Negative effects of care tend to be found mainly for behavioral outcomes, while positive effects are often found for cognitive outcomes. An important aspect of the NICHD study is the ability to separately examine the type, quality, and quantity of care, as well as its timing. Thus, based on NICHD data, it can be said that spending more than ten hours per week in care at a young age is correlated with less-secure attachment for children whose mothers are not sensitive. Similarly, longer hours in care are related to more problem behaviors at age two. However, time spent in *quality* care was related to fewer problem behaviors at ages two and three. In fact, quality was positively related with both better behavioral outcomes and better cognitive outcomes. When quality is measured by language stimulation and caregiver interactions, children's language skills are observed to be higher at ages fifteen, twenty-four, and thirty-six months. Similarly, when quality is measured mainly by child-staff ratio, group size, teacher training, and teacher education, language comprehension and school readiness are higher for two- and three-year-old children. Interestingly, when focusing simply on type of care, center-based care was found to have a positive relationship to cognitive outcomes, but it was also related to poor behavioral outcomes.

These relationships between day care and child outcomes generally appear to be long lasting, especially for cognitive outcomes. Children in higher quality care were still scoring better on vocabulary tests in the fifth grade than were those in lower quality care. At the same time, those who had been in center-based care still exhibited more problem behaviors in sixth grade. By this age, however, there was no longer any relationship between behavior and having been in any care (versus parental care). Based on the NICHD studies, then, it appears possible that subsidizing high quality care has the potential to increase children's cognitive outcomes (and ultimately their adult labor market outcomes). However, it is impossible to draw causal conclusions based on the nonrepresentative NICHD sample with self-selection into types of care.

An alternate type of nonexperimental study is one that uses existing data but implements econometric techniques that are meant to allow the estimated effects to be interpreted causally. Recall that the NLSY and NICHD studies discussed in the preceding do nothing more than control for as many observable characteristics as possible and admit that the results cannot be interpreted as causal impacts of child care. Bernal (2005) uses the same NLSY data as other studies but estimates a structural model to allow for joint estimation of the employment and child care decisions. While fairly strong assumptions must be maintained to estimate the model, the results confirm the negative impacts of early child care on later cognitive outcomes

4. Discussion of the NICHD results is based on Belsky et al. (2007) and Waldfogel (2002), which contain references to the full range of the past literature.

Table 3.1   Nonexperimental studies of child care (review papers and selected studies)

Study	Evaluation design	Sample	Outcomes	Effects
Waldfogel (2002)—review of Desai et al. (1989); Baydar and Brooks-Gunn (1991); Belsky and Eggebeen (1991); Blau and Grossberg (1992); Vandell and Ramanan (1992); Parcel and Menaghan (1994); Greenstein (1995); Harvey (1999); Han, Waldfogel, and Brooks-Gunn (2001); Waldfogel, Han, and Brooks-Gunn (2000); Ruhm (2000)	Literature review.	NLSY several cross-sections of mainly preschoolers; one cross-section of 2nd graders, one cross-section of 12 year-olds; several longitudinal studies of children up to age eight.	Cognitive outcomes including PPVT-R, PIAT-Reading, PIAT-Math test scores; behavioral outcomes measured by BPI.	Majority of studies find negative effects on cognitive outcomes, behavior. A small number of studies find insignificant effects on outcomes. Some evidence that negative effects are not significant for minority groups.
Waldfogel (2002)—review of NICHD Early Child Care Research Network (1996, 1997, 1998, 1999, 2000)	Literature review.	NICHD study children through age three.	Language comprehension, school readiness, language skills, problem behaviors.	High quality care associated with better cognitive skills and school readiness, fewer problem behaviors.
Bernal (2005)	Estimation structural model of employment and child care.	NLSY children age five, six, and seven.	PPVT, PIAT-Reading, PIAT-Math.	Full-time care over first five years leads to 10.4% reduction in test scores.
Baker, Gruber, and Milligan (2005)	Natural experiment of Quebec providing $5 a day child care.	NLSCY children aged zero–four and six–eleven years old.	Behavioral outcomes including hyperactivity, anxiety, and aggression; developmental outcomes including motor and social development score, PPVT; health outcomes including overall, injuries, asthma.	Positive impacts on problem behaviors; negative impact on motor and social development; negative impacts on good health; no significant effect on PPVT.

Baker and Milligan (2008)	Natural experiment of Canada extending maternity leave to one year.	NLSCY children aged six–twenty-nine months old.	Child temperament (irritability, crying, etc.); security (response to new things, overall difficulty, etc.); development (motor/ social score, age sat up, age took first step).	Little impact of increased maternal care found on children's outcomes.
Brooks (2002)	Comparison of low-income mothers in Georgia receiving child care subsidies with those left on a waiting list.	Fifty-two families with subsidies and fifty demographically matched families on a waiting list.	School readiness, personal maturity scale, general health.	No significant differences between groups.

Note: NLSY = National Longitudinal Survey of Youth 1979 Mother-Child Matched file; PPVT = Peabody Picture Vocabulary Test; PIAT = Peabody Individual Achievement Test; BPI = Behavior Problems Index; NICHD = National Institute of Child Health and Development; NLSCY = National Longitudinal Survey of Children and Youth.

that were found in most of the observational studies using the NLSY. Note, however, that this study focuses only on young children and, thus, cannot speak to whether the cognitive effects of early exposure to child care persist.

Two papers using Canadian data try to approximate an experimental study design by taking advantage of "natural experiments" in which a change in the environment exogenously changes a child's exposure to day care. Baker, Gruber, and Milligan (2005) take advantage of a policy change in Quebec that provided government-sponsored child care for an out-of-pocket cost of just $5 per day. The effect of this policy was to increase the use of preschool-aged child care by 14 percentage points. This increase in child care, though, led to clear negative effects on child outcomes. In particular, increases in hyperactivity, anxiety, and aggression were reported, with declines in motor and social development and health outcomes. Based on this natural experiment, one might conclude that there are clear negative effects of child care. However, one major drawback to this study is the inability to control for quality. There is some evidence that the rapid expansion of child care slots necessary to implement this program resulted in most of the children who ended up in care due to the new program being in low quality care. Because disadvantaged children in Quebec generally already had access to subsidized child care, the children taking up this lower-quality care were generally middle class. Additionally, the largest labor supply changes were seen among married mothers, implying the program mainly resulted in middle-class children from intact families being placed in low-quality care. Thus, it is not clear that we can draw conclusions from this quasi-experiment on what the impact on disadvantaged children of spending on high-quality care would be.

Baker and Milligan (2008) study an expansion of maternity leave in Canada that resulted in mothers spending about 50 percent more time not working in the first year of a child's life. Thus, this natural experiment reduced the use of early child care. If such care were to cause negative (positive) child outcomes, then we would expect to observe positive (negative) outcomes in the wake of this change. However, at least over the first two years of the child's life, there appeared to be no developmental impacts, either positive or negative. While it is possible that effects will appear at older ages or are already present in outcomes not able to be measured with the existing data, this study currently provides some of the best nonexperimental data on child care impacts, and it implies that investing in either extended maternity leave or in more early child care is unlikely to have significant impacts on child developmental outcomes.

Finally, one other approach to estimating causal impacts using nonexperimental data is based on rationing of government child care subsidies. Brooks (2002) is able to compare low-income Georgia mothers who received day care subsidies with those who remained on a waiting list. The fact that both sets of mothers wanted child care obviates the major source of selection in the observational studies. While the mothers receiving the subsidies were more likely to be employed, and their children were more likely to be in stable, center-based care, there were no significant differences in school readiness or socioemotional development between these children and those remaining on the waiting list. The main drawback to this study is an inability to measure quality. The Georgia subsidy level was fairly low, so even though the subsidized mothers were more likely to use center-based care, the children may still have been in relatively low-quality care.

3.4   Experimental Studies Providing Evidence on the Effects of Day Care

Given the drawbacks of the nonexperimental studies described in the preceding, it is unfortunate that there are no experimental studies in which children are randomly assigned into a treatment group that is placed into day care and into a control group which is not. However, there are a range of randomized control trials in which child care subsidies are part of a package of benefits given to a treatment group and withheld from a control group. These experimental studies are summarized in table 3.2. These types of trials were carried out in the 1990s as part of states' experimentation with welfare reform, prior to the federal Personal Responsibility and Work Opportunity Reconciliation Act of 1996 (PRWORA). The goal of PRWORA and the demonstrations that preceded it were to transition women off of welfare by emphasizing "work first." The demonstrations experimented with different programs to investigate what types of welfare-to-work services worked best. These experimental services typically incorporated carrots (earnings supplements), sticks (mandatory employment services and welfare time limits), or both in order increase mothers' labor force participation. Given this emphasis on maternal employment, an important component to most of these experiments was expanded child care assistance, in the form of such things as subsidies and direct payments to providers and increased access to information and help with bureaucratic hurdles. Typically, there was an emphasis on formal care, especially center-based care.

All of the demonstrations were successful in pulling mothers into the labor force and increasing their earnings[5]. However, not all programs increased family income because in some cases, earnings gains were matched by decreases in benefit payments. Only the programs that included earnings supplements uniformly increased income. Perhaps not surprisingly, given the uniform increases in maternal employment, the use of child care also increased. No serious negative impacts on children appear for the experimental group although for some age groups in some demonstrations, there

5. This discussion of the programs as a whole is based mainly on the summary study of Morris, Gennetian, and Duncan (2005), but also draws from the individual program studies referenced in table 3.2.

Table 3.2　　　　**Experimental studies with a child care component**

Study	Intervention	Evaluation design	Sample
Bloom et al. (2000)	Florida's Family Transition Program (FTP), 1994–1999	Random assignment into FTP versus standard AFDC.	Four-year follow-up of 2,800 single parents; children who were aged 0–4 initially are split 331/325 for FTP/AFDC.
Gennetian, Miller, and Smith (2005)	Minnesota Family Investment Program (MFIP), 1994–1999	Random assignment into MFIP versus standard AFDC.	Six-year follow-up of 3,554/3,848 (MFIP/AFDC) single parent and 1,109/1,147 two-parent households. Focus here on single-parent effects, where increased child care was observed during program years.
Miller et al. (2008)	Milwaukee's New Hope Project, 1994–1998	Random assignment into New Hope versus standard AFDC.	Eight-year follow-up of 366/379 (New Hope/AFDC) families with child aged one–ten at enrollment.
Michalopoulos et al. (2002)	Canada's Self-Sufficiency Project (SSP), 1992–2002	Random assignment into SSP versus standard Income Assistance.	Thirty-six-month and fifty-four-month follow-ups of children from 9,000 single-parent Income Assistance recipients in British Columbia and New Brunswick.
Bloom et al. (2002)	Connecticut's Jobs First (CT Jobs First), 1996–1999	Random assignment into Jobs First versus standard AFDC.	Three-year follow-up of 2,381/2,392 (Jobs First/AFDC) welfare applicants and recipients.
Freedman et al. (2000)	Los Angeles Jobs-First GAIN (LA GAIN), 1995–1998	Random assignment into LA GAIN versus standard AFDC.	Two-year follow-up of 15,683 single-parent and 5,048 two-parent families.
Hamilton et al. (2001)	National evaluation of Welfare-to-Work Strategies (NEWWS), 1991–1999	Evaluation of eleven different programs, all with random assignment into program versus standard AFDC.	Five-year follow-up of 40,000 single parents and their children across seven locations.
Quint, Bos, and Polit (1997)	New Chance, 1989–1992	Random assignment of mothers aged sixteen–twenty-two into New Chance versus standard AFDC.	Three-year follow-up of 1,401/678 (treatment/control) mothers.
Morris, Gennetian, and Duncan (2005)	Next Generation Project	Meta-analysis of seven random assignment studies (FTP, MFIP, New Hope, SSP, CT Jobs First, LA GAIN, NEWWS).	27,180 observations from 15,779 children aged two–nine years old at random assignment from 11,502 families.

Note: AFDC = Aid to Families with Dependent Children.
SD = standard deviation.

Outcomes	Effects
Parental outcomes of employment, family income, welfare receipt; child outcomes of child care, academic functioning, social behavior and emotional well-being, health, and safety.	FTP increases employment and earnings, reduces welfare receipt. More child care, more hours, and more stable arrangements. No impact on quality of care. Few significant impacts on child development.
Parental outcomes of employment, family income, and welfare receipt; child outcomes of 3rd and 5th grade math and reading achievement.	MFIP increased employment, earnings, and welfare receipt through four years; no overall impacts, but .2 SD increase in 3rd grade reading for long-term welfare recipients, .4 SD for reading and .5 SD for math in 5th grade for the most disadvantaged.
Parental outcomes of employment, family income, welfare receipt; child outcomes of child care, academic functioning, social behavior and emotional well-being, health, and safety.	New Hope increased employment and income, impacts fade at program end; more time in center-based care, care more stable; .12 SD increase in reading scores; more positive parent-reported behavior, teachers report more problem behavior for girls; no health impacts.
Parental outcomes of employment, family income, welfare receipt; child outcomes of child care, academic functioning, social behavior and emotional well-being, health, and safety.	SSP increased full-time employment and earnings through the 4th year; increased use of nonmaternal care, increased instability for three–four-year-old care; no impact on outcomes for those one–two years old at intake, .1 increase in portion of math skills questions correct for those three–four years old.
Parental outcomes of employment, family income, welfare receipt; child outcomes of child care, academic functioning, social behavior and emotional well-being, health, and safety.	Jobs First increased employment and earnings; increased use of child care; positive effects on children's behavior; no effect on academic outcomes.
Parental outcomes of employment, family income, welfare receipt; child outcomes of child care, academic functioning, social behavior and emotional well-being, health, and safety.	LA GAIN increased employment and earnings; increased use of child care (formal and informal) and problems with child care; no systematic effects on child outcomes, but some evidence of increased grade repetition for the youngest children.
Parental outcomes of employment, family income, welfare receipt; child outcomes of child care, academic functioning, social behavior and emotional well-being, health, and safety.	Increases in employment and earnings, smaller for education-focused programs, mandate enforcement necessary for impacts; increases in child care use fade over time as employment effects fade; few impacts on academic outcomes, some gains in social skills and behavior; impacts vary greatly across programs.
Parental outcomes of employment, family income, welfare receipt; child outcomes of child care, academic functioning, social behavior and emotional well-being, health, and safety.	Short-term increase in employment, no increase in earnings; more use of center care in first 1.5 years, few care differences in second 1.5 years; no impact on cognitive development; some evidence of more behavioral problems.
Cognitive outcomes and school achievement.	Positive improvements in school achievement (.05 SD if aged two–three at start, .07 if 4–5) appear due to increased income (since mainly seen in programs with an earnings supplement component); some possibility that increased center-based care can impact school achievement.

are small increases in problem behavior. There also do not appear to be many important positive effects although there are some indications of small increases in academic outcomes, especially for the children who were the youngest at the start of the demonstration. The biggest impacts on cognitive development appear in programs that increase family income. Given that the use of center-based care increases strongly with income, it is difficult to sort out how much of the observed positive effects are due to higher income versus more exposure to center-based care. Recall that observational studies based on the NICHD data found a positive correlation between cognitive development and high-quality center-based care.

In thinking about whether it is possible that subsidizing child care might improve child outcomes purely by the increase in family income achieved via a working mother, it is important to consider the literature on the effect of family income on children. Poor outcomes observed for children living in poverty are often pointed to as an indication that higher family income can improve children's outcomes (e.g., Berger, Paxson, and Waldfogel 2005). However, a range of recent studies have cast doubt on the idea that there is a causal effect of income. For example, Blau (1999) concludes that the effect of current income on child development is very small, and that while changes in permanent income are larger, they are still not meaningful in a policy sense. That is, politically infeasible income transfers would be necessary to have any important effects on child development. Mayer (1997) comes to similar conclusions. Additionally, Dooley and Stewart (2004) use econometric methods similar to Mayer and to Blau (family-fixed effects, including future income, instrumental variables, etc.) on Candian data and also discount the importance of family income as a causal mechanism for child development. Finally, and perhaps most convincingly, Sacerdote (2007) examines outcomes for Korean adoptees who were essentially randomly placed with families beginning in the 1950s. He found no significant effect of family income on any of the adult adoptees' outcomes (education levels, income, etc.). Note that for their nonadopted siblings, there was a significant effect of income. Thus, it does not appear that any significant returns to subsidized child care would come purely via the transmission of parental income to child income as an adult.[6]

That said, studies using convincing methods to estimate causal impacts of income have found significant, but short-term, effects on children's test scores. Dahl and Lochner (2008) take advantage of expansions in the Earned Income Tax Credit (EITC) to determine that an extra $1,000 in family income increases children's test scores in reading and math by 6 percent of a standard deviation. However, these positive effects appear to fade out

6. Note that in Sacerdote (2007), the transmission coefficient from family income to child adult income is 0.246 and significant for biological children, but only 0.186 and insignificant for adopted children. At best, then, we would expect a 10 percent increase in parental income to increase future adult income by only about 2 percent.

about a year after the income shock. Similarly, looking at the Canadian Child Benefit Expansions, Milligan and Stabile (2009) find that $1,000 in additional family income results in math and vocabulary test scores increasing by about 7 percent of a standard deviation. They also find that children's emotional and mental health is improved, which has the potential for longer-term effects.

3.5   Discussion and Extensions

Despite the limited evidence on the causal impacts of child care on children's developmental outcomes, the Child Care and Development Fund (CCDF) made $5 billion in federal funds available in fiscal year 2008 to states, territories, and tribes.[7] As seen in figure 3.1, federal CCDF spending is only a part of total government spending on child care, with over 50 percent of funding coming from state funds (matching and maintenance of effort [MOE] for CCDF, excess state Temporary Assistance to Needy Families [TANF] MOE funds) and TANF funds (direct and transfer to CCDF). Figure 3.2 shows that government spending on child care has risen dramatically over time, more than tripling since 1996.

States are required to spend at least 4 percent of their CCDF allocation on "quality activities" meant to increase the provision and use of quality child care (CCDF report to Congress). Among other things, quality activities can include such things as providing training to providers, increasing provider compensation, and providing consumer education. Quality activities can also involve programs that are better categorized as early learning programs that are discussed in the child development chapter.

As might be surmised from the large increase in child care spending since the beginning of welfare reform, a major governmental interest in child care is allowing single mothers to enter the work force, while still insuring that their children are cared for in a safe environment. Based on experimental evidence from welfare-to-work demonstrations, it seems safe to conclude that child care used in this manner does no harm to children, and those placed in center-based care may even see slight benefits. However, the small positive impacts on academic achievement seen in some demonstrations may not be due solely to increased use of center-based care, but rather to the combination of changes engendered by the move from welfare to work. Additionally, the positive aspects of center-based care may be less due to the type of care than the quality. That is, center-based care may be much more likely to implement early learning activities that are specifically designed to positively impact children's development.

Given that our main evidence on the impacts of child care come either

---

7. Information is available from the CCDF Web site at http://www.acf.hhs.gov/programs/ccb/ccdf/index.htm.

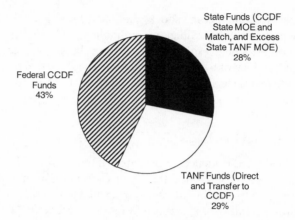

Fig. 3.1   FY2005 Child Care and Development Fund (CCDF) and Temporary Assistance for Needy Families (TANF) funding available for child care
Source: CCDF report to Congress for FY2005 and FY2006.

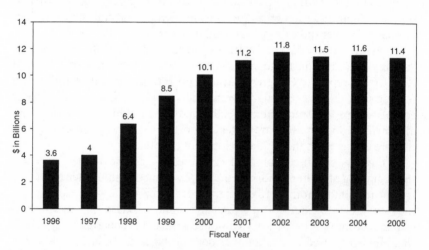

Fig. 3.2   State and federal child care funding over time
Source: CCDF report to Congress for FY2005 and FY2006.

Notes: Estimates of funds available for child care include mandatory and discretionary Child Care and Development Fund (CCDF) federal appropriations; state matching and mainte- nance of effort (MOE) funds for CCDF, Temporary Assistance for Needy Families (TANF) transfers to CCDF, and direct spending on child care; state excess MOE funds for child care in the TANF program; and Social Services Block Grant (SSBG) funds for child care.

from observational studies that are contaminated by self-selection into child care, or welfare-to-work demonstrations that confound child care effects with other program effects, it would be useful to implement randomized control trials geared specifically at child care. Within the context of TANF, for example, mothers could be randomly assigned to use center-based care or not to determine if it is type of care, per se, that matters. Because the observational studies provide evidence of the importance of quality measures, it would be worthwhile to implement randomization on this dimension. One possibility might be to experiment at child care centers with changes in child-staff ratios, group sizes, provision of additional caregiver training, and so on. Randomization into treatment and control centers (or care groups within a center) would need to be carefully done to convincingly maintain comparability.

Based on current evidence, however, it does not seem that spending on child care itself can be considered a front-line approach to poverty fighting. Conditional on the fact that children will be in nonparental care, however, spending on quality may pay dividends. The unanswered question is whether quality improvements that do not reach the level of actually being child development programs would be worth the cost. It is here that carefully done experiments on the relatively straightforward aspects of quality highlighted in observational studies such as those from the NICHD would be quite useful.

References

Baker, Michael, Jonathan Gruber, and Kevin Milligan. 2005. Universal childcare, maternal labor supply and family well-being. NBER Working Paper no. 11832. Cambridge, MA: National Bureau of Economic Research, December.

Baker, Michael, and Kevin Milligan. 2008. Evidence from maternity leave expansions of the impact of maternal care on early child development. NBER Working Paper no. 1382. Cambridge, MA: National Bureau of Economic Research, February.

Baydar, Nazil, and Jeanne Brooks-Gunn. 1991. Effects of maternal employment and child care arrangements in infancy on preschoolers' cognitive and behavioral outcomes: Evidence from the children of the NLSY. *Developmental Psychology* 27:918–31.

Belsky, Jay, Margaret Burchinal, Kathleen McCartney, Deborah Lowe Vandell, K. Alison Clarke-Stewart, and Margaret Tresch Owen. 2007. Are there long-term effects of early child care? *Child Development* 78 (2): 681–701.

Belsky, Jay, and David Eggebeen. 1991. Early and extensive maternal employment/child care and 4–6-year-olds socioemotional development: Children of the National Longitudinal Survey of Youth. *Journal of Marriage and the Family* 53:1083–99.

Berger, Lawrence M., Christina Paxson, and Jane Waldfogel. 2005. Income and child development. *Center for Research on Child Wellbeing Working Paper no. 05-16-FF*, June.

Bernal, Raquel. 2005. The effects of maternal employment and child care choices on children's cognitive development. Northwestern University. Mimeograph.

Blau, D. M. 1999. The effect of income on child development. *Review of Economics and Statistics* 81 (2): 261–76.

Blau, Francine D., and Adam J. Grossberg. 1992. Maternal labor supply and children's cognitive development. *Review of Economics and Statistics* 74 (3): 474–81.

Bloom, Dan, James J. Kemple, Pamela Morris, Susan Scrivener, Nandita Verma, Richard Hendra, Diana Adams-Ciardullo, David Seith, and Johanna Walter. 2000. *The Family Transition Program: Final report on Florida's initial time-limited welfare program.* New York: MDRC.

Bloom, Dan, Susan Scrivener, Charles Michalopoulos, Pamela Morris, Richard Hendra, Diana Adams-Ciardullo, Johanna Walter, and Wanda Vargas. 2002. *Jobs first: Final report on Connecticut's welfare reform initiative.* New York: MDRC.

Brooks, Fred. 2002. Impacts of child care subsidies on family and child well-being. *Early Childhood Research Quarterly* 17:498–511.

Dahl, Gordon, and Lance Lochner. 2008. The impact of family income on child achievement: Evidence from the Earned Income Tax Credit. NBER Working Paper no. 14599. Cambridge, MA: National Bureau of Economic Research, December.

Desai, Sonalde, P. Lindsey Chase-Lansdale, and Robert T. Michael. 1989. Mother or market?: Effects of maternal employment on cognitive development of four-year-old children. *Demography* 26:545–61.

Dooley, M., and J. Stewart. 2004. Family income and child outcomes in Canada. *Canadian Journal of Economics* 37 (4): 898–917.

Freedman, Stephen, Jean Tansey Knab, Lisa A. Gennetian, and David Navarro. 2000. *The Los Angeles Jobs-First GAIN evaluation: Final report on a work first program in a major urban center.* New York: MDRC.

Gennetian, Lisa A., Cynthia Miller, and Jared Smith. 2005. *Turning welfare into a work support.* New York: MDRC.

Greenstein, Theodore N. 1995. Are the "most advantaged" children truly disadvantaged by early maternal employment? Effects on child cognitive outcomes. *Journal of Family Issues* 16 (2): 149–69.

Hamilton, Gayle, Stephen Freedman, Lisa Gennetian, Charles Michalopoulos, Johanna Walter, Diana Adams-Ciardullo, Anna Gassman-Pines, et al. 2001. *National evaluation of welfare-to-work strategies: How effective are different welfare-to-work approaches? Five year adult and child impacts for eleven programs.* New York: MDRC.

Han, Wen-Jui, Jane Waldfogel, and Jeanne Brooks-Gunn. 2001. The effects of early maternal employment on later cognitive and behavioral outcomes. *Journal of Marriage and the Family* 63 (2): 336–54.

Harvey, Elizabeth A. 1999. Short-term and long-term effects of early parental employment on children of the National Longitudinal Survey of Youth. *Developmental Psychology* 35 (2): 445–59.

Mayer, S. 1997. *What money can't buy: Family income and children's life chances.* Cambridge, MA: Harvard University Press.

Michalopoulos, Charles, Doug Tattrie, Cynthia Miller, Philip K. Robins, Pamela Morris, David Gyarmati, Cindy Redcross, Kelly Foley, and Reuben Ford. 2002. *Making work pay: Final report on the Self-Sufficiency Project for long-term welfare recipients.* New York: MDRC.

Miller, Cynthia, Aletha C. Huston, Greg J. Duncan, Vonnie C. McLoyd, and Thomas S. Weisner. 2008. *New hope for the working poor: Effects after eight years for families and children.* New York: MDRC.

Milligan, Kevin, and Mark Stabile. 2009. Do child tax benefits affect the wellbeing of children? Evidence from Canadian child benefit expansions. Canadian Labour Market and Skills Researcher Network, Working Paper no. 12.

Morris, Pamela A., Lisa A. Gennetian, and Greg J. Duncan. 2005. Effects of welfare and employment policies on young children: New findings on policy experiments conducted in the early 1990s. *Social Policy Report* 19 (2): 1–17.

NICHD Early Child Care Research Network. 1996. Characteristics of infant child care: Factors contributing to positive caregiving. *Early Childhood Research Quarterly* 11:269–306.

———. 1997. The effects of infant child care on infant-mother attachment security: Results of the NICHD Study of Early Child Care. *Child Development* 68:860–79.

———. 1998. Early child care and self-control, compliance, and problem behavior at 24 and 36 months. *Child Development* 69 (3): 1145–70.

———. 1999. Child outcomes when child-care center classes meet recommended standards for quality. *American Journal of Public Health* 89:1072–77.

———. 2000. The relation of child care to cognitive and language development: Results from the NICHD Study of Early Child Care. *Child Development* 71 (4): 960–80.

Parcel, Toby L., and Elizabeth G. Menaghan. 1994. Early parental work, family social capital, and early childhood outcomes. *American Journal of Sociology* 99 (4): 972–1009.

Quint, Janet C., Johannes M. Bos, and Denise F. Polit. 1997. *New chance: Final report on a comprehensive program for young mothers in poverty and their children.* New York: MDRC.

Ruhm, Christopher J. 2000. Parental employment and child cognitive development. University of North Carolina at Greensboro. Mimeograph.

Sacerdote, B. 2007. How large are the effects from changes in family environment? A study of Korean American adoptees. *The Quarterly Journal of Economics* 121 (1): 119–58.

U.S. Census Bureau. 2007. *Statistical abstract of the United States: 2008 (127th edition).* Washington, DC: GPO. Available at: http://www.census.gov/compendia/statab/2008/2008edition.html.

Vandell, Deborah Lowe, and Janaki Ramanan. 1992. Effects of early and recent maternal employment on children from low-income families. *Child Development* 63 (4): 938–49.

Waldfogel, Jane. 2002. Child care, women's employment, and child outcomes. *Journal of Population Economics* 15:527–48.

Waldfogel, Jane, Wen-Jui Han, and Jeanne Brooks-Gunn. 2000. Early maternal employment and child outcomes: A longitudinal analysis of children from the NLSY. Columbia University. Mimeograph.

4

Child Health

Lara Shore-Sheppard

4.1 Introduction

The connection between poor health and low income has long been recognized. Along almost any dimension, the poor suffer from worse health. Even among children, who are generally healthy, poorer individuals report worse health outcomes, and this relationship only sharpens in adulthood. According to data from the National Health Interview Survey, while nearly 90 percent of nonpoor children report very good or excellent health, fewer than 70 percent of poor children do, and, among adults aged forty-five to sixty-four, the percentages range from slightly over 60 percent among the nonpoor to under 30 percent among the poor (see figure 4.1). Similar patterns hold for severe health problems, with significantly more poor adults and children reporting a condition that limits their daily activities (see figure 4.2). From the cradle to the grave, poverty and poor health are closely entwined.

Determining whether interventions targeting childhood health are likely to have a beneficial long-run effect on a child's life chances is more difficult, however.[1] Perhaps even more than most individual characteristics, health is a "black box"—a complicated and only partially understood function of genes, other biological factors, environment, and behavior. Moreover, health interacts with various other inputs provided by the child's family or society, such as income and education, to determine a child's life chances. While there is evidence linking poor health in childhood to worse adult nonhealth

Lara Shore-Sheppard is an associate professor of economics at Williams College, and a faculty research fellow of the National Bureau of Economic Research.

1. See Currie (2008) for a thoughtful survey of this question and of the question whether parental circumstances affect child health.

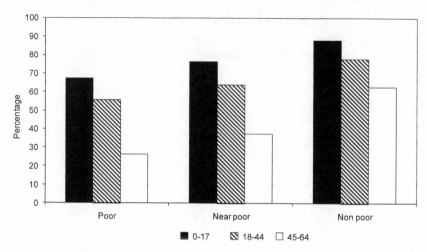

Fig. 4.1   Individuals reporting very good or excellent health, by poverty status and age

Source: Centers for Disease Control Health Data Interactive calculation from National Health Interview Survey 2004–2006.

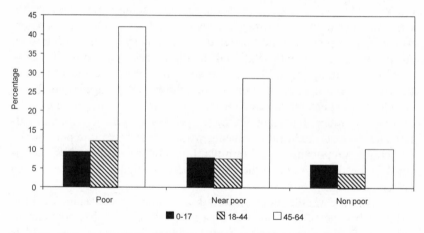

Fig. 4.2   Percent of individuals with an activity limitation, by poverty status and age

Source: Centers for Disease Control Health Data Interactive calculation from National Health Interview Survey 2004–2006.

outcomes, the direction of causality is unclear. For example, Case, Lubotsky, and Paxson (2002) find that having one of a set of identified medical conditions is associated with fewer years of completed schooling but that the association is smaller for children with higher incomes. While this evidence is consistent with poor health having a causal effect on education (perhaps through days of school missed or difficulty studying), it is also consistent with poverty or some other related factor causing both the poor health and the reduction in schooling, with little or no direct link between health and education. Currie et al. (2009) address this issue to some extent by including maternal fixed effects in a study of the association between health in childhood and early adult outcomes using administrative data from Manitoba. They find that siblings with poorer health in childhood—particularly with problems of mental health—are more likely to participate in public assistance and to have worse educational outcomes than their healthier siblings. Similarly, Smith (2009), using retrospective data from the Panel Study of Income Dynamics, finds that adults who report having good or excellent health as children have higher adult socioeconomic outcomes than their siblings who did not report having good health. These results give some support to the possibility that there is a causal relationship between health in childhood and adult outcomes.

In figure 4.3, I outline the possible causal links between child health and adult income as well as the possible intermediaries by which child health may be affected. There are three main pathways by which child health can affect adult income. Probably the most direct way is through the impact child health has on adult health, which, in turn, will affect adult earnings capacity. However, child health may also affect adult earnings even if the child does not become an unhealthy adult if the child's ill health affects the quantity or quality of education the child receives. If, for example, the child misses a great deal of school or is unable to learn while in school because of health problems, the child will have accumulated lower amounts of human capital

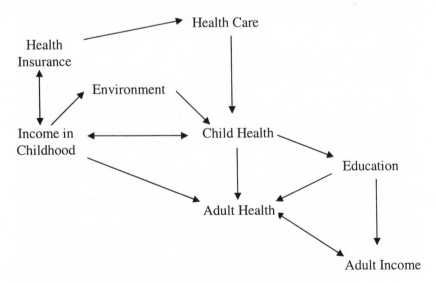

Fig. 4.3   Possible causal links between child health and adult income

than he or she would have otherwise. Finally, child health may affect adult earnings more indirectly, through the income the child's family has available. For example, having a severely or chronically ill child to take care of may reduce the amount of work the child's parent is able to do. Income in childhood, in turn, affects childhood health—by enabling the purchase of health insurance or health care, better environment, and other goods such as nutritious food.

In this chapter, I present and analyze evidence on whether and how child health interventions affect adult labor market outcomes. This evidence has two parts. First, the interventions must actually affect child health in a measurable way. Second, there must be a link between that improvement in health and adult labor market outcomes. This link may be direct (e.g., the improvement in health permits higher levels of earnings) or indirect (e.g., the improvement in health permits greater levels of education). It is important to emphasize that even if an intervention does not show measurable effects on factors affecting adult labor market outcomes, it may have benefits beyond the scope of this book. I discuss such benefits briefly at the end of the chapter.

To keep the length of this chapter manageable, I focus on major health-related interventions and on a set of conditions that have relatively high prevalence in the U.S. population. I do not focus on interventions that have targeted less prevalent (though possibly more severe) conditions. For example, folic acid fortification of grain products, which targeted neural tube defects (such as spina bifida and anencephaly), was associated with a reduction in neural tube defect prevalence from 0.0378 percent of all births to 0.0305 percent (Honein et al. 2001). Prevalence rates such as these are so small they preclude sizeable impacts on poverty reduction at the population level. In addition, I do not survey the literature on successful interventions from the past that have resulted in the near complete elimination of particular diseases or conditions in the United States (such as public health infrastructure to provide clean water and sanitation or widespread immunization for particular diseases). Finally, I do not survey the quite substantial literature on the relationships between child health and adult functioning in developing country contexts because the health problems faced by children in developing countries are, in most cases, more severe than the health problems of U.S. children.

I begin this survey with a discussion of interventions intended to promote general health among children, including expanded access to health insurance through Medicaid and the State Children's Health Insurance Program (SCHIP) and nutritional supplements to pregnant women and infants through the Special Supplemental Nutrition Program for Women, Infants, and Children (WIC). I then move on to discuss a few specific conditions with relatively high prevalence in the population that have been the focus both of interventions and research on the links between health and adult outcomes.

These conditions are asthma, mental health (particularly Attention-Deficit/ Hyperactivity Disorder), dental health, obesity or overweight, and exposure to environmental toxins (including elevated blood lead levels and air pollution). While some of these conditions are also targeted by the general health care interventions of Medicaid and SCHIP, they are sufficiently important to merit separate discussion.

4.2   Interventions Targeting General Health

4.2.1   Medicaid and the State Children's Health Insurance Program

In terms of number of children affected, the most significant intervention targeting children's health since the mid-1960s has been the Medicaid program. It is a joint federal-state program; generally, the federal government sets mandatory and optional provisions within which states must act. Initially Medicaid covered two groups of low-income individuals: recipients of Aid to Families with Dependent Children (AFDC) and low-income elderly (for services not covered by Medicare, such as some out of pocket expenditures and nursing home care). A few years later, when the Supplemental Security Income (SSI) program was created to aid poor, disabled individuals, Medicaid coverage was required for SSI recipients as well.[2]

The services Medicaid provides to covered children include a rich set of preventative and curative care services under the Early and Periodic Screening, Diagnostic, and Treatment (EPSDT) requirement. However, there were two factors that limited the potential effectiveness of the program. First, by tying Medicaid eligibility for children almost entirely to eligibility for AFDC, eligibility for the program was limited to the very poorest children and, moreover, only to children in single parent families. Second, the program has typically reimbursed doctors at rates that are well below the rates paid by private insurers, which has led to very low participation rates among physicians, particularly in some areas and among some specialties.

Beginning in the mid- to late-1980s, Congress passed a series of laws intended to address the first issue—that many poor children were ineligible for the program. These laws substantially reduced the link between Medicaid eligibility and AFDC eligibility by extending Medicaid coverage to children and pregnant women in families with incomes above the AFDC thresholds (generally to levels between 100 percent and 185 percent of the federal poverty level, depending on the state and age of the child). Following these expansions of Medicaid, in 1997, a new program was passed that further expanded access to health insurance for low-income children. The State Children's Health Insurance Program (SCHIP) is also a state-federal

---

2. See http://www.kff.org/medicaid/timeline/pf_entire.htm for further information on the history of the Medicaid program.

partnership although it was designed to give states somewhat more flexibility in designing their programs. States could either expand Medicaid eligibility or create a new program for children who did not qualify for Medicaid. In either case, income eligibility limits moved further up the income distribution, with the eligibility limits ranging between one and four times the poverty line depending on the state. In total, expansions of Medicaid eligibility and implementation of SCHIP increased eligibility rates for public insurance, from about 16 percent of all children prior to the expansions to roughly 40 percent of all children.[3]

4.2.2 The Impact of Medicaid Expansions and SCHIP for Children

Along with the increase in access to additional low-income children, the Medicaid expansions and SCHIP implementation have offered researchers an opportunity to assess the impact of public health insurance for poor children. Prior to the expansions, Medicaid was linked so tightly to receipt of AFDC and SSI that it was not possible to distinguish between the effects of Medicaid and the effects of the other programs on children's outcomes. Moreover, there was no variation in eligibility along any dimension that was not plausibly related to outcomes directly. By contrast, the form of the Medicaid expansions provided useful variation along the dimensions of age, state, and time, permitting researchers to examine the impact of Medicaid and SCHIP using quasi-experimental approaches.[4]

An obvious first question to ask when examining the impact of a health insurance expansion is whether, in fact, any additional children gained insurance as a result of the policy. There has been a fairly substantial literature on this question, with some debate over the relative importance of "crowding out"—the phenomenon whereby children who already have the option of health insurance through a private source enroll in Medicaid instead. Although researchers remain divided on the relative importance of crowding out versus take-up behavior among the uninsured, there is consensus that the expansions did indeed increase health insurance coverage among low-income children. Researchers have generally found around an 8 to 10 percentage point reduction in uninsurance due to the Medicaid expansions, and a 5 to 8 percentage point reduction in uninsurance due to SCHIP (see table 4.1). This increase in insurance coverage rates largely occurred for children with family incomes between 30 and 150 percent of the federal

---

3. For the most part, the second issue—that of physician reimbursement and participation—has remained largely unaddressed, although in designing their SCHIP programs, some states have chosen to provide a somewhat less complete benefits package while attempting to reimburse physicians at closer to private market rates.

4. A particularly good example of exogenous variation in the expansions is the expansion enacted in the Omnibus Budget Reconciliation Act of 1990, in which for historical reasons the essentially random birth date cutoff for eligibility (only children born after September 30, 1983, were eligible) was chosen.

poverty level, as can be seen in an updated version of figure 1 from Card and Shore-Sheppard (2004) (see figure 4.4).

As the intervention represented by Medicaid and SCHIP is to provide health insurance, rather than health per se, it is worth considering what having health insurance may do to improve a child's chances of being out of poverty in adulthood. Conceptually, health insurance may work to improve the health of the child, through preventative care, early detection of problems, and access to treatment. Indeed, several of the interventions discussed later in the sections on specific health conditions require access to health care, which is made easier with health insurance. Health insurance is also likely to play a financial role, protecting income and assets against the risk of bad health shocks. To the extent that family income in childhood reduces the chance a child will be poor in adulthood, the financial protection afforded by health insurance may be important.

In a useful survey of the literature on the relationship between health insurance and health, Levy and Meltzer (2004) show that while there are a wealth of studies on this relationship, the bulk of them are purely observational, suggesting a positive association but not demonstrating a causal relationship. The evidence from the smaller number of quasi-experimental and truly experimental (i.e., the RAND Health Insurance Experiment) studies is somewhat mixed, but, in general, Levy and Meltzer conclude that vulnerable populations (such as infants, children, and low-income individuals) have the most to gain from having health insurance and that they do indeed benefit. Research on the Medicaid expansions (some of which is surveyed by Levy and Meltzer) bears this out.

One mechanism by which health insurance can improve health is by improving access to health care. Because all children are supposed to have at least one visit to the doctor per year, one measure of access is whether expanded health insurance coverage increased the fraction of children who visited the doctor at least once. By this measure, the Medicaid expansions and SCHIP did indeed improve access. Estimates of the impact of the expansions range from a 1 percentage point increase to a 9 percentage point increase in the fraction of children with at least one visit to the doctor in the past year, depending on which expansion is being considered (see table 4.1). The values in the upper range of these estimates are fairly large, suggesting that making a child eligible for Medicaid lowers the probability the child goes without a visit by almost half. However, it is worth noting that the standard errors on these estimates are also fairly large, enabling the researchers to rule out no effect, but leaving a wide range of possible effects. Other measures of utilization of care increased as well. In particular, hospital use increased among children made eligible for the expansions, with the existing evidence suggesting that the Medicaid expansions led to an increase in overall hospitalization rates but a reduction in ambulatory-care-sensitive hospitalizations (see table 4.1).

Table 4.1   Selected studies of Medicaid expansions and State Children's Health Insurance Program (SCHIP) implementation

Study	Intervention	Design
Cutler and Gruber (1996)	Medicaid expansion	Quasi-experimental; instrumental variables based on exogeneity of state coverage levels for different groups.
Card and Shore-Sheppard (2004)	Medicaid expansion	Regression discontinuity; children born before and after 9/30/1983 cutoff and children older and younger than six.
Ham and Shore-Sheppard (2005)	Medicaid expansion	Quasi-experimental; instrumental variables based on exogeneity of state coverage levels for different groups.
Shore-Sheppard (2008)	Medicaid expansion	Quasi-experimental; instrumental variables based on exogeneity of state coverage levels for different groups, controlling for coverage trends.
LoSasso and Buchmueller (2004)	SCHIP implementation	Quasi-experimental; instrumental variables based on exogeneity of state coverage levels for different groups.
Hudson, Selden, and Banthin (2005)	SCHIP implementation	Quasi-experimental; instrumental variables and differences in trends based on exogeneity of state coverage levels for different groups.
Gruber and Simon (2008)	SCHIP implementation	Quasi-experimental; instrumental variables based on exogeneity of state coverage levels for different groups.
Currie and Gruber (1996a)	Medicaid expansion	Quasi-experimental; instrumental variables based on exogeneity of state coverage levels for different groups.
Currie, Decker, and Lin (2008)	Medicaid expansion, SCHIP implementation	Quasi-experimental; instrumental variables based on exogeneity of state coverage levels for different groups.
Banthin and Selden (2003)	Medicaid expansion	Quasi-experimental; difference in differences (eligible vs. ineligible children, where ineligible consisted of two groups: children who eventually became eligible, and those who were never eligible).
Dafny and Gruber (2005)	Medicaid expansion	Quasi-experimental; instrumental variables based on exogeneity of state coverage levels for different groups.
Kaestner, Joyce, and Racine (2001)	Medicaid expansion	Quasi-experimental; difference in differences: hospitalization of children from low income zip codes vs. higher income zip codes before and after expansion.
Aizer (2007)	Medicaid outreach effort	Quasi-experimental; instrumental variables based on exogeneity of outreach program at zip code level.

Note: CPS = Current Population Survey; pp = percentage points; SIPP = Survey of Income and Program Participation; NHIS = National Health Interview Survey; OBRA = Omnibus Budget Reconciliation Act; MEPS = Medical Expenditure Panel Survey; NMES = National Medical Expenditure Survey; NHDS = National Hospital Discharge Survey; HCUP-3 HIS = Healthcare Cost and Utilization Project Nationwide Inpatient Sample; ACS = ambulatory care sensitive.

Sample	Outcomes	Effects
March CPS 1988–1993, children zero–eighteen, women fifteen–forty-four.	Any coverage, Medicaid coverage, private coverage.	Children: probability uninsured reduced 8–12 pp; women: no statistically significant changes in coverage.
SIPP 1990–1993, March CPS 1990–1996, NHIS 1992–1996, children zero–eighteen.	Any coverage, Medicaid coverage, private coverage, any doctor visit last year.	Probability uninsured reduced 1–9 pp (more for OBRA 1990 expansion, less for OBRA 1989 expansion); probability doctor visit/year increased 1–4 pp.
SIPP 1986–1993, children zero–fifteen.	Any coverage, Medicaid coverage, private coverage.	Probability uninsured reduced 10–12 pp.
March CPS 1988–1996, children 0–18.	Any coverage, Medicaid coverage, private coverage.	Probability uninsured reduced 8–10 pp.
March CPS 1996–2000.	Any coverage, public coverage, private coverage.	Probability uninsured reduced by 5–8 pp.
MEPS 1996–2002.	Any coverage, public coverage, private coverage.	Probability uninsured reduced by 6–10 pp.
SIPP 1996, 2001 (partial).	Any coverage, public coverage, private coverage.	Probability uninsured reduced by 5 pp.
NHIS 1984–1992.	Any doctor visit last year, any visit last two weeks, hospital admission last year, child mortality rate.	Probability doctor visit/year increased by 10 pp; probability hospital visit/year increased by 4 pp; child mortality rate reduced by 0.13 pp for each 10 pp increase in Medicaid eligibility.
NHIS 1985–2005.	Less than excellent health, no doctor visit in last year.	No effect of concurrent eligibility on probability (less than excellent health), probability (doctor visit/year) increased by 6 pp; 10 pp higher eligibility in state at ages 2–4 → 0.4 pp reduction in probability (less than excellent health) and 0.6–0.8 pp reduction in probability (no doctor visit/year).
NMES 1987, MEPS 1996.	Any doctor visit last year, any dentist visit last year, usual source of care, any visit to the emergency room.	Probability doctor visit/year increased by 8–9 pp, probability dentist visit/year increased by 5–6 pp, no statistically significant effect on usual source of care or emergency room.
NHDS 1983–1996, discharges for children <16, grouped into age–state–year cells.	Hospitalization rate, unavoidable hospitalization rate, avoidable hospitalization rate.	10 pp increase in eligibility → 8.4% increase in hospitalization, 8% increase in unavoidable hospitalization, statistically insignificant increase in avoidable hospitalization.
HCUP-3 HIS 1988, 1992.	Incidence of ACS hospitalizations.	Decline in ACS hospitalizations (except asthma) for two–six-year-olds; little change for seven–nine-year-olds.
California hospital discharge data 1996–2000.	Incidence of ACS hospitalizations.	10% increase in enrollment → 2–3% reduction in ACS hospitalizations.

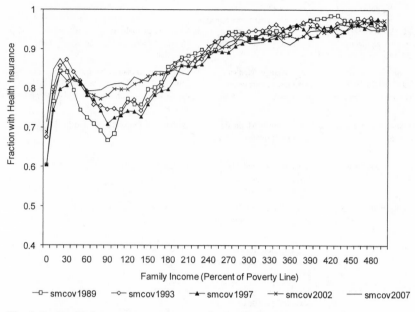

Fig. 4.4   Health insurance coverage rates by family income (smoothed)
Source: Author's calculation from March Current Population Surveys, 1989, 1993, 1997, 2002, and 2007.

Ideally, increased access to care would lead to improved health both in the short run and in the longer run. To date, there has been little research on whether this is the case, largely because of a lack of data available to answer the question. Because incidence rates of even relatively widespread conditions and diseases are fairly low among young children, it is difficult to detect effects in the sample sizes available in national survey data. Currie and Gruber (1996a) examine child mortality in the U.S. vital statistics data, which have the advantage of being calculated from the universe of U.S. death certificates. They find that the child mortality rate fell in the wake of the Medicaid expansions, with a reduction of 0.13 percentage points in mortality for every 10 percentage point increase in Medicaid eligibility. While this estimate is fairly imprecisely measured, it does indicate that there was an effect of Medicaid on child health. This conclusion is reinforced by the fact that Currie and Gruber find no evidence of an effect on deaths from "external causes" (accidents, homicides, suicides, etc.) but do find an effect on deaths from "internal causes." Looking at health in later childhood (ages nine to seventeen), Currie, Decker, and Lin (2008) find some evidence of an effect of Medicaid eligibility in early childhood. They find that children ages nine to seventeen who lived in states that had more generous Medicaid eligibility when they were ages two to four had a lower probability of being in less than excellent health. This effect is small, however—a 20 percentage point increase in eligibility (roughly the increase in eligibility over the entire period of the expansions) is associated with only a 1 percentage point reduction in the likelihood of being in less than excellent health. Further examination of the impact of the expansions on short-run and long-run health outcomes is needed to assess more fully the impact of the expansions for children.

4.2.3   The Impact of Medicaid Expansions for Pregnant Women and Infants

One question that has received somewhat more attention is whether the expansions for pregnant women and infants have improved infant health outcomes. While existing research generally indicates that the expansions increased prenatal care use or its adequacy (see table 4.2), the evidence for an effect on infant health outcomes is much weaker.[5] Probably the strongest evidence for an effect on infant health comes from Currie and Gruber (1996b). Using vital statistics data on the fraction of births that are low birth weight (LBW) and the infant mortality rate by state and year, they find evidence both for a reduction in low birth weight incidence and a reduction in infant mortality. However, these reductions appear only to come from the earliest expansions that were aimed at women well below the poverty line; later expansions aimed at women with incomes as high as the poverty line or slightly higher show no statistically significant effect. A series of state-level case studies (see table 4.2) find similarly equivocal results, as does a later study by Currie and Grogger (2002). Overall, the effects of expanded access to Medicaid for pregnant women on infant health appear to be weakly positive though the results vary depending on the group targeted and the outcome studied.

In considering whether the Medicaid expansions for pregnant women and infants are likely to affect poverty, additional information is needed beyond the expansions' impacts on prenatal care and infant health. In particular, a link between infant health and long-run outcomes must be established. The key issue in establishing this link is determining whether a causal relationship can be shown. In the case of birth weight, such a causal relationship appears to exist. The bulk of the literature examining this causal relationship relies on within-twin variation in birth weight. Most studies in this literature find that increases in birth weight lead to small but statistically significant increases in outcomes such as education, IQ scores, and earnings (see table 4.2 for a summary of these studies).[6]

When considering the results from twin studies such as these, two caveats

5. "Adequate" prenatal care is care that begins early in the pregnancy and continues for a minimum number of visits.
6. An exception is the study by Berhman and Rosenzweig (2004), which finds effects that are much larger. However, Behrman and Rosenzweig use birth weight divided by gestational length as their measure of infant health, which, as Royer (2009) points out, may lead to biased estimates because gestational length is measured with considerable error.

Table 4.2   **Selected studies of infant health care and outcomes**

Study	Intervention	Design
Currie and Gruber (1996b)	Medicaid expansion	Quasi-experimental; instrumental variables based on exogeneity of state coverage levels for different groups.
Piper, Ray, and Griffin (1990)	Tennessee Medicaid expansion to married women in 1985	Observational: outcomes in groups with large enrollment increases.
Haas et al. (1993)	Massachusetts Healthy Start	Quasi-experimental; difference in differences (before/after and eligible for new program/ Medicaid eligible or private).
Piper, Mitchel, and Ray (1994)	Tennessee Medicaid expansion in 1987	Observational: difference over time.
Ray, Mitchel, and Piper (1997)	Tennessee Medicaid expansion 1983–1991	Observational: outcomes in groups with large enrollment increases.
Long and Marquis (1998)	Florida Medicaid expansion of 1989	Quasi-experimental; difference in differences (before/after and enrollees/privately insured).
Currie and Grogger (2002)	Medicaid expansions	Quasi-experimental; instrumental variables based on exogeneity of state coverage levels for different groups.
Hanratty (1996)	Canadian National Health Insurance implementation	Quasi-experimental; based on exogeneity of province-level adoption of national health insurance.
Behrman and Rosenzweig (2004)	NA (Link study)	Regressions of adult outcomes on fetal growth controlling for twin-fixed effects.
Black, Devereux, and Salvanes (2007)	NA (Link study)	Regressions of adult outcomes on ln(birth weight) controlling for twin-fixed effects.
Oreopoulos et al. (2008)	NA (Link study)	Regressions of adult outcomes on birth weight in categories or APGAR score controlling for twin- or sibling-fixed effects.

Sample	Outcomes	Effects
NLSY (prenatal care); aggregate Vital Statistics (health outcomes).	Delay prenatal care; incidence of LBW and infant mortality by state and year.	Becoming eligible → 50% reduction in probability delay (large s.e.); 1 pp increase in eligibility rate due to expansion to very low-income pregnant women → 17 pp reduction in LBW incidence, and 3 pp reduction in infant mortality. No effect for later expansion.
TN birth certificates linked to Medicaid enrollment records.	Use of early prenatal care; birth weight; neonatal mortality.	No effect for any outcome.
MA birth certificates.	Satisfactory prenatal care; prenatal care before third trimester; adverse infant outcomes.	No effect on either prenatal care or infant outcomes.
TN birth certificates, death certificates, Medicaid enrollment files.	No first trimester prenatal care; no care or third trimester care; inadequate care; LBW rate; perinatal, neonatal, infant mortality rates.	Reduction in probability received no or third trimester care; no effect on any other outcome.
TN birth certificates linked to Medicaid enrollment records.	Enrolled in first trimester; adequate prenatal care; preterm birth.	27 pp increase in first trimester enrollment; 6.4 pp reduction in inadequate prenatal care; no effect on preterm birth.
FL birth, death certificates, hospital discharge records, Medicaid enrollment and claims files.	No prenatal care; third trimester care only; inadequate care; LBW; infant mortality.	Improvements in all measures, but not all statistically significantly different from 0.
Vital Statistics detailed natality and fetal death data 1990–1996.	Prenatal care begun in first trimester; adequate prenatal care.	No effect on first trimester care start; doubling income eligibility cutoff (100–200%) increased probability adequate care by 0.4% for whites; no effect on birth weight; reduction in fetal death for blacks.
Vital Statistics natality data, county-level infant mortality data.	Infant mortality rate; incidence of LBW.	National Health Insurance in province → 4% decline in infant mortality rate; 1.3% decline in LBW; 8.9% decline in LBW for single mothers.
804 twins from Minnesota Twins Registry.	Years of schooling; body mass index; height; log(wage).	1 lb increase in birth weight → 1/3 more years of education; 0.6 inches in height; ~7% higher wages; no effect on body mass index.
Data on twins from Norwegian administrative data, (1,862–13,106 twins, depending on outcome; some outcomes are only for different genders).	Height; body mass index; IQ score; ≥ 12 years education; earnings; birth weight of 1st child.	10% increase in birth weight (~250 g) → 0.57 cm increase in height; 0.11 increase in body mass index; 1/20 stanine increase in IQ; 1 pp increase in probability finish high school; 1% increase in full-time earnings; 1.5% increase in birth weight of 1st child.
Data on siblings from administrative data from Manitoba province (880–40,514 dependent on outcome and whether twins or siblings).	Language arts test score; probability (reach grade 12 by age 17); social assistance take-up and length.	Worse infant health → reduction probability (reach grade 12 by 17); increased social assistance take-up and length; little consistent effect on test score.

(continued)

Table 4.2 (continued)

Study	Intervention	Design
Royer (2009)	NA (Link study)	Regressions of adult outcomes on birth weight controlling for twin-fixed effects.
Smith (2009)	NA (Link study)	Regressions of adult outcomes on recalled health in childhood controlling for family-fixed effects.
Currie, Manivong, and Roos (2009)	NA (Link study)	Regressions of young adult outcomes on health problems in childhood.
Sikorski et al. (1996)	Reduced schedule of prenatal visits	Randomized controlled trial.
McDuffie et al. (1996)	Reduced schedule of prenatal visits	Randomized controlled trial.
Clement et al. (1999)	Reduced schedule of prenatal visits	Randomized controlled trial.
Villar et al. (2001)	Reduced schedule of prenatal visits	Randomized controlled trial.
Evans and Lien (2005)	Reduced access to prenatal care	Quasi-experimental; instrumental variables based on public transit strike as exogenous variation in access to care.

Note: NLSY = National Longitudinal Survey of Youth; LBW = low birth weight; pp = percentage points; NA = not applicable; APGAR score = measure of newborn health developed in 1952 by Dr. Virginia Apgar based on five criteria (Appearance, Pulse, Grimace, Activity, Respiration); PSID = Panel Study of Income Dynamics.

must be kept in mind. First, differences in birth weight within a twin pair cannot be due to preterm delivery because twins have the same gestational length. Instead, they must arise from differences in fetal growth rates. These differences are believed to arise primarily because of unequal nutritional intake. Therefore, if the reason for low birth weight matters in the effect of low birth weight on long-run outcomes, the results from the twin studies cannot necessarily be extrapolated more broadly. The results of Almond, Chay, and Lee's (2005) study of short-run effects of low birth weight suggest that the reason for low birth weight may indeed matter. They examine two different sources of variation in birth weight—that arising from within-twin

Sample	Outcomes	Effects
Data on twins from intergenerationally linked California birth records (5,670 twins).	Education; birth weight of child; public payment for delivery of child; zip code characteristics.	500 g increase in birth weight (~1 lb) → .06–.08 of a year increase in education; 30 g increase in birth weight of child; no effect on public payment, characteristics of zip code.
2,248 siblings in 1999 PSID.	Years of completed education, ln income, ln wealth, ln earnings, weeks worked.	Health excellent or very good has positive effect on all adult outcomes.
Administrative records from 50,404 siblings born between 1979 and 1987 in Manitoba, Canada.	On Social Assistance, grade 12 by age seventeen, took college math, literacy measure.	Mental health diagnosis at age four or later, major injury at age nine or later, major conditions at age fourteen or later, LBW all associated with worse young adult outcomes.
2,794 women with low risk pregnancies randomly assigned to standard care or reduced number of visits.	Measures of fetal and maternal morbidity; health service use; satisfaction.	No effect on morbidity; reduced health service use; reduced satisfaction.
2,764 women with low risk pregnancies randomly assigned to standard care or reduced number of visits.	Preterm delivery; preeclampsia; cesarean delivery; LBW; satisfaction.	No effect on any outcome.
1,117 women with low risk pregnancies randomly assigned to standard care or reduced number of visits.	Post-birth maternal and child well-being, health service use, health-related behavior.	No effect on any outcome.
Sample of women obtaining prenatal care at clinics randomized to receive standard care or fewer visits.	Referral rates; hospital admissions; LBW; measures of maternal and fetal morbidity.	Higher referral rates in new model; no effect on any other outcome.
Women in Allegheny County (women in other Pittsburgh area counties and other similar city counties as controls).	Number of prenatal visits; birth weight; gestation length; maternal weight gain; smoking behavior.	One-half visit reduction for black inner-city residents, 1/3 visit reduction for black suburban residents; no statistically significant effect on birth weight, gestation length, or maternal weight gain; increase in maternal smoking prevalence.

(and, hence, nutritional) variation and that arising from maternal smoking behavior among singleton births—and find substantial differences in outcomes both across these two sources of variation and when compared to typical cross-sectional regression estimates. A second, and related, caveat is that the effects of variation in birth weight between twins may not accurately predict the effects of variation in birth weight across singleton births if parents of twins behave differently as a result of the difference in birth weight. If, for example, parents favor the heavier twin, then part of the estimated effect of birth weight is actually an effect of differential investment in childhood. In addition, twins tend to be lighter at birth, often substantially so, than singletons, so a given reduction in birth weight for a twin may have a larger effect than the same reduction from a higher initial level for a singleton. For example, a 100-gram reduction in birth weight may matter less for a singleton weighing 3,500 grams than for a twin weighing 2,500 grams.

Despite these caveats, based on twin studies, there seems to be a clear link between birth weight and adult outcomes that may plausibly affect poverty. The question then becomes how birth weight can be affected. Biologically, there are two basic mechanisms for increasing birth weight: extending the length of gestation and increasing the weight of the infant conditional on gestational length. The intervention discussed thus far, public provision of health insurance through Medicaid (and SCHIP), is intended to provide access to prenatal care, which arguably could affect both gestational length (for example, through the provision of antibiotics to treat genitourinary tract infections, which have been shown to increase the probability of preterm birth) and weight conditional on gestation (for example, through smoking cessation interventions). An important point made by Currie and Grogger (2002) is that little is known about the content of prenatal care. The available measures of prenatal care "adequacy" tend to be quantitative (involving number of visits and spacing of visits), so wide variability in content and quality of care may exist even among care generally counted as adequate. This is one of the problems researchers have faced as they have tried to determine whether prenatal care does, in fact, lead to improved birth outcomes. Another problem is that the evidence linking prenatal care and birth outcomes is generally observational so that studies of the effectiveness of prenatal care are hampered by the possibility of selection bias. Selection bias in this context may work in two directions: women who are more health conscious and likely to take better care of themselves even in the absence of prenatal care are also more likely to obtain prenatal care, leading to overestimates of the effectiveness of prenatal care; and women who have high-risk pregnancies are also more likely to obtain prenatal care, leading to underestimates of the effectiveness of prenatal care.

Random or quasi-random variation in prenatal care is difficult to obtain. Because of ethical concerns about denying possibly beneficial care to pregnant women, there have been only a handful of randomized trials, and these trials tested typically recommended levels of prenatal care against a regimen of somewhat fewer visits for women identified as having low-risk pregnancies (see Sikorski et al. 1996; McDuffie et al. 1996; Clement et al. 1999; and Villar et al. 2001). Consequently, none of the trials showed any effect of the reduced number of visits on infant health. Evans and Lien (2005) exploit variation in prenatal care access for a somewhat higher risk sample. In 1992, there was a month-long public transit strike in Pittsburgh, which Evans and Lien argue caused exogenous variation in access to prenatal care. Evans and Lien find evidence that black, inner-city residents lost on average one-half a prenatal visit due to the strike. This reduction appears to be statistically significantly correlated with an increase in maternal smoking behavior, but Evans and Lien are unable to identify precise estimates of any other outcome.

Overall, the evidence presented here suggests that infant health—birth weight in particular—can matter for long-run outcomes, but that changing infant health is difficult. While there is consistent evidence that expanding access to public health insurance can increase prenatal care, evidence on the impact of prenatal care on infant health is much weaker. Aside from the findings of Currie and Gruber (1996b) of an improvement in low birth weight rates associated with the earliest Medicaid expansions, few researchers have found compelling evidence of improvements in infant health from prenatal care use. Researchers have suggested this may be because the content of prenatal care is seldom measured, and, indeed, there is some evidence that augmented prenatal care services can be beneficial for the health of the infants of the least-well-off mothers (see, e.g., Long and Marquis 1998; Joyce 1999). This evidence also suggests that prenatal care is an intervention for which the effects on the average and marginal infants are not the same, but, unfortunately, data limitations often preclude precise identification of the effects for the marginal infants.

4.2.4   Other Effects of Expanded Public Insurance Eligibility

In addition to direct effects on health through access to health care, expanded eligibility for public insurance may have an impact on the life chances of children through the "insurance component" of health insurance. By providing public insurance to low-income families for their children, the government provides an in-kind transfer of resources. This transfer has an impact on the economic circumstances of the family through the reduction in medical insurance costs and out-of-pocket expenses that a family would otherwise have to incur for its children. Despite its potential importance, this effect of public health insurance has been surprisingly little studied (see table 4.3 for a summary of studies). Gruber and Yelowitz (1999) examine Medicaid expansions between the mid-1980s and the mid-1990s and find that the average increase in dollars of medical expenditure eligible to be paid by Medicaid over this period led to an approximately $538 increase in annual consumption. They also find evidence for a reduction in wealth holdings, presumably due to a reduction in precautionary saving as a result of the expanded access to Medicaid. Taking a somewhat different approach, Banthin and Selden (2003) compare children who became eligible under the Medicaid expansions to children who were slightly better off financially. They find that there was a 7 percentage point reduction in the fraction of families with a financial burden from family health care of at least 10 percent of disposable family income. These are fairly substantial effects, indicating that this is an important area for further research. In particular, it would be useful to know whether these results hold for later expansions of health

Table 4.3   Financial effects of expanded public health insurance eligibility

Study	Intervention	Design	Sample	Outcomes	Effects
Gruber and Yelowitz (1999)	Medicaid expansion	Quasi-experimental; instrumental variables based on exogeneity of state coverage levels for different groups.	SIPP 1984–1993, CEX 1983–1993.	Probability (positive net worth); net worth; annual consumption.	Reduced probability (positive net worth); reduced wealth holdings by $567–$722; increased consumption by $538.
Banthin and Selden (2003)	Medicaid expansion	Quasi-experimental; difference in differences (eligible vs. ineligible children, where ineligible consisted of two groups: children who eventually became eligible, and those who were never eligible).	NMES 1987, MEPS 1996.	Family out-of-pocket spending; financial burden.	Reduction in out-of-pocket spending of ~$600; 7–8 pp reduction in probability health care expenditure >10% of disposable family income.

Note: SIPP = Survey of Income and Program Participation; CEX = Consumer Expenditure Survey; NMES = National Medical Expenditure Survey; MEPS = Medical Expenditure Panel Survey; pp = percentage points.

insurance eligibility as well and whether the effect of public health insurance availability continues at the same level over time.

4.2.5   The Special Supplemental Nutrition Program for Women, Infants, and Children (WIC)

Although not a health program per se, the WIC program is intended to improve the health of infants and children through the provision of food and nutrition education to mothers. Pregnant women, infants, and young children in families with incomes below 185 percent of the federal poverty line or who participate in certain programs for low-income families including Medicaid are eligible for WIC. The WIC program has been in existence since 1972 and has been evaluated often, but virtually all research on WIC has relied on observational research designs, comparing WIC participants with nonparticipants. Attempts to use quasi-experimental variation (such as different state policies) have proven unsuccessful as such studies have been unable to eliminate the possibility that the results were driven by other factors varying at the state level.

More recently, a group of studies have relied on large administrative data sets with extensive controls, arguing that any selection bias in WIC participation conditional on these controls is likely to be negative because observable selection appears negative. These studies find an association between WIC participation and improvements in birth weight, with some studies finding substantial birth weight improvements (see table 4.4). However, these results have engendered considerable debate as it appears that most improvements in birth weight associated with WIC participation have occurred via the mechanism of longer gestations rather than greater fetal growth. Researchers such as Joyce and his collaborators have argued that WIC effects on gestation length are implausible given results from the medical literature (Joyce, Gibson, and Colman 2005; Joyce, Racine, and Yunzal-Butler 2008). Moreover, effects on gestation length may be subject to "gestational age bias," the fact that women with longer gestations have more opportunity to enroll in WIC prenatally. Evidence that this may indeed confound estimates of WIC's effect comes from results showing that women who enrolled in the third trimester of their pregnancies had larger "WIC effects" than did women who enrolled in the first or second trimesters (Joyce, Racine, and Yunzal-Butler 2008). Controlling for gestational age results in much smaller estimated WIC effects though, as Ludwig and Miller (2005) point out in their survey of the debate, if WIC *does* have an effect on gestational length, this approach would be likely to underestimate WIC's effect. In a recent paper, Figlio, Hamersma, and Roth (2009) are able to solve the problem of endogeneity of WIC participation using an instrumental variable strategy that compares the differential effects of a state policy change on women identified as marginally eligible with women who were marginally ineligible for WIC. While their empirical strategy is preferable in several ways to the strategies

Table 4.4   Selected studies of the Special Supplemental Nutrition Program for Women, Infants, and Children (WIC)

Study	Intervention	Design	Sample	Outcomes	Effects
Kowaleski-Jones and Duncan (2002)	WIC	Family-fixed effects (siblings with and without maternal prenatal WIC participation).	NLSY children born 1990–1996 (1,984 children, 969 siblings, seventy-one discordant sibling groups)	ln(birth weight)	WIC participation associated with statistically insignificant increase in birth weight at the mean.
Bitler and Currie (2005)	WIC	Observational (Medicaid deliveries with and without WIC).	PRAMS deliveries paid by Medicaid, 1992–1999 (60,731 women from nineteen states).	Birth weight; gestation length, probability (prenatal care beginning 1st trimester); probability (preterm); probability (LBW); probability (VLBW).	WIC participation associated with 63.7 g increase in birth weight; 0.28 of a week increase in gestation length; 44% increase in probability (1st trimester care); 29% decrease in probability (preterm); 27% decrease in probability (LBW); 54% decrease in probability (VLBW).
Joyce, Gibson, and Colman (2005)	WIC	Observational (Medicaid deliveries with and without WIC).	New York City birth certificates, 1988–2001 (811,190 births).	Birth weight; gestation length; birth weight for gestational age.	WIC participation associated with 25.5 g increase in birth weight; 0.12 of a week increase in gestation length; 7.3 g increase in birth weight for gestational age; results not consistent over time.

Study	Program	Design	Data (sample)	Outcomes	Findings
Joyce, Racine, and Yunzal-Butler (2008)	WIC	Observational (women who enrolled in WIC during vs. after pregnancy).	PNSS deliveries ever enrolled in WIC, 1995–2004 (3,311,976 women from nine states).	Birth weight; probability (LBW); probability (VLBW); probability (preterm); birth weight for gestational age; probability (small for gestational age); probability (term LBW).	Prenatal WIC associated with 63 g increase in birth weight; 2.7 pp decrease in LBW; 0.9 pp decrease in VLBW; 2.7 pp decrease in probability (preterm); 39.5 g increase in birth weight for gestational age; 1.7 pp decrease in probability (small for gestational age); 0.7 pp decrease in probability (term LBW).
Figlio, Hamersma, and Roth (2009)	WIC	Quasi-experimental; instrumental variables based on differential impact of new documentation requirement in marginally eligible and marginally ineligible groups.	Florida linked administrative data: births to women with a child already in school, 1997–2001 (4,190 women).	Birth weight; probability (LBW); gestational age; probability (preterm).	WIC associated with statistically insignificant increase in birth weight; 12.9 pp decrease in LBW; statistically insignificant effect on gestational age and probability (preterm).

Note: NLSY = National Longitudinal Survey of Youth; PRAMS = Pregnancy Risk Assessment Monitoring System; LBW = low birth weight; VLBW = very low birth weight; PNSS = Pregnancy Nutritional Surveillance System; pp = percentage points.

used in previous research, their work is hampered by the fact that their resulting analysis sample is quite small, so most of the effects they estimate have very wide confidence intervals. The only statistically significant effect they identify is a reduction in the probability of low birth weight; effects on average birth weight, gestational age, and prematurity are all statistically indistinguishable from zero. Overall, the preponderance of existing evidence suggests that WIC is likely to have an effect on birth weight though that effect is likely to be somewhat below the large effects identified in the observational studies. Consequently, while WIC is a potentially compelling intervention given the evidence on long-run effects of low birth weight from the twin studies discussed in the preceding, the lack of certainty about the magnitude and nature of any WIC effects precludes any strong conclusion about WIC's effect.

4.3   Interventions Targeting Specific Health Conditions

4.3.1   Asthma

Asthma is one of the most common chronic illnesses among children, with a national current prevalence rate of 8.9 percent in 2005 (Akinbami 2006). This level represents a historic high, with gradually increasing rates over the 1980s and 1990s. The disease is most prevalent among minority children, particularly non-Hispanic black children, who have prevalence rates that are nearly 50 percent higher than white prevalence rates (Akinbami 2006). It can be sufficiently severe as to result in disability (defined as an inability to conduct a major activity such as school or a limitation in the amount or kind of the activity performed; see Newacheck and Halfon 2000). Asthma is, however, controllable for most children with medication and behavior modification. In assessing the importance of asthma-oriented interventions with the goal of poverty reduction in mind, there are two components to consider: first, can interventions successfully reduce symptom days among children with asthma, and, second, are reductions in asthma symptom days likely to lead to improved long run outcomes?

From the extensive literature on treating asthma, the answer to the first question appears to be yes: even children in very difficult economic circumstances can have their asthma controlled. The Centers for Disease Control's Web site on Potentially Effective Interventions for Asthma provides information on over forty interventions that have been evaluated with randomized trials and shown indications of effectiveness.[7] Based on these interventions, it is clear that access to health care (such as provided by Medicaid) is a necessary, but not sufficient, condition to ensure adequate asthma control; the interventions reviewed typically involve patient education, counseling,

---

7. See http://www.cdc.gov/asthma/interventions/interventions_info.htm.

and possibly provision of additional resources. For example, as part of the National Cooperative Inner-City Asthma Study, Evans et al. (1999) incorporated a randomized trial of an asthma management program in an inner-city setting. This program included social workers as asthma counselors, asthma education, referrals to community resources (e.g., smoking cessation programs), pillow and mattress covers, and insecticide to reduce cockroaches in the home. Evans et al. find a reduction of 0.5 symptom days per two-week period in treatment versus control group and some reduction in unscheduled visits to physicians and emergency rooms by the second-year follow-up. Moreover, these effects persist after the end of the intervention.

While effective interventions exist, the answer to the second question, whether interventions targeting asthma are likely to have long-run impacts on poverty reduction, is much less clear. One issue is that while there is a clear link between asthma and days of school missed (see the comprehensive review by Milton et al. 2004), few studies have found effects of asthma on academic achievement. Milton et al. (2004) review eleven studies that compare the academic achievement of children with asthma to the achievement either of matched controls or the general population and find no evidence of differential academic performance between children with and without asthma. There are several problems with these studies, however. The measures of academic achievement are fairly limited, there is no experimental or even quasi-experimental variation available, and it is not always clear in the study whether the child's asthma is well controlled or poorly controlled. Moreover, the studies typically do not focus on low-income children, who suffer disproportionately from asthma and may be more at risk for differential academic performance. There is some evidence for worse labor market outcomes among individuals with childhood-onset asthma (see the review by Milton et al. [2004] and the citations therein), although the outcomes studied have been limited to employment (individuals with asthma are less likely to be employed and more likely to be out of the labor force), and the methods are limited to including (sometimes extensive) controls as there is no quasi-experimental variation available. Overall, this is an area in which additional research is necessary to determine convincingly the extent of the relationship between asthma in childhood, asthma control in childhood, and long-run economic outcomes.

4.3.2   Mental Health

One area in which links between child health status and outcomes potentially affecting adult poverty have been fairly convincingly identified is mental health and, particularly, Attention-Deficit/Hyperactivity Disorder (ADHD, see table 4.5). Attention-Deficit/Hyperactivity Disorder is a neurobehavioral disorder characterized by the presence of at least six symptoms of inattention or hyperactivity-impulsivity that are sufficiently severe and inconsistent with the child's level of development (American

Academy of Pediatrics Committee on Quality Improvement, Subcommittee on Attention-Deficit/Hyperactivity Disorder 2000). Based on the 2003 National Survey of Children's Health, in which parents were asked about whether their child had been diagnosed with ADHD, the Centers for Disease Control (CDC) estimate a prevalence rate of nearly 8 percent among children four to seventeen years old in 2003 (CDC 2005a).

The most common approach to examining the effect of ADHD symptoms on various outcomes is to control for family-fixed effects. Using this approach, Currie and Stabile (2006) find that children with symptoms of ADHD are more likely to repeat a grade, score lower on math and reading tests, and are more likely to be placed in special education, with some evidence of stronger effects for boys than girls. Using the same methods, for comparison they examine the effects of the presence of chronic conditions and poor health and find no statistically significant relationship between physical conditions and their outcome measures. In an extension of this work, Currie and Stabile (2007) examine other behavioral problems symptoms and find qualitatively similar, though substantially smaller, effects for antisocial or aggressive symptoms and depressive symptoms.[8]

In an examination of whether the Currie and Stabile (2006, 2007) results hold for longer-term outcomes, Fletcher and Wolfe (2008) examine the effects of retrospectively reported ADHD symptoms among eighteen to twenty-eight year-olds on an array of high school outcomes, years of education, and whether the person attended college. Like Currie and Stabile, they find evidence of effects on short-run outcomes, particularly increased probabilities of grade repetition and special education placement. They find little evidence of effects on longer-run outcomes, however. Moreover, Fletcher and Wolfe find statistically significant effects in ordinary least squares (OLS) models but no statistically significant effects in the family-fixed effects models (with the exception of an increase in the probability an individual was suspended). They argue that this finding indicates the possible existence of spillover effects on long-run outcomes for siblings of individuals with ADHD. While this is certainly a possibility, it does call into question the assumption underlying the use of sibling-fixed effect models to eliminate family-level unobservables.

Ding et al. (2007) and Fletcher and Lehrer (2008) use an alternative approach, using variation in the presence of genetic markers (either across or within families) believed to be correlated with symptoms of ADHD, depression, and obesity. Ding et al. (2007) find evidence of an approximately 1 standard deviation reduction in grade point average due to the presence of depression or obesity, but the effect is statistically significant only for

---

8. Similar, though larger, results are found for a sample of Australian twins by Le et al. (2005) and Vujić et al. (2008), who find that symptoms of conduct disorder are associated with reduced human capital accumulation and greater likelihood of violent or criminal behavior in adulthood.

girls and the combined sample. Unlike the previous studies, they find no statistically significant effect of ADHD. One concern with this study is its external validity as the data come from five high schools from a single county in Northern Virginia. Finally, the study by Fletcher and Lehrer (2008) combines the use of genetic instruments with family-fixed effects in data from the National Longitudinal Study of Adolescent Health. They find statistically significant effects of a diagnosis of attention deficit disorder on grade point average (GPA), though no statistically significant effects for the combined ADHD diagnosis nor for depression nor obesity. Interestingly, the results for the family-fixed effects only, instrumental variables only, and fixed effects and instrumental variables models differ substantially, raising concerns about the assumptions underlying the use of both models. The assumption underlying the use of genetic markers is that they are unrelated to other (omitted) characteristics affecting human capital outcomes (such as cognitive ability), while the assumption underlying family fixed effects is that any omitted factors correlated with both mental health conditions and human capital outcomes vary only at the family, rather than the individual, level. At this point, little is known about whether these assumptions are likely to hold.

While the use of genetic markers as instruments is intriguing, it does raise the question of whether the presence of these health problems is manipulable by interventions. That is, while the use of genetic markers may help researchers establish a statistical relationship between mental health problems and later outcomes, they do less to help researchers or policymakers determine what an effective intervention targeting these health problems would be. This problem is not limited to the genetic markers studies but holds for the studies using family-fixed effects as well.[9]

Because drug treatments for ADHD exist (psychostimulant therapy), the effects of ADHD may plausibly be affected by public health insurance interventions, particularly the availability of health insurance through Medicaid and the State Children's Health Insurance Program. Indeed, Medicaid spending on stimulant drugs (most used to treat ADHD) increased fourteenfold between 1991 and 2000 (Frank, Goldman, and Hogan 2003). However, a review of studies of the impact of drug treatment for ADHD by Wigal et al. (1999) indicates that while there is convincing evidence of symptom reduction from randomized placebo-controlled trials, there is little to no evidence of improvement in academic achievement. Wigal et al. discuss three studies, two of which found no effect on academic achievement and one which found an effect. All three of the studies have problems that limit their validity: the two studies finding no effect had very limited follow-up

9. As noted by the Surgeon General's Report on Mental Health (U.S. Department of Health and Human Services 1999), even mental health problems believed to have a significant genetic component are affected by environmental factors. The Surgeon General's Report suggests that early childhood interventions such as Head Start may work to prevent mental health problems from developing. See chapter 2 in this volume for an extensive review of these interventions.

Table 4.5   Selected studies of child mental health

Study	Intervention	Design	Sample	Outcomes	Effects
Currie and Stabile (2006)	NA (Link study)	Family-fixed effects (siblings with and without ADHD symptoms).	NLSY (3,969 children ages five–eleven, 2,406 siblings); NLSCY (3,925 children ages four–eleven, 1,540 siblings).	Math, reading test scores; probability of grade repetition, special education placement.	(U.S.): median → 90th percentile in ADHD symptom scale → 10 point reduction (on mean of ~50) in math and reading scores; increase probability of grade repetition and special education placement.
Currie and Stabile (2007)	NA (Link study)	Family-fixed effects (siblings with and without reported behavioral problems).	NLSY (3,758 children ages five–eleven, 2,358 siblings); NLSCY (5,604 children ages four–eleven, 2,374 siblings).	Math, reading test scores; probability of grade repetition, special education placement.	(U.S.): median → 90th percentile in hyperactivity symptom scale → 0.2 s.d. reduction in math and reading scores, increased probability grade repetition, special education; median → 90th percentile in antisocial/aggressive symptom scale → 0.1 s.d. reduction in math and reading scores, increased probability grade repetition; median → 90th percentile in depressive symptom scale → no significant relationship to math and reading scores, increased probability grade repetition.

Fletcher and Wolfe (2008)	NA (Link study)	Family-fixed effects (siblings with and without ADHD symptoms).	Add Health (retrospective survey of ~14,000 individuals ages eighteen–twenty-eight, ~2,900 siblings).	GPA; probability repeat grade, special education placement, suspended, expelled, drop out; years of education, probability attend college.	Increased probability repeat grade, placed in special education, drop out; no other statistically significant results in fixed effects models.
Ding et al. (2007)	NA (Link study)	Instrumental variables (genetic markers as instruments).	Georgetown Adolescent Tobacco Research study (2,576 adolescents from a county in northern Virginia).	GPA.	Depression and obesity → ~1 s.d. reduction in GPA, statistically significant for combined sample and girls only; No statistically significant effect for ADHD.
Fletcher and Lehrer (2008)	NA (Link study)	Instrumental variables (genetic markers as instruments) and family-fixed effects.	Add Health (1,684 individuals with genetic information, 1,068 siblings).	Peabody Picture Vocabulary Test (Revised).	~2 s.d. reduction from ADD; ~1 s.d. reduction from ADD when sample limited to same gender twins.
Wigal et al. (1999)	Drug treatment for ADHD	Review of three placebo-controlled randomized studies.		No effect on test scores in short term; possible long-run effect but study inconclusive.	

Note: ADD = attention-deficit disorder; ADHD = attention-deficit/hyperactivity disorder; NLSY = National Longitudinal Survey of Youth; NLSCY = Canadian National Longitudinal Survey of Children and Youth; s.d. = standard deviation; Add Health = National Longitudinal Study of Adolescent Health.

times (five to six weeks of treatment), so it is possible that an effect could emerge over a longer period, while the study that found an effect had a longer follow-up period (fifteen months) but had a 72 percent drop-out rate among the placebo group, so that the results may be biased. The conclusion that there is little evidence of long-term academic benefits of stimulant therapy has been drawn in other reviews as well (see Pelham, Wheeler, and Chronis [1998] and the citations therein).

4.3.3   Dental Health

Dental caries—a bacterial infection of the tooth—is the most prevalent chronic disease of childhood—five times more common than asthma (U.S. Department of Health and Human Services 2000). As with many chronic diseases, it is even more prevalent among low-income and minority children. For example, the mean number of decayed and filled surfaces of primary (baby) teeth among five-year-olds was approximately two among children with family incomes above twice the poverty level and over six among children with family incomes below the poverty level (Dye et al. 2007, figure 2,4). This disparity has been increasing for primary teeth although other data in this report indicate that disparities in caries rates for permanent teeth have not widened substantially (Dye et al. 2007). Rates of treatment also differ substantially by income and minority status, with the odds of having at least one untreated decayed tooth nearly double among poor children (see figure 4.5, from U.S. Department of Health and Human Services 2000, 63).

In addition to causing pain, absence from school, difficulty learning, playing, eating, and poor appearance, untreated dental disease can have long-term economic consequences. While there is a wealth of anecdotal evidence that tooth loss may lead to greater difficulty finding a job or getting a promotion (see, e.g., Sered and Fernandopulle 2007; Shipler 2005), recent research by Glied and Neidell (2008) provides compelling empirical evidence that this is indeed the case, at least for women. Using variation in dental health caused by variation in community water fluoridation levels during childhood, Glied and Neidell find that women whose childhood counties had fluoridated water earn approximately 4 percent more than women who did not. They find no evidence of a relationship for men. They show evidence that this relationship is most likely due to tooth loss, finding that residence in a fluoridated community is associated with approximately one-third of a tooth more in adulthood.

There are three types of interventions targeting dental health among children: fluoridation (either at the community level or via provision of fluoride to individual children), provision of dental sealants (coating the teeth to make them more resistant to caries), and dental insurance through Medicaid or SCHIP. The first two interventions have received extensive study and review by the Task Force on Community Preventive Services at the Centers for Disease Control. Based on this review (Task Force on Community Pre-

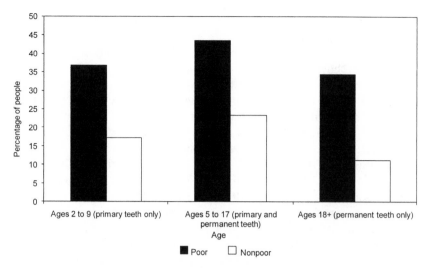

Fig. 4.5   Percentage of people with at least one untreated decayed tooth
Source: U.S. Department of Health and Human Services (2000, 63).

ventive Services 2005, chapter 7) community water fluoridation has been shown to be very effective, reducing dental caries by 30 percent to 50 percent among children four to seventeen years old in communities with fluoridated water. It is also a relatively inexpensive intervention, with a per capita cost of between $0.68 and $3.00 per person depending on the size of the population served (U.S. Department of Health and Human Services 2000, 161). Among communities without community water fluoridation, children may be prescribed dietary supplements for home use, or there may be a school-based dietary supplement program. The evidence on the effectiveness of home use supplements is weak, with no well-designed clinical trials of home-based supplementation and difficulties with self-selection bias and compliance arising in observational studies (U.S. Department of Health and Human Services 2000, 164). School-based programs (again in communities without water fluoridation) have been shown to be more effective, with randomized controlled trials showing caries reductions of 20 to 28 percent over periods of three to six years although optimal effectiveness is only attained when administration of the supplement is tightly controlled, and cost-effectiveness is only attained in schools with children at high risk of dental caries (U.S. Department of Health and Human Services 2000, 164–65).

Dental sealants are a somewhat more recently considered intervention. Sealants are plastic resinous materials that are applied to the molars and harden into a protective coating, providing a physical barrier against bacteria and food particles. For the most part, sealants are provided by individual dentists although school-based sealant programs also exist. Sealants have been shown to reduce the incidence of "pit-and-fissure caries" (caries on the chewing surfaces of the molars) by 52 percent after fifteen years (Simonsen [1991] as cited in U.S. Department of Health and Human Services 2000, 167). Sealants have been shown to be cost-effective as well as effective when used on children at high risk for caries. Sealants are a required service under Medicaid's Early Periodic Screening, Diagnosis, and Treatment (EPSDT) rules, as is routine dental care from a dental professional. Medicaid is thus a potentially important dental health intervention for low-income children, as is SCHIP in many states.[10] However, compelling research on the effect of the Medicaid/SCHIP intervention on dental health is relatively scarce. Based on state reports on EPSDT compliance, it is clear that the Medicaid/SCHIP intervention is reaching few children—among children enrolled in Medicaid, states report that only 30 percent received any dental service in 2004 (Gehshan and Wyatt 2007). The U.S. Department of Health and Human Services Office of the Inspector General attributes this low level of service use primarily to low levels of dentist participation in the Medicaid program, most likely because of low reimbursement rates (less than half the private rates) and the hassles involved in dealing with the Medicaid program. Another commonly cited factor is that Medicaid families place a low priority on dental services although this may be due in part to the difficulty such families have in finding a dentist willing to accept Medicaid. Nevertheless, researchers have found evidence that having Medicaid or SCHIP yields higher levels of dental care services than being uninsured. For example, Wang, Norton, and Rozier (2007) show that children with Medicaid or SCHIP are less likely than uninsured children to report unmet dental care need and more likely to have visited a dentist in the past six months. Further research in this area is necessary to establish a definitive causal link and to examine the role of recent changes in public health insurance provision of dental care (such as increased use of private insurers to provide SCHIP dental coverage in some states).

4.3.4   Childhood Overweight

Perhaps the most discussed issue in children's health in recent years has been the sharp rise in the percentage of children overweight (defined for children as a body mass index [BMI] at or above the 95th percentile for children of the same age and sex) or at risk of overweight (defined as being between the 85th and 95th percentiles). According to data from the National Health and Nutrition Examination Survey (NHANES), the fraction of overweight children in both age groups six to eleven and twelve to nineteen has risen from roughly 5 percent in the 1976 to 1980 period to nearly 20 percent in the 2003 to 2004 period (see figure 4.6). Children who are overweight

10. Unlike Medicaid, states are not required to include dental services in their SCHIP plans although many do include these services.

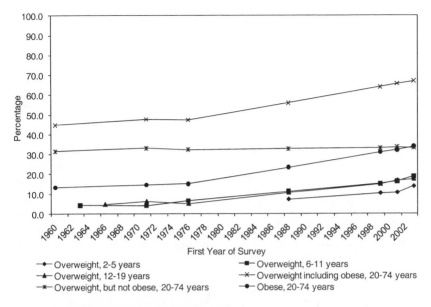

First Year of Survey

—◆— Overweight, 2-5 years   —■— Overweight, 6-11 years
—▲— Overweight, 12-19 years   —✕— Overweight including obese, 20-74 years
—✳— Overweight, but not obese, 20-74 years   —●— Obese, 20-74 years

Fig. 4.6   Overweight and obesity, 1960–2004
Source: National Center for Health Statistics (2007, 41).

have a higher risk of various health problems including diabetes and cardiovascular problems (Gidding et al. 1996). In addition, there is a strong
association between being overweight in childhood and being overweight as
an adult.

Although the research is conflicting, there is some evidence that being
overweight as an adult leads to worse economic outcomes among women
(see table 4.6). The difficulty in establishing whether such a relationship
exists and is causal is, of course, the endogeneity of obesity and labor market
outcomes. While obese individuals tend to have worse labor market outcomes, this correlation could come from the reverse causality (low wages
causing obesity), for which there is some empirical support. Or there may be
an additional factor that causes both obesity and lower wages. Studies have
attempted to account for these possibilities largely in three ways: sibling-
fixed effects (thus assuming that any omitted factors vary only at the family
level), using lagged values of weight instead of current values (eliminating
the reverse causality issue but not dealing with the third-factor possibility),
and instrumental variables that are correlated with the individual's weight
but not his or her labor market outcomes. The most convincing studies have
tended to use a combination of these approaches. For example, Cawley
(2004) uses sibling weight as an instrument as well as using lagged weight
and sibling-fixed effects and finds evidence in the NLSY of a negative effect
of weight on labor market outcomes for women. However Norton and Han

Table 4.6   Selected studies of overweight and obesity

Study	Intervention	Design	Sample	Outcomes	Effects
Averett and Korenman (1996)	NA (Link study)	Sibling fixed effects, lagged values of BMI.	NLSY (1990).	Family income; probability (marriage); spouse's income; hourly wages.	Higher BMI category → reduction in family income, probability (marriage), only for women.
Cawley (2004)	NA (Link study)	Individual and sibling-fixed effects, sibling weight as instrument for own weight.	NLSY (thirteen years).	Log(wage).	IV est: 1 s.d. increase in weight 36 lb) associated with 10% decrease in wages for white women; no significant effect for other groups.
Norton and Han (2007)	NA (Link study)	Instrumental variables (genetic markers as instruments).	Add Health.	probability (employed); log(wage).	No statistically significant effect on either outcome for women or men.

Note: NA = not applicable; BMI = body mass index; NLSY = National Longitudinal Survey of Youth; Add Health = National Longitudinal Study of Adolescent Health; s.d. = standard deviation.

(2007) also use a combination of approaches including genetic markers as instruments (similar to the approach described earlier for mental health) and find no statistically significant effect of weight on labor market outcomes for any group. One issue with this study is its relatively small sample size—there are only 524 observations in the log wage regression, so the standard errors are fairly large.

Given that there is some evidence for labor market impacts of adult overweight and evidence for a relationship between childhood overweight and adult overweight, the next question is whether successful interventions to target overweight in children exist. While there is research that shows that it is possible to reduce weight among overweight children in the short run (see, e.g., Savoye et al. [2007] for a well-evaluated weight management program targeting inner-city minority children that shows evidence of successful weight management sustained for up to a year), the more difficult question is whether these short-run interventions have long-run effects. The American Academy of Pediatrics' Committee on Nutrition takes a fairly pessimistic view about this possibility, stating "Prevention of overweight is critical, because long-term outcome data for successful treatment approaches are limited" (American Academy of Pediatrics Committee on Nutrition 2003, 427). However, there is as yet little evidence of convincingly evaluated interventions targeting prevention that have long-term success—for example, none of the eighty-eight citations in the Committee on Nutrition's Policy

Statement describes such a study. Consequently, while it is possible that a causal link exists between childhood overweight and adult poverty, further research on possible interventions is needed before any recommendations can be made.

4.3.5 Exposure to Environmental Toxins

The final set of child health interventions I consider in this chapter are interventions targeting reduction in exposure to environmental toxins. I focus on two interventions in particular: improvements in air quality and reductions in lead exposure. According to findings from the Environmental Protection Agency cited by the American Academy of Pediatrics Committee on Environmental Health (2004), in 2002, roughly half of the American population was living in areas where monitored air did not meet air quality standards for at least one of six key pollutants. There are biological reasons to believe that children, and particularly infants, may be more susceptible to health problems as a consequence of air pollution. Lung development continues after birth and through adolescence, and children's recommended activities (such as outdoor play and exercise) tend to increase their exposure to pollution (American Academy of Pediatrics Committee on Environmental Health 2004). Associations between most air pollutants and health problems in children (particularly respiratory problems such as asthma) have been well documented (see American Academy of Pediatrics Committee on Environmental Health [2004] and the citations therein). Recent research has shown that there is a causal link (and that the associations are not solely due to the fact that areas with higher pollution also tend to have other characteristics such as higher population densities that may have effects on health). Moreover, this research has shown that there are effects on children at moderate levels of pollution (see table 4.7). Pollution, particularly carbon monoxide, ozone, and particulate matter, has been shown to cause increased hospitalizations for asthma and other respiratory illness (Ransom and Pope 1995; Friedman et al. 2001; Neidell 2004); increased absenteeism (Ransom and Pope 1992; Gilliland et al. 2001; Currie et al. 2007); and increased infant mortality (Chay and Greenstone 2003; Currie and Neidell 2005; Currie, Neidell, and Schmieder 2009). Thus, interventions to reduce air pollution appear to be effective in improving children's health. Unfortunately, this is an area for which there is little to no information on long-term effects. Detailed data over a long period of time is necessary to determine an individual's exposure to pollution in order to relate that exposure to adult outcomes. Recognizing this need, the Children's Health Act of 2000 established the National Children's Study to examine long-term (birth to age twenty-one) environmental effects on the health and development of more than 100,000 children (http://www.nationalchildrensstudy.gov).

Another environmental hazard that has historically been significant for

Table 4.7   Selected studies of air pollution

Study	Intervention	Design	Sample	Outcomes	Effects
Ransom and Pope (1992)	Reduction in pollution due to steel mill closure	Quasi-experimental; mill closed/opened due to labor strike, compared to adjacent valley.	Utah Valley school districts weekly or daily attendance records, 1985–1990.	Absenteeism.	~1% of students absent each day as a result of particulate pollution exposure; effect of high pollution on absenteeism persisted for 3–4 weeks.
Ransom and Pope (1995)	Reduction in pollution due to steel mill closure	Quasi-experimental; mill closed/opened due to labor strike, compared to adjacent valley.	Hospital administrative records, Vital Statistics.	Hospital admissions; mortality rate.	120% increase in bronchial and asthma admissions for preschool children; 17% increase in pneumonia admissions for preschool children; no statistically significant effect on mortality.
Gilliland et al. (2001)	Daily variation in pollution levels	Observational; variation across twelve California communities.	Children's Health Study: 4th graders in 12 communities within 200 miles of LA; school records and survey data.	Absenteeism.	20 ppb of ozone increase associated with 62.9% increase for illness-related absence rates, especially respiratory illness.
Chay and Greenstone (2003)	Reduction in pollution due to recession	Quasi-experimental; variation across counties and over time in pollution levels.	U.S. Vital Statistics and pollution data from the Environmental Protection Agency.	Infant mortality.	1 $\mu g/m^3$ decrease in particulates associated with 5 fewer infant deaths/100,000 live births.

Study	Intervention	Method	Data	Outcome	Findings
Neidell (2004)	Seasonal reduction in pollution	Quasi-experimental; seasonal variation in pollution by zip code and year.	California hospitalization data at zip code-month level.	Hospitalization for asthma.	CO increase asthma hospitalization for children over one.
Currie and Neidell (2005)	Seasonal reduction in pollution	Quasi-experimental; seasonal variation in pollution by zip code and year.	California vital statistics data, 1989–2000.	Infant mortality.	One-unit reduction in CO decreased infant mortality by 34 per 100,000 live births.
Currie et al. (2007)	Seasonal reduction in pollution	Quasi-experimental; seasonal variation in pollution by school, attendance period, and year.	School-level average absentee rates by 6-week attendance period, Texas, 1996–2001.	Absenteeism.	Absentee rates increase with increasing days CO is within 75% of EPA threshold.
Currie, Neidell, and Schmieder (2009)	Seasonal reduction in pollution	Quasi-experimental; seasonal variation in pollution by pregnancy trimester.	New Jersey Vital Statistics data, 1989–2003, mothers <10 km from pollution monitor.	Birth weight, gestation.	One-unit (1 ppm) reduction in average CO during 3rd trimester increased birth weight 16.65 g, no statistically effect for ozone and PM10.
Currie and Schmieder (2009)	Reduction in release of toxic chemicals	Quasi-experimental; variation in release of toxic chemicals at county level over time.	Vital Statistics data at county level matched with EPA's Toxics Release Inventory.	Gestation, birth weight, infant death.	Chemical releases associated with small reductions in gestation and birth weight, larger effect on probability of low or very low birth weight.

children's health is lead. Lead is a potent neurotoxin, causing effects on brain development and functioning even at doses originally believed to be safe. Over the twentieth century, scientists and clinicians gradually realized that lead had negative effects on children's brain development even at levels below that causing acute lead poisoning, but because of lead's usefulness in various materials (including pipes, paint, and, most notably, gasoline), there was great unwillingness to discontinue its use (Silbergeld 1997). (The decision to permit lead additives in fuel has been described as a public health catastrophe, while the banning of lead additives in fuel has been widely recognized as a triumph of public health intervention.) Important for considering interventions to combat lead damage, lead damage is long lasting and difficult to treat after it has occurred (Silbergeld 1997). However, it is entirely preventable by limiting exposure. Between 1960 and 1990, the blood lead level at which the CDC recommended individual intervention in children was lowered from 60 μg/dL to 25 μg/dL, and in 1991 it was lowered further, to 15 μg/dL, with a "level of concern" at 10 μg/dL (CDC 2005b). While there is evidence of lead toxicity at levels below 10 μg/dL, this evidence is all based on observational studies. Because children disadvantaged for other reasons are also more likely to have higher lead levels, it is difficult to determine whether the relationship is causal at levels below 10 μg/dL (CDC 2005b). The evidence for a causal relationship between higher levels of lead exposure and both cognitive functioning and behavioral change is more widely accepted, although still not definitive at moderate levels of lead (see Silbergeld [1997] and Rhoads et al. [1999] and the citations therein). The magnitude of the effect of increasing blood lead from 10 to 20 μg/dL has been shown to be associated with a mean deficit in full scale IQ of around 1 to 2 IQ points based on a systematic review of the literature (Pocock, Smith, and Baghurst 1994). A compelling causal relationship between reduction in childhood lead exposure and crime has been shown by Reyes (2007), who finds that the reduction in childhood lead exposure in the late 1970s and early 1980s was responsible for significant declines in violent crime in the 1990s. Reyes (2005) also shows that the phaseout of leaded gasoline led to 3 to 4 percent reductions in infant mortality and low birth weight.

Nationwide, blood lead levels among children have dropped precipitously as bans on lead in various uses have been instituted. According to data from the National Health and Nutrition Examination Surveys (NHANES), the percentage of children ages one to five with blood lead levels exceeding 10 μg/dL fell from 88.2 percent in the 1976 to 1980 wave to 8.6 percent in the 1988 to 1991 wave, to 4.4 percent in the 1991 to 1994 wave, and to 2.2 percent in the 1999 to 2000 wave (Centers for Disease Control and Prevention n.d., table 1). However, this nationwide fall masks an increasing spread in the distribution of elevated blood lead levels, with minority children and low-income children at much higher risk (Silbergeld 1997, table 5). Low-income minority children living in areas with older housing stocks are the most at risk, as lead paint in deteriorating housing is the most significant source of lead exposure remaining for children. Interventions targeting these children include blood lead screening (not sufficient by itself to reduce lead exposure), removal to lead-free housing, lead abatement, and effective cleaning methods. Widespread removal to lead-free housing is effective but has not been tested as a policy due to its cost. Abatement has been shown to be effective (Charney et al. 1983), but it is also quite expensive. Rhoads et al. (1999) conducted a randomized controlled trial of a maternal education and cleaning intervention and showed that blood lead fell 17 percent as a result, with higher reductions for children whose homes were cleaned more frequently. This decrease is modest, but it does show that cleaning is an effective intervention that may be more economically feasible.

4.4   Discussion and Extensions

This chapter has surveyed a wide range of child health-related interventions and the links between them and long-run outcomes. There is fairly clear evidence that several of these interventions "work" in the sense of improving children's health, notably interventions targeting dental health, childhood asthma, and exposure to environmental toxins. However, the evidence on links between children's health and adult poverty is much weaker. While it exists, researchers have faced some important challenges in estimating the magnitude of these links. These challenges include data availability (particularly the availability of data spanning long time periods); the almost complete lack of true experiments; the limited availability of quasi-experiments affecting long-run outcomes; and the intrinsic difficulty of measurement of the outcomes of interest. Consequently, long-term effects of many types of health-related outcomes are, for the most part, not yet established. While enough evidence exists to indicate that at least some child health measures are causally related to long-run outcomes, it remains an open question whether the interventions investigated have long-run effects at levels of child health currently existing (a good example is blood lead: while it is clear that reducing blood lead from the previous high levels had significantly positive long-run effects, it is less clear whether further reductions in blood lead would have a sizeable impact on the probability of adult poverty). Despite this fairly pessimistic assessment of the state of knowledge about the poverty-related benefits of health interventions, it would be irresponsible not to consider the nonpoverty related benefits when assessing such interventions. It is undisputed that health is an intrinsic part of individual well-being, and the reduction in pain and suffering (both physical and in some cases, financial) offered by the health interventions surveyed here is in some cases substantial. The fact that poor children suffer from worse health gives further impetus not only to an effort to improve the research environment for determining the long-run effects of child health, but also to public policies to ameliorate poor health among poor children if only for its short-run benefits.

References

Akinbami, Lara J. 2006. The state of childhood asthma, United States, 1980–2005. *Advance Data from Vital and Health Statistics* no. 381, December 12. http://www.cdc.gov/nchs/data/ad/ad381.pdf.

Aizer, Anna. 2007. Public health insurance, program take-up, and child health. *Review of Economics and Statistics* 89 (3): 400–415.

Almond, Douglas, Kenneth Y. Chay, and David S. Lee. 2005. The costs of low birth weight. *Quarterly Journal of Economics* 120 (3): 1031–83.

American Academy of Pediatrics Committee on Environmental Health. 2004. Policy statement: Ambient air pollution: Health hazards to children. *Pediatrics* 114 (6): 1699–1707.

American Academy of Pediatrics Committee on Nutrition. 2003. Policy statement: Prevention of pediatric overweight and obesity. *Pediatrics* 112 (2): 424–30.

American Academy of Pediatrics Committee on Quality Improvement, Subcommittee on Attention-Deficit/Hyperactivity Disorder. 2000. Clinical practice guideline: Diagnosis and evaluation of the child with Attention-Deficit/Hyperactivity Disorder. *Pediatrics* 105 (5): 1158–70.

Averett, Susan, and Sanders Korenman. 1996. The economic reality of the beauty myth. *Journal of Human Resources* 31 (2): 304–30.

Banthin, Jessica S., and Thomas M. Selden. 2003. The ABCs of children's health care: How the Medicaid expansions affected access, burdens, and coverage between 1987 and 1996. *Inquiry* 40:133–45.

Behrman, Jere R., and Mark R. Rosenzweig. 2004. Returns to birthweight. *Review of Economics and Statistics* 86 (2): 586–601.

Bitler, Marianne P., and Janet Currie. 2005. Does WIC work? The effects of WIC on pregnancy and birth outcomes. *Journal of Policy Analysis and Management* 24 (1): 73–91.

Black, Sandra E., Paul J. Devereux, and Kjell G. Salvanes. 2007. From the cradle to the labor market? The effect of birth weight on adult outcomes. *Quarterly Journal of Economics* 122 (1): 409–39.

Card, David, and Lara D. Shore-Sheppard. 2004. Using discontinuous eligibility rules to identify the effects of the federal Medicaid expansions on low-income children. *Review of Economics and Statistics* 86 (3): 752–66.

Case, Anne, Darren Lubotsky, and Christina Paxson. 2002. Economic status and health in childhood: The origins of the gradient. *American Economic Review* 92 (5): 1308–34.

Cawley, John. 2004. The impact of obesity on wages. *Journal of Human Resources* 39 (2): 451–74.

Centers for Disease Control and Prevention (CDC). 2005a. Mental health in the United States: Prevalence of diagnosis and medication treatment for Attention-Deficit/Hyperactivity Disorder—United States, 2003. *MMWR* 54 (34): 842–47. http://www.cdc.gov/mmwr/preview/mmwrhtml/mm5434a2.htm.

———. 2005b. Preventing lead poisoning in young children. Atlanta: CDC. http://www.cdc.gov/nceh/lead/publications/PrevLeadPoisoning.pdf.

————. n.d. Children's blood lead levels in the United States. http://www.cdc.gov/nceh/lead/research/kidsBLL.htm.

Charney, Evan, Barry Kessler, Mark Farfel, and David Jackson. 1983. Childhood lead poisoning: A controlled trial of the effect of dust-control measures on blood lead levels. *New England Journal of Medicine* 309 (18): 1089–93.

Chay, Kenneth Y., and Michael Greenstone. 2003. The impact of air pollution on infant mortality: Evidence from geographic variation in pollution shocks induced by a recession. *Quarterly Journal of Economics* 118 (3): 1121–67.

Clement, Sarah, Bridget Candy, Jim Sikorski, Jenny Wilson, and Nigel Smeeton. 1999. Does reducing the frequency of routine antenatal visits have long term effects? Follow-up of participants in a randomised controlled trial. *British Journal of Obstetrics and Gynaecology* 106 (4): 367–70.

Currie, Janet. 2008. Healthy, wealthy, and wise: Is there a causal relationship between child health and human capital development? NBER Working Paper no. 13987. Cambridge, MA: National Bureau of Economic Research.

Currie, Janet, Sandra Decker, and Wanchuan Lin. 2008. Has public health insurance for older children reduced disparities in access to care and health outcomes? *Journal of Health Economics* 27:1567–81.

Currie, Janet, and Jeffrey Grogger. 2002. Medicaid expansions and welfare contractions: Offsetting effects on prenatal care and infant health? *Journal of Health Economics* 21 (2): 313–36.

Currie, Janet, and Jonathan Gruber. 1996a. Health insurance eligibility, utilization of medical care, and child health. *Quarterly Journal of Economics* 111 (2): 431–66.

————. 1996b. Saving babies: The efficacy and cost of recent changes in the Medicaid eligibility of pregnant women. *Journal of Political Economy* 104 (6): 1263–96.

Currie, Janet, Eric Hanushek, E. Megan Kahn, Matthew Neidell, and Steven Rivkin. 2007. Does pollution increase school absences? NBER Working Paper no. 13252. Cambridge, MA: National Bureau of Economic Research.

Currie, Janet, and Matthew Neidell. 2005. Air pollution and infant health: What can we learn from California's recent experience? *Quarterly Journal of Economics* 120 (3): 1003–30.

Currie, Janet, Matthew Neidell, and Johannes F. Schmieder. 2009. Air pollution and infant health: Lessons from New Jersey. *Journal of Health Economics* 28:688–703.

Currie, Janet, and Johannes F. Schmieder. 2009. Fetal exposures to toxic releases and infant health. *American Economic Review: Papers and Proceedings* 99 (2): 177–83.

Currie, Janet, and Mark Stabile. 2006. Child mental health and human capital accumulation: The case of ADHD. *Journal of Health Economics* 25 (6): 1094–1118.

————. 2007. Mental health in childhood and human capital. NBER Working Paper no. 13217. Cambridge, MA: National Bureau of Economic Research.

Currie, Janet, Mark Stabile, Phongsack Manivong, and Leslie L. Roos. 2009. Child health and young adult outcomes. *Journal of Human Resources,* forthcoming.

Cutler, David M., and Jonathan Gruber. 1996. Does public insurance crowd out private insurance? *Quarterly Journal of Economics* 111 (2): 391–430.

Dafny, Leemore, and Jonathan Gruber. 2005. Public insurance and child hospitalizations: Access and efficiency effects. *Journal of Public Economics* 89 (1): 109–29.

Ding, Weili, Steven F. Lehrer, J. Niels Rosenquist, and Janet Audrain-McGovern. 2007. The impact of poor health on education: New evidence using genetic markers. Queen's University. Mimeograph. http://post.queensu.ca/~lehrers/genes.pdf.

Dye, Bruce A., Sylvia Tan, Vincent Smith, Brenda G. Lewis, Laurie K. Barker, Gina Thornton-Evans, Paul I. Eke, Eugenio D. Beltraín-Aguilar, Alice M. Horowitz, and Chien-H. Li. 2007. Trends in oral health status: United States, 1988–1994 and 1999–2004. National Center for Health Statistics. *Vital and Health Statistics* 11 (248).

Evans, Richard, Peter J. Gergen, Herman Mitchell, Meyer Kattan, Carolyn Kercsmar, Ellen Crain, John Anderson, Peyton Eggleston, Floyd J. Malveaux, and H. James Wedner. 1999. A randomized clinical trial to reduce asthma morbidity among inner-city children: Results of the National Cooperative Inner-City Asthma Study. *Journal of Pediatrics* 135 (3): 332–38.

Evans, William N., and Diana S. Lien. 2005. The benefits of prenatal care: Evidence from the PAT bus strike. *Journal of Econometrics* 125:207–39.

Figlio, David, Sarah Hamersma, and Jeffrey Roth. 2009. Does prenatal WIC participation improve birth outcomes? New evidence from Florida. *Journal of Public Economics* 93:235–45.

Fletcher, Jason M., and Steven F. Lehrer. 2008. Using genetic lotteries within families to examine the causal impact of poor health on academic achievement. Queen's University. Mimeograph. http://post.queensu.ca/~lehrers/genelotto.pdf.

Fletcher, Jason M., and Barbara Wolfe. 2008. Child mental health and human capital accumulation: The case of ADHD revisited. *Journal of Health Economics* 27:794–800.

Frank, Richard G., Howard H. Goldman, and Michael Hogan. 2003. Medicaid and mental health: Be careful what you ask for. *Health Affairs* 22 (1): 101–13.

Friedman, Michael S., Kenneth E. Powell, Lori Hutwagner, LeRoy M. Graham, and W. Gerald Teague. 2001. Impact of changes in transportation and commuting behaviors during the 1996 Summer Olympic Games in Atlanta on air quality and childhood asthma. *Journal of the American Medical Association* 285 (7): 897–905.

Gehshan, Shelly, and Matt Wyatt. 2007. Improving oral care for young children. National Academy for State Health Policy. Unpublished Manuscript. http://www.nashp.org/Files/improving_oral_health.pdf.

Gidding, Samuel S., Rudolph L. Leibel, Stephen Daniels, Michael Rosenbaum, Linda Van Horn, and Gerald R. Marx. 1996. Understanding obesity in youth: A statement for healthcare professionals from the Committee on Atherosclerosis and Hypertension in the Young of the Council on Cardiovascular Disease in the Young and the Nutrition Committee, American Heart Association. *Circulation* 94: 3383–87.

Gilliland, Frank D., Kiros Berhane, Edward B. Rappaport, Duncan C. Thomas, Edward Avol, W. James Gauderman, Stephanie J. London, et al. 2001. The effects of ambient air pollution on school absenteeism due to respiratory illnesses. *Epidemiology* 12 (1): 43–54.

Glied, Sherry, and Matthew Neidell. 2008. The economic value of teeth. NBER Working Paper no. 13879. Cambridge, MA: National Bureau of Economic Research.

Gruber, Jonathan, and Kosali Simon. 2008. Crowd-out 10 years later: Have recent public insurance expansions crowded out private health insurance? *Journal of Health Economics* 27 (2): 201–17.

Gruber, Jonathan, and Aaron Yelowitz. 1999. Public health insurance and private savings. *Journal of Political Economy* 107 (6, pt. 1): 1249–74.

Haas, Jennifer S., I. Steven Udvarhelyi, Carol N. Morris, and Arnold M. Epstein. 1993. The effect of providing health coverage to poor uninsured pregnant women in Massachusetts. *Journal of the American Medical Association* 269 (1): 87–91.

Ham, John C., and Lara D. Shore-Sheppard. 2005. The effect of Medicaid expansions for low-income children on Medicaid participation and private insurance coverage: Evidence from the SIPP. *Journal of Public Economics* 89 (1): 57–83.

Hanratty, Maria J. 1996. Canadian National Health Insurance and infant health. *American Economic Review* 86 (1): 276–84.

Honein, Margaret A., Leonard J. Paulozzi, T. J. Mathews, J. David Erickson, and Lee-Yang C. Wong. 2001. Impact of folic acid fortification of the U.S. food supply on the occurrence of neural tube defects. *Journal of the American Medical Association* 285 (23): 2981–86.

Hudson, Julie L., Thomas M. Selden, and Jessica S. Banthin. 2005. The impact of SCHIP on insurance coverage of children. *Inquiry* 42 (Fall): 232–54.

Joyce, Theodore. 1999. Impact of augmented prenatal care on birth outcomes of Medicaid recipients in New York City. *Journal of Health Economics* 18 (1): 31–67.

Joyce, Theodore, Diane Gibson, and Silvie Colman. 2005. The changing association between prenatal participation in WIC and birth outcomes in New York City: What does It mean? *Journal of Policy Analysis and Management* 24 (4): 661–85.

Joyce, Theodore, Andrew Racine, and Cristina Yunzal-Butler. 2008. Reassessing the WIC effect: Evidence from the Pregnancy Nutrition Surveillance System. *Journal of Policy Analysis and Management* 27 (2): 277–303.

Kaestner, Robert, Theodore Joyce, and Andrew Racine. 2001. Medicaid eligibility and the incidence of ambulatory care sensitive hospitalizations for children. *Social Science and Medicine* 52:305–313.

Kowaleski-Jones, Lori, and Greg J. Duncan. 2002. Effects of participation in the WIC program on birthweight: Evidence from the National Longitudinal Survey of Youth. *American Journal of Public Health* 92 (5): 799–804.

Le, Anh T., Paul W. Miller, Andrew C. Heath, and Nick Martin. 2005. Early childhood behaviours, schooling and labour market outcomes: Estimates from a sample of twins. *Economics of Education Review* 24:1–17.

Levy, Helen, and David Meltzer. 2004. What do we really know about whether health insurance affects health? In *Health policy and the uninsured,* ed. Catherine G. McLaughlin, 179–203. Washington, DC: Urban Institute Press.

Long, Stephen H., and M. Susan Marquis. 1998. The effects of Florida's Medicaid eligibility expansion for pregnant women. *American Journal of Public Health* 88 (3): 371–76.

LoSasso, Anthony T., and Thomas C. Buchmueller. 2004. The effect of the State Children's Health Insurance Program on health insurance coverage. *Journal of Health Economics* 23 (5): 1059–82.

Ludwig, Jens, and Matthew Miller. 2005. Interpreting the WIC debate. *Journal of Policy Analysis and Management* 24 (4): 691–701.

McDuffie Jr., Robert S., Arne Beck, Kimberly Bischoff, Jean Cross, and Miriam Orleans. 1996. Effect of frequency of prenatal care visits on perinatal outcome among low-risk women. *Journal of the American Medical Association* 275 (11): 847–51.

Milton, B., M. Whitehead, P. Holland, and V. Hamilton. 2004. The social and economic consequences of childhood asthma across the lifecourse: A systematic review. *Child: Care, Health and Development* 30 (6): 711–28.

National Center for Health Statistics. 2007. *Health, United States, 2007 With chartbook on trends in the health of Americans.* DHHS Pub. no. 2007-1232. Hyattsville, MD. http://www.cdc.gov/nchs/data/hus/hus07.pdf.

Neidell, Matthew. 2004. Air pollution, health, and socio-economic status: The effect of outdoor air quality on childhood asthma. *Journal of Health Economics* 23:1209–36.

Newacheck, Paul W., and Neal Halfon. 2000. Prevalence, impact, and trends in childhood disability due to asthma. *Archives of Pediatric and Adolescent Medicine* 154:287–93.

Norton, Edward C., and Euna Han. 2007. Genetic information, obesity, and labor market outcomes. Health, Econometrics and Data Group Working Paper no. 07/15. University of York.

Oreopoulos, Philip, Mark Stabile, Randy Walld, and Leslie L. Roos. 2008. Short-, medium-, and long-term consequences of poor infant health. *Journal of Human Resources* 43 (1): 88–138.

Pelham Jr., William E., Trilby Wheeler, and Andrea Chronis. 1998. Empirically supported psychosocial treatments for Attention Deficit Hyperactivity Disorder. *Journal of Clinical Child and Adolescent Psychology* 27 (2): 190–205.

Piper, Joyce M., Edward F. Mitchel, Jr., and Wayne A. Ray. 1994. Expanded Medicaid coverage for pregnant women to 100 percent of the federal poverty level. *American Journal of Preventive Medicine* 10 (2): 97–102.

Piper, Joyce M., Wayne A. Ray, and Marie R. Griffin. 1990. Effects of Medicaid eligibility expansion on prenatal care and pregnancy outcome in Tennessee. *Journal of the American Medical Association* 264 (17): 2219–23.

Pocock, Stuart J., Marjorie Smith, and Peter Baghurst. 1994. Environmental lead and children's intelligence: A systematic review of epidemiological evidence. *British Medical Journal* 309:1189–96.

Ransom, Michael R., and C. Arden Pope, III. 1992. Elementary school absences and PM_{10} pollution in Utah Valley. *Environmental Research* 58:204–19.

———. 1995. External health costs of a steel mill. *Contemporary Economic Policy* 13 (2): 86–97.

Ray, Wayne A., Edward F. Mitchel, Jr., and Joyce M. Piper. 1997. Effect of Medicaid expansions on preterm birth. *American Journal of Preventive Medicine* 13 (4): 292–97.

Reyes, Jessica Wolpaw. 2005. The impact of prenatal lead exposure on infant health. Amherst College, Working Paper.

———. 2007. Environmental policy as social policy? The impact of childhood lead exposure on crime. *The B.E. Journal of Economic Analysis & Policy:* 7 (1): Article 51. http://www.bepress.com/bejeap/vol7/iss1/art51.

Rhoads, George G., Adrienne S. Ettinger, Clifford P. Weisel, Timothy J. Buckley, Karen Denard Goldman, John Adgate, and Paul J. Lioy. 1999. The effect of dust lead control on blood lead in toddlers: A randomized trial. *Pediatrics* 103 (3): 551–55.

Royer, Heather. 2009. Separated at girth? U.S. twin estimates of the effects of birth weight. *American Economic Journal: Applied Economics* 1 (1): 49–85.

Savoye, Mary, Melissa Shaw, James Dziura, William V. Tamborlane, Paulina Rose, Cindy Guandalini, Rachel Goldberg-Gell, et al. 2007. Effects of a weight management program on body composition and management parameters in overweight children: A randomized controlled trial. *Journal of the American Medical Association* 297 (24): 2697–2704.

Sered, Susan Starr, and Rushika Fernandopulle. 2007. *Uninsured in America: Life and death in the land of opportunity.* Los Angeles: University of California Press.

Shipler, David K. 2005. *The working poor: Invisible in America.* New York: Vintage Books.

Shore-Sheppard, Lara D. 2008. Stemming the tide? The effect of expanding Medicaid eligibility on health insurance coverage. *The B.E. Journal of Economic Analysis and Policy:* 8 (2): Article 6. http://www.bepress.com/bejeap/vol8/iss2/art6.

Sikorski, Jim, Jennifer Wilson, Sarah Clement, Sarah Das, and Nigel Smeeton. 1996. A randomized controlled trial comparing two schedules of antenatal visits: The antenatal care project. *British Medical Journal: Clinical Research Edition* 312 (7030): 546–53.

Silbergeld, Ellen K. 1997. Preventing lead poisoning in children. *Annual Reviews of Public Health* 18:187–210.

Simonsen, Richard J. 1991. Retention and effectiveness of dental sealant after 15 years. *Journal of the American Dental Association* 122 (11): 34–42.

Smith, James P. 2009. The impact of childhood health on adult labor market outcomes. *Review of Economics and Statistics* 91 (3): 478–89.

Task Force on Community Preventive Services. 2005. *The guide to community preventive services: What works to promote health?* ed. Stephanie Zaza, Peter A. Briss, and Kate W. Harris, New York: Oxford University Press. http://www.thecommunity guide.org/library/book/.

U.S. Department of Health and Human Services. 1999. Mental health: A report of the surgeon general. Rockville, MD: U.S. Department of Health and Human Services, Substance Abuse and Mental Health Services Administration, Center for Mental Health Services, National Institutes of Health, National Institute of Mental Health. http://www.surgeongeneral.gov/library/mentalhealth/home.html.

———. 2000. Oral health in America: A report of the surgeon general. Rockville, MD: U.S. Department of Health and Human Services, National Institute of Dental and Craniofacial Research, National Institutes of Health.

U.S. Department of Health and Human Services, Office of Inspector General. 1996. Children's dental services under Medicaid: Access and utilization. Pub. no. OEI-09-93-00240. http://www.oig.hhs.gov/oei/reports/oei-09-93-00240.pdf. San Francisco: Office of Evaluation and Inspection.

Villar, Jose, Hassan Ba'aqeel, Gilda Piaggio, Pisake Lumbiganon, José Miguel Belizan, Ubaldo Farnot, Yagob Al-Mazrou, Guillermo Carroll, Alain Pinot, Allan Donner, Ana Langer, et al. 2001. WHO antenatal care randomized trial for the evaluation of a new model of routine antenatal care. *Lancet* 357 (9268): 1551–64.

Vujić, Sunčica, Pierre Koning, Dinand Webbink, and Nick Martin. 2008. The effect of childhood conduct disorder on human capital. CPB Netherlands Bureau for Economic Policy Analysis Working Paper no. 13. http://www.cpb.nl/eng/pub/cpbreeksen/discussie/113/disc113.pdf.

Wang, Hua, Edward C. Norton, and R. Gary Rozier. 2007. Effects of the State Children's Health Insurance Program on access to dental care and use of dental services. *Health Services Research* 42 (4): 1544–63.

Wigal, Tim, James M. Swanson, Roland Regino, Marc A. Lerner, Ihab Soliman, Ken Steinhoff, Suresh Gurbani, and Sharon B. Wigal. 1999. Stimulant medications for the treatment of ADHD: Efficacy and limitations. *Mental Retardation and Developmental Disabilities Research Reviews* 5:215–24.

Middle Childhood Interventions

After-School Care

Phillip B. Levine and David J. Zimmerman

5.1 Introduction

Support for investments in after-school programs is motivated by a few central concerns. Principally, there is a concern that a large number of children end their formal school-day activities and enter a period of time during which they are unsupervised until the time their parents return home from work. As Delaware U.S. Representative Michael Castle stated during a congressional hearing on March 11, 2008, "each afternoon, millions of students around the nation leave school with no place to go because they lack affordable, accessible, after-school opportunities."[1] Providing structured after-school programs to these "latch-key" children during this critical time period, it is argued, would enhance children's physical safety, discourage risky behavior, and—depending on the emphasis of the after-school program—nurture various other desirable outcomes. These benefits might include improved academic outcomes, physical fitness, or artistic creativity.

From the perspective of this volume, after-school programs might then be viewed as a potential investment in poverty reduction if the programs alter outcomes that either directly or indirectly improve the adult labor market outcomes of the participants.[2] Indeed, after-school programs may be regarded as an essential component of a policy framework promoting equal

Phillip B. Levine is the Class of 1919 Professor and chair of department of economics at Wellesley College, and a research associate of the National Bureau of Economic Research. David J. Zimmerman is a professor of economics and Orrin Sage Professor of Political Economy at Williams College, and a research associate of the National Bureau of Economic Research.

1. See http://edlabor.house.gov/hearings/ecese-2008-03-11.shtml.
2. After-school care may also impact parent's labor supply, which may impact family income and, hence, children's later outcomes. This link is covered in another chapter in this volume.

opportunity, as articulated in the annual report of The After-School Corporation (TASC)—a significant funder of after-school programs in New York:

> The resources that families with means treat as routine extensions of their kids' education—music lessons, sports, academic help—are out of reach for kids in broad swaths of the city. Kids on the wrong side of the opportunity gap face limited possibilities to develop the talents, skills, breadth of learning that would prepare them for college and careers. (TASC 2007).

Obviously, the merit of this intervention strategy hinges on several key issues. The marginal benefit of participation will likely depend critically on the subset of the child population that elects to participate in the programs. The economic benefits are likely to be greater if participants come from high-risk families or environments than if they come from stable supportive families or environments. After-school programs, generally voluntary in nature, may have a limited effect if the alternative to a formal supervised after-school program is simply supervised care at home and not unsupervised self-care. Further, potential benefits will hinge on the types of programs provided and the impact they have on children's ability to achieve self-sufficiency later in life. Programs emphasizing recreational activities may foster self-esteem or physical fitness but may have a less significant effect on academic performance. Last, it is critical to understand the cost of after-school programs so that the benefits per dollar spent might compare with other interventions competing for scarce funding. Does an investment in after-school care reap high returns in reducing poverty when the participants attain adulthood?

This chapter reviews the literature on after-school programs with an eye to offering advice on whether these programs are likely candidates for an effective antipoverty program. The chapter is organized as follows: in the next section, we discuss the motivation for interest in after-school programs. We then examine some of the main nonexperimental evaluations that have been conducted on "flagship" after-school programs. Next we summarize the evidence on the key experimental evaluations that have been conducted. Finally, we'll discuss the implications of these findings and offer conclusions.

5.2   Background

Over the past three decades, there has been a significant increase in female labor force participation. In 1975, just over half of women with children aged between six and seventeen were active in the labor force. For women with children under the age of six, the participation rate was just under 40 percent. By 2006, almost 80 percent of women with children aged six to seventeen were active in the labor force, and 63 percent of mothers with children six years or younger were working (U.S. Bureau of Labor Statistics 2007). These trends, shown in figure 5.1, have implications for the care of

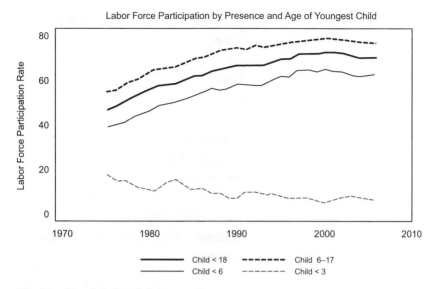

Fig. 5.1   **Trends in female labor supply**
Source: Women in the Labor Force: A Databook, September 2007.

children when parents are at work. There is a large literature considering the provision of child care for younger children, but less research has been done on the impact of different child care arrangements for school-aged children (see chapter 3 in this volume). Data from the Survey on Income and Program Participation, administered by the U.S. Census Bureau, indicate that roughly 14 percent (or 5.2 million) of children between the ages of five and fourteen were spending time in "self-care" on a regular basis during 2005 (U.S. Census Bureau 2005). Rates of self-care rise with the age of the child and are highest for women who are windowed, separated, or divorced (19.5 percent) and for those employed full time (18 percent). The distribution of regular child care arrangements is shown in figure 5.2.

Concerns over children being unsupervised during the after-school time period of roughly 3 p.m. to 6 p.m. are supported by data on the temporal incidence of crime. Figure 5.3 shows that violent crimes, sexual assault, and aggravated assault by juveniles show a distinct peak during the after-school hours (cf. Fox and Newman 1997). Trends for nonstudents (not shown) do not show this peak. After-school care, when appropriately supervised, would then hold the potential to provide children with a safe environment during the after-school hours and reduce the odds that they engage in various crimes. Beyond safety, after-school programs are often suggested as a way to help students improve their academic performance, reduce risky behavior such as drug use or sexual activity, or to enhance their social and emotional well-being (cf. Catalano et al. 1998; Durlak and Weissberg 2007).

This suggests that a prima facie case can be made for the provision

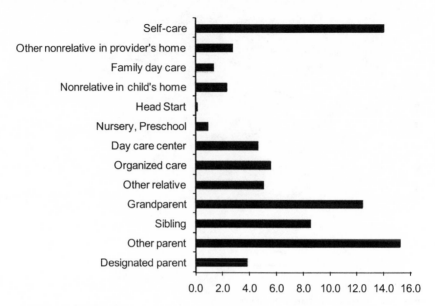

Fig. 5.2   Child care arrangements of grade-schoolers 5–14 years old living with mother
Source: "Who's Minding the Kids" 2005 data, U.S. Bureau of the Census.

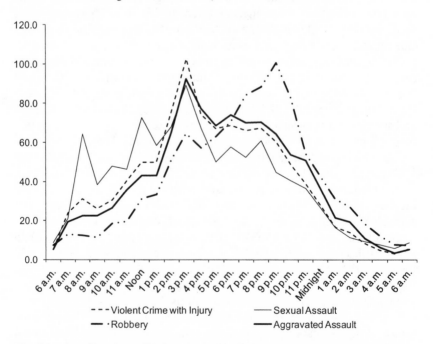

Fig. 5.3   Juvenile crime, offenders per 1,000 offenders in age group by time of day
Sources: Snyder and Sickmund (2006); U.S. Department of Justice (2006).

of after-school programs of some sort. The federal role in this endeavor comes primarily through the 21st Century Community Learning Centers (21CCLC) program, which is the only federal funding source, directed solely at after-school programs. The program, which began in 1998, is described as follows by the U.S. Department of Education:

> This program supports the creation of community learning centers that provide academic enrichment opportunities during non-school hours for children, particularly students who attend high-poverty and low-performing schools. The program helps students meet state and local student standards in core academic subjects, such as reading and math; offers students a broad array of enrichment activities that can complement their regular academic programs; and offers literacy and other educational services to the families of participating children. (http://www2 .ed.gov/programs/21stcclc/index.html)

Funds from the 21CCLC program are granted on a competitive basis by the U.S. Department of Education to state education agencies, who then grant funds on a competitive basis to eligible organizations. Each state, therefore, funds a variety of programs with these funds.

The 21CCLC program began with $40 million in appropriations in 1998. Funding rose rapidly to $453 million in 2000 and then to approximately $1 billion in 2002. Funding has remained roughly steady in recent years; however, pressure for reductions in spending have recently mounted. Figure 5.4 shows the trends in funding since the programs inception with predicted appropriations inserted for 2009.[3] Beyond federal funding, after-school programs may receive funding from state and local governments, private foundations, businesses, and fees. Funding from a variety of these sources is common.

5.3   Evaluations

The Harvard Family Research Project provides a national database on a large number of evaluations of after-school programs.[4] Evaluations may be for a particular (singular) program or for a group of programs. Of the roughly 150 evaluations that are reviewed, only 9 programs that were classified as either "after-school," "comprehensive," or "mentoring" were evaluated

---

3. There are a few other federal programs that support after-school programs, though to a lesser extent. Snacks served at after-school programs may qualify for reimbursement from the U.S. Department of Agriculture (USDA). The Child Care and Development Fund may be used by states to provide after-school care. Further, Temporary Assistance for Needy Families (TANF) funds may be used to support after-school programs if they meet the programs requirements. Government support for childcare, however, is minimal. Indeed, only 4.1 percent of children under the age of fifteen received support from a federal, state, or local government agency, or a welfare office in 2002 (U.S. Census Bureau 2002).

4. See http://www.hfrp.org/.

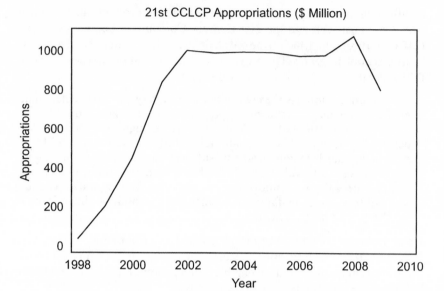

Fig. 5.4   Trends in federal funding of after-school programs
Sources: http://www.ed.gov/about/overview/budget/statetables/index.html and http://www.afterschoolalliance.org/21stcclc.cfm.
Note: 2008–2009 are estimated.

using an experimental design.[5] The remainder utilized either a quasi- or non-experimental framework for their evaluation. This highlights the fact that there is a limited research base from which to draw in forging an assessment of the efficacy of after-school programs.

5.3.1   Nonexperimental Evaluations

Nonexperimental evaluations of particular programs typically contrast the outcomes of participants and "similar" nonparticipants. These comparisons may utilize a regression framework with "program participation" or "self-care" specified as an independent variable or may simply compare the outcomes of participants to those of a set of nonparticipants who are selected for their similarity in terms of age, gender, prior grades, and so on. The principal empirical task facing these studies is selection bias; that is, participants and nonparticipants may differ in a myriad of ways—some of which (e.g., parental concern, child's academic motiva-

5. These programs include the 21st Century Learning Centers—national evaluation, Across Ages Program, Children's Aid Society Carrera-Model Teen Pregnancy Prevention Program, Louisiana State Youth Opportunities Unlimited Summer Program, Quantum Opportunities Program, Woodrock Youth Development Project, Big Brothers Big Sisters of America Program, and the Howard Street Tutoring Program. Some of these programs are significantly more comprehensive than most after-school programs or are only tangentially targeted at academic enrichment.

tion, etc.) may be important predictors of participation and performance but may be unobservable to the researcher. Selection may bias the effects of program participation up or down depending on its nature. For example, suppose children left in self-care are from homes that, on average, place less emphasis on academic achievement. If these children perform more poorly on a reading test than children in supervised care, it may have little to do with "self-care" per se and more to do with other aspects of the child's home environment. Alternatively, parents may only opt for self-care if their children are particularly responsible. In that case, the self-care children may actually outperform children in supervised settings. But the superior performance may have nothing to do with the particular child care option selected. An experimental protocol, with random assignment into the program, on the other hand, provides the necessary control that participants and nonparticipants should be similar, on average, except for their participation in the program. Including a variety of control factors in a regression model may not capture these unobservable differences (c.f. Vandell and Corasaniti 1988; Posner and Vandell 1999). Aizer (2004) makes a serious attempt to address these issues by using a family fixed effects model that contrasts siblings who have experienced different child care histories. She finds that adult supervision reduces a range of risky behavior including drug use or school attendance. This estimation strategy, as she notes, would produce biased estimates if "the decision to allocate time to certain children within the family is correlated with the child's propensity to engage in negative behavior" (Aizer 2004, 1840). Aizer provides some simple tests for this possibility, but they cannot rule out the possibility of selection.

5.3.2 Meta-Analyses

A variety of studies attempt to synthesize the large and conflicting literature on after-school programs (cf. Fashola 1998; Eccles and Templeton 2001; Redd, Cochran, and Moore 2002; Scott-Little, Hamann, and Jurs 2002; Miller 2003; Catalano et al. 1998; Lauer et al. 2006; Durlak and Weissberg 2007; Little, Wimer, and Weiss 2008). These reviews suffer from a common problem: how can studies of varying credibility be aggregated to form a conclusion? These syntheses often combine evaluations that are scientifically credible with studies that are not methodologically compelling—sometimes then using the results to conduct further evaluations on what program features are likely to be important in constructing an effective program. Clearly, the weights placed on the validity of the various evaluations will play a critical role in any conclusions that are drawn, making a clear synthesis of the literature difficult to accomplish. One survey, for example, limits the population of studies considered to those with "effects demonstrated on behavioral outcomes." Studies with "no effect" effectively get a weight of zero in the analyses (Catalano et al. 1998). Fashola, in her study of thirty-four programs concludes: "Our review shows that research on after-school programs is at a very rudimentary stage. Few studies of the effects of after-school programs on achievement or other outcomes meet minimal standards of research design" (Fashola 1998, 54). Scott-Little, Hamann, and Jurs, in a comprehensive survey of the literature, note that most existing evaluation studies "were published outside of peer-reviewed journals" and that "few programs have utilized experimental designs, a problem common in educational research" (Scott-Little, Hamann, and Jurs 2002, 410–12). Of the thirty studies used in Lauer et al. (2006) to investigate the effect of out-of-school time programs on improving reading, only four are published in peer-reviewed journals (Lauer et al. 2006). Miller notes that one reason for this shortage of credible information is that the "standards of rigorous scientific research require resources that are not available to most providers" (Miller 2003, 85).

5.3.3   Flagship Nonexperimental Evaluations

Perhaps the best-known and largest scale nonexperimental evaluations are those done for the Los Angeles' Better Educated Students for Tomorrow (LAB) program and for programs conducted by The After-School Corporation (TASC).

Los Angeles' Better Educated Students for Tomorrow (LAB)

The LAB program, a partnership between the City of Los Angeles, the Los Angeles School District, and the private sector, is a comprehensive school-based after-school program targeted at children aged five to twelve years old. The program began in 1988 and now has over 100 sites located primarily in high-risk, low-income areas throughout the City of Los Angeles. The program provides children with homework help, recreational activities, snacks, and a variety of enrichment programs through to 6 p.m. each weekday. A brief description of the program and its evaluations can be found in table 5.1. The first evaluation used a nonrandom sample and contrasted a set of outcomes for eighty program participants to those for sixty-six comparison group members who were selected based on similarity in age, family income, and education of their parents, and their parent's willingness to let them participate in the evaluation (Brooks, Mojica, and Land 1995). The authors note, however, that the "lack of comparability between the control and program children can only in part be compensated by statistical adjustments" (7). They also indicate a concern about "the representativeness of these groups." The results are difficult to interpret as no statistically significant differences in improvements in math, reading, composition, social studies, or science were found until the sample was adjusted to remove "outliers." As noted in Blau and Currie (2004), "from the pattern of the results, it appears that the effect of deleting these outliers was to raise the mean scores of the LA's Best kids relative to the controls" (58). There were, however, positive effects on attitudinal effects such as feeling "safer during school" and "[liking] school more this year than last year." A second larger study (n = 19,322) compared participants to nonparticipants controlling for ethnicity, gender, language proficiency, eligibility for free or reduced school lunch, and disability status. Participants were differentiated based on their participation (high, medium, low) in the program (Huang et al. 2000). The evaluation showed improvements in standardized tests in math, reading, language arts, and attendance. Differences in grades, however, disappeared by grades eight and nine. Other work considering the LAB program describes the evidence on academic achievement as "uneven" while reporting reductions in criminal behavior by program participants (Goldschmidt, Juang, and Chinen 2007). Importantly, the design utilized in these studies leaves open the possibility that unobserved characteristics that lead the students into the program could be the causal factors behind any differences in outcomes. Further, it is possible that the selection issues are strongest for those students who persist in the program. If, for example, students with more supportive family backgrounds are those that exhibit the most regular attendance, then what might be regarded as a "dosage" effect is really the result of stronger selection effects. Huang et al. (2000) recognize this possibility, noting "it may be that high-level attenders do so because they and their parents are more highly motivated, and this interest transfers to achievement. But it is equally likely that coming to school and to the LA's Best program regularly is the reason for good performance and persisting impact subsequent to leaving LA's best" (10). Unfortunately, the research design does not allow us to distinguish between these possibilities. Other research, however, suggests that students with riskier profiles are more likely to drop out of after-school programs (Weisman and Gottfredson 2001). This suggests that program attrition may taint comparisons using high-level attenders with selection bias.

The After-School Corporation (TASC)

The After-School Corporation is a nonprofit organization that began in 1998 and by 2003 spent almost $100 million supporting 50,000 students in 242 after-school programs in New York—with 186 of the projects located in New York City. Programs are typically located in schools serving a high-fraction of "at-risk" students. The programs place emphasis on homework assistance, academic enrichment, reading, fitness and sports, artistic development, and life skills. The After-School Corporation's objective has been described as follows:

> TASC's mission, in effect, calls for it to demonstrate that high-quality after-school programs can be created, operated, and sustained in partnership with public schools and with other public and private partners. A central proposition of this mission is that after-school programs can attract significant numbers of children on a regular basis and can offer these children important developmental opportunities, all at no

Table 5.1 Review of evidence

Study	Intervention	Evaluation design	Sample	Outcomes	Effects
			Selected nonexperimental studies		
Brooks, Mojica, and Land (1995)	Los Angeles's Best After-School Program	Comparison group design.	Non-random sample. Program participants (n = 80 in year 1, n = 69 in year 2) were in 5th and 6th grades with 2+ years in program. Comparison group (n = 66 in year 1, n = 58 in year 2) was similar in terms of age, family income, age, and education of parents, but with <3 months in program.	Grades in math, reading, composition, social studies, and science. Safety. Enjoyment of school and other attitudinal measures.	No significant effect. Improved sense of safety. Improvement in several attitudinal areas.
Huang et al. (2000)	Los Angeles's Best After-School Program	Multiple regression. Controls include ethnicity, gender, language proficiency status, eligibility for free/reduced lunch, and disability status.	Non-random sample. Program participants in grades 2–5 (n = 4,312) and schoolmate nonparticipants (n = 15,010). Participants divided into high (75% days present), medium (26–74% days present), and low (<26% days present) levels of participation.	Comprehensive Test of Basic Skills and Stanford-9 Achievement Test in reading, math, and language arts. School absenteeism.	Positive effect (increases with participation). no significant effect by grades 8 and 9.
Reisner et al. (2004)	The After-School Corporation (TASC)	Multiple regression. Controls include baseline test scores, family income, gender, race, and eligibility for specialized educational services.	Data collected for over four school years from ninety-six TASC after-school projects and their host schools in New York City with 52,000 after-school participants and 91,000 students who were enrolled in TASC host schools but not participating in TASC projects.	Math. Reading.	+.06 sigma after 1 year, +.42 sigma after 2 years; active participants: +.13 sigma after 1 year, +.79 sigma after 2 years. No significant effect.

Selected experimental studies

James-Burdumy et al. (2005)	21st Century Community Learning Centers Program	Elementary school: experimental. Middle school: comparison group.	Mostly low-income schools with large proportions of minority students. Elementary school study based on random assignment of students from twelve school districts and twenty-six centers that had excess demand for the programs in 1999. First cohort of elementary students first year (2000–2001) had treatment n = 589 and control n = 384 for seven school districts. Second cohort (2001–2002) had treatment n = 693 and control n = 666 for five districts. Test scores administered at baseline and follow-up. Average attendance 2.7 days/week for students continuing into second year. These students were more likely to come from two-parent families and had higher baseline reading test scores. Middle school study is based on a nationally representative sample of program participants (n = 1782) and a matched sample of nonparticipants (n = 2482). Participants in second year had more educated mothers. Extensive controls.	Second year results (note: participant and intent-to-treat effects are similar). Frequency of self-care. Maternal employment, reading test-score (SAT-9), English grade, math grade, science and social science grades, TV viewing time, homework completion, attendance. Behavioral problems. Sense of safety. Frequency of self care. Math, English, or science grade. Social Studies grades. School absences.	No significant effect. Increased for treatment students. Fewer treatments (2.5% vs 7.1%) felt "not at all safe" after school. No significant effect. Treatment higher in second year. More behavioral problems with treatment students.
Morris, Shaw, and Perney (1990)	Howard Street Tutoring Program	Experimental.	Bottom 1/3 of 2nd and 3rd grade readers identified by teachers. Students are ranked based on several reading tests administered by outside evaluators and ranked from high to low. Students with similar rank are randomly assigned to program or control groups. Two years evaluated. Treatment: n = 30, control: n = 30. Students are from a low-socioeconomic status school.	Word recognition. Basal word recognition and spelling.	No significant effect. Statistically significant gains.

(*continued*)

Table 5.1 (continued)

Study	Intervention	Evaluation design	Sample	Outcomes	Effects
Hahn, Leavitt, and Aaron (1994)	Quantum Opportunity Program (QOP)	Experimental.	Twenty-five students from each site were randomly selected to participate in the program from 9th–12th grade. Targeted at disadvantaged families. Launched in five sites: Philadelphia, Milwaukee, San Antonio, Saginaw, and Oklahoma City.	High-school graduation rate. Drop out of school. Pursue post-secondary education. Attend a four-year college. Participants less likely to become teen parents (24% vs. 38%; $p<.01$). Trouble with police.	Higher for participants (63% vs. 42%; $p<.01$). Participants less likely to drop out (23% vs. 50%; $p<.01$). Participants more likely (42% vs. 16%; $p<.01$). Participants more likely (18% vs. 5%) or two-year college (19% vs. 9%; $p<.01$). Participants had less trouble with police ($p = .09$).
Maxfield et al. (2003)	QOP	Experimental.	Demonstration evaluation in seven sites conducted by U.S. Department of Labor and the Ford Foundation between 1995–2001. Single cohort of 580 ninth grade in 9th grade program participants and 489 controls. Sites included six inner-city sites and one rural community. There were 100 youth participants in four sites, 80 in one site, and 50 in two sites.	Achievement test scores, grades, high school graduation rates, or behavioral issues.	No significant effect.

Study	Program	Design	Sample	Outcomes	Results
Schirm, Stuart, and McKie (2006)	QOP	Experimental.	Follow up of U.S. Department of Labor and Ford Foundation study. Participants aged twenty-three and twenty-five years old.	High school graduation or postsecondary education. Earnings or employment.	Participants no more likely to graduate from high school or engage in post-secondary education or training. No impact on earnings or employment.
Tierney, Grossman, and Resch (1995)	Big Brothers Big Sisters of America (BBBS)	Experimental	Sample includes youth aged ten–sixteen (more than half minority) from eight sites with excess demand. Agencies were among largest in BBBS organization. Students randomly assigned to treatment (n = 571) or to control (a waiting list where they remained for the study duration; n = 567) were surveyed. At one-year follow-up survey, samples were treatment n = 487 and control n = 472.	Stealing, damaging property, hours spent on homework, hours spent reading. Initiating drug use, hitting another person, perceived ability to complete homework, skipping school/class, lying to parents. Grades.	No significant effect. Significant beneficial impact. Grade effect was .08 (p<.1; both genders). Grade effect was .17 (p<.05; girls).

Herrara et al. (2007) BBBS   Fourth through 9th graders; 565 treatments, 574 controls. Academic performance.   Academic performance was .11 points higher (on 1–5 scale) for treatments at one-year follow-up; impacts largely disappeared at 15-month follow-up.

out-of-pocket cost to participants or their families. Finally, according to this mission, these programs and the opportunities they offer can increase the likelihood that participants will succeed in school and in life generally (Reisner et al. 2004, 2).

Several evaluations of TASC have been conducted by Policy Studies Associates (PSA) (c.f. Reisner et al. 2002; Reisner et al. 2004). An evaluation conducted in 2003 by PSA summarized impacts for 96 TASC projects over four school years. The analyses employed a regression based approach including a large number of covariates including baseline test scores, family income, gender, race, and eligibility for special education services. The report argues that inclusion of baseline test scores and baseline attendance measures should control for any self-selection bias in estimates for grade and attendance, respectively. This assumption is true only if the factors generating self-selection are constant over time. If, for example, a child's family actively decided to place more emphasis on education and that emphasis included after-school participation, then selection bias would still be present. The evaluation further distinguished between regular and "active" participants who attended at least 60 percent of the possible days and attended at least sixty days during the school year. Estimates for reading and math achievement tests were calculated for two separate years for children in grades three to eight. Math test gains were not statistically significant in the first year but rose by .42 "standardized scale points" in the second year. Gains were higher still for "active" participants—reporting gains of .79 standardized scale points in the second year. Again, reliance on evidence for "active" participants relies on selection not dictating the degree of participation. Interestingly, no significant gains were found for reading tests. School attendance, after two-years, was approximately half a day more per year for the participants. And, similar to the LAB study, TASC participants report improvements in various attitudinal measures. Participants, for example, are show an increased likelihood in claiming they "like school more" than nonparticipants.

5.3.4   Experimental Evaluations

21st Century Community Learning Centers (21CCLC) Programs

Given the problematic nature of interpreting evaluation evidence gathered in a nonexperimental setting, it is important to investigate evidence generated from an experimental design. Certainly the most influential of the experimental studies is a study done of the 21st Century Community Learning Centers Program (21CCLC) conducted by Mathematica Policy Research (James-Burdumy et al. 2005; James-Burdumy et al. 2007). The 21CCLC study had two components. First was a study of elementary students based on a random assignment of students from twelve school districts and twenty-six program centers that had excess demand for their programs in 1999. These schools were not regarded as nationally representative of programs serving elementary school students. The excess demand allowed the use of random assignment in admission to the program to create treatment and control groups for two cohorts.[6] Test scores were administered at the baseline for both treatments and controls. Importantly, this study considered the child care arrangements of students assigned to the control group. This allowed the researchers to observe the extent to which those students randomly denied access to the after-school program ended up in "self-care." The results were considerably less favorable than those frequently cited for the nonexperimental evaluations. While the programs were serving mostly low-income schools, treatments did not differ from controls in frequency of self-care, maternal employment, reading test scores, math grades, English grades, science or social science grades, TV viewing time, homework completion, or attendance. There were positive benefits measured for in English and science for low baseline students. Further, behavioral problems were *higher* for the treatment students. And treatments were more likely to report feeling "not at all safe" after school. A nationally representative, but nonexperimental, evaluation of 4,264 middle school students with 1,782 in 21CCLC programs—using controls similar to those used in the TASC study—also found no impact on self-care, math, English, or science grades. Social studies grades were higher in the second year, and school absences were lower for the participants. Again, behavioral problems were *higher* for program participants.

Clearly, these results offer a very different picture of after-school efficacy than the nonexperimental studies. Indeed, rather than observing latch-key care for the controls, a full 75 percent of controls were home with a parent after school. Only 1 percent were in self-care three or more days per week. Not surprisingly, a variety of criticisms have been launched against this influential study (cf. Bissell et al. 2003; Dynarski et al. 2003). Kane (2004) provides an excellent summary and evaluation of the merits of the various criticisms. One possible explanation for the lack of significant impacts is that attendance rates at the 21CCLC programs were quite low with students participating only one to two days per week (Kane 2004). This participation was lower than that at the TASC sites where elementary school participation averaged almost four days per week. This suggests that the "treatment" being considered was not very strong. Second, it is apparent that most of the students electing to participate were not latch-key children. The alternative to after-school supervision was most often parental care, which might well provide similar impacts on risky behavior or academic enhancement. Third, the sample size may not have been adequate to identify a statistically

---

6. For the 2000 cohort, there were 589 students in the treatment group and 384 in the control group. For the 2001 cohort, there were 693 students in the treatment group and 666 in the control group.

significant effects on test scores. It is important to distinguish between "no effect" and an inability to reject the null hypothesis of "no effect." Kane points out that the typical gain in standardized reading test scores between the fourth and fifth grades is approximately a third to a half a standard deviation. If after-school programs are regarded as adding an additional hour of time on task each day (and assuming an attendance rate of 100 percent), that would imply an addition of approximately one-sixth of academic time each day. Assuming after-school academic time impacts learning in the same fashion as time spent during the regular school day, we'd expect an impact on the order of .05 to .08 standard deviations. The sample size established for the 21CCLC evaluation, however, was set to capture effects only as small as .20 standard deviations (Kane 2004).

Other Studies

Other experimentally structured studies have offered somewhat more positive results. A good example of a small scale intervention is provided by the Howard Street Tutoring Program (Morris, Shaw, and Perney 1990). Unlike the multisite evaluations discussed in the preceding, this is a careful evaluation of a single program. The Howard Street program began in 1979 and had adult volunteers working after school one-on-one with low achieving second and third grade readers all attending a poor inner-city school. The mentors met with the students for 1.5 hours after school twice each week and followed a structured lesson with emphasis on contextual reading, word study, writing, and reading to the child. Thirty students each were randomly assigned to the treatment and control groups. The program showed improvements in the children's reading with "a one-half year difference in reading achievement between the tutored and comparison group" being generated by "50 hours per child of well-planned, closely supervised one-to-one tutoring" (Morris, Shaw, and Perney 1990, 146).

While the Howard Street program employed a simple strategy for improving students outcomes other programs have offered significantly more comprehensive interventions. The Quantum Opportunities (QOP) program is a good example of a program that is comprehensive in nature and that was evaluated using an experimental protocol (Hahn, Leavitt, and Aaron 1994). The QOP program was a multiyear program—beginning in the ninth grade—that included homework help, tutoring, life and family skills counseling (including counseling on alcohol and drug abuse, sex, and family planning), a significant community service requirement, and "meaningful relationships with adults . . . without fear of having bonds abruptly severed when the programs ended" (Hahn, Leavitt, and Aaron 1994, 3). In addition, students received financial incentives to encourage them to persist in the program. It is important to realize that while QOP was significantly more comprehensive than a generic after-school program, it did incorporate regular program activities from 3 p.m. to 6 p.m.

A pilot study of QOP was launched in 1989 in five sites with twenty-five students from disadvantaged families each being randomly assigned to the treatment or control groups. The results, pooled for the five sites, found significant improvements in high school graduation rates (63 percent for the treatments versus 42 percent for the controls), reduced drop out rates (23 percent versus 50 percent) and higher rates of college attendance (18 percent versus 5 percent for four-year colleges). Further, participants were less likely to become teen parents and had "less trouble with the police." It is noteworthy that a careful reading of the report shows that the statistically significant pooled results were driven largely, though not exclusively, by results from one of the implementation sites (Philadelphia). Indeed, at the Philadelphia site, over three-quarters of the participants completed high school with 72 percent of those who graduated from high school attending a postsecondary educational institution. Only 8 percent of the treatments dropped out of high school compared to 44 percent of the controls. Other sites showed positive—though often not statistically significant results. The evaluation report attributed the success in Philadelphia to its ability to create a "consistent group identity and design tangible program services to support QOP members throughout their high school years" (Hahn, Leavitt, and Aaron, 16). Based on enthusiasm for the results of the pilot project, a larger scale demonstration—with 580 participants and 489 controls—of QOP was conducted in seven sites by Mathematica Policy Research (Maxfield et al. 2003) and funded by the U.S. Department of Labor and the Ford Foundation. Participants were virtually all African American or Hispanic and entered the program when they were fourteen years old. The evaluation showed heterogeneity across sites in the implementation of the QOP model. Programs sometimes deviated from the intended QOP model in terms of the depth of mentoring or the hours of community service, for example. While some elements of the program were diluted relative to the programs goals, it was still regarded by "school administrators, faculty, and CBO managers [as the] most intensive program they had ever encountered" (Maxfield et al. 2003, 54). Unfortunately, the demonstration reported little in the way of program impact. In particular, there were no differences between the treatment and control groups in achievement test scores, grades, high school graduation rates, or behavioral issues in school. These disappointing findings may be caused by deviations from the intended intervention, the depth of the academic disadvantage of the participants, or the larger size of the programs (Milton S. Eisenhower Foundation 2005). These concerns, of course, raise questions about the scalability of such comprehensive interventions as well as their efficacy in serving highly disadvantaged populations.

    The fourth and final report on QOP by Mathematica Policy Research (Schirm, Stuart, and McKie 2006) measures impacts when most of the participants are between the ages of twenty-three and twenty-five years old. This report echoes earlier reports concluding that QOP did not increase the likelihood that participants had higher grades or achievement scores, were no less likely to engage in risky behaviors, and were not more likely to graduate from high school or engage in postsecondary education or training. In addition, there was no impact on employment or earnings in this latest follow-up. There was some evidence that participants who were fourteen or younger when they entered ninth grade may have benefited from participating in the QOP program. This subgroup of younger participants were 7 percentage points more likely to graduate from high school (significant at the 10 percent level). Similar to the earlier evaluations, QOP's impacts were found to vary significantly across sites.

Mentoring, a critical component of the original QOP pilot, has been shown to generate positive results in an evaluation of the Big Brothers Big Sisters Program (Tierney, Grossman, and Resch 2000). In this community-based mentoring program, children aged ten to sixteen were matched with carefully screened voluntary mentors. The majority of these children were from "relatively poor households"—44 percent reported that their family had received welfare. Participants met with the mentors at least two to four times each month for between two and five hours per meeting. A waiting list of interested youth created the opportunity to randomly assign applicants into treatment and control groups. The data used for the analyses contained 959 youth, with 487 treatments and 472 controls. At the time of the evaluation, program participants had had participated in the program for, on average, one year. The average participant was about twelve years old.

Comparing outcomes for the two groups eighteen months later showed statistically significant reductions in the initiation of drug abuse (–45.8 percent) and an improvement in grades (+.08). The grade improvement was largely driven by a .17 grade point increase in grades for the female participants. Participants also reported skipping about one-half fewer days of school. No statistically significant impact was found on, stealing, damaging property, or hours spent doing homework or reading. The cost per participant was $1,000 in 1992 (or $1,480 in 2007$).

The promising results found for community-based mentoring programs have led to a variety of school-based mentoring programs. In the school-based programs, mentors are paired with students whom they typically visit in or after school for an hour a week. A study by Public/Private Ventures conducted an experimental evaluation of the Big Brothers Big Sisters school-based mentoring system (Herrera et al. 2007). The study involved seventy-one schools, ten Big Brother Big Sister Agencies, and 1,139 students in grades four through nine. A total of 565 students were randomly assigned to the treatment group and 574 to the control group. A significant portion of the participants were economically disadvantaged, with 60 percent of the participants receiving free or reduced lunch during the first year of the study. About half of the students were identified as experiencing academic difficulties. The mentors were typically younger than in community based mentoring. About half of the mentors were eighteen years old or younger, with 72 percent being female. A little under a half were currently enrolled in high school. Further, only 27 percent of the mentors reported spending "a lot or most" of their time on tutoring or homework help.

At the end of the first year, participant's academic performance had risen relative to the controls. Improvements were seen in Written and Oral Language, Science, and in the Quality of Class Work and Number of Assignments Completed. Overall, academic performance increased by .11 points on a 1 to 5 scale. Participants were also less likely to skip school or engage in Serious School Misconduct. Improvements were not concentrated on any particular gender, grade, race, or ethnicity subgroups in the treatment population. A follow-up at fifteen months suggested that about half the children discontinued mentoring in their second year. For those children, the academic benefits seen at twelve months follow-up, only about half of the treatments were receiving mentoring. The academic gains that had been seen at the first follow-up had now largely disappeared. Indeed, academic performance at the start of the second school year for students who continued mentoring into the second year was not generally statistically different than the controls, though this may have been because the follow-up occurred early in the second school year and most had not met with their mentors over the summer.

5.4   Discussion and Extensions

Forging a simple assessment of the efficacy of after-school programs is difficult. Rob Hollister, in a survey of several evaluation studies states: "In short, in response to the question . . . what do we know about what works— our answer has to be: *not much*" (Hollister 2003, 12). We concur with that assessment. The current literature on after-school programs raises serious concerns about selection bias. This concern makes it difficult to draw lessons from the prevailing nonexperimental evaluations of flagship program or from programs evaluated using comparison groups. The concern about selection is likely endemic in programs that are voluntary in nature.

While the experimental evidence helps mitigate concerns about selection, a careful reading of this evidence suggests several other possibilities for why the estimated impacts on academic achievement may be muted. First, programs may pay limited attention to academic goals. If the primary focus of an after-school intervention is physical exercise or recreation, then impacts may not be seen in the academic domain. This would also be the case if the time spent on academics was limited. Further, as noted by Kane (2004), the effects may be too small to detect using the sample sizes selected. Another concern is that control groups gathered from overenrolled programs may have reasonably good after-school care alternatives compared to the treatment program. If, as seems to be the case, the controls are not simply "home alone," then we might not expect to see differential impacts on academic outcomes. More generally, program effects, may be small if the control population is relatively privileged (as in the 21CCLC program) or of the treatment group is extremely disadvantaged (as in the QOP demonstration). In the first case, the counterfactual may not differ much from the treatment. In the second case, after-school programs may not be sufficient to overcome other disadvantages. It is also worth noting that benefits from noncognitive outcomes may be exist. Several studies we've reviewed show improvements in various attitudinal measures. Students, for example, may have an improved enthusiasm for school. While this may not translate into any measureable effect on grades, it may provide benefits that support their future odds at achieving self-sufficiency. Recent work by James Heckman suggests that these noncognitive benefits may be substantial.

Of course, these possible explanations for the no-effect finding are speculative. It is also possible that there is simply no effect. More research is needed to investigate whether the concerns raised are substantive. To that end, the evaluation of after-school programs would benefit from something of a "model evaluation" much like that of the Perry Preschool Project evaluation (Belfield et al. 2006). It would be useful to have an upper bound on what benefits a "high-end" after-school program might provide. It would also be useful to gauge the effect for participants of varying degrees of depravation.

References

Aizer, Anna. 2004. Home alone: Supervision after school and child behavior. *Journal of Public Economics* 88:1835–48.
Belfield, Clive R., Milagros Nores, Steve Barnett, and Lawrence Schweinhart. 2006. The High/Scope Perry Preschool Program: Cost-benefit analysis using data from the age-40 follow-up. *Journal of Human Resources* 41 (1): 162–90.
Bissell, Joan S., Christopher Cross, Karen Mapp, Elizabeth Reisner, Deborah Lowe Vandell, Constancia Warren, and Richard Weissbourd. 2003. Statement Released by Members of the Scientific Advisory Board for the 21st Century Community Learning Center Evaluation. http://www.gse.harvard.edu/hfrp/content/projects/afterschool/resources/21stcclc_statement.doc.
Blau, David, and Janet Currie. 2004. Preschool, day care, and after-school care: Who's minding the kids. NBER Working Paper no. 10670. Cambridge, MA: National Bureau of Economic Research.
Brooks, Pauline, Cynthia Mojica, and Robert Land. 1995. Final evaluation report. Longitudinal study of LA's best after-school education and enrichment program, 1992–94. http://www.cse.ucla.edu/products/misc.html.
Catalano, Richard F., M. Lisa Berglund, Jeanne A. M. Ryan, Heather S. Lonczak, and J. David Hawkins. 1998. Positive youth development in the United States: Research findings on evaluations of positive youth development programs. Seattle, WA: Social Development Research Group, University of Washington.

Durlak, Joseph, and Roger Weissberg. 2007. *The impact of after-school programs that promote personal and social skills.* Chicago: CASEL.

Dynarski, Mark, Mary Moore, John Mullens, Philip Gleason, Susanne James-Burdumy, Linda Rosenberg, Carol Pistorino, Tim Silva, John Deke, Wendy Mansfield, Sheila Heaviside, Daniel Levy. 2003. When schools stay open late: The national evaluation of the 21st Century Community Learning Centers Program. Washington, DC: U.S. Department of Education, Office of the Under Secretary.

Eccles, Jacquelynne S., and Janice Templeton. 2001. Community-based programs for youth: Lessons learned from general developmental research and from experimental and quasi-experimental evaluations. Urban Seminar on Children's Health and Safety. John F. Kennedy School of Government, Harvard University.

Fashola, Olatokunbo. 1998. Review of extended-day and after-school programs and their effectiveness. Baltimore, MD: CRESPAR.

Fox, J. A., and S. A. Newman. 1997. *After-school crime or after-school programs: Tuning into the prime time for violent juvenile crime and implications for national policy. A report to the United States Attorney General.* Washington, DC: Fight Crime: Invest in Kids. ED 412 319.

Goldschmidt, Pete, Denise Juang, and Majorie Chinen. 2007. The long-term effects of after-school programming on educational adjustment and juvenile crime: A study of LA's best after-school program. Los Angeles: UCLA Center for the Study of Evaluation, Graduate School of Education and Information Studies.

Hahn, Andrew, Tom Leavitt, and Paul Aaron. 1994. Evaluation of the Quantum Opportunities Program. Did the program work? Waltham, MA: Brandeis University, Center for Human Resources.

Herrera, Carla, Jean Baldwin Grossman, Tina J. Kauh, Amy F. Feldman, Jennifer McMaken, and Linda Z. Jucovy. 2007. Making a difference in schools. The Big Brothers Big Sisters school-based mentoring impact study. Public Private Ventures. http://www.ppv.org/ppv/publications/assets/220_publication.pdf.

Hollister, Rob. 2003. The growth in after-school programs and their impact. Mimeograph. Paper commissioned by the Brookings Roundtable on Children.

Huang Denise, Barry Gribbons, Kyung Sung Kim, Charlotte Lee, and Eva Baker. 2000. A decade of results. The impact of LA's best after-school enrichment program on subsequent student achievement and performance. Los Angeles: UCLA Center for the Study of Evaluation, Graduate School of Education and Information Studies.

James-Burdumy, Susanne, Mark Dynarski, Mary Moore, John Deke, and Wendy Mansfield. 2005. *When schools stay open late: The National Evaluation of the 21st Century Community Learning Centers Program. Final report.* Washington, DC: U.S. Department of Education.

James-Burdumy, Susanne, Mark Dynarski, and John Deke. 2007. When elementary schools stay open late: Results From the National Evaluation of the 21st Century Community Learning Centers Program. *Educational Evaluation and Policy Analysis* 29 (4): 296–313.

Kane, Thomas. 2004. The impact of after-school programs: Interpreting the results of four recent evaluations. William T. Grant Foundation, Working Paper.

Lauer, P., M. Akiba, S. Wilkerson, H. Apthrop, D. Snow, and M. Martin-Glenn. 2006. Out-of-school-time programs: A meta-analysis of effects for at-risk students. *Review of Educational Research* 76 (2): 275–313.

Little, Priscilla M. D., Christopher Wimer, and Heather B. Weiss. 2008. After-school programs in the 21st century. Their potential and what it takes to achieve it. Issues and Opportunities in Out-of-School Time Evaluation no. 10. Cambridge, MA: Harvard Family Research Project.

Maxfield, Myles, Laura Castner, Vida Maralani, and Mary Vencill. 2003. The Quantum Opportunity Program demonstration: Implementation findings. Washington, DC: Mathematica Policy Research.

Maxfield, Myles, Allen Schirm, and Nuria Rodriguez-Planas. 2003. The Quantum Opportunities Program demonstration: Implementation and short-term impacts. U.S. Department of Labor Contract no. K-5547-5-00-80-30. Washington, DC: Mathematica Policy Research.

Miller, Beth. 2003. *Critical hours.* New York: Nellie Mae Foundation.

Milton S. Eisenhower Foundation. 2005. Quantum Opportunities Program 2003 forum: Lessons learned. Washington, DC.

Morris, Darrell, Beverly Shaw, and Jan Perney. 1990. Helping low readers in grades 2 and 3: An after-school volunteer tutoring program. *Elementary School Journal* 91 (2): 132–50.

Posner, Jill, and Deborah Lowe Vandell. 1999. After-school activities and the development of low-income urban children: A longitudinal study. *Developmental Psychology* 35 (3):868–79.

Redd, Zakia, Stephanie Cochran, and Kristin Moore. 2002. *Academic achievement programs and youth development: A synthesis.* Washington, DC: Child Trends.

Reisner, Elizabeth R., Christina Russell, Megan Welsh, Jennifer Birmingham, and Richard White. 2002. Supporting quality and scale in after-school services to urban youth: Evaluation of program implementation and student engagement in the TASC After-School Program's third year. Policy Studies Associates report to The After-School Corporation.

Reisner, Elizabeth R., Richard White, Christina Russell, and Jennifer Birmingham. 2004. Building quality, scale, and effectiveness in after-school programs. Policy Studies Associates report to The After-School Corporation.

Schirm, All, Elizabeth Stuart, and Allison McKie. 2006. The Quantum Opportunities Program demonstration: Final impacts. U.S. Department of Labor Contract no. K-5547-5-00-80-30. MPR Reference no. 8279-932. Washington, DC: Mathematica Policy Research.

Scott-Litte, Catherine, Mary Sue Hamann, and Stephen G. Jurs. 2002. Evaluations of after-school programs: A meta-evaluation of methodologies and narrative synthesis of findings. *American Journal of Evaluation* 23 (4): 387–419.

The After-School Corporation (TASC). 2007. Annual report. New York: The After School Corporation.

Tierney, Joseph, Jean Baldwin Grossman, and Nancy L. Resch. 2000. *Making a difference. An impact study of Big Brothers Big Sisters.* Public Private Ventures. http://www.ppv.org/ppv/publications/assets/111_publication.pdf.

U.S. Bureau of Labor Statistics. 2007. *Women in the labor force: A databook. Report 1002.* Washington, DC: U.S. Bureau of Labor Statistics.

U.S. Census Bureau. 2002. *Who's minding the kids? Child care arrangements: Winter 2002.* Washington, DC: U.S. Census Bureau.

U.S. Census Bureau. 2005. *Who's minding the kids? Child care arrangements: Spring 2005.* http://www.census.gov/population/www/socdemo/child/ppl-2005.html.

Weisman, Stephanie, and Denise Gottfredson. 2001. Attrition from after-school programs: Characteristics of students who drop out. *Prevention Science* 2 (3): 201–5.

Vandell, Deborah Lowe, and Mary Anne Corasaniti. 1988. The relation between third graders' after-school care and social, academic, and emotional functioning. *Child Development* 59 (4): 868–75.

Education Reforms

Susanna Loeb and Patrick J. McEwan

6.1 Introduction

Over 55 million children and adolescents attend elementary and secondary schools in the United States, 89 percent in public schools. These students spend approximately 1,000 hours each year in schools across the country, for which local, state, and federal governments spend over \$550 billion (National Center for Education Statistics [NCES] 2008).[1] Education is an intensive and costly enterprise. It also has the potential to dramatically improve opportunities for students. In the United States, estimates of the return to an additional year of schooling are in the neighborhood of 10 percent, depending on the data and method (Card 1999).[2] Educational attainment is also associated with differences in individual health, incarceration, and dependence on public assistance (Belfield and Levin 2007). While schooling improves children's lifetime opportunities, the debate on how to use scarce time and resources to maximize outcomes while in school is not settled.

Even so, the terms of debate have improved markedly from a time when researchers asked whether "money mattered" using mainly nonexperimental

Susanna Loeb is professor of education at Stanford University, and a faculty research fellow of the National Bureau of Economic Research. Patrick J. McEwan is an associate professor of economics at Wellesley College.

We are grateful to Phil Levine and David Zimmerman for their comments.

1. See http://nces.ed.gov/pubs98/yi/y9638a.asp for data on hours.
2. Economists have long worried that estimates of the return to schooling do not have a causal interpretation. High-ability individuals may earn more, in addition to being more likely to continue in school, perhaps leading to a spurious association between schooling and wages. A large literature, including twins studies and other attempts to isolate exogenous variation in schooling, rarely suggest that the return to years of schooling is biased upward. Indeed, they frequently yield even larger estimated returns, perhaps because the methods estimate returns for a unique subpopulation (Card 1999).

studies.[3] In the last decade, the breadth and quality of education research has improved (Angrist 2004; Barrow and Rouse 2005). In the late 1990s, economists published influential reanalyses of experimental data on the impact of class size reduction in Tennessee (Krueger 1999) and private school vouchers in Milwaukee (Rouse 1998). The next ten years yielded even more and better research, catalyzed by three factors. First, the data improved, especially with collection of longitudinal administrative data on students in several U.S. states and cities (Loeb and Strunk 2003). Second, formerly hypothetical policies—especially related to choice and accountability—were implemented and studied with good research designs (Figlio and Ladd 2008; Zimmer and Bettinger 2008). Third, the U.S. Department of Education and other funders increasingly required the use of research designs able to yield credible causal findings, especially randomized experiments and regression-discontinuity designs.

Education polices comprise a vast array of programs and approaches. To make our task manageable, we categorize them into one of three groups: (a) direct investments in schools, including school improvement grants and class size reductions; (b) interventions that target the teacher workforce through wages, recruitment, or professional development programs; and (c) interventions that aim to increase accountability and change decision-making in schools through either enhancing parental choice or increasing test-based accountability. This chapter selectively reviews the high-quality evidence on the effects of different approaches within each of these three groups.

6.2   Estimating Policy Effects

Economists have traditionally used nonexperimental data to estimate education production functions, in which student test scores are regressed on a "kitchen sink" of explanatory variables. These include attributes of students and their families (e.g., ability and income), attributes of teachers and schools (e.g., preservice training and expenditures), and attributes of peers and communities. The usual goal is to isolate the causal effect of school inputs that can potentially be manipulated by school authorities. The empirical task is complicated by the fact that observed test scores are the cumulative result of investments by families and schools throughout a child's life (Todd and Wolpin 2003). Only a fraction of these investments are observed in most data sets. It is common, in such cases, to include a lagged test score in regressions as an implicit control for prior family or school variables. Even if this does control for prior influences on test scores,

---

3. The early, nonexperimental literature often showed little consistent evidence of correlations between expenditures and achievement (Hanushek 1986, 2006), though others interpreted the same literature more optimistically (Greenwald, Hedges, and Laine 1996; Krueger 2003).

the models must fully control for contemporaneous factors associated with student participation in different policies or programs, and this is very difficult. Researchers are often left wondering whether their regressions effectively adjust for the selection of different students into different policy environments.

Alternatively, researchers attempt to identify "clean" variation in policy variables (like class size) that is uncorrelated with unobserved variables that affect test scores. In experiments, the researcher randomly assigns a subset of students, classrooms, or schools to receive a policy treatment and randomly denies it to others. By design, in large studies, this randomization ensures that treated subjects are similar to untreated ones, except for their exposure to the policy, and that subsequent comparisons of outcomes will likely yield unbiased effects. In a few cases, randomized assignment is a natural byproduct of program implementation, as in lotteries to allocate private school vouchers.

When randomization is not feasible, it is sometimes possible to identify variation in policy treatments that is "as good as random." Among the many varieties of quasi-experiments, the regression-discontinuity design can yield convincing causal results (Shadish, Cook, and Campbell 2002; Angrist and Krueger 1999). Treatments are assigned on the basis of a single variable and an assignment cutoff (i.e., schools receive a program if their poverty rate is below a fixed threshold, but not above). Assuming that schools or students on either side of the cutoff are otherwise similar, comparisons of the two groups' outcomes are a reasonable estimate of the causal effect. It is akin to very local randomized experiment (Lee 2008).

When feasible, we focus on research that uses experimental and discontinuity research designs. Still, it bears emphasis that our goal is to generalize these effects beyond the immediate research setting and that doing so is sometimes more art than science. First, policy effects may be heterogeneous across students. If effects are heterogeneous, then randomized experiments succeed in identifying the average effect among students (or occasionally within subgroups of students in large experiments). However, the research participants are often unique in ways that could increase or decrease their treatment effects, relative to the typical student that the real-world policy would eventually target. Experimental subjects often volunteer to be randomly assigned, are drawn disproportionately from a particular race or income-level, or reside in compact geographic areas with unique institutions (e.g., school finance and accountability rules).

Regression-discontinuity studies may face a stricter version of this problem because they identify local average effects for the subpopulation or students or schools in the vicinity of the assignment cutoff. Often this is policy relevant because decision-makers might raise or lower eligibility cutoffs. But for broader decisions about the cost-effective targeting of resources, it would be useful to understand whether treatment effects are different for subjects far away from eligibility cutoffs (i.e., the poorest schools that qualify for Title I funds, rather than just-poor-enough schools).

Second, the best causal research is frequently conducted on a small scale. However, scaling up an intervention can provoke unanticipated general equilibrium effects. Sometimes this undermines a policy's original objectives. The best-known case in education is California's statewide class size reduction in the late 1990s (Jepsen and Rivkin 2009), which sharply increased demand for teachers and may have lowered teacher quality in some schools. In other cases, the potential general equilibrium effects in scale-ups are of greater policy interest than the treatment effects actually identified in the small-scale research. For example, private school voucher experiments identify the effects of private school attendance on the few students who are offered vouchers. Yet most policymakers are at least as interested in how a large voucher offer (and the concomitant reshuffling of students across schools) would affect the outcomes of all students through increasing market competition or school stratification (Hsieh and Urquiola 2006; Hoxby 2000a).

6.3 Direct Resource Investments

The next sections review the best recent evidence on four types of direct resource investments (see table 6.1 for a summary of studies). First, we consider three policies that affect the level of per-pupil revenues or expenditures in schools: the Federal Title I program which directs additional funds to high-poverty schools; a California policy of school bonuses for high-performing schools; and a range of school equity reforms that leveled up (or down) the expenditures in schools. Second, we briefly review the experimental evidence on whether class size reduction increases test scores. Third, we review whether specialized instructional packages—often referred to as "whole-school" reforms—can raise test scores, focusing on the Success for All reading program. Fourth, we consider whether computer-assisted instruction causes test score improvements.

6.3.1 Dollars

Title I is the largest Federal education program in K-12 education, with $12 billion allocated in fiscal year 2005 (van der Klaauw 2008). Besides its scale, it is notable for its objective targeting of resources toward counties and schools with larger numbers of poor students. Title I's distribution rule is intended to promote a transparent and well-targeted resource allocation, but it also facilitates a regression-discontinuity design.[4] van der Klaauw (2008)

---

4. Similar evaluation strategies have been applied to programs in Chile and the Netherlands that allocated additional resources to schools based on measures of achievement or disadvantage (Chay, McEwan, and Urquiola 2005; Leuven et al. 2007). The Chilean program found moderately positive test score effects of intensive after-school tutoring, while the Dutch program found some negative effects of extra funding for computers and software.

applies this strategy to school-level data on New York City public schools. Schools with poverty rates below a threshold have sharply higher probabilities of receiving Title I funds (about 5 percent of a school's budget) but are otherwise similar to schools just above the threshold.[5] The author finds that Title I designation did not produce achievement gains in 1993, 1997, or 2001 and may even have led to achievement declines in the earlier years. However, Title I schools also do not appear to have higher expenditures, perhaps because the state or local authorities remove other funds (for related evidence, see Gordon 2004). van der Klaauw (2008) further notes that a popular use for Title I funds was "pull-out" remedial instruction. Despite its easier compliance with federal rules, it has little demonstrated effectiveness as an instructional strategy.

In 2000 and 2001, California offered financial rewards to schools that met specified achievement targets (Bacolod, Dinardo, and Jacobson 2008). Upon winning, schools received one-time, unrestricted bonuses that amounted to about 5 percent of per-pupil expenditures. Though apparently intended for computers or other instructional purposes, it appears that most funds were returned to teachers in the form of bonuses. Using a discontinuity approach, Bacolod, Dinardo, and Jacobson (2008) compare subsequent achievement of schools that barely qualify for an award with those that barely miss one. After confirming that schools above and below cutoffs are observationally similar, they find no gains in student achievement.

Finally, we consider school finance reforms, which constitute one of most significant attempts in the last thirty years to influence the resources available to schools enrolling disadvantaged children.[6] Most reforms were mandated by state courts, following successful challenges to the state constitutionality of locally based systems of school finance. Because these "experiments" were initiated by courts and legislatures, and not researchers, their causal effects are harder to identify. Corcoran and Evans (2008) compare the evolution of expenditures in states with and without reforms, finding that finance reforms typically reduced within-state inequality in per-pupil expenditures by 15 to 19 percent. Further, this does not appear to have occurred through a simple leveling down of higher-spending schools.

Although one anticipates that additional resources should affect student outcomes, there is mixed evidence on this fundamental question (Corcoran and Evans 2008). In a cross-state analysis, Card and Payne (2002) find that states with court-mandated reforms experienced reductions in test score inequality, but the researchers are hampered by the use of SAT scores that

5. One might be concerned that schools could manipulate poverty rates and their treatment status, but the eligibility cutoff was not preannounced in this case, leaving little scope for strategic behavior (van der Klaauw 2008). Further, there is no evidence of discontinuities around the eligibility cutoff in observed characteristics that influence outcomes.

6. Another class of finance reform, not considered here, is tax limitations, which removed resources from schools (Downes and Figlio 2008).

Table 6.1 The effects of direct resource investments

Study	Intervention	Grades(s) (length) of intervention	Research design	Sample and year(s) of intervention	Outcomes (posttest grade)	Effects
van der Klaauw (2008)	Title I funding allocations (~5% of expenditures)	K–12	Discontinuity assignment based on poverty	New York City public schools, 1993, 1997, 2001	School pass rates in reading and math	n.s. or negative effects, but offsetting effects on school expenditures
Bacolod, Dinardo, and Jacobson (2008)	Unrestricted school awards (~5% of expenditures)	K–12	Discontinuity assignment based on composite test scores	California public schools, 2000–2001	School-mean composite test score	n.s.
Guryan (2003)	Added state funding	K–12	Discontinuity assignment based on funding formula variables	Massachusetts public school districts, 1994–1996	District-mean math (4th)	.15σ per $500 (1996)
					district-mean reading (4th)	.06σ per $500 (1996)
					District-mean math (8th); district-mean reading (8th)	Positive but non-robust effects in 8th

Study	Treatment	Grade (years)	Research design	Sample	Outcome measure	Effect size
Schanzenbach (2007)	"Small" classes (thirteen–seventeen) vs. "regular" classes (22–25)	K (four yrs.)	Randomization of students/teachers within schools	Seventy-nine Tennessee schools, students, 1985–1989	Composite test (3rd)	$.15\sigma$ (full sample); $.24\sigma$ (black students); $.12\sigma$ (white students)
					composite test (8th)	n.s
					Took college entrance exam (change in probability)	.02 (full sample); .05 (black students); n.s. (white students);
Borman et al. (2007)	Success for All reading program	K (three yrs.)	Randomization of schools	Forty-one schools in eleven states, 2001–2004	Multiple reading tests (2nd)	$.21–.36\sigma$
Dynarski et al. (2007)	Sixteen technology products for reading/math instruction	1, 4, 6 (one yr.)	Randomization of products/training to teachers within schools	132 schools, 439 teachers, 2004–2005	Multiple reading and math tests	n.s.
Barrow, Markman, and Rouse (2008)	Computer-assisted math instructional package	8–10 (one yr.)	Randomization to class periods within schools	Seventeen schools, sixty-one teachers, 2004–2005	Algebra test	$.17\sigma$

Notes: n.s. = not statistically significant at 5%. Reported estimates from Schanzenbach (2007); Borman et al. (2007); and Barrow, Markman, and Rouse (2008) are intent-to-treat effects.

are taken by a subset of students. Other authors working with cross-state data find no effects (Downes and Figlio 1998).

The most credible studies are typically conducted in a single or small number of states, but here, too, the evidence is conflicting (Corcoran and Evans 2008). Researchers have found no effect on test scores in Kentucky (Flanagan and Murray 2004) but found positive effects on pass rates in Michigan (Papke 2005; Cullen and Loeb 2004). Of state-specific studies, Guryan's (2003) is one of the most convincing. His discontinuity study assesses how increased spending, induced by changes in the Massachusetts school funding formula, affected test scores. Specifically, he relies on spending variation created when districts fall on one side or another of funding thresholds established by the formula. He finds that increasing per-pupil expenditures by $500 per student,[7] about half a standard deviation, yields tests score increases in fourth grade mathematics and reading of roughly 0.06 to 0.15 standard deviations, respectively.[8] The eighth grade test score results are also positive but not robust to alternative specifications.

6.3.2   Class Size Reduction

Given the popularity of class size reduction, there are surprisingly few high-quality studies of its effects on test scores. Researchers have focused on a large randomized experiment conducted in Tennessee during the mid-1980s (Schanzenbach 2007).[9] Within seventy-nine volunteer schools, researchers randomly assigned students and teachers to "small" classes (thirteen to seventeen students) and "regular" classes (twenty-two to twenty-five students).[10] This treatment was maintained for four years (between kindergarten and third grade), though not all students participated in all years. For example, some new students entered the school after kindergarten, and a small proportion moved between classes within schools.

On average, the Tennessee results suggest that students who were initially assigned to smaller classes have test score gains of 0.15 standard deviations by the end of third grade, though similar achievement gains were already in evidence by the end of kindergarten. The effects are even larger for the subset of black students, or lower-income students. In follow-up studies, these effects were much smaller and statistically insignificant by the end of eighth

---

7. These appear to be 1996 dollars.

8. The coefficient estimates are from the fixed-effects specification in column (2) of table 4. Guryan (2003) divides these coefficients by the standard deviation of district-level test score means, which tends to inflate effect sizes when between-district test score variation is small. To make the effect size comparable to others, and in the absence of a student-level standard deviation of test score, we assume it to be (district-level SD)/sqrt (intradistrict correlation coefficient), where the second term in parentheses is the proportion of variance in test scores accounted for by between- rather than within-district variation (What Works Clearinghouse 2007). We assume it to be 0.2, which is likely overstated.

9. For earlier analyses of the Tennessee experiment, see Krueger (1999) and Krueger and Whitmore (2001).

10. They also considered a third group, consisting of regular classes with teachers' aides.

grade. In a surprising finding, however, it appears that students eventually had a higher probability of taking a college entrance exam (0.02), again larger for black or lower-income students.

Despite these findings, reducing class size can be a costly endeavor. Following Schanzenbach (2007), we can assume that a seven-student reduction in the typical class size increased per-pupil expenditures ($10,551 in 2005) by 47 percent, an annual per-pupil increase of $4,959. The intervention lasted four years, but the average student participated for 2.3. Assuming a 3 percent discount rate and inflating dollar estimates to 2007, the discounted per-pupil cost of the STAR intervention is $11,865. This is just under $16,000 per 0.2 standard deviation gain in test scores (but just under $10,000 per 0.2 among black students).

As California's experience has shown, general equilibrium factors could moderate potentially positive effects of large-scale class size reduction. When California reduced class size in kindergarten through third grade across the state, new teaching positions opened up in traditionally easy-to-staff schools, drawing teachers from other more difficult-to-staff schools. Schools with high shares of low-income and minority students saw a decrease in the proportion of teachers with prior teaching experience and full credentials (Jepsen and Rivkin 2009).

The results on the effects of class size are also inconsistent across studies. As an example, Hoxby (2000b) finds no class size effects in Connecticut, using different quasi-experimental approaches, including variation in class size driven by plausibly random changes in the size of local populations. She also implements a discontinuity analysis, using sharp decreases in class size caused when enrollments exceed specified caps. The evaluation approach has been applied in several other countries, notably Israel (Angrist and Lavy 1999) and Bolivia (Urquiola 2006), showing positive tests score effects of reducing class size. Some doubt is cast on the collected discontinuity findings, however, because it is plausible that schools can manipulate the discrete assignment variable (school enrollment) in the vicinity of class size caps.[11] Urquiola and Verhoogen (2009) provide concrete evidence of this in Chile, implying a scope for violations of the identifying assumptions of the discontinuity design in related settings.

6.3.3   Curriculum and Instructional Programs

To educators and parents, an obvious avenue for improving schools is to improve the curriculum and instruction offered by schools. There are hundreds of different curricular and instructional reform approaches. Many are piecemeal add-ons to existing school programs, few of which are supported

---

11. In contrast, it is less plausible that schools could precisely manipulate continuous assignment variables, such as test scores because there is an error component that may ensure locally randomized assignment (Lee 2008).

by high-quality studies. Some of these approaches, however, are whole-school reforms that consist of comprehensive and coordinated efforts to overhaul the curriculum, instruction, technology, training, and other aspects of school operations (Levin 2002). These reforms are varied in their strategies and goals, and only a few have been subjected to rigorous evaluation.

As an example, randomized experiments have assessed the effectiveness of the School Development Program of James Comer, finding mixed results on student achievement (Cook et al. 1999; Cook, Murphy, and Hunt 2000). However, these experiments were hampered by relatively small samples of participating schools, which were the unit of randomization. A quasi-experimental, interrupted time-series analysis of Henry Levin's Accelerated Schools Project showed positive effects, but the study lacked an untreated comparison group to verify the robustness of these results (Bloom 2003). In New York City, researchers have compared achievement over time in a varied group of reform schools (without random assignment) to nonreform schools. This research yields mixed achievement results, and it is unclear whether nonreform schools are an adequate comparison group (Bifulco, Duncombe, and Yinger 2004; Schwartz, Stiefel, and Kim 2004).

To date, the most rigorous evaluation has been conducted on the Success for All reform, which focuses on improving reading skills. Success for All is a package of materials, training, and a scripted blueprint for implementing the program, generally targeted at high-poverty and low-achieving schools (Borman et al. 2007). In a random assignment study, forty-one schools were randomly assigned to apply the reform (or not) in early grades. After three years, the reading scores of students in Success for All treatment schools were 0.21 to 0.36 standard deviations higher than students in the control schools, depending on the test. Borman and Hewes (2002) estimate that Success for All has annual per-pupil costs of $795 (in 2000).[12] Assuming a discount rate of 3 percent in a three-year intervention, and inflating dollars to 2007, the discounted per-pupil cost of the intervention is $2,789. Thus, depending on the effect size estimate, it costs from $1,500 to $2,600 per 0.2 standard deviations.

6.3.4   Computer-Assisted Instruction

Many countries and states have embarked on costly plans to increase the number of computers in schools, ranging from placement of computers in classrooms to thoughtful efforts to integrate computers into schools' instructional plans. A small number of high-quality studies have assessed the extent to which the latter efforts have a causal effect student learning. The mixed evidence suggests that results depend vitally on the program details.

---

12. Barnett (1996) reports slightly lower per-pupil costs. They may underestimate full social costs because Success for All incurs opportunity costs for volunteering parents and existing staff (King 1994).

As examples, two randomized experiments have tested the effects of the Fast ForWord program, a popular computer-based approach to raising reading and language ability (Borman, Benson, and Overman 2009; Rouse and Krueger 2004). Neither finds meaningful effects for the program. A large, federally funded randomized experiment also finds no effects, using a diverse array of instructional products in both math and reading (Dynarski et al. 2007). This study randomly assigned teachers within 132 schools to use one of sixteen of computer-based approaches. After one year, there were no detectable test score effects.

In contrast, a recent evaluation of a computer-based algebra program (I Can Learn) found modest effects on student test scores (Barrow, Markman, and Rouse 2008). The researchers randomly assigned teachers (or class periods) within schools, roughly following the design of Dynarski et al. (2007), and identified test score effects of 0.17 standard deviations. Barrow, Markman, and Rouse (2008) calculate a per-student intervention cost of $283 for a single variety of computer-assisted instruction in math, or $333 per 0.2 standard deviations.[13] While encouraging, the mixed evidence on the effects of computer-assisted instruction suggests that specific features of the treatment and its implementation play a decisive role in its success.

6.3.5 Summary

Research on direct investments in schools finds great variation in effects. Given the much-improved quality of these studies (relative to a decade ago), the mixed patterns of evidence cannot be attributed entirely to bad methods or data. Rather, it suggests that the debate has usefully shifted to questions of how and when resources matter for student outcomes, rather than whether they matter at all.

Most evidence on increases in per-pupil expenditures does not show test score improvements for students; however, this lack of impact may reflect funds being used for ineffective interventions such as pull-out tutoring or one-time bonuses. The literature on school finance reforms suggests that the subsequent increases in funding in formally low-spending areas may have diminished test score inequality, but our understanding of how these gains occurred or failed to occur is surprisingly modest. Further progress rests on obtaining a more nuanced understanding of how resources are used in specific policy settings.

Class size reduction can have positive effects on student learning, but at a substantial cost. There is no shortage of innovative attempts to reform curriculum and instruction, but few have been rigorously evaluated. Still, it appears that intensive efforts to improve reading skills can successfully raise test scores. Computers also are no panacea for schools especially in the

---

13. Though the upfront costs of a computer lab and training are relatively high, they are amortized across seven years.

absence of clear instructional goal, but a well-conceived math program that integrates computers can demonstrate robust effects in one year.

6.4   Teachers and Teaching

Schools spend more on teachers than on any other budget category, and there is mounting evidence that these expenditures affect student achievement. As one example, Rivkin, Hanushek, and Kain (2005) find that a 1 standard deviation increase in average teacher quality for a grade raises average student achievement in the grade by at least 0.11 standard deviations of the total test score distribution in mathematics and 0.095 standard deviations in reading. There is some controversy over the accuracy of using regression-adjusted changes on student test performance as measure of teacher effectiveness (Rothstein 2009). However, Kane and Staiger (2008) show that regression-based value added estimates of teacher effects are consistent with estimates using random assignment of teachers to classrooms, and Boyd et al. (2009) show that the instructional practices of high value added teachers differ meaningfully from those of lower value added teachers.

Despite this growing body of research, knowing that teachers vary meaningfully in their effectiveness does not provide a policy roadmap for how to increase teacher quality. In this section, we summarize the current knowledge of the effects of three types of policies aimed at improving teacher quality: wage increases, recruitment, and professional development (see table 6.2 for a summary of studies).

6.4.1   Wages

Teachers' choices about jobs are responsive to wages. A large literature finds that teachers are more likely to choose teaching when starting wages are high relative to wages in other occupations. Approximately 16.5 percent of public school teachers who decided to move to another school between 2003 to 2004 and 2004 to 2005 reported having done so for better salary or benefits (National Center for Education Statistics [NCES] Schools and Staffing Surveys). For those who left teaching in 2004 to 2005, nearly 15 percent cited salary-related reasons. Teacher wages have increased dramatically over the last forty years. Nevertheless, since the 1970s, they have fallen behind salaries in nonteaching jobs for individuals with similar qualifications. Lawyers, doctors, scientists, and engineers earn substantially more, as do managers and sales and financial service workers (Corcoran, Schwab, and Evans 2004). Bacolod (2007) finds that highly qualified teachers are especially sensitive to changes in relative wages. The less teachers are paid, relative to professionals, the less likely high-ability women are to choose teaching. The opportunity cost of becoming a teacher, in terms of salary forgone in alternative professions, is high. However, teachers likely work fewer hours and fewer days, at least partially compensating for this forgone income.

While the evidence on the effects of wages on teachers' decisions is persuasive, high-quality evidence on the effects of teacher wage increases on students is sparse. Loeb and Page (2000) use state-level panel data from the 1960 to 1990 Public Use Microdata Samples from the U.S. Census to examine changes in teacher wages over time. They identify the effect of wages from both changes in relative teacher salaries and changes in only the salaries of nonteaching college graduates, the opportunity cost of becoming a teacher. The study finds that increases in teacher wages of 10 percent led to a 3 to 4 percent drop in student dropout rates and a 1 to 2 percent increase in college enrollment. The authors' simple calculations suggest that the benefits of a 10 percent wage increase would slightly outweigh the costs.

The Loeb and Page (2000) study examines the effects of average wage increases, but wage increases can also be targeted to specific needs and outcome goals. Conceptually, directly linking wage increases to improved outcomes for students is a logical means of maximizing their effects. By paying teachers more when their students learn more, performance-based pay creates incentives for teachers to focus their efforts on student learning, and it can create incentives for the most effective teachers to enter or remain in the teaching professions. There are also potential drawbacks of performance-based pay. We do not measure all aspects of student learning that we care about, and, thus, by creating incentives to focus on the measured outcomes, we may be hurting students on unmeasured dimensions. Similarly, it is difficult to create performance-based pay systems that provide teachers with incentives to treat their students equitably. The reward formulas often make it beneficial to concentrate more on some students, perhaps those who are performing quite close to an achievement cutoff, to the detriment of other students. In addition, if cooperation among teachers is important to student learning, then performance-based pay systems can have detrimental effects if they reduce incentives for teachers to cooperate.

There is very little solid evidence on performance-based pay in the United States, so we briefly discuss the higher-quality and mixed evidence from developing countries. Two studies use experimental methods to estimate the effects of performance pay for teachers in India and Kenya. Muralidharan and Sundararaman (2006) report effects from a randomized experiment in 500 schools in the rural Indian state of Andhra Pradesh. The schools were divided into five groups: the control group, schools with individual teacher bonuses tied to student test-score gains, school-based bonuses, teacher aides, and extra funds. The average bonus was approximately 4 percent of average salary but could reach a maximum of 29 percent for the individual bonuses and 14 percent for the school-based bonuses. The study finds that students in schools with either incentive program performed better than those in the

Table 6.2   The effects of investments in teachers

Study	Intervention	Research design	Sample and year(s) of intervention	Outcomes (posttest grade)	Effects
Loeb and Page (2000)	Across-the-board wage increase	State-level difference-in-difference analysis with IV	1970–1990	High school graduation, college enrollment	3–4% drop in dropouts and 1–2 percent college enrollment increase for 10% wage increase
Glazerman, Mayer, and Decker (2006)	Teachers selected and trained by TFA	Randomized assignment of students to TFA or non-TFA teachers within grades	Six cities, seventeen elementary schools, 100 classrooms	Reading Math	n.s $.15\sigma$
Boyd et al. (2006)	Teachers selected and trained by TFA	School-fixed effects	New York City student-level data, grades 4–8, 1998–2004	Reading Math	$-.03\sigma$ n.s

Xu, Hannaway, and Taylor (2008)	Teachers selected and trained by TFA teachers	Student-fixed effects	North Carolina student-level data, high school, 2000–2006	Math and Science	.07σ
Jacob and Lefgren (2004)	Externally provided training to schools (seventeen firms)	Discontinuity assignment of training subsidies to low-performing schools	Chicago public schools, grades 3–6, 1996–1999	Reading Math	n.s. n.s.
Carpenter et al. (1989)	Professional development workshop	Randomized assignment	First grade teachers	Math	.5 "σ" in complex addition and subtraction (positive but not significant overall)
Saxe, Gearhart, and Nasir (2001)	Professional development	Randomized assignment	Upper elementary math teachers	Math	1.5 "σ" on the conceptual scale, n.s. in computation

Note: n.s. indicates not statistically significant at 5%; TFA = Teach for America other schools. Relative to the control schools, these students gained 0.19 and 0.12 standard deviations more in math and language tests, respectively.

Glewwe, Ilias, and Kremer (2003) implement a smaller experiment in 100 rural schools in Kenya. In this case, all the bonuses were schoolwide and represented approximately 21 to 43 percent of teacher wages. The authors found that students in schools with merit bonuses were more likely to pass their exams during the two years of the program but that the students did not perform better in subsequent years. In addition, the researchers found little evidence that teachers increased their effort or focus on instruction as a result of the program. It is clearly difficult to generalize from rural India and Kenya to schools in the United States. Current performance-based pay programs in Denver, Nashville, and other cities are likely to provide useful evidence on this approach in the relatively near future.

6.4.2   Recruitment

Wage changes are a straightforward means of affecting the teacher workforce, but they are not the only means and they may not be the most cost-effective. Teach for America (TFA) and other recruitment programs such as the New York City Teaching Fellows have demonstrated that recruitment combined with reorganization of the timing of entry requirements for teaching can drastically change the pool of teacher candidates. As an example, for the 2006 school year, TFA received approximately 19,000 applications for approximately 2,400 openings received, including 10 percent of the senior classes at Spelman and Yale and 8 percent of the senior class from the California Institute of Technology (Teach for America 2006).

Studies of the effects of Teach for America teachers on student achievement have tended to find more positive effects in math than in reading or English language arts, and more positive effects when comparing TFA teachers to the average teacher in the school, than to teachers who obtained certification through traditional teacher education programs. Decker, Mayer, and Glazerman (2004) designed a within-school random assignment study in seventeen schools (100 classrooms) during the 2002 to 2003 school year. They found that the test scores of students of TFA teachers improved by approximately 0.15 standard deviations more in math than those of other students in the school. They found no difference in reading.

Teach for America teachers are paid by the district in which they work as are other teachers. However, there are additional program costs. Teach for America reports that it must raise $20 million annually to support 1,000 members in New York City schools (some of which may be reimbursed by school districts).[14] Of these funds, 21 percent goes to recruitment and selection, 21 percent to preservice training, and 27 percent to professional

---

14. See https://www.teachforamerica.org/about/regions/new_york_city.htm#financial_sustainability.

development. TFA is also a member of AmeriCorps, which provides their members with loan forbearance and interest payment on qualified student loans for the two years of participation and an education award of $4,725 at the end of each year for future educational expenses or to repay qualified student loans. Assuming a typical TFA class size of eighteen (Decker, Mayer, and Glazerman 2004), the annual per-pupil cost of supporting a TFA teacher is $1,374 (including TFA's costs and the AmeriCorps stipend). This is roughly $1,800 per 0.2 standard deviation in math scores although it bears emphasis that there are no measured reading effects, and these results come from comparing TFA teachers to a range of teachers, many of whom had very little preservice training.

The Decker study has strong internal validity because students were randomly assigned to teachers within their school. However, the variety of non-TFA teachers in sampled schools facilitates some conclusions, but not others. For example, it is clear that TFA teachers perform approximately as well in reading and better in math than the other teachers in the school in which they teach but not necessarily better than teachers who had fulfilled the traditional requirements for teaching. The effects of TFA teachers also may differ across schools and across grade levels, and, thus, the results for elementary schools in the Decker study may not reflect the effects in other contexts.

Several studies have used state and district longitudinal data on students to assess whether TFA teachers produce greater test-score gains among their students than other teachers: two studies in a Texas district, one in rural North Carolina, and two in New York City. These studies confirm some of the Decker study's findings and shed further light on the relative effectiveness of TFA teachers. Raymond, Fletcher, and Luque (2001) and Darling-Hammond et al. (2005) use data on elementary schools in the same district in Texas and find some positive effects in math but not in reading. Xu, Hannaway, and Taylor (2008) is the only study of TFA teachers to assess effects in high school. The authors find that rural North Carolina students of TFA teachers learn more during the course of the year than students of teachers from traditional routes. They estimate that the difference in effectiveness between the routes is approximately equal to twice the difference between the average first-year and average second-year teachers.[15]

Boyd et al. (2006) study TFA in New York City, comparing TFA teachers to teachers who had completed a traditional teacher certification program. They find that students of TFA teachers gained 0.31 standard deviations *less* in English language arts and about the same in math as traditionally certified teachers in the same schools, though students of TFA teachers did

15. There is not a large enough sample size of TFA teachers in North Carolina high schools to separate the effects by subject area and the results are an average of teachers in algebra I, algebra II, biology, chemistry, geometry, physics, physical science, and English I.

have greater learning gains in math than other not-traditionally-certified teachers, such as those who entered teaching through individual evaluation, emergency certification, and other alternative routes.

Teach for America teachers largely replace other not-traditionally-prepared teachers, so the comparison with traditionally prepared teachers may not be the most policy-relevant comparison. As an example, in the Decker, Mayer, and Glazerman (2004) experimental study, while only 4 percent of TFA teachers reported having spent ten or more weeks student teaching compared with 31 percent of other teachers with three or fewer years of experience, all TFA teachers had at least four weeks of student teaching experience during their summer institute, while over half of other novice teachers had no student teaching experience. Boyd et al. (Forthcoming) found that as a result of eliminating emergency certification and implementing intensive recruitment efforts through the New York City Teaching Fellows program and, to a lesser extent, through TFA, the gap between the qualifications of teachers in high-poverty schools and low-poverty schools narrowed substantially between 2000 and 2005. The authors estimate that this change in measured qualifications of teachers alone is likely to have improved the test-score performance of students in the poorest schools approximately 0.03 standard deviations, about half the difference between being taught by a first-year teacher and a more-experienced teacher.

6.4.3 Professional Development

Recruitment programs such as TFA concentrate on new teachers, but a variety of professional development policies aim to improve the effectiveness of teachers already in the classroom. The average effect of these policies and programs are not promising. In a summary of this research, Hill (2007, 121) writes, "there is little evidence that the system of professional development, taken as a whole, improves teaching and learning in the United States." In one of the best large-scale studies, given its reliance on discontinuity assignment, Jacob and Lefgren (2004) find little evidence that in-service programs in Chicago affected student performance in either math or reading.

There is little argument that professional development programs, on average, have not had positive effects on students. Exceptions to this rule seem to appear only when programs are concentrated and intensive. Yoon et al. (2007) reviewed more than 1,300 studies of professional development programs. Of these, only nine met the standards established by the Department of Education's What Works Clearinghouse for estimating causal effects. Combining the results from these studies, the authors conclude that *concentrated* professional development opportunities—in this case, programs that required an average of forty-nine hours of teacher participation—can improve student achievement by approximately 21 percentile points, or approximately 0.55 standard deviations for a student starting at the mean.

Carpenter et al. (1989) is one example of the studies meeting the criteria in the Yoon report. They randomly assigned forty first-grade teachers to either a control group or a month-long workshop focused on children's development of problem-solving skills in addition and subtraction. Teachers in the control group participated in workshops focused on nonroutine problem solving. The program required teachers to attend twenty workshop hours a week for four weeks during the summer and one brief meeting in October, taught by two professors and three graduate students. The researchers found that teacher in who participated in the workshop taught problem solving significantly more and number facts significantly less than did control teachers. Students were given a standardized mathematics achievement pretest in September and a series of posttests in April and May. Students in the treatment group scored approximately 0.4 standard deviations higher on the posttest (the Iowa Test of Basic Skills). This difference, though large, was not statistically significant; however, on the subscore of complex addition and subtraction, the treatment groups did score a statistically significant 0.5 standard deviations higher.

Using a pretest-posttest design and some random assignment, Saxe, Gearhart, and Nasir (2001) also found positive effects of professional development interventions for mathematics teaching. They compared three sets of classrooms studying a unit on fractions. Two sets used the same reform curriculum, but the teachers in one group were randomly assigned to participate in an integrated professional development program, while the teachers in the other group had no organized professional development although they met regularly to discuss implementation of the curriculum. The professional development included a five-day summer institute and thirteen additional meetings. A third set of classroom teachers, not randomly assigned, used a traditional curriculum. The study analyzed changes in conceptual understanding and computation. They found no difference between groups on the computation scale but did find systematic variation on the conceptual scale, with the reform group receiving professional development scoring substantially higher, more than a standard deviation, than the other two groups.

6.4.4   Summary

The evidence shows that policies aimed at influencing who becomes a teacher and what teachers do once they enter the classroom can change the teacher workforce and student outcomes. Wages influence teachers decisions; recruitment influences the pool of interested candidates; professional development, in some instances, can change teachers' behaviors and student outcomes. This said, we know little about the optimal design of teacher policies.

Across the board wage increases are extremely expensive. Among 3.5 million teachers staff classrooms in the United States, even a small across-the-board increase in wages is a huge expense. Targeted wage changes are more promising but difficult to design, given the many factors that influence a student's learning in a given year, the multitude of dimensions of learning that we care about (only some of which we measure), and the difficulty of designing a reward system that benefits students equitably. Recruitment programs have dramatically changed the teaching force, particularly in large urban districts. Such approaches are likely to be a part of any effective comprehensive plan to improve teaching, but they only affect the pool of new teachers (not the substantial number of individuals already teaching), and the evidence on how to select the best teachers from this growing pool of candidates is sparse. Finally, it is evident that professional development can improve student performance but that this professional development must be both intensive and targeted on specific tasks. Designing professional development that works on a large scale is a daunting task.

6.5   School Choice and Accountability

Even if endowed with sufficient resources, schools may not have incentives to use their money wisely, and they may be focusing on student outcomes that parents and communities do not value. Two sets of policies aim to realign incentives in order to improve opportunities for students: test-based accountability programs and market-based accountability programs.

In test-based accountability schemes, governments measure schools' achievement, judge whether they are successful, and attach a variety of rewards or sanctions to these judgments (Figlio and Ladd 2008).[16] The best known of these policies is the Federal No Child Left Behind (NCLB) law of 2001, which required schools to make "adequate yearly progress" toward 100 percent student proficiency. But even before NCLB, many states and large cities had implemented accountability policies, which coexist with NCLB in states like California. Studies using pre-NCLB, cross-state variation in the timing of these state laws suggest some positive effects on test scores (Carnoy and Loeb 2002; Hanushek and Raymond 2005). Research within states has generally been limited in its ability to identify convincing comparison groups against which to compare the outcomes of students subjected to accountability provisions (Figlio and Ladd 2008).[17] The strongest

16. Conceptually, measuring "success" involves estimating the causal effect of thousands of individual schools on test scores. In practical terms, accountability systems measure either the level of student performance in a given year and compare it a specified goal (e.g., the Federal No Child Left Behind law) or measure changes in schools' or students' performance between years (e.g., California's state accountability scheme). The dilemma in either case is that schools might be held accountable for variance in test score measures that is due to factors beyond schools' control (e.g., family poverty or randomness in test score fluctuations from year to year).

17. One exception is a range of studies that examine effects of accountability pressures on schools judged to be failing in Florida. These studies, which use variants of discontinuity design, based on the formula for calculating "failure," suggest that test scores improved in these schools. See Rouse and Barrow (2008) and the citations therein.

study uses variation in accountability pressures across schools in Florida and shows that schools facing greater pressure were more likely to implement a range of new instructional practices such as lengthening instructional time, focusing more on low-performing students, and improving low-performing teachers. Moreover, improvements in student achievement in the schools are likely the result of these policy changes (Rouse et al. 2007).

Market-based policies constitute a second approach to holding schools accountable. Broadly speaking, these policies enhance the ability of parents to choose a preferred public or private school. In so doing, they create incentives for school authorities to cater to parental preferences for certain features of schools and their students. There is already much choice through families' choice of residence and its neighborhood public school, which already creates competition (Hoxby 2000a; Rouse and Barrow 2008). But moving costs are high, and not all parents have the resources and information needed to move to the neighborhood of their preferred school. Variants of other choice policies, such as private school vouchers and charter schools, are grafted onto this system of residential choice. The next two sections consider recent evidence on the effects of each policy on student outcomes.

6.5.1   Private School Vouchers

Private school vouchers are tuition coupons that students can redeem at a participating private school. In the few existing U.S. programs, voucher eligibility is typically restricted to small numbers of low-income students, and the participating schools are mostly Catholic (except on the occasions, such as the early phases of the Milwaukee program, when sectarian participation was restricted). The accompanying research has thus attempted to identify test score effects on low-income students who are offered or actually use a voucher to attend such private schools. A separate literature, not considered here, considers how to estimate the general equilibrium effects of large school voucher plans.[18]

In the 1980s, when voucher plans were mostly hypothetical, authors used nonexperimental methods and data to estimate the effect of Catholic school attendance on test scores. This literature, reviewed by McEwan (2000) and Neal (2002), showed no or very small effects on test scores but more substantial effects on eventual high school attainment. Its results were somewhat inconclusive because of concerns that omitted variables like student motivation or ability were biasing estimates of private school effects.

As publicly and privately funded voucher programs were implemented in several U.S. cities, the evidence base improved. In 1990, Milwaukee's Parental

---

18. The most compelling evidence on large-scale voucher plans is only available from countries like Chile that have actually implemented such plans (McEwan 2001; Hsieh and Urquiola 2006). For reviews of the wider literature on vouchers, see McEwan (2000), Zimmer and Bettinger (2008), and Rouse and Barrow (2008).

Choice Program began offering vouchers of $2,446 (later increased) to low-income students for attendance at nonsectarian schools (Witte 2001). Subsequent versions of the program included more students and private schools, but the best research was conducted in the program's early phase. Rouse (1998) compared achievement gains of students offered vouchers to gains of two comparison groups: a random sample of low-income students in Milwaukee Public Schools and, more compellingly, a group of unsuccessful applicants who were randomly denied admission to private schools. The results consistently suggested no statistically significant effects on reading scores and small annual effects on math scores of no more than 0.11 standard deviations (Rouse and Barrow 2008).

Privately funded voucher programs have been implemented and evaluated with randomized experiments in several U.S. cities (Howell and Peterson 2002; Rouse and Barrow 2008). Most prominently, a New York City program offered $1,400 to poor children for private school attendance (if necessary, families were expected to contribute further toward private school tuition). Beginning in Fall 1997, a random subset of eligible applicants was offered vouchers and followed for three years by researchers. Two independent analyses found no effects of voucher offers on test scores after three years in the full sample of students (Mayer et al. 2002; Krueger and Zhu 2004). The first study did find effects among the subsample of African American students. Krueger and Zhu found that this result disappeared when using the full sample of data and alternative methods of defining student race in the sample.

The best recent evidence of voucher effects is from the randomized evaluation of a federally funded voucher program in Washington, D.C. (the Opportunity Scholarship Program). The scholarships are worth up to $7,500 and can be used to cover tuition, fees, and transportation to any participating private school. As in New York City, the vouchers were restricted to poor students and were awarded by lottery. After two years, the effect of the voucher offer on math scores is close to zero, and the reading estimates are 0.05 to 0.08 standard deviations, but none of these are statistically different from zero at the 5 percent level (Rouse and Barrow 2008; Wolf et al. 2008).

6.5.2   Charter Schools

Charter schools are publicly funded schools of choice that enjoy some degree of autonomy from local school authorities. They receive state or local funding based on the number of students that they attract. If they receive more applications than spaces, then students are usually admitted by lottery. Charter schools are not a homogeneous "treatment." In the 2007 to 2008 school year, forty states and the District of Columbia had enacted charter school laws with wide variation in charter authorization, finance, regulation, and accountability (Bifulco and Bulkley 2008). Currently, about 4,100 charter schools enroll 1.2 million children (2 percent of the total) although they are concentrated in a small number of states.[19]

The best research to date has focused on particular states or cities and has followed one of two evaluation approaches, each with drawbacks. The first set of studies takes advantage of large samples of administrative data from states that track all students' test scores over time. The authors of these studies identify the subset of students that switch between public and charter schools and compare their test scores, before and after, to the non-switching comparison group.[20] They are generally consistent in their findings, despite being conducted in Texas, North Carolina, Florida, and two large California cities (Hanushek et al. 2007; Bilfulco and Ladd 2006; Sass 2006; Zimmer and Buddin 2006). Switching to charter schools often has negative effects, usually small, on student test scores (see table 6.3). They tend to be largest when the charter school is relatively new and closer to zero otherwise. The generalizability of these effects is uncertain because they refer only to students that switch between grades and not students who both start and complete their schooling in charter schools. In a more recent report including more than 70 percent of charter school enrollment across the country Center for Research on Education Outcomes ([CREDO] 2009) compares students in charter schools with students in nearby public schools and finds similar results to those in the preceding: charter schools vary in their effectiveness with some better than the average local public school and some worse; however, on average, student achievement gains are somewhat lower in charter schools.

A second set of studies, using a more convincing approach to causal inference, relies on the fact that charter schools are usually required to admit students by lottery when faced by excess demand. Hoxby and Rockoff (2004) compare the test score outcomes of students who won or lost in admissions lotteries at three Chicago charter schools. Overall, there were no statistically significant differences in reading or math scores between winners or losers although this could mask some positive effects in earlier grades. There is little national or state data collected on how many charter schools are oversubscribed, though even generous estimates conclude it is only a small portion (McEwan and Olsen 2007). By revealed preference of families, oversubscribed schools are perhaps the most effective of a city's charter schools. Thus, the Chicago results are surprising, but still broadly consistent with a more ambitious study that analyzed 194 admissions lotteries at nineteen Chicago high schools (Cullen, Jacob, and Levitt 2006). Though not charter schools, the high schools allow open enrollments in the same local schooling

19. National charter school data are regularly compiled by an advocacy group, the Center for Education Reform (http://www.edreform.com).

20. Authors apply variants of student fixed effects specifications. The exact specifications adopted by the authors differ, but the broad results are not sensitive to these decisions.

Table 6.3   The effects of vouchers and charter schools

Study	Intervention	Grades (length) of intervention	Research design	Sample and year(s) of Intervention	Outcomes	Effects
Rouse (1998); Rouse and Barrow (2008)	Offer of private school vouchers (up to $2,985 in 1993)	K–8 (annual gains)	Comparison groups of unsuccessful applicants and random sample of Milwaukee public students	Milwaukee, 3,163–8,751 students (depending on comparison group), 1990–1994	Reading Math	n.s. (annually) n.s. to .11σ (annually)
Krueger and Zhu (2004)	Offer of private school vouchers (up to $1,400)	K–4 (three yrs.)	Random assignment of vouchers to eligible (poor) applicants	New York City, 2,080 students, 1997–1998	Reading Math	n.s. n.s. (small, non-robust effects for black subsample)
Wolf et al. (2008)	Offer of private school vouchers (up to $7,500)	K–12 (two yrs.)	Random assignment of vouchers to eligible (poor) applicants	Washington, DC, 2,308 students, 2004–2006	Reading Math	n.s. n.s.
Hanushek et al. (2007)	Student switching between public and charter school	4–8	Student-fixed effects	Texas administrative data, 1996–2002	Composite reading and math	–.32σ to n.s.
Bifulco and Ladd (2006)	Student switching between public and charter school	3–8	Student-fixed effects	North Carolina administrative data, 1996–2002	Reading Math	–.18σ to –.06σ –.31σ to –.08σ
Sass (2006)	Student switching between public and charter school	3–10	Student-fixed effects	Florida administrative data, 1999–2003	Reading Math	–.04.σ to –.01σ –.08σ to –.02σ

Zimmer and Buddin (2006)	Student switching between public and charter school	Elementary and secondary	Student-fixed effects	Los Angeles and San Diego administrative data, 1997–2002	Reading	-2.1 to n.s. (elementary); -1.2 to 1.5 (secondary)
					Math	-5.0 to n.s. (elementary); -1.7 to 1.3 (secondary)
Hoxby and Rockoff (2004)	Offer of place in one of three Chicago international charter schools	1–8 (one yr.)	Lottery admissions	Chicago, 2,668 students	Reading	n.s.
					Math	n.s. (some positive and significant effects for younger students)
Hoxby and Murarka (2007)	One yr. of attendance in a New York City charter school	3–8 (one yr.)	Lottery admissions, two-stage least squares	New York City	Reading	.04σ
					Math	.09σ
Dobbie and Fryer (2009)	Offer of place in Promise Academy	6 (three yrs.)	Lottery admissions	New York City (Harlem), 269 students	Reading	.24σ
					Math	.73σ

Notes: n.s. = not statistically significant at 5%. Reported estimates from **Rouse** (1998), **Krueger and Zhu** (2004), **Wolf et al.** (2008), **Hoxby and Rockoff** (2004), and **Dobbie and Fryer** (2009) are intent-to-treat effects. Hoxby and Murarka (2007) is a treatment-on-the-treated effect obtained from a two-stage least squares regression. Effects in Zimmer and Buddin (2006) are reported in test score percentiles.

market. Despite evidence that participating families appear to choose better schools along a range of measures like test scores, the authors do not any evidence that lottery winners experience benefits on a wide range of achievement measures.

Recent lottery research in New York City has turned up very different results. Hoxby and Murarka (2007) use multiple lotteries for charter schools in New York City and find modest annual test-score gains in both math (0.09 standard deviations) and reading (0.04 standard deviations) for students that actually attend charter schools. Similarly, Dobbie and Fryer (2009) find substantial achievement gains for students attending the charter schools in the Harlem Children's Zone, a ninety-seven-block area of central Harlem in New York City. In particular, for middle school students, they find that winning a lottery to attend the Promise Academy increases achievement by 0.73 standard deviations in math and 0.24 in English language arts over three years, with most of the gains in the third year. The New York City results provide convincing evidence that *some* charter schools are very effective. It is quite possible that oversubscribed charter schools in New York City are, on average, more effective than other city schools and perhaps many charter schools in other states. The results highlight the fact that charter school policies across states, and the schools themselves, are quite heterogeneous and prevent easy generalizations about effectiveness or costs.

6.5.3   Summary

One premise of choice and accountability is that public schools lack incentives to use resources efficiently. In the logic of test-based accountability systems, this inefficiency may arise from poor management or from schools aiming to produce outcomes other than test scores for students. In choice systems, the inefficiency could similarly be due to poor management or to schools aiming to produce outcomes that parents do not care as much about. In either case, there is underproduction of student outcomes, which are presumably valued by parents and society.

Substantial recent research has asked whether test-based and market accountability programs have improved student outcomes. The evidence on test-based accountability programs is mixed. However, it is clear that some systems can change school practices and, in turn, affect student learning (Rouse et al. 2007). The evidence on the average effects of private school vouchers and charter schools is quite mixed. Few studies have shown positive and meaningful effects of private school voucher programs. The charter school evidence has also shown few positive effects across many states, but these results are tempered by recent evidence of successes in New York City. As a final caveat, large-scale voucher and charter school policies may increase competition which, in the long run, can benefit schools and students. The present research is not well-suited to uncovering these effects.

6.6   Conclusions

We have known for some time that additional years of schooling are a good investment, but we know less about how to design education systems to use resources to maximize student outcomes. Fortunately, the volume and quality of research has accelerated in the past decade. This chapter's review focused on high-quality evidence on the impact and costs of interventions in three areas: direct resource investments, investments in the teacher workforce, and school choice and accountability.

Among direct investments, there is no consistent evidence that simply increasing expenditures will increase test scores although such investments can increase achievement if used well. The research on class size reduction and intensive reading programs like Success for All provide evidence of the potential benefits of increased investments. In general, computer-assisted instruction is no panacea, though a recent study found it can be effective if coherently integrated with instructional goals and intensively applied. Among teacher policies, there is some evidence that across-the-board teacher wage increases can improve student outcomes although this approach is quite costly. Evidence on targeted wage increase policies (like performance pay) is still sparse in the United States. The mounting evidence is more consistent in suggesting that popular alternative routes for teacher recruitment, such as Teach for America, can raise test scores, at least in math, if they replace teachers with few formal qualifications. The vast literature on teacher professional development only suggests effects when the programs are intensive and targeted at improving specific student outcomes. Finally, a growing number of randomized and natural experiments suggest zero or very small effects of receiving a private school voucher or gaining admission to a public school of choice, except in the emerging evidence on New York City charter schools.

This summary masks potentially large variation in the cost-effectiveness of the subset of "effective" programs and policies. Section 6.3 suggested that schools might have to invest upward of $10,000 on class size reduction to obtain increases in test scores of at least 20 percent of a standard deviation in test scores. In other cases, such as Success for All or Teach for America, the same test score increases might be obtained for one-quarter the cost or less. Indeed, prior work has found, among a subset of effective interventions, that class size reduction is less cost-effective than others in raising test scores. These include computer-assisted instruction (Levin, Glass, and Meister 1987) and investments in teacher resources (Grissmer et al. 2000).

These results might appear to suggest that class size reduction in not a worthwhile investment. However, this can only be judged by converting test-score gains into a reasonable estimate of monetary benefits that can be weighed against costs. For example, Schanzenbach (2007) assumes that class size reduction raises test scores by 0.15 standard deviations and that a 1 standard deviation increase in test scores causes annual earnings to increase by 20 percent.[21] Under these assumptions, class size reduction shifts discounted annual earnings upward by 3 percent. Weighed against the substantial costs of the Tennessee intervention, the internal rate of return is 4.8 percent, assuming no real wage growth. Krueger (2003) makes slightly different assumptions and finds an internal rate of return of 5.2 percent. Harris (2007) applies further sensitivity analysis and finds that the internal rate of return does not fall below 3 percent, equal to a commonly applied discount rate.

The final chapter of this volume conducts a more careful cost-benefit comparison of class size reduction and other interventions. For the moment, however, the results illustrate that class size reduction—one of the *least* cost-effective education interventions—can at least pass a basic cost-benefit test (which only includes only a single category of benefits, private earnings). This implies substantial scope for identifying other economically reasonable investments in the quality of education. However, as the chapter's review suggested, the research literature still has far to go in separating the effective investments from the ineffective and in thinking carefully about how to scale-up pilot interventions.

References

Angrist, Joshua D. 2004. American education research changes tack. *Oxford Review of Economic Policy* 20 (2): 198–212.

Angist, Joshua D., and Alan B. Krueger. 1999. Empirical strategies in labor economics. In *Handbook of Labor Economics.* Vol. 3A, ed. Orley Ashenfelter and David Card, 1277–1366. Amsterdam: Elsevier.

Angrist, Joshua D., and Victor Lavy. 1999. Using Maimonides' rule to estimate the effect of class size on scholastic achievement. *Quarterly Journal of Economics* 114 (2): 533–75.

Bacolod, Marigee. 2007. Do alternative opportunities matter? The role of female labor markets in the decline of teacher quality. *Review of Economics and Statistics* 89 (4): 737–51.

Bacolod, Marigee, John Dinardo, and Mireille Jacobson. 2008. Beyond incentives: Do schools use accountability rewards productively? University of California, Irvine, and University of Michigan. Unpublished Manuscript.

Barnett, W. Steven. 1996. Economics of school reform: Three promising models. In *Holding schools accountable: Performance-based reform in education,* ed. Helen F. Ladd, 299–326. Washington, DC: Brookings Institution.

Barrow, Lisa, Lisa Markman, and Cecilia E. Rouse. 2008. Technology's edge: The educational benefits of computer-aided instruction. NBER Working Paper no. 14240. Cambridge, MA: National Bureau of Economic Research.

---

21. The estimate is taken from Neal and Johnson (1996), who relate Armed Forces Qualification Test (AFQT) scores to subsequent earnings.

Barrow, Lisa, and Cecilia E. Rouse. 2005. Causality, causality, causality: The view of education inputs and outputs from economics. Federal Reserve Bank of Chicago Working Paper no. 2005-15. Chicago: Federal Reserve Bank of Chicago.

Belfield, Clive, and Henry M. Levin. 2007. *The price we pay: Economic and social consequences of inadequate education.* Washington, DC: Brookings Institution.

Bifulco, Robert, and Katrina Bulkley. 2008. Charter Schools. In *Handbook of research in education finance and policy,* ed. Helen F. Ladd and Edward B. Fiske, 425–46. New York: Routledge.

Bifulco, Robert, William Duncombe, and John Yinger. 2004. Does whole-school reform boost student performance? The case of New York City. *Journal of Policy Analysis and Management* 24 (1): 47–72.

Bifulco, Robert, and Helen F. Ladd. 2006. The impacts of charter schools on student achievement: Evidence from North Carolina. *Education Finance and Policy* 1 (1): 50–90.

Bloom, Howard S. 2003. Using "short" interrupted time-series analysis to measure the impacts of whole-school reforms: With applications to a study of accelerated schools. *Evaluation Review* 27 (1): 3–49.

Borman, Geoffrey D., James G. Benson, and Laura Overman. 2009. A randomized field trial of the Fast For Word Language computer-based training program. *Educational Evaluation and Policy Analysis* 31 (1): 82–106.

Borman, Geoffrey D., and Gina M. Hewes. 2002. The long-term effects and cost-effectiveness of Success for All. *Educational Evaluation and Policy Analysis* 24 (4): 243–66.

Borman, Geoffrey D., Robert E. Slavin, Alan C. K. Cheung, Anne M. Chamberlain, Nancy A. Madden, and Bette Chambers. 2007. Final reading outcomes of the national randomized field trial of Success for All. *American Educational Research Journal* 44 (3): 701–31.

Boyd, Don, Michelle Brown, Julie Cohen, Pam Grossman, Hamilton Lankford, Susanna Loeb, Dan Mindich, Sinead Mullen, and James Wyckoff. 2009. Measure for measure: A pilot study linking English language arts instruction and teachers' value-added to student achievement. Unpublished Manuscript. Stanford University.

Boyd, Don, Pamela Grossman, Hamilton Lankford, Susanna Loeb, and James Wyckoff. 2006. How changes in entry requirements alter the teacher workforce and affect student achievement. *Education Finance and Policy* 1 (2): 176–216.

Boyd, Don, Hamilton Lankford, Susanna Loeb, Jonah Rockoff, and James Wyckoff. Forthcoming. The narrowing gap in New York City teacher qualifications and its implications for student achievement in high-poverty schools. *Journal of Policy Analysis and Management.*

Card, David. 1999. The causal effect of education on earnings. In *Handbook of labor economics.* Vol. 3A, ed. Orley Ashenfelter and David Card, 1801–63. Amsterdam: Elsevier.

Card, David, and A. Abigail Payne. 2002. School finance reform, the distribution of school spending, and the distribution of student test scores. *Journal of Public Economics* 83:49–82.

Carnoy, Martin, and Susanna Loeb. 2002. Does external accountability affect student outcomes? A cross-state analysis. *Educational Evaluation and Policy Analysis* 24 (2): 305–31.

Carpenter, Thomas P., Elizabeth Fennema, Penelope L. Peterson, Chi-Pang Chiang, and Megan Loef. 1989. Using knowledge of children's mathematics thinking in classroom teaching: An experimental study. *American Educational Research Journal* 26 (4): 499–531.

Center for Research on Education Outcomes (CREDO). 2009. *Multiple choice: Charter school performance in 16 states.* Stanford, CA: CREDO.

Chay, Kenneth Y., Patrick J. McEwan, and Miguel Urquiola. 2005. The central role of noise in evaluating interventions that use test scores to rank schools. *American Economic Review* 95 (4): 1237–58.

Cook, Thomas D., Farah N. Habib, Meredith Phillips, Richard A. Settersten, Shobha C. Shagle, and Serdar M. Degirmencioglu. 1999. Comer's School Development Program in Prince George's County, Maryland: A theory-based evaluation. *American Educational Research Journal* 36 (3): 543–97.

Cook, Thomas D., Robert F. Murphy, and H. David Hunt. 2000. Comer's School Development Program in Chicago: A theory-based evaluation. *American Educational Research Journal* 37 (2): 535–97.

Corcoran, Sean P., Robert M. Schwab, and William N. Evans. 2004. Women, the labor market and the declining relative quality of teachers. *Journal of Policy Analysis and Management* 23 (3): 449–70.

Corcoran, Sean P., and William N. Evans. 2008. Equity, adequacy and the evolving state role in education finance. In *Handbook of research in education finance and policy,* ed. Helen F. Ladd and Edward B. Fiske, 332–56. New York: Routledge.

Cullen, Julie Berry, Brian A. Jacob, and Steven Levitt. 2006. The effect of school choice on participants: Evidence from randomized lotteries. *Econometrica* 74 (5): 1191–1230.

Cullen, Julie Berry, and Susanna Loeb. 2004. School finance reform in Michigan: Evaluating Proposal A. In *Helping children left behind: State aid and the pursuit of educational equity,* ed. John Yinger, 215–49. Cambridge, MA: MIT Press.

Darling-Hammond, Linda, Deborah J. Holtzman, Su Jin Gatlin, and Julian Vasquez Heilig. 2005. Does teacher preparation matter? Evidence about teacher certification, Teach for America and teacher effectiveness. *Education Policy Analysis Archives* 13 (42): http://epaa.asu.edu/epaa/v13n42/.

Decker, Paul T., Daniel P. Mayer, and Steven Glazerman. 2004. The effects of Teach For America on students: Findings from a national evaluation. MPR no. 8792-750. Mathematica Policy Research. Princeton, NJ.

Dobbie, Will, and Roland G. Fryer, Jr. 2009. Are high-quality schools enough to close the achievement gap? Evidence from a bold social experiment in Harlem. Harvard University. Unpublished Manuscript.

Downes, Thomas A., and David N. Figlio. 1998. School finance reforms, tax limits, and student performance: Do reforms level-up or dumb down? Tufts University. Unpublished Manuscript.

———. 2008. Tax and expenditure limits, school finance and school quality. In *Handbook of research in education finance and policy,* ed. Helen F. Ladd and Edward B. Fiske, 373–88. New York: Routledge.

Dynarski, Mark, Roberto Agodini, Sheila Heaviside, Timothy Novak, Nancy Carey, Larissa Campuzano, Barbara Means, et al. 2007. Effectiveness of reading and mathematics software products: Findings from the first student cohort. NCEE no. 2007-4005. Washington, DC: National Center for Education Evaluation and Regional Assistance, Institute of Education Sciences.

Figlio, David F., and Helen F. Ladd. 2008. School accountability and student achievement. In *Handbook of research in education finance and policy,* ed. Helen F. Ladd and Edward B. Fiske. New York: Routledge.

Flanagan, Ann E., and Sheila E. Murray. 2004. A decade of reform: The impact of school reform in Kentucky. In *Helping children left behind: State aid and the pursuit of educational equity,* ed. John Yinger, 195–213. Cambridge, MA: MIT Press.

Glazerman, Steven, Daniel Mayer, and Paul Decker. 2006. Alternative routes to teaching: The impacts of Teach for America on student achievement and other outcomes. *Journal of Policy Analysis and Management* 25 (1): 75–96.

Glewwe, Paul, Nauman Ilias, and Michael Kremer. 2003. Teacher incentives. NBER Working Paper no. 9671. Cambridge, MA: National Bureau of Economic Research.

Gordon, Nora. 2004. Do federal grants boost school spending? Evidence from Title I. *Journal of Public Economics* 88 (9–10): 1771–92.

Greenwald, Rob, Larry V. Hedges, and Richard D. Laine. 1996. The effect of school resources on student achievement. *Review of Educational Research* 66 (3): 361–96.

Grissmer, David, Ann Flanagan, Jennifer Kawata, and Stephanie Williamson. 2000. *Improving student achievement: What state NAEP test scores tell us.* Santa Monica, CA: RAND.

Guryan, Jonathan. 2003. Does money matter? Estimates from education finance reform in Massachusetts. University of Chicago. Unpublished Manuscript.

Hansushek, Eric A. 1986. The economics of schooling: Production and efficiency in public schools. *Journal of Economic Literature* 24 (3): 1141–77.

———. 2006. School Resources. In *Handbook of the economics of education.* Vol. 2, ed. Eric A. Hanushek and Finis Welch, 865–908. Amsterdam: Elsevier.

Hanushek, Eric A., John F. Kain, Steven G. Rivkin, and Gregory F. Branch. 2007. Charter school quality and parental decision making with school choice. *Journal of Public Economics* 91:823–48.

Hanushek, Eric A., and Margaret E. Raymond. 2005. Does school accountability lead to improved student performance? *Journal of Policy Analysis and Management* 24 (2): 297–327.

Harris, Douglas N. 2007. Class size and school size: Taking the trade-offs seriously. In *Brookings Papers on Education Policy:* 137–61. Washington, DC: Brookings Institution.

Hill, Heather. 2007. Learning in the teaching workforce. *Future of Children* 17: 111–28.

Hoxby, Caroline M. 2000a. Does competition among public schools benefit students and taxpayers? *American Economic Review* 90 (5): 1209–38.

———. 2000b. The effects of class size on student achievement: New evidence from popular variation. *Quarterly Journal of Economics* 115 (4): 1239–85.

Hoxby, Caroline M., and Sonali Murarka. 2007. Charter schools in New York City: Who enrolls and how they affect their students' achievement. Stanford University. Unpublished Manuscript.

Hoxby, Caroline M., and Jonah E. Rockoff. 2004. The impact of charter schools on student achievement. Harvard University and Columbia University. Unpublished Manuscript.

Howell, William G., and Paul E. Peterson. 2002. *The education gap: Vouchers and urban schools.* Washington, DC: Brookings Institution.

Hsieh, Chang-Tai, and Miguel Urquiola. 2006. The effects of generalized school choice on achievement and stratification: Evidence from Chile's voucher program. *Journal of Public Economics* 90:1477–1503.

Jacob, Brian A., and Lars Lefgren. 2004. The impact of teacher training on student achievement: Quasi-experimental evidence from school reform efforts in Chicago. *Journal of Human Resources* 39 (1): 50–79.

Jepsen, Christopher, and Steven Rivkin. 2009. Class size reduction and student achievement: The potential trade-off between teacher quality and class size. *Journal of Human Resources* 44 (1): 223–50.

Kane, Thomas J., and Douglas O. Staiger. 2008. Estimating teacher impacts on student achievement: An experimental evaluation. NBER Working Paper no. 14607. Cambridge, MA: National Bureau of Economic Research.

King, Jennifer, A. 1994. Meeting the educational needs of at-risk students: A cost analysis of three models. *Educational Evaluation and Policy Analysis* 16 (1): 1–19.

Krueger, Alan B. 1999. Experimental estimates of education production functions. *Quarterly Journal of Economics* 114 (2): 497–532.

———. 2003. Economic considerations and class size. *Economic Journal* 113:F34–F63.

Krueger, Alan B., and Diane M. Whitmore. 2001. The effect of attending a small class in the early grades on college-test taking and middle school test results: Evidence from Project Star. *Economic Journal* 111 (468): 1–28.

Krueger, Alan B., and Pei Zhu. 2004. Another look at the New York City school voucher experiment. *American Behavioral Scientist* 47 (5): 658–98.

Lee, David S. 2008. Randomized experiments from non-random selection in U.S. house elections. *Journal of Econometrics* 142 (2): 675–97.

Leuven, Edwin, Mikael Lindahl, Hessel Oosterbeek, and Dinand Webbink. 2007. The effect of extra funding for disadvantaged pupils on achievement. *Review of Economics and Statistics* 89 (4): 721–36.

Levin, Henry M. 2002. Issues in designing cost-effectiveness comparisons of whole-school reforms. In *Cost-effectiveness and educational policy.* Yearbook of the American Education Finance Association, ed. Henry M. Levin and Patrick J. McEwan, 71–96. Larchmont, NY: Eye on Education.

Levin, Henry M., and Patrick J, McEwan. 2001. *Cost-Effectiveness Analysis.* 2nd ed. Thousand Oaks, CA: Sage.

Levin, Henry M., Gene V. Glass, and Gail R. Meister. 1987. Cost-effectiveness of computer-assisted instruction. *Evaluation Review* 11 (1): 50–72.

Loeb, Susanna, and Marianne E. Page. 2000. Examining the link between teacher wages and student outcomes: The importance of alternative labor market opportunities and non-pecuniary variation. *Review of Economics and Statistics* 82 (3): 393–408.

Loeb, Susanna, and Katharine Strunk. 2003. The contribution of administrative and experimental data to education policy research. *National Tax Journal* 56 (2): 415–38.

Mayer, Daniel P., Paul E. Peterson, David E. Myers, Christina Clark Tuttle, and William G. Howell. 2002. School choice in New York City after three years: An evaluation of the School Choice Scholarships Program. MPR no. 8404-045. Mathematica Policy Research. Princeton, NJ.

McEwan, Patrick J. 2000. The potential impact of large-scale voucher programs. *Review of Educational Research* 70 (2): 103–49.

———. 2001. The effectiveness of public, Catholic, and non-religious private schools in Chile's voucher system. *Education Economics* 9 (2): 103–28.

McEwan, Patrick J., and Robert Olsen. 2007. Admissions lotteries in charter schools. Wellesley College and Urban Institute. Unpublished Manuscript.

Muralidharan, Karthik and Venkatesh Sundararaman. 2006. Teacher incentives in developing countries: Experimental evidence from India. Harvard University. Unpublished Manuscript.

National Center for Education Statistics (NCES). 2008. *Digest of education statistics 2007.* Washington, DC: U.S. Department of Education.

Neal, Derek. 2002. How vouchers could change the market for education. *Journal of Economic Perspectives* 16 (4): 25–44.

Neal, Derek A., and William R. Johnson. 1996. The role of premarket factors in black-white wage differences. *Journal of Political Economy* 104 (5): 869–95.

Papke, Leslie E. 2005. The effects of spending on test pass rates: Evidence from Michigan. *Journal of Public Economics* 89:821–39.

Raymond, Margaret, Stephen H. Fletcher, and Javier Luque. 2001. *Teach for America: An evaluation of teacher differences and student outcomes in Houston, Texas.* Stanford, CA: The Hoover Institute, Center for Research on Education Outcomes [CREDO]. http://credo.stanford.edu/downloads/tfa.pdf.

Rivkin, Steven G., Eric A. Hanushek, and John F. Kain. 2005. Teachers, schools, and academic achievement. *Econometrica* 73 (2): 417–58.

Rothstein, Jesse. 2009. Student sorting and bias in value added estimation: Selection on observables and unobservables. NBER Working Paper no. 14666. Cambridge, MA: National Bureau of Economic Research.

Rouse, Cecilia Elena. 1998. Private school vouchers and student achievement: An evaluation of the Milwaukee Parental Choice Program. *Quarterly Journal of Economics* 113 (2): 553–602.

Rouse, Cecilia Elena, and Lisa Barrow. 2008. School vouchers and student achievement: Recent evidence, remaining questions. NCSPE Occasional Paper no. 163. New York: Teachers College and National Center for the Study of Privatization in Education.

Rouse, Cecilia Elena, Jane Hannaway, Dan Goldhaber, and David Figlio. 2007. Feeling the Florida heat? How low-performing schools respond to voucher and accountability pressure. NBER Working Paper no. 13681. Cambridge, MA: National Bureau of Economic Research.

Rouse, Cecilia Elena, and Alan B. Krueger. 2004. Putting computerized instruction to the test: A randomized evaluation of a "scientifically based" reading program. *Economics of Education Review* 23:323–38.

Sass, Tim R. 2006. Charter schools and student achievement in Florida. *Education Finance and Policy* 1 (1): 91–122.

Saxe, Geoffrey B., Maryl Gearhart, and Na'ilah S. Nasir. 2001. Enhancing students' understanding of mathematics: A study of three contrasting approaches to professional support. *Journal of Mathematics Teacher Education* 4:55–79.

Schanzenbach, Diane Whitmore. 2007. What have researchers learned from Project STAR? In *Brookings Papers on Education Policy:* 205–28. Washington, DC: Brookings Institution.

Schwartz, Amy Ellen, Leanna Stiefel, and Dae Yeop Kim. 2004. The impact of school reform on student performance: Evidence from the New York Network for School Renewal Project. *Journal of Human Resources* 39 (2): 500–22.

Shadish, William R., Thomas D. Cook, and Donald T. Campbell. 2002. *Experimental and quasi-experimental designs for generalized causal inference.* Boston: Houghton Mifflin.

Teach for America. 2006. In strong job market, record number of graduating seniors apply to Teach for America. http://www.teachforamerica.org/newsroom/documents/TeachForAmerica_News_20060601.html.

Todd, Petra E., and Kenneth I. Wolpin. 2003. On the specification and estimation of the production function for cognitive achievement. *Economic Journal* 113 (485): F3–F33.

Urquiola, Miguel. 2006. Identifying class size effects in developing countries: Evidence from rural Bolivia. *Review of Economics and Statistics* 88 (1): 171–77.

Urquiola, Miguel, and Eric Verhoogen. 2009. Class size caps, sorting, and the regression-discontinuity design. *American Economic Review* 99 (1): 179–215.

van der Klaauw, Wilbert. 2008. Breaking the link between poverty and low student achievement: An evaluation of Title I. *Journal of Econometrics* 142:731–56.

What Works Clearinghouse. 2007. Technical details of WWC-conducted computations. Washington, DC: Institute of Education Sciences, What Works Clearing-house.

Witte, John F. 2001. *The market approach to education: An analysis of America's first voucher program.* Princeton, NJ: Princeton University Press.

Wolf, Patrick, Babette Gutmann, Michael Puma, Brian Kisida, Lou Rizzo, Nada Eissa, and Marsha Silverberg. 2008. Evaluation of the DC Opportunity Scholarship Program: Impacts after two years. NCEE no. 2008-4023. Washington, DC: National Center for Education Evaluation and Regional Assistance, Institute of Education Sciences.

Xu, Zeyu, Jane Hannaway, and Colin Taylor. 2008. Making a difference: The effects of TFA in high schools. CALDER Working Paper.

Yoon, Kwang Suk, Teresa Duncan, Silvia Wen-Yu Lee, Beth Scarloss, and Kathy L. Shapley. 2007. *Reviewing the evidence on how teacher professional development affects student achievement.* Report REL 2007–no. 033. Washington, DC: National Center for Education Evaluation and Regional Assistance, Institute of Education Sciences, U.S. Department of Education.

Zimmer, Ron, and Eric P. Bettinger. 2008. Beyond the rhetoric: Surveying the evidence on vouchers and tax credits. In *Handbook of research in education finance and policy,* ed. Helen F. Ladd and Edward B. Fiske. New York: Routledge.

Zimmer, Ron, and Richard Buddin. 2006. Charter school performance in two large urban districts. *Journal of Urban Economics* 60:307–26.

IV

Adolescent Interventions

7

Preventing Drug Use

Beau Kilmer and Rosalie Liccardo Pacula

7.1 Introduction

There is a wealth of evidence suggesting that substance use and poverty are closely connected. Surveys of the homeless show staggering rates of alcohol and drug dependence among this marginalized population (Greene, Ennett, and Ringwalt 1997; Wenzel et al. 2004). Similarly, studies of the household population find that female welfare recipients are twice as likely to report illicit drug use when compared to women with dependent children who did not receive assistance (Jayakody, Danziger, and Pollack 2000; Pollack et al. 2002). Even data from the 2007 National Survey of Drug Use and Health (NSDUH), which generally reflects the household population (although efforts are taken to include individuals living in homeless shelters and other group homes), supports the positive association between illicit drug use and poverty. As shown in figure 7.1, individuals living below the federal poverty line are 50 percent to 100 percent more likely to report use of an illicit drug in the past month or dependence/abuse in the past year than individuals with incomes exceeding 200 percent of the federal poverty threshold. Alcohol dependence or abuse also appears to be slightly higher among those with incomes below the federal poverty threshold, but the results are not statistically significant. Only current use of alcohol in the previous month, which combines casual drinkers with heavy users, shows a negative association between use and poverty.

What is not clear from these data is whether substance use and abuse actually cause poverty. It may be that those experiencing severe poverty

Beau Kilmer is Co-Director of the RAND Drug Policy Research Center. Rosalie Liccardo Pacula is Co-Director of the RAND Drug Policy Research Center and a senior economist at RAND, and a faculty research fellow of the National Bureau of Economic Research.

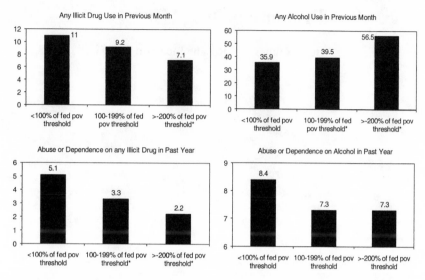

Fig. 7.1   Substance use and dependence by income level, 2007 National Survey on Drug Use or Health (NSDUH)

Notes: Based on online analysis of the 2007 National Survey on Drug Use and Health (N = 55,435). Asterisks (*) after a bar label indicate statistical significance at the 95 percent level. The sample is selected from the civilian, noninstitutionalized population of the United States aged twelve and older, including residents of noninstitutional group quarters such as college dormitories, group homes, shelters, rooming houses, and civilians dwelling on military installations. The federal poverty measure used here was reported in the public use data. According to SAMHSA's codebook, the measure is constructed using information about the family size, number of children, and total family income. The federal threshold is based on data in 2006, as reported by the U.S. Census. Abuse and dependence are based on DSM-IV criteria.

use alcohol and illicit drugs to cope with the stress of being poor. Also, some argue that public programs may foster economic dependency and even encourage substance use by providing resources to support a drug habit and reducing incentives to work (Shaner et al. 1995; Phillips, Christenfeld, and Ryan 1999); however, recent evidence does not fully support this notion (Rosen et al. 2006; Chatterji and Meara 2007).

The limited scientific literature examining a causal connection between poverty and substance use remains unsettled. Most studies examining the topic examine the contemporaneous relationship between substance use and labor market participation and/or current earnings, and the results are generally mixed. Part of the problem is that substance use can influence both earnings and labor market participation indirectly through health, education, marriage and fertility, and job experience (e.g., Kandel, Chen, and Gill 1995; Kaestner 1999; Fergusson, Horwood, and Swain-Campbell 2002; Ringel, Ellickson, and Collins 2006). So it can be difficult to ascertain the full effect of substance use on poverty status in a manner in which causality can be clearly attributed to the use of substances. Importantly, one study finds that reducing drug use among Aid to Families with Dependent Children (AFDC) participants to the level of nonparticipants would actually reduce welfare participation by 3 to 5 percent (Kaestner 1998). This study suggests that current substance use does influence welfare participation.

The question remains, however, whether adolescent substance use contributes to adult poverty. The direct connection is difficult to make given the large number of potentially confounding factors, such as criminal involvement, early pregnancy, and not finishing high school. While a few studies have shown through analyses of selective cohorts that adolescent use of hard drugs during high school is correlated with lower job stability and/or higher unemployment later in life (Kandel et al. 1986; Newcomb and Bentler 1988; Schulenberg et al. 1996; Ellickson, Tucker, and Klein 2003), the samples are typically small, lack a quasi-experimental design, suffer from attrition bias, and only use vague outcomes correlated with poverty rather than poverty status itself.

This chapter considers whether substance use prevention programs targeted at adolescents can influence the probability of experiencing poverty as an adult. Because we are not aware of any studies that have directly addressed this question, we draw conclusions from two different literatures: (a) The literature on the effectiveness of programs intended to prevent substance use among adolescents, and (b) the literature on the effect of substance use on educational attainment and labor market outcomes. The next section begins with a discussion of the etiology of substance use, which helps the reader understand why the timing of substance use initiation and escalation complicates studies attempting to assess the causal effect of this use on later life outcomes. Section 7.3 presents an overview of interventions intended to prevent adolescent substance use, and section 7.4 presents our specific exclusion criteria for the program review we conduct. Section 7.5 reviews the experimental studies of these prevention programs, with a special emphasis on the long-term outcomes. Section 7.6 reviews the literature on how substance use influences labor market outcomes as well as how substance use influences educational attainment. Section 7.7 summarizes these findings and lists some ideas for future research in this field.

7.2   Background on the Etiology of Substance Use

According to information from NSDUH, 29 percent of sixteen- to seventeen-year-old adolescents report use of alcohol in the past thirty days, and approximately one in five (19.4 percent) report binge drinking in the past thirty days (Substance Abuse and Mental Health Services Administration

[SAMHSA] 2008).[1] Rates of illicit drug use are similar to binge drinking rates as 16 percent of youth ages sixteen to seventeen report use of an illicit substance (mostly marijuana) in the past month. Given the illegality of alcohol and drugs for this particular age group, the relatively high use rates are often viewed as troubling. When considered within the context of other decisions made by youths at this age regarding finishing high school, applying to college, and engaging in unprotected sex, the relatively high prevalence rates become even more disconcerting.

Figures 7.2 and 7.3 illustrate the trends in consumption among tenth grade students from the Monitoring the Future Survey since 1991.[2] Figure 7.2 shows that the current use rate for any illicit drug (primarily marijuana) in 2007 is below its peak but still nearly 50 percent higher than it was in 1992. Figure 7.3 shows that daily use of marijuana in 2007 (2.8 percent) is also below its peak value (4.5 percent), but still more than three times as high as its low value in 1991 (0.075 percent). There have also been fluctuations in the prevalence rates for being drunk over this period, but they have not been as dramatic as the fluctuations in marijuana use.

Rates of initiation for the various substances confirm the notion that substance abuse is often a problem that begins at a very early age. Whether discussing cigarettes, alcohol, or illicit substances, substance use typically begins during adolescence for many, peaks during early adulthood (ages eighteen to twenty-five), and then (in the case of illegal substances) diminishes in the late twenties and early thirties (Kandel and Logan 1984; Johnston et al. 2005; SAMHSA 2008). These patterns of use across substances in the general population are amazingly consistent across time, locations, gender, and race/ethnicity, although the age of initiation can differ in important ways across the substances. For example, cigarettes, alcohol, and inhalants are generally substances that are initiated prior to illicit substances and can begin as early as fifth and sixth grade (Chen and Kandel 1995; Johnson and Gerstein 1998). As for "harder" substances, the average age of first use among the household population for marijuana was 17.6 years, for cocaine and ecstasy 20.2 years, for heroin and pain relievers 21.2 years, and for tranquilizers 24.5 years (SAMHSA 2008).

Age of initiation is a particularly important indicator of problematic substance use. Numerous studies have shown that early initiates are at greater risk of serious mental illness, poor schooling outcomes, and dependence (Bray et al. 2000; Patton et al. 2002; Wells, Horwood, and Fergusson 2004;

---

1. Binge drinking refers to the consumption of five or more drinks in a single drinking occasion (i.e., within a few hours). Rates are even higher among eighteen- to twenty-year-olds, where 50.7 percent report drinking in the past thirty days and 35.7 percent report binge drinking in the past month.

2. The Monitoring the Future survey is a school-based survey of students while the NSDUH is a survey of the household population. By focusing on use rates among tenth graders, we hope to capture those who are still required to stay in school due to their age.

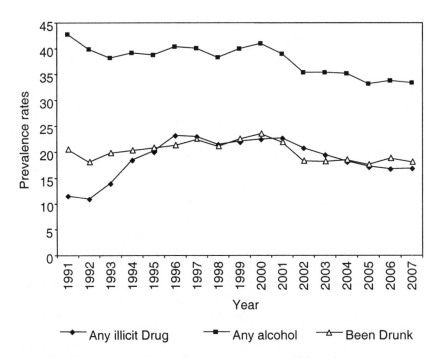

Fig. 7.2   Thirty-day prevalence of substance use among 10th graders
Source: Johnston et al. (2008).

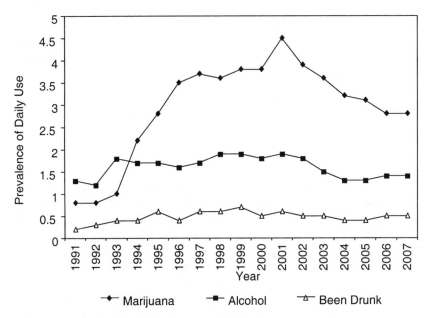

Fig. 7.3   Rates in daily use of substances among 10th graders
Source: Johnston et al. (2008).

Patton et al. 2007). Importantly, these are all outcomes that are also highly associated with poor labor market outcomes and reduced income. In the case of mental health problems and poor schooling outcomes, the evidence regarding the direction of the causal association remains mixed, as many studies show that heavy substance use precedes these outcomes (Hawkins, Catalano, and Miller 1992; Fergusson and Horwood 1997; Coffey et al. 2003). In the case of dependence (which is a diagnosable mental disorder) the causal association is actually clear and descriptive evidence from the NSDUH survey confirms the result. In 2007, 15.9 percent of adults who reported that they initiated alcohol use at fourteen years or younger met DSM-IV criteria for alcohol abuse or dependence, compared to only 3.9 percent of adults who first had alcohol at age eighteen or older. Similarly, 12.9 percent of adults who reported first trying marijuana prior to the age of fifteen met DSM-IV abuse or dependence for an illicit substance, whereas only 2.7 percent of adults who initiated marijuana after age eighteen met the criteria. The link between early initiation and subsequent dependence as well as duration of dependence has held up in multivariate analyses of data from the United States and other countries (Fergusson, Horwood, and Beautrais 2003; Pudney 2004; van Ours 2006; Patton et al. 2007; van Ours and Williams 2007). Thus, programs that can delay initiation past certain critical ages will reduce subsequent dependence on these substances, which may improve future labor market outcomes and reduce poverty.

7.3   Taxonomy of Interventions to Prevent Adolescent Substance Use

Prevention programs are typically divided into three categories: Universal (for the general population), selective (for those at risk or just beginning to use), and indicated (for those already using). When discussed among policymakers, they can also be thought of in terms of the context in which they are provided (school-based prevention, family-based prevention, and community prevention). We focus on this alternative categorization here.

7.3.1   School-Based Programs

The vast majority of middle school students receive some sort of universal school-based prevention designed to reduce short-run and long-run demand for alcohol, tobacco, and illegal drugs (Gottfredson and Wilson 2003). Universal and selective school-based programs have also been developed for elementary and high school students. The more successful programs typically include booster sessions for kids as they progress in school. Decisions about the type of program to adopt are usually made at the school-district level, where officials are often courted by vendors for particular programs. The curriculum of these programs can be classified into three general types: information only, skill building (understanding social influences and learning how to respond to different situations, including resistance training), and normative education (changing perceptions about substance use norms) (Manski, Pepper, and Petrie 2001). Programs are taught by teachers, peers, outside speakers (e.g., police officers, trained health educators), or some combination of these depending on the program. Sessions can occur within classrooms or in auditoriums with the entire student body.

7.3.2   Family-Based Programs

These programs generally focus on families with a child or parent who is currently using drugs or is at high risk of doing so. Interventions can range from psychotherapy to programs intended to improve intra-family communication and promote a discussion about the consequences of consumption. Sessions can occur in a variety of locations, including a physician's/therapist's office or inside the home. It is also important to note that many school-based prevention programs include components intended to extend the discussion about substance use to the home.

7.3.3   Targeted Community-Based Programs

Targeted community-based programs are those that target a specific population within a community that may be at particularly high risk for drug use and abuse. Mentoring programs, like the YMCA and Big Brothers Big Sisters, which are intended to promote healthy relationships by offering positive role models to disadvantaged youth, are one such example.[3] Other types of programs that also fall into this category include specific law enforcement activities (such as neighborhood policing), drug treatment, and criminal justice interventions. While not frequently viewed as prevention, these programs do in fact aim at preventing access to drugs (e.g., preventing street markets in certain neighborhoods in the case of law enforcement) or relapse of drug use among youths who have already initiated (in the case of treatment and criminal justice interventions). A wide range of tools have been used through these alternative systems. For example, criminal justice interventions targeting high-risk youth vary from drug education, to treatment diversion programs, to boot camps.

7.3.4   Universal Community-Based Programs

This category includes programs and policies that provide universal coverage to all individuals living within a community, regardless of their risk of use. Examples of universal programs include mass media campaigns, restrictions on sales to minors, policies raising the price of legal and illicit substances (including general drug enforcement), and advertising restrictions. All of these approaches represent community-wide attempts to prevent the initiation of or reduce use of alcohol, tobacco, and/or illicit drugs.

---

3. The popularity of these programs has grown six-fold in the past ten years and it is now estimated that over 3 million adolescents currently have adult mentors (Rhodes 2008).

Also included in this category of programs are multipronged community-level initiatives intended to provide comprehensive strategies for reducing substance use. While this chapter focuses on specific interventions rather than attempts to combine many interventions, it is important to recognize that the reported effectiveness of an initiative may differ if it is part of a comprehensive strategy.

Two additional types of programs that are frequently referred to in prevention circles have not yet been mentioned: drug and alcohol testing, and brief interventions. These programs can be implemented in a variety of different settings, including schools, health care facilities, places of employment, and community criminal justice settings, and hence do not fall neatly into the aforementioned classification. Drug and alcohol testing involves testing urine, sweat, breath, blood, or hair to identify the use of these substances. It is important to note that simply detecting whether someone is using alcohol or drugs does not influence consumption itself; a change in behavior depends on how that information is used. If an individual believes there will be sanctions associated with testing positive (e.g., exclusion from after-school sports), this could influence use if the expected sanction is larger than the expected benefit of consumption (Becker 1968). If detection forces someone into treatment or into a fruitful discussion with a caring adult, this may also influence future consumption.

Often rooted in motivational interviewing, the goals of brief interventions (BIs) are to help the users identify problem use and enhance their motivation to change this behavior (Tevyaw and Monti 2004). These short interventions (often less than thirty minutes) range considerably in terms of their content, target population, delivery mechanism, setting, and goals (e.g., reduced risk-taking behavior, engagement in treatment); thus, they represent a heterogeneous group of programs. While BI is often associated with primary care settings and emergency rooms, the model has recently been adapted to several different settings for adolescents, including schools, shelters, and teen courts (Baer, Peterson, and Wells 2004; D'Amico and Edelen-Orlando 2007; D'Amico and Stern 2008).

7.4   Inclusion Criteria Used for Review of Prevention Program Effects

Since many policies and programs can be construed as having preventive effects, the list of potential programs to evaluate is quite extensive. Thankfully, many reviews and meta-analyses of a variety of prevention programs already exist (e.g., Manski, Pepper, and Petrie 2001; Caulkins et al. 2002; Gottfredson and Wilson 2003; Faggiano et al. 2005; Gates et al. 2006). Most conclude that skills-based prevention programs (in schools or elsewhere) are effective at deterring early-stage drug use, by delaying initiation and reducing the frequency of tobacco, alcohol, and marijuana use among young adolescents during the period in which the youth are engaged in the programs, but the effect sizes are small (Manski, Pepper, and Petrie 2001; Faggiano et al. 2005). More importantly, few studies provide evidence of sustained effects after the programs end (Manski, Pepper, and Petrie 2001; Caulkins et al. 2002; Faggiano et al. 2005). Even fewer are independently evaluated in terms of their long-term effects. Indeed, a recent National Research Council (NRC) panel was quite pessimistic when summarizing their review of the prevention literature, stating:

> At least 20 reviews and meta-analyses of drug prevention programs were published during the 1980s and 1990s. The most recent of these generally conclude that substance abuse prevention efforts are 'effective' for preventing substance use, in the sense that the studies reviewed report statistically significant differences between subjects receiving and not receiving the preventive intervention on some measure of substance use, at least immediately following the termination of the prevention activity, and in rare cases months or years beyond that point. However, certain practices in the reporting of original research and in the summaries of these findings have tended to overstate the effectiveness of prevention activities. (Manski, Pepper, and Petrie 2001, 213)

Because we are interested in considering whether drug prevention programs can be used as a means of reducing adult poverty, we are particularly interested in understanding whether drug prevention can result in either (a) sustained reductions in substance use, or (b) delayed initiation past the end of the program. Either of these outcomes might then translate into positive schooling and labor market outcomes, which should reduce the likelihood of experiencing poverty as an adult. We therefore limit our review of adolescent prevention programs to those that meet the following three criteria: (a) they have been evaluated using a randomized-controlled trial, thereby increasing the reliability of findings even if conducted by the developer of the program; (b) they include follow-up information related to substance use at least twelve months after the end of the program; and (c) they were conducted within the United States. To identify programs included here, we conducted our own literature review and drew on reviews by Skara and Sussman (2003); Foxcroft et al. (2003); Faggiano et al. (2005); Gates et al. (2006); and D'Amico and Stern (2008).

Application of these inclusion criteria means that some prevention programs are not considered. In particular, law enforcement strategies are excluded as most are not rigorously analyzed with a focus on longer-term outcomes. We similarly do not include brief interventions as we are unaware of studies examining the long-term outcomes from these programs for adolescents. Interventions that were not generally considered drug prevention (e.g., Head Start) are also not included. The notable exception is Big Brothers Big Sisters, which has been evaluated using a large sample, randomized design, long-term follow-up, and has demonstrated sustained effects on substance use over time.[4] We do not consider multicomponent community-level prevention since is it is extremely difficult to identify the main mechanism driving the change (the message itself, parental involvement, accountability, etc.). Finally, as the focus of this chapter is on more traditional prevention programs, we do not review the extensive literature on treatment programs. Readers interested in reviews of the treatment literature should consult Manski, Pepper, and Petrie (2001, chapter 8); Aos et al. (2006); and the National Institute on Drug Abuse (2009).

Most program evaluations considered in this chapter do not include outcome information related to education and adult employment because (a) they are usually not the primary outcomes of interest, and (b) they tend to focus on short-term outcomes. When available, we do report this information. We also include a summary of the long-term effects of one nonexperimental program, the Seattle Social Development Program, since it includes rich information on substance use as well as on work and school outcomes.

7.5   Review of the Long-Term Effects of Prevention

7.5.1   School-Based Programs

Table 7.1 presents the results from long-term evaluations of randomized controlled prevention experiments with schools or students. The first column includes the name of the program and the second column includes information about grades covered, number of sessions, and theoretical approach of the program.[5] All programs included in the table have a follow-up evaluation that takes place at least one year after the prevention program ended. For programs that included multiple follow-ups (i.e., "waves"), we only present the information from the last wave available since we are primarily interested in whether program effects can be sustained over time.[6]

There is no evidence suggesting that school-based prevention programs have any long-term effect (> five years) on marijuana use. While some of these programs do appear to have an impact several months after the intervention (e.g., Adolescent Alcohol Prevention Trial [AAPT], ALERT), the six-year follow-up for ALERT and Life Skills as well as the four/five-year follow-up for Project Towards No Drug Use (TND) showed no effect on marijuana use. An independent evaluation of the Project ALERT curriculum delivered to students in eight Pennsylvania middle schools by outside

---

4. The Head Start program is evaluated for its long-term effects on poverty in another chapter in this monograph.

5. We heavily rely on Skara and Sussman (2003) for their descriptions of the program approach (e.g., comprehensive social influences, resistance education) and refer readers to their review for more specific details on many of the programs listed in table 7.1.

6. The one exception is AAPT, where the five-year evaluation did not include information about marijuana use; thus we include information from the one-year follow-up (Hansen and Graham 1991).

program leaders demonstrated no effects of the curriculum on substance use at the twelve-month follow-up (St. Pierre et al. 2005). However, the authors admit that lack of an effect may be attributable to differences in how the program was administered (particularly the use of outside program leaders rather than teachers familiar with the students). The study raises important questions regarding the reliability of prevention programs when diffused broadly and the importance of independent evaluations of the programs. Because no other prevention programs were similarly evaluated under alternative conditions by independent evaluators, we do not dismiss the results of Project ALERT vis-à-vis the other program effects. Finally, while Project Towards No Drug Use did find a small effect of the program on hard drug use at the four- or five-year evaluation, the authors note that this effect should be interpreted cautiously because they did not find a sustained program effect in years two and three, suggesting that their result in waves 4 and 5 might only apply to the selective sample that remained in the study over the full period (i.e., "attrition bias").

The effect of these programs on long-term alcohol use is slightly better. The evaluation of Life Skills found no effect on frequency of use, but that it did reduce the probability of being drunk in the previous thirty days at the six-year follow-up. An evaluation of the Adolescent Alcohol Prevention Trial (AAPT) using five waves of data and latent growth curve modeling produced more promising results (Taylor et al. 2000). The analysis found that the seventh grade program had a beneficial effect on lifetime alcohol use, recent alcohol use, and lifetime drunkenness through the eleventh grade. The authors also found that those randomly assigned to the normative education program had lower rates of growth for self-reported alcohol use. The long-term evaluations of ALERT and TND found no effects on alcohol.

The results with respect to smoking appear to be very program-specific. The Hutchinson Smoking Prevention Program is based on the social influence model and includes sixty-five sessions over the course of fourth to tenth grades (Peterson et al. 2000). The authors were able to follow-up with 94 percent of the original sample at two years after high school and found that the program had no effect on daily smoking or other smoking outcomes. Projects ALERT and TND also did not find any long-term effects of prevention on smoking behaviors; however, both of these programs had lower retention rates (57 percent and 46 percent, respectively) that may have influenced these results.

The six-year wave of Know Your Body (two hours per week of teacher instruction for every school week from fourth through ninth grades; 384 total sessions) found that 13.1 percent of the control group initiated use in ninth grade, compared to 3.1 percent of those assigned to the intervention (Walter, Vaughan, and Wynder 1989). However, it should be noted that they were only followed up with 65 percent of those surveyed at baseline and the evaluation was conducted at the end of the program (ninth grade). Thus,

Table 7.1   **Long-term results of experimental evaluations of school-based prevention programs in the United States**

Study	Program description	Evaluation design and sample
Adolescent Alcohol Prevention Trial (Taylor et al. 2000; Hansen and Graham 1991)	Ten sessions in 7th grade; comprehensive social influences.	Students in twelve schools in Los Angeles were randomly assigned to one of four prevention conditions (by school). Five waves of longitudinal data were obtained for 33.5% of the 3,027 students (through 11th grade). Authors use structural equation modeling to address data missing from waves 2–5.
D.A.R.E. (Perry et al. 2003)	Ten sessions in 7th grade; resistance education is taught by a police officer in the classroom.	Twenty-four middle schools in Minnesota were randomly assigned to D.A.R.E., D.A.R.E. Plus, or a delayed program. There were 6,237 students at baseline, and 84% were surveyed at the one-year follow-up. Used growth curve models to account for missing data.
D.A.R.E. Plus (Perry et al. 2003)	D.A.R.E., plus four sessions of a peer-led program, extra-curricular activities, and neighborhood action teams.	
Hutchinson Smoking Prevention Program (Peterson et al. 2000)	Sixty-five sessions between 4th and 10th grades; comprehensive social influences.	Forty school districts in Washington were randomly assigned to intervention or control condition. The study started with 8,388 3rd grade students who were followed to two years after high school (94% follow-up).
Keeping it R.E.A.L. (Hecht et al. 2003)	Ten sessions in middle school (with booster activities and advertising); resistance and life skills.	Thirty-five school districts were randomly assigned to intervention or control condition (n = 6,035 respondents; used multiple imputation to address attrition and missing values). Final wave of interviews was conducted fourteen months postintervention.
Know Your Body (Walter, Vaughan, and Wynder 1989)	Two hours of instruction each week during the school year from 4th to 9th grade; normative and stress management.	Fifteen schools in the vicinity of New York City were assigned to either an intervention or a nonintervention group (n = 1,105 eligible children, 911 participated at baseline, and 593 were interviewed at six years).
Life Skills Program (Botvin et al. 1995)	Fifteen sessions in 7th grade (boosters in 8th and 9th); cognitive behavioral resistance skills.	Fifty-six schools were randomly assigned to intervention or control; 3,597 12th grade students represented 60.61% of the initial 7th-grade sample.
Life Skills Program (Botvin et al. 2001)	Fifteen sessions in 7th grade (boosters in 8th); cognitive behavioral resistance skills.	Twenty-nine New York City schools were randomized to receive the intervention or be in the control group; 5,222 students (predominantly minority) participated in the study, and 69% provided data at the one-year follow-up.

Alcohol use	Tobacco use	Illegal drug use
"Students receiving the normative education program had significantly lower average levels of reported cigarette and alcohol use, lower rates of growth for reported cigarette and alcohol use, and less deceleration of reported levels of cigarette and alcohol use as compared with the control group (information about consequences of use)."		Analyses based on five waves of data did not discuss illegal drug use. At one-year follow-up, normative education group demonstrated lower rates of recent marijuana use (2.2% vs. 6.2%; p < 0.001).

No significant differences in outcomes between students assigned to D.A.R.E. and students assigned to the control condition.

"Among boys, those in the D.A.R.E. Plus schools were less likely than those in the control schools to show increases in alcohol use behavior and intentions, past year or past month alcohol use, tobacco use behavior and intentions, multidrug use behavior and intentions, and victimization" (p < 0.05). There were no significant effects for girls.

Alcohol use	Tobacco use	Illegal drug use
	"No significant difference in prevalence of daily smoking was found between students in the control and experimental districts . . . Moreover, no intervention impact was observed for other smoking outcomes, such as extent of current smoking or cumulative amount smoked, or in *a priori* specified variables, such as family risk for smoking."	
Mean difference in past month use between intervention and control after accounting for baseline level: –0.232 (p < 0.001).	Mean difference in past month use between intervention and control after accounting for baseline level: no significant difference.	Mean difference in past marijuana month use between intervention and control after accounting for baseline level: –0.175 (p < 0.001).
	13.1% of control group had initiated use in 9th grade compared to 3.1% of those assigned to the intervention (P < 0.005).	
The intervention did not influence frequency of use at the six-year follow-up, but it did reduce the probability of being drunk (40% vs. 34, p < 0.05; vs. 0.33, p < 0.01).	The intervention reduced past-week smoking (33% vs. 27, p < 0.05; vs. 0.26 p < 0.01) and past-month smoking (27% vs. 23, p < 0.05; vs. 0.21 p < 0.05).	Had no effect on marijuana use at the six-year follow-up.

The authors measure substance use on a variety of scales, with 1 = "Never" or "I don't drink," and a maximum ranging from 6–11, depending on the measure. The mean scores for treatment and control groups both hovered between 1 and 2. The scores for the control group were marginally higher and statistically significant for the following measures: smoking frequency*, smoking quantity**, drinking frequency**, drunkenness frequency*, drinking quantity**, inhalant frequency*; p ≤ 0.05*; p ≤ 0.01**. There was no statistically significant difference for marijuana frequency or getting "high" frequency.

(*continued*)

Table 7.1 (continued)

Study	Program description	Evaluation design and sample
Project ALERT (Ellickson, Bell, and McGuigan 1993)	Eight sessions in 7th grade (boosters in 8th grade); social influence model—resistance skills training curriculum.	Thirty schools in California and Oregon were randomly assigned to three conditions: ALERT taught by health educators, ALERT taught by health educators with help from students, and a control; ~4,000 students were assessed in 7th grade, and six times thereafter through grade 12. The analysis sample at grade 12 constitutes 57% of baseline sample.
Project ALERT Plus (Ellickson et al. 2003)	Eleven sessions in 7th grade (boosters in 8th grade); social influence model—resistance skills training curriculum.	Fifty-five middle schools in North Dakota were randomly assigned to ALERT, ALERT Plus (with high school booster sessions), or control. Of the 5,412 students enrolled in these schools, 4,689 completed baseline survey and 4,276 completed follow-up at eighteen months after baseline.
Project ALERT (St. Pierre et al. 2005)	Eleven sessions in 7th grade (three boosters in 8th grade); social influence model—resistance skills training curriculum.	Eight schools in Pennsylvania randomly assigned two 7th-grade classrooms to each of three conditions: (1) adult-led Project ALERT; (2) adult-led, teen-assisted Project ALERT; and (3) control. Participants were recruited before 7th grade and followed-up through 9th grade. There were 1,649 participants, and 88% completed the questionnaire in at least four out of five waves.
Project SHOUT (Elder et al. 1993; Eckhardt, Woodruff, and Elder 1997)	Eighteen sessions in 7th and 8th grade (boosters in 9th and 11th grade); comprehensive social influence.	Twenty-two schools in San Diego were randomly assigned to intervention or control condition. There were 3,655 participants, and 2,688 (73%) were available to be surveyed at the end of 9th grade.
Project toward No Tobacco Use (Dent et al., 1995)	Ten sessions in 7th grade (one booster in 8th grade); comprehensive social influence.	Forty-eight schools were randomly assigned to the intervention or control group (N = 6,716); 52% of the sample was interviewed at the twenty-four-month follow-up.
Project towards No Drug Use (Sun et al. 2006)	Twelve sessions in one year of high school; health motivation, social skills, and decision making curriculum.	Twenty-one schools were randomly assigned to control, classroom only, or classroom + (SAC). Of 1,578 baseline subjects, four–five-year follow-up data were available for 46%.
Start Taking Alcohol Risks Seriously (Werch et al. 2003)	One session in 6th grade and one in 7th grade. Materials sent to home. Second session is with nurse.	650 sixth-grade students were randomly assigned to the intervention or a minimal intervention control (a booklet to read at school).

Source: Heavily based on table 4 in Skara and Sussman (2003).

Alcohol use	Tobacco use	Illegal drug use

At the six-year follow-up: "Once the lessons stopped, the program's effects on drug use stopped. Effects on cognitive risk factors persisted for a long time (many through grade 10), but were not sufficient to produce corresponding reductions in use" (856).

ALERT Plus did not influence alcohol initiation or current use, but it did lead to lower alcohol misuse scores (p < 0.05), and students were less likely to engage in drinking that resulted in negative consequences (p < 0.04).

ALERT Plus reduced cigarette initiation by 19% (p < 0.01) and past-month smoking by 23% (p < 0.01).

ALERT Plus reduced marijuana initiation by 24% (p < 0.01).

Analyses failed to yield any positive effects for substance use or mediators for use in the adult or teen-assisted delivery of the curriculum.

"At the end of the third year, the prevalence of tobacco use within the past month was 14.2% among the intervention students and 22.2% among the controls . . ." (p < 0.001).

Weekly cigarette use increased 9% for controls and 5% for those assigned to intervention (p < 0.05). Trial cigarette use increased 23% for controls and 16% for intervention (p < 0.05).

"[S]ignificant reductions were not found for 30-day use of cigarettes, alcohol, or marijuana use" (191).

Adjusted mean levels of 30-day hard drug use at 4/5 year follow-up: control (1.51%); class (0.66%), SAC (0.3%), p = 0.02. The authors note that this effect was evident at one-year follow-up, but not at the two–three-year follow-up.

At the one-year follow-up: "While mean alcohol consumption on all four measures of use was lower for neighborhood students receiving the intervention as compared to the control condition, these differences were not significant."

it is unclear whether these effects persist after the program is over and how attrition influences the results. The six-year Life Skills evaluation included 61 percent of the initial seventh-grade sample and also found that it decreased smoking. Finally, AAPT noted a significant effect on cigarette use for those receiving the normative education program.

There is a long-term evaluation that did not utilize a randomized controlled design that should be mentioned because it directly assessed the impact of the intervention on substance use and schooling outcomes. The Seattle Social Development Project focused on teacher training, skill development for students, and parent training. There were three conditions: "Full"—at least one semester of intervention in grades one to four and at least one semester of intervention in grades five to six; "Late"—at least one semester of intervention in grades five to six; and the "Control" received no intervention. Hawkins et al. (2005) were able to follow-up with 94 percent of the participants ($n = 605$) when they were twenty-one years old (nine years after the intervention). While they did not find noticeable effects on substance use,[7] they did find statistically significant effects in terms of functioning at school or work at age twenty-one among the treatment group. The authors attempt to reconcile the contradictory findings by stating that "it is also possible that at twenty-one years of age, the use of various substances is relatively normative, even among those progressing positively in the domains of school and work" (Hawkins et al. 2005; 30). If this argument is correct, it may be the case that the programs highlighted in table 7.1 do influence human capital development even if they have no noticeable long-term effect on substance use.

It is also important to acknowledge that even if these school-based prevention programs do not have a long-term effect on consumption, the fact that they delay initiation of particular substances for some students may influence subsequent educational attainment and labor market outcomes. Using two-to-three year follow-up data from a variety of middle school-based prevention evaluations (both randomized and nonrandomized), Caulkins et al. (2002) calculated the initiation effects of a composite, hypothetical "best practice" prevention program on alcohol, tobacco, and marijuana use.[8] They estimate that a 1 percent reduction in substance use observed twelve months after the end of a good prevention program could generate anywhere from a 14 to 51 percent reduction in lifetime quantity consumed of that substance, depending on the substance targeted by the prevention program. Even if the true effect on initiation is indeed the lower bound, this is not negligible.

7. Specifically, they note that the full-intervention group participants "were also less likely to have used a substance in the recent past (alcohol or tobacco in the past month or any other illicit drug in the past year), but this finding did not achieve statistical significance ($p = 0.09$). Subsequent analyses examining different substances separately found no significant effects of the full- or the late-intervention condition, compared with controls, for past month alcohol or tobacco use or for past year marijuana or other illicit drug use" (29).

8. The authors considered four approaches for generating these ranges and fully acknowledge the limitations.

A further point to consider about these programs is that school-based drug prevention programs are relatively inexpensive to implement on a per child basis. A study by Aos et al. (2004) reports the cost of a variety of school-based substance abuse prevention programs and compares these program costs to that of a variety of general prevention programs, community initiatives, and mentoring programs. They show that the per child cost of many of the school-based programs just mentioned range from a low of ~$5 dollars per child (for Project ALERT and TNT, respectively) to a high of only $112 (for DARE).[9] In all cases, however, the costs exclude the cost of teachers' time spent training and preparing lessons, as well as the opportunity cost of the time that could have been used teaching alternative subjects. Most of the school-based programs are on the lower end of the range, with Life Skills and Start Taking Alcohol Risk Seriously (STARS) costing $33 and $20, respectively. The one exception was the Seattle Social Development project, for which they report a per child cost of $5,172, but these program costs include teacher training and parent training on top of the interventions planned in early and later grades.

The fact that the average cost per child of implementing these programs is so low means that the programs do not have to have very large outcome effects in order to have a benefit-cost ratio greater than one. Caulkins et al. (2002) point out in their assessment of an ideal school-based drug prevention program that 95 percent of the time the benefits are more than twice the cost of actually implementing the program on a per child basis, even when programs are assumed to have small effects. Of course, the fact that something creates cost savings does not mean that it is desirable to implement, as it depends on several factors, including the relative cost-effectiveness of other approaches that could be used to achieve the same end.

7.5.2   Family-Based Programs

As previously noted, many prevention programs include a school and home component. The latter can be as passive as sending anti-drug materials home to something as active as including parent training on how to talk to adolescents about substance use. This section focuses on those interventions that primarily focus on the family, and like the earlier section, we focus on the latest wave of outcome data.

The program that receives the most attention in the review literature is the Iowa Strengthening Families Program (ISFP). The program lasts seven weeks, with parents and students meeting for two hours per week with trained program staff. In the first hour the parents and students are separated for their sessions, and in the second hour they are all brought together. Sessions primarily focus on parenting skills, peer resistance, and communication skills. Schools were randomly assigned to ISFP or a minimal contact control condition and "nonlinear growth curve analyses were

9. Aos et al. (2004) report all figures in 2003 dollars and we converted them to 2007 dollars.

conducted with school-level outcome variables aggregated over the available respondents in each school . . ." (Spoth et al. 2004). Analyses based on the six-year follow-up (for students with a data available at all waves, case-wise deletion was used for those missing any information) found that time to alcohol use without parental permission, drunkenness, and cigarette use was significantly longer for those assigned to ISFP ($p < 0.05$).

As part of the evaluation, Spoth et al. (2004) also randomly assigned some schools to a related program called Preparing for the Drug Free Years (PDFY), which primarily focuses on the parents separately and includes fewer sessions. Compared to the same control group, there was no difference in time to initiation for any of the substances for those assigned to PDFY, but there was a statistically significant difference in growth rates for tobacco use ($p < 0.05$).

The Focus on the Family program is intended to prevent substance use for children of heavy drug users in treatment (Catalano et al. 1999). The program included thirty-three hours of parental skills training and nine months of home-based case management. A total of 140 adult methadone patients (and their 178 children, ranging from three to fourteen years) were recruited and either assigned to the intervention or a no-intervention control. The program did not have much of an effect on the children at the one-year follow-up interview, but it did influence parental drug use.

Family-based programs are generally more expensive per youth than school-based prevention programs because they involve more people and management. For example, Aos et al. (2004) report that the average cost per youth of the Iowa Strengthening Families Program was $959, which is substantially higher then the school-based prevention programs mentioned before, but lower in cost than the Seattle Social Development Project, which included a school and family component.

7.5.3   Community-Based Programs

In addition to the benefits discussed in chapter 5, participation in the Big Brothers Big Sisters (BBBS) mentoring program has the effect of reducing and/or delaying initiation of substance use. Grossman and Tierny (1998) report that the adolescents assigned to the treatment condition were 46 percent less likely to initiate drug use and 27 percent less likely to initiate alcohol use during the eighteen-month follow-up period (information was not reported for the intensity of use). There are at least two reasons to believe that this study may underestimate the effects of mentoring. First, the authors present intent-to-treat results and nearly 20 percent of the treatment group was not matched to a mentor. Second, it is not clear whether those in the control group were mentored somewhere else, thus possibly diluting the treatment effect.

An experimental evaluation of a related BBBS mentoring program based in schools did not yield the same results (Herrara et al. 2007). Utilizing a similar waiting list approach with over 1,000 students in ten sites across the country, the study found only one major difference between the control and treatment groups at the fifteen-month follow-up: those in the treatment group were less likely to skip school and more confident that they would attend and complete college.[10] They attribute the lack of effect to attrition from the mentoring (many students switched schools) and noted that the mentors did not have as much time to cultivate relationships as they did in the previous BBBS community intervention.

Aos et al. (2004) estimate that the average cost of BBBS to taxpayers is $1,392 per youth participant; however, this does not include the opportunity costs associated with being a mentor or a mentee. We refer readers to chapter 5 of this volume for a more detailed discussion of these costs and note that the benefits of the community-based BBBS extend beyond a decrease in the initiation substance use.

Another important community-wide prevention strategy is mass media campaigns. Studies have shown these campaigns to be effective at deterring cigarette smoking, binge drinking, and selected drug use in small communities, particularly when coupled with other prevention strategies (Flynn et al. 1994, 1997; Flay 2000; Pentz 2003). However, a careful multiyear evaluation of the National Youth Anti-Drug Campaign, a national campaign funded by the Office of National Drug Control Policy (ONDCP) to prevent kids from using illegal substances, found that the campaign had absolutely no impact on marijuana use among youth (Hornik, Maklan, Cadell, Barmada, Jacobsohn, and Henderson 2003; Hornik, Maklan, Cadell, Barmada, Jacobsohn, and Prado 2003). This was consistent with results obtained from another group of researchers examining the effects of weekly exposure to media ads from the campaign on marijuana use in a single Midwestern state (Longshore, Ghosh-Dastidar, and Ellickson 2006). What is interesting about this latter study is that the researchers found that youth who also received the ALERT Plus drug prevention program, a universal classroom-based social influences and resistance training program, did report lower past-month marijuana use than adolescents exposed to either alone (Longshore, Ghosh-Dastidar, and Ellickson 2006). Thus, there appeared to be synergistic effects of these two programs.

7.5.4   Drug Testing

There are very few studies of the effectiveness of student drug testing (MacCoun 2007; Levy 2009), and fewer still that employ a randomized design. We are aware of only one study using a randomized design to evaluate the effects of student drug testing in schools (Goldberg et al. 2007).

---

10. Specifically, they note: "We did not see benefits in any of the out-of-school areas we examined, including drug and alcohol use, misconduct outside of school, relationships with parents and peers, and self-esteem . . ." (iv).

The researchers recruited eleven schools near Portland that wanted to start student athlete drug-testing programs. Five of these schools were randomly assigned to implement testing programs and the other six were assigned to defer implementation until the study was completed (653 student athletes in testing schools and 743 student athletes in the deferred testing schools). Substance use was serially assessed with voluntary, confidential questionnaires. The results of the two-year prospective study were mixed: testing did not influence past-month drug use among student athletes, but "prior year drug use was reduced in two of four follow-up self reports, and a combination of drug and alcohol use was reduced at two assessments as well" (421). Even though this study used a randomized design, we cannot draw strong conclusions from the results for at least three reasons: (a) five of the eleven schools were removed from the study after originally agreeing to participate and being selected; (b) two of the remaining schools altered their testing programs during the study; and (c) those schools that remained in the sample experienced high attrition among the student athletes.[11]

Another drug testing experiment conducted by the California Youth Authority (CYA) also generated inconclusive results. Nearly 2,000 young parolees (twelve to twenty-four years old, mean nineteen years) were randomly assigned to one of five different levels of testing (including no testing), and graduated sanctions were supposed to be applied to those testing positive (Haapanen and Britton 2002). Those assigned to higher levels of testing were more likely to be arrested for a violent crime and less likely to have a "good" parole outcome at twenty-four months postrelease (Haapanen and Britton 2002). The study could not address the causal effect on drug use since self-reported drug use information was not collected, although the authors noted that parolees assigned to lower levels of testing were more likely to test positive.

A follow-up analysis of this experiment focusing on human capital outcomes and accounting for noncompliance found that parolees randomly assigned to testing were more likely to be employed or in school in the month after being released from prison, with the effect being large for Hispanics and nonexistent for blacks (Kilmer 2008). The lack of long-run employment and schooling data for these parolees makes it difficult to reconcile these findings, but it suggests we have more to learn about the heterogeneous and dynamic effects of drug testing in criminal justice settings.

Drug testing costs vary greatly depending on the testing method, the substances being tested, and whether the entity purchasing the test receives a quantity discount. For example, urine tests conducted by criminal justice

---

11. An important study by Yamaguchi, Johnston, and O'Malley (2003) using a quasi-experimental design to examine whether students who attended schools that drug tested students reported less drug use found no significant relationship. The study did not account for the method for drug testing (random or for "just cause"), and hence the results may be biased toward zero because of grouping these two types of drug testing together.

agencies can cost less than $2 per test (with a quantity discount) while over-the-counter hair tests can exceed $60. Full cost evaluations of testing programs should also include the costs associated with addressing positive tests (e.g., additional probation supervision, admission to a treatment program, incarceration).

7.6   Review of the Literature on Substance Use, Educational Attainment, and Labor Market Outcomes

Considerable attention has been given by social scientists to the impact of substance use on worker productivity and labor market outcomes. Substance use is believed to diminish a worker's productivity and lead to poor labor market outcomes for several reasons.[12] First, it may delay initiation into the workforce, thereby reducing experience and human capital accumulation associated with on-the-job training (Johnson and Herring 1989). Second, it may decrease the probability of being employed which, again, may interfere with human capital accumulation (Gill and Michaels 1992; Register and Williams 1992). Third, it may increase absenteeism, which directly influences the productivity of not only the worker himself, but also those individuals who work with him (French, Zarkin, and Dunlap 1998). Finally, substance abuse may reduce an individual's productivity at the job, which should translate directly into lower wages if wages are indeed a good indicator of the worker's marginal productivity.

Empirical studies that analyze the direct effect of substance use and abuse on earnings have generated very mixed findings. Even after accounting for the endogeneity of substance use, earnings of substance users are found to be higher by some researchers (Kaestner 1991; Gill and Michaels 1992; Register and Williams 1992; French and Zarkin 1995; Zarkin et al. 1998), and lower by others (Mullahy and Sindelar 1993; Kenkel and Ribar 1994; Burgess and Propper 1998). The lack of a robust finding has led many economists to focus on other measures of a worker's productivity, such as the probability of being employed or unemployed (Kandel and Davies 1990; Register and Williams 1992). Here, too, the evidence is mixed. Using the 1984 and 1985 waves of the National Longitudinal Surveys of Youth (NLSY), Kandel and Davies (1990) find that use of marijuana and cocaine in the past year is positively associated with the total number of weeks unemployed. However, Register and Williams (1992) find, using data from the 1984 wave of the NLSY, that use of marijuana on the job in the past year and long-term use of marijuana both have a positive impact on the probability

12. There is also research examining whether income-support programs encourage substance use by providing resources to support a drug habit, and the evidence is mixed (Shaner et al. 1995; Phillips, Christenfeld, and Ryan 1999; Rosen et al. 2006; Chatterji and Meara 2007).

of being employed. General use of marijuana, on the other hand, did lower the probability of being employed.

The lack of a robust finding is driven by a number of factors. First, studies examine the impact of substance use on earnings and labor market outcomes for populations of varying ages. While some studies focus on young adults (Kandel and Yamaguchi 1987), others focus on mature young adults (Kandel and Davies 1990; Register and Williams 1992), while others focus on the full adult population (Zarkin et al. 1998). It is quite possible that the nature of the relationship between substance use and labor market outcomes changes over the life cycle as job market experience and job tenure begin to dominate the effects of other individual determinants of labor market outcomes. Indeed, a few studies have explicitly considered this fact and noted the differential effects of substance use on wages conditional upon age (Mullahy and Sindelar 1993; French and Zarkin 1995), but it is not a factor that is consistently considered in the literature.

A second factor complicating the interpretation of findings from the literature is the inconsistent treatment of indirect mechanisms through which substance abuse could impact earnings; for example, through educational attainment, health, fertility, and occupational choice. Given that these inputs have been established as important determinants of labor market participation and wages (Becker 1964; Mincer 1970; Willis and Rosen 1979), and that there are strong findings in the literature about associations with each of these (Cook and Moore 1993; Mullahy and Sindelar 1994; Kenkel and Wang 1998; Bray et al. 2000; Chatterji 2006), it is important to consider whether analyses looking at the impact of substance abuse on earnings consider the indirect effects as well.

Finally, the literature is inconsistent in terms of its definition of substance use. "Current" use has been defined as daily use (Kandel and Yamaguchi 1987), use in the past month (Cook and Moore 1993; Chatterji 2006), and use in the past year (Kandel and Davies 1990; Register and Williams 1992; Mullahy and Sindelar 1993). A few studies attempt to differentiate the effects of chronic use from casual use (Kenkel and Ribar 1994; Roebuck, French, and Dennis 2004), or proxy chronic use with measures of early initiation (Bray et al. 2000; Ringel, Ellickson, and Collins 2006). Given all the different ways that substance use can be operationalized, with some representing more chronic or persistent use while others represent more casual use, it is not surprising that findings vary across the studies.

It is clear that the relationship between substance use and abuse and labor market outcomes is dynamic and can be potentially influenced by the relationship between early substance use and human capital production. The potential for reverse causality is also real. Just as substance use and abuse can lead to job separations and other poor labor market outcomes, job separations may lead to increased substance use and abuse. Statistical methods used to date to try to separate out these two effects include event history analysis (e.g., Kandel and Yamaguchi 1987; Ringel, Ellickson, and Collins 2006), fixed-effects modeling (Cook and Moore 1993; Kaestner 1994a, 1994b; Kenkel and Ribar 1994), and instrumental variable (IV) techniques (e.g., Bray et al. 2000). The problem, however, is not purely statistical in nature. At least some of the problem stems from how and when substance use is measured.

In table 7.2, we highlight rigorous studies that attempt to address issues relevant for understanding the link between substance use and employment, earnings, and schooling. The table is far from exhaustive, as there are many more studies that have been done in this area. However, these particular studies represent major steps forward in the literature in attempting to deal with the statistical and measurement problems so as to get cleaner estimates of the causal associations.

The top of table 7.2 focuses on studies examining the relationship between substance use and employment or earnings. For most of these studies, the major issue has been dealing with the simultaneity of current substance use and current labor market outcomes. The main approach for dealing with the problem is to employ IV methods. The difficulty comes in trying to identify appropriate instruments, and the particular choice of instruments (religiosity, family stability, nonearned income, or illegal acts) used in the first few studies could all be viewed as problematic.[13] The Register and Williams (1992) study, however, remains particularly insightful because it was the first (and, as far as we know, only) study that differentiated the effects of on-the-job substance use from off-the-job substance use. Indeed, they find that in the case of marijuana, off-the-job use was positively associated with earnings, while they find on-the-job use and long-term use to be associated with lower wages. They interpret their results as evidence that recreational marijuana use may help reduce stress in a fashion similar to moderate alcohol consumption. However, since current substance use was instrumented, not long-term use, there is still a possibility that simultaneity bias influences some of their findings.

The results from the two Kaestner studies (1994a, 1994b) demonstrate how substance abuse can differentially influence different aspects of labor market outcomes even for the same population being considered. In the first study, for example, Kaestner (1994a) finds a positive effect of cocaine use on earnings for young adult women, but in his second study (Kaestner 1994b) he shows no effect of the same measure of cocaine use on women's hours

13. The robustness of IV methods depends critically on the validity of assumptions regarding the independence (i.e., lack of correlation) between the identifying "instrument" and the primary outcome of interest (labor market outcome or educational attainment, in this instance) except through its affect on substance use. A variable that is believed to be associated with substance use could also be related to labor market outcomes if it picks up on an unobserved character trait that is relevant to both (such as rates of time preference or acceptance of authority). Instruments used in early studies have been called into question in later analyses that included statistical tests of these assumptions.

Table 7.2   Literature on the effects of substance use and abuse (SA) on employment, earnings, and educational attainment

Study	Data	Outcome	SA measure	Methods	SA and other intermediate factors controlled for?	Key insight from study	Effects
				Employment and Earnings			
Register & Williams (1992)	Young (ages eighteen–twenty-six), male workers in the 1984 NLSY	Log annual earnings, hours worked, and probability of employment	Continuous measures of the number of times cocaine and marijuana are used in the past thirty days. Also include long-term use, defined as use eight (five) years for marijuana (cocaine).	Two-stage least square. Identifying instruments include religious affiliation and attendance, divorce status, parental education, and urban status. None are tested for validity or overidentification.	Education, marital status, and health are included as additional controls. Education and marital status are negatively associated with substance use in the first stage.	Cocaine use has no impact on wages or employment. Long-term and on-the-job use of marijuana are negatively related to wages, but off-the-job use is positively associated with wages.	An additional day of off-the-job marijuana use in the past month is associated with a 3% to 5% increase in wages. On-the-job use and long-term use associated with a 73% and 17% reduction in wages, respectively.
Kaestner (1994a)	1984 and 1988 waves of the NLSY79 (sample was twenty-three–thirty-two years old in 1988). Models are estimated separately for men and women.	Log annual earnings	Measures of lifetime and past thirty day frequency of use of cocaine and marijuana. Heavy use measures based on lifetime frequency of use.	Both cross-sectional and panel (fixed effects) estimates are obtained using two-stage least square estimation. Identifying variables include frequency of religious attendance and nonearned income.	Education, experience, health status, and marital status are all included.	No statistically significant association was found between marijuana and log wages in the panel data analysis for males or females. For cocaine, the panel data models show a positive effect of lifetime frequency of use on log wages for females only (significant at 10% level). Women who never use cocaine have significantly higher wages in panel analysis.	A one-unit increase in cocaine use increases wages for women between 28% (cross-sectional model) and 75% (fixed-effect model).

Study	Data	Dependent variable	Substance use measure	Methods	Covariates	Results	Conclusion
Kaestner (1994b)	1984 and 1988 waves of the NLSY79 (sample was twenty-three–thirty-two years old in 1988). Models are estimated separately for men and women.	Usual number of hours worked in the past twelve months.	Measures of lifetime frequency of use of cocaine and marijuana were examined. Heavy use measures based on lifetime frequency of use were also constructed.	Cross-sectional and panel estimates obtained using two-stage least squares. Identifying variables include frequency of religious attendance and number of illegal acts committed prior to 1980.	Education, experience, and health status are all included. Panel data models are estimated separately by marital status.	The parameter estimates of the effect of illicit drug use were imprecisely estimated and had different signs depending on measure of drug use and the sample evaluated.	No effect.
Kenkel and Ribar (1994)	NLSY 1979 cohort. Separate analyses were done for men and women.	Earnings, labor market hours	Four alternative measures of problem drinking, including DSM-III criteria for abuse, DSM-III criteria for dependence, binge drinking in the past thirty days, and number of days they had a drink.	OLS baseline estimates, individual- and sibling-fixed effects models, and IV models. IV models use price of beer and percentage of state population living in dry counties as identifying instruments.	Marital status, schooling, AFQT IQ test, and health problem indicators that could interfere with work.	When individual fixed effects models are estimated, they find that problem alcohol use is associated with a 1.3% increase in earnings for men and a 1.5% increase for women. When IV methods are used, they find large but statistically insignificant effects of problem drinking on income for males, but large positive and statistically significant effects of problem drinking on females' labor supply.	Given the inconsistent results using alternative methods for handling the problem, no general conclusion drawn.

(continued)

Table 7.2 (continued)

Study	Data	Outcome	SA measure	Methods	SA and other intermediate factors controlled for?	Key insight from study	Effects
Mullahy and Sindelar (1996)	Alcohol Supplement of the 1988 National Health Interview Survey, individuals between twenty-five–fifty-nine years of age. Models for men and women estimated separately.	Employed, unemployed, or out of the labor force in the past two weeks before the survey.	Alcohol dependence (DSM-III-R criteria), an indicator of total ethanol consumed, and heavy drinking (90th and 95th percentile for gender-specific distribution).	IV methods. Instruments include state excise tax on beer, state ethanol consumption, and state excise tax on cigarettes.	Schooling, health, and marital status are all included as additional controls.	IV results for males do not support the conclusion that heavy drinking reduces employment or unemployment relative to being OLF. Findings for women is that problem drinking increases both probability of being employed and unemployed (hence lowers likelihood of being OLF). Net effect is ambiguous.	Unclear.
Zarkin et al. (1998)	1991 and 1992 cross sections of the NSDUH, focusing exclusively on young males between the ages of eighteen and twenty-four.	Self-reported hours worked at all jobs in the past month.	Alcohol, cigarette, marijuana, cocaine, and other drug use in the past month and in one's lifetime. Past month alcohol and marijuana use controlled for quantity and frequency using categorical variables.	OLS IV estimation. Instruments include self-reported health risk and difficulty obtaining each substance. Only past month use was instrumented out.	Education, marital status, nonlabor income, number of children, and self-reported health status were all included as additional controls.	In general, they find no consistent relationship between drug use and hours worked. However, light marijuana use (one–three joints in the last month) is positively and statistically associated with hours worked in the 1991 data and negatively and statistically associated with hours worked in the 1992 data. Specification tests support the 1992 results, but the inconsistency in results in adjacent cross sections of the same data is revealing.	1992 results show that smoking between one and three marijuana joints in the past month is associated with forty-one fewer hours worked. 1991 results (although viewed less reliable than 1992 results) suggest that light marijuana use is associated with working forty-two hours more in the past month than nonusers.

Study	Data	Outcome	Substance Use Measure	Methods	Controls	Results	Findings
DeSimone (2002)	Males from the 1984 and 1988 NLSY79	Binary indicator of having worked at all in the past year.	Binary indicators of any past year cocaine or marijuana use, so frequency or chronic use not captured.	IV methods. Instruments include regional cocaine prices and state decriminalization policies.	Labor force experience, marital status, and number of children are omitted, but educational attainment is included.	Results from the IV models are consistently negative and statistically significant across the years in which the relationship is evaluated.	The probability of being employed is reduced by 15–17 percentage points by marijuana and 23–32 percentage points by cocaine.

Educational Attainment

Study	Data	Outcome	Substance Use Measure	Methods	Controls	Results	Findings
Cook and Moore (1993)	Various waves of the NLSY79 data	High school completion, college entry, and college completion	Heavy and binge drinking in high school.	IV and reduced form methods. Instruments include state variation in beer taxes and minimum legal purchase ages for alcohol.	No.	Heavy drinking during senior year of high school reduces likelihood of finishing high school and graduating college.	Frequent drinkers complete 2.3 fewer years of college compared to nonfrequent drinkers.
Dee and Evans (2003)	NELS:88, repeated cross sections of the 1977–1992 Monitoring the Future Surveys and 1990 Public-Use Microdata Sample	Educational attainment.	Use of alcohol in the past thirty days, binge drinking in the past two weeks.	IV methods and reduced form models. Instruments include beer tax and state minimum legal drinking ages.	No.	Reduced form estimates based on PUMS data show that teen exposure to MLDA of 18 had a small but statistically insignificant effect on high school completion, college entrance, and college completion.	No effect.
Bray et al. (2000)	Longitudinal survey of 1,392 adolescents ages sixteen–eighteen in a southeastern school system.	Dropped out of high school between the ages of sixteen and eighteen (evaluated for each age).	Initiation of each of four substances prior to age sixteen, seventeen, and eighteen. Substances are alcohol, cigarettes, marijuana, and other illicit drugs.	Logistic models of the probability of dropping out of school. Although IV models were tested and rejected, instruments used for identification of age of first use were not described.	One of the first economic studies to fully consider polysubstance use.	Marijuana initiation is positively related to dropping out of high school, although the magnitude and significance of this relationship varies with age of dropout and other substances used.	Marijuana users are at 2.3 times greater odds of dropping out of school than nonusers.

(continued)

Table 7.2 (continued)

Study	Data	Outcome	SA measure	Methods	SA and other intermediate factors controlled for?	Key insight from study	Effects
Chatterji (2006)	Year 2000 follow up of the NELS:88. Models estimated separately for men and women.	Four measures of educational attainment by age twenty-six: high school completion, GED, some college, finished college.	Alcohol use in the past thirty days in the 10th and 12th grade, as well as an indicator of binge drinking in the past two weeks from both waves.	Bivariate probit techniques. IVs include state beer taxes and percentage of the state population living in a dry county.	Prior cigarette use in 8th grade.	Results from the bivariate probit models relying on her IVs are unreliable because of the poor performance of her IVs. Attempts to bound the causal association using Altonji et al. (2005) method provide no evidence of a causal interpretation.	No effects.
McCaffrey et al. (Forthcoming)	Project ALERT Plus sample of middle school students in South Dakota	High school dropout status (as reported by school administrator as well as self-reports).	Persistent and heavy marijuana use in the past thirty days in both 9th and 10th grade. Quantity-frequency index of alcohol use in the past month and year.	Propensity score weighting adjusts sample for baseline differences in 7th grade as well as differential participation in the Project ALERT curriculum.	Cigarette use at baseline (7th) and in each wave during high school is considered.	Even after adjusting for propensity weights, marijuana users are 2.3 times more likely to drop out. Statistical significance disappears when measures of cigarette use, family bonds, or peer effects are included.	No effects.

Note: NLSY = National Longitudinal Survey on Youth; DSM = Diagnostic and Statistical Manual of Mental Disorders; OLS = ordinary least squares; AFQT = Armed Forces Qualification Test; OLF = Out of the Labor Force; NSDUH = National Survey of Drug Use and Health; NELS = National Educational Longitudinal Study; PUMS = Public Use Microdata Sample; MLDA = Minimum Legal Drinking Age.

worked. Interestingly, Mullahy and Sindelar (1996) also show a positive effect of heavy drinking on women's labor market participation, suggesting that women with a serious substance abuse problem may be more tied to the labor market.

Findings for men are less clear. Neither of the Kaestner studies shows a consistent result for the effects of cocaine on employment or wages, nor does Register and Williams (1992). However, DeSimone (2002), using the same data set as Kaestner, does find a large statistically significant negative association between marijuana and cocaine use and labor market participation for men. DeSimone emphasizes in his work the importance of instruments satisfying exclusion restrictions and overidentification tests, which he argues are not met by Kaestner's instruments.[14] DeSimone uses external measures of availability, including cocaine prices and marijuana state decriminalization status, for his identifying instruments rather than internal measures of religious attendance, prior delinquent behavior, and unearned income, which were used by Kaestner (1994a, 1994b) and could reflect the same unobserved character trait that motivates both drug use and poor labor market outcomes. DeSimone also employs more proximal measures of substance use, capturing frequency of use in the past year rather than in the lifetime. However, DeSimone does not account for a number of intermediate mechanisms through which substance use might impact labor markets, most notably labor market experience and marital status. So, the omission of these intermediate factors may also contribute to the finding of a large effect.

The Mullahy and Sindelar (1996) paper, which was the last in a series of papers they coauthored examining alcohol dependence and labor market outcomes, was one of the first to carefully test the validity and appropriateness of the instruments used for estimation and consider the extent to which the relationship between alcohol dependence and labor market outcomes might differ over the life course. In another paper they show that the relationship between alcohol dependence and earnings clearly differs by age (Mullahy and Sindelar 1993), but in this study they find no statistically significant or consistent evidence that alcohol dependence influences employment or unemployment, at least for men.

Another question is whether alcohol dependence might influence the types of jobs people get, not just whether or not they work. Kenkel and Wang (1998) use data from the 1979 NLSY to compare job attributes of alcoholic and nonalcoholic men. They find that male alcoholics are less likely to be in white-collar occupations, less likely to receive fringe benefits, and tend to work for smaller firms than their nonalcoholic counterparts.

---

14. In Kaestner's defense, statistical tests empirically evaluating exclusion restrictions and overidentification in IV models became standard outputs of statistical software estimating these models after Kaestner's work got published.

They also find that alcoholic men who work in white-collar occupations earn about as much as nonalcoholics, while alcoholic men working in blue-collar professions earn about 15 percent less on average. If substance users are able to self-select into specific job occupations that enable them to continue their substance use, then studies that examine the relationship between substance use and wages and other measures of productivity may be biased because they are attributing differences to substance use behavior instead of characteristics of the job.

Finally, using data from the 1991 and 1992 National Household Survey on Drug Abuse, Zarkin et al. (1998) examine the effects of current use (i.e., in the past thirty days) and previous substance use on hours worked in the past month. They use an IV approach, identifying instruments within the survey using information on self-reported risks and availability. They estimate the models separately for 1991 and 1992, both years representing an independent nationally representative cross-section of U.S. households. In general they find no consistently significant effect of any of the substances examined. However, their results for light marijuana users (those reporting use of one to three joints in the past thirty days) were particularly interesting. Using the 1991 cross-section, they found that light marijuana use was statistically significantly associated with working *more* hours (forty-two hours more per month than nonusers). However, using the exact same method, same controls, and the same measure of substance use with the 1992 cross-section, they found that light marijuana use was statistically significantly associated with working *fewer* hours (forty-one fewer hours than nonusers). The authors interpret these completely opposite results despite the same methodology and controls as evidence of the necessity to continue investigating the relationship and the need for careful inspection of models that get estimated.

Schooling outcomes, which are shown in the latter part of table 7.2, are of particular interest because of their close proximity to the delivery of adolescent prevention programs and because educational attainment is such an important factor for labor market outcomes. As in the literature just reviewed on earnings and employment, much of the focus of the schooling literature in economics remains focused on the identification of causal effects, but a much more serious debate over the proper variables for identification of causal effects using IV methods has ensued (Cook and Moore 1993; Dee and Evans 2003; Chatterji 2006). For example, Cook and Moore (1993) use cross-state variation in the minimum legal drinking age and beer taxes, two significant predictors of adolescent drinking behaviors, to identify the causal effects of teen drinking on educational attainment. They find that after controlling for sociodemographic factors and family environment, high school seniors who are frequent drinkers complete 2.3 fewer years of college compared to seniors who are not frequent drinkers. Dee and Evans (2003), however, contend that the approach employed by Cook and Moore is flawed because it relies on cross-state variation from a single year. They contend that a study of variation in state regulations over time is needed to distinguish these effects from other state-level factors that might affect educational attainment, such as state expenditures on education. Using matched cohorts from the Monitoring the Future Survey and 1990 Public-Use Microdata Sample, they use two-sample IV technique and find that teen drinking has no independent effect on educational attainment. A limitation of their analysis, however, is that average population effects could be driving their null finding as opposed to the nonexistence of a true relationship between schooling and educational attainment at the individual level.

The debate regarding the usefulness of instruments and IV approaches was addressed again by Chatterji (2006), who used data from the 2000 National Educational Longitudinal Study (NELS:88) to model educational attainment at age twenty-six conditional upon current alcohol use in tenth and twelfth grade. Chatterji employed a bivariate probit technique to simultaneously model substance use and specific educational outcomes (high school completion, GED, some college or college completion—each separately), and used as additional instruments state beer taxes and the percentage of the state population living in dry counties. She finds through diagnostics of these instruments that they perform poorly as instruments and decides instead to explore plausibility of a causal relationship using Altonji's et al. (2005) bounding technique. She finds no evidence supporting a causal association using this method. Other strategies have emerged to try to deal with the problem of identification of causal associations in this strand of the literature. Bray et al. (2000), for example, use information from a longitudinal survey and assess whether the age of first use of alcohol, cigarettes, marijuana, and other illicit drugs are statistically associated with the probability of dropping out of school. This sort of prospective approach relies heavily on the notion that early use of these substances (prior to age sixteen) is highly correlated with dependent use later. While this notion is well supported in the literature, it may also be the case that adolescents who initiate at a young age have environmental or personality factors that make them less likely to complete high school (e.g., less parental supervision, bad peers, etc.). They attempt to control for some of these factors, and find that marijuana initiation in particular is positively related to dropping out of high school, although the magnitude and significance varied in a nonlinear fashion with age. What is perhaps most surprising about the study is that early initiation of the other substances was not negatively and statistically associated with high school dropout status, which raises serious questions as to whether it is truly the drug use that is being picked up by these measures or something behavioral.

McCaffrey et al. (forthcoming) use a different approach for evaluating the relationship between substance abuse and schooling. Using a very rich set of panel data from the Project ALERT evaluation, they examine whether persistent and heavy marijuana use over the tenth and twelfth grade is associated with high school completion using propensity score weighting. They also consider separately the effect of drinking through a continuous quantity-frequency measure of use in the past month and year. They are able to obtain baseline information on the adolescents in seventh grade, before the kids participated in the Project ALERT drug prevention curriculum, and account for a variety of observable differences. When they conduct analyses that simply correct for baseline differences between the groups, including participation in the ALERT program, they find that heavy and persistent marijuana use is still positively associated with high school dropout (odds ratio of 2.3). However, when additional time varying measures are added to a propensity score weighted regression, they find that the statistically significant association between marijuana use and schooling disappears, suggesting that much of the observed association between marijuana use and high school completion can be explained by peer influences and family bonds. The study does not speak directly to the issue of causality, but provides interesting evidence of the mechanisms through which marijuana use might be indirectly associated with schooling. Importantly, the authors find no direct effect of participation in the prevention program on dropping out of high school.

Overall, the findings remain fairly mixed in terms of the effects of substance use on schooling as well as on earnings and labor force participation. While methods that attempt to deal with the endogeneity of substance use generally lead to a reduction in the observed association, the studies using these methods also have problems and instruments have subsequently been found to be either weak or invalid. Thus, the literature continues to evolve, in part because the negative associations remain so strong in observational data and studies are so inconsistent in their treatment of mechanisms through which substance use is allowed to affect the outcomes.

7.7   Summary and Next Steps

This chapter reviews the literatures on the effectiveness of substance use prevention and the effect of substance use on education, employment, and earnings. While there is a fair amount of evidence suggesting that prevention programs for adolescents have short-term effects on consumption, there is very little evidence suggesting these effects remain through high school. But as noted by Caulkins et al. (2002), program effects that last just a year post-program completion can still potentially translate into important changes in terms of lifetime substance use. Research also shows that delaying the age in which a substance is initiated can have a large effect on the probability of becoming dependent and the duration in which the substance is used (Douglas 1998; van Ours 2006; Patton et al. 2007). Thus, it is possible that these programs could translate into improved schooling or employment outcomes, although the evidence is weak and uncertain.

The economic literature on the casual effect of substance use on education attainment and labor market outcomes remains mixed. While we discussed many factors that have contributed to this situation, perhaps the most important one to keep in mind is how substance use and abuse gets defined in these studies. Clearly, the level of consumption, duration of consumption, and timing of consumption all have important implications in terms of whether we should expect to see an impact on employment or earnings. Rarely have such factors been considered in an analysis.

Another important factor relevant for studying the association between substance use and earnings is the extent to which statistical models are correctly specified for identification of mechanisms that are being considered. While the literature suggests that chronic substance abusers are less likely to be employed, it also suggests that chronic substance abusers are less likely to finish school and more likely to engage in crime. Analyses of the effects of substance abuse on later life cycle outcomes needs to carefully consider the indirect mechanisms through which substance use might also influence those outcomes. The potential for endogeneity bias, caused by unaccounted for differences in ability, antisocial disorders, deviance, mental health problems, rates of time preference, or some other unobserved factor, to impact results abound and few studies have adequately dealt with all of this using IV or other methods.

Information is desperately needed to better inform policymakers of the role substance use might play in contributing to adult poverty. If chronic substance use lowers educational attainment and/or earnings, either directly or indirectly, then programs that prevent or delay substance abuse during adolescence may be an effective way of raising future income and deterring some from becoming economically dependent on the social safety net system or on others. Even if chronic substance use is just an indication of some other third factor that is really driving the correlation between substance use and future labor market outcomes, prevention programs may still be an effective way of reducing poverty—not because they stop substance abuse, but because they teach valuable life skills, resistance training, and coping mechanisms that help empower youth to make better life choices. Moreover, because so many of the prevention programs are relatively inexpensive to implement on a per student basis, they could prove to be an extremely cost-effective strategy for reducing future levels of poverty.

We strongly support additional research on the long-term effects of prevention programs and a more serious look at the direct effect of participation in these prevention programs on economic variables, such as educational attainment and early job entry. These programs are relatively inexpensive and some do show promising results in the short run. If we had to design the next round of experiments to improve our understanding of prevention programs, we would focus on the following:

• Comprehensive, evidence-based school programs that begin with middle school students and provide sessions through high school. While many prevention programs do have booster sessions after seventh or eighth grade, the typical age for initiation into hard drug use does not come until after high school. One could imagine randomly assigning the grade when school-based prevention stops so we could get a better understanding of whether the timing of booster sessions matters.

• Additional long-term follow-up studies (through senior year of high school) of treatment and control groups for the "evidence-based" programs, with a special focus on human capital accumulation. This would allow us to determine whether program participation shows any real effect on school performance and health by the end of high school, not just substance use. Additionally, this would allow us to better understand the extent to which there is an immediate or slow decay of program effects for youth impacted by the prevention program, and whether additional boosters could prolong program effects.

• A large-scale replication of the Big Brothers Big Sisters community-based mentoring experiment, with a special focus on long-term human capital outcomes, to more carefully evaluate the effect of this program on substance use and economic well-being.

• An experimental evaluation of school-based drug testing that is coupled with a curriculum-based prevention program, paying close attention to alcohol consumption, attendance, and the probability of dropping out of school. Special attention should also be given to the consequences associated with testing positive. Indeed, if the expected sanction for testing positive is small, we would expect the intervention to have very small effects, if any.

• Experimental evaluation of various brief interventions targeted to at-risk youth that examine long-run outcomes. While some of the short-run results are impressive (e.g., D'Amico and Edelen-Orlando 2007), it is unclear whether these approaches have a lasting effect on substance use patterns.

References

Altonji, J., T. Conley, T. Elder, and C. R. Taber. 2005. Selection on observed and unobserved variables: Assessing the effectiveness of Catholic schools. *Journal of Political Economy* 113 (1): 151–84.

Aos, S., R. Lieb, J. Mayfield, M. Miller, and A. Pennucci. 2004. *Benefits and costs of prevention and early intervention programs.* Olympia: Washington State Institute for Public Policy. Available at: http://www.wsipp.wa.gov/rptfiles/04-07-3901.pdf.

Aos, S., J. Mayfield, M. Miller, and W. Yen. 2006. *Evidence-based treatment of alcohol, drug, and mental health disorders: Potential benefits, costs, and fiscal impacts for Washington State.* Olympia: Washington State Institute for Public Policy. Available at: http://www.wsipp.wa.gov/rptfiles/06-06-3901.pdf.

Baer, J. S., P. L. Peterson, and E. A. Wells. 2004. Rationale and design of a brief substance use intervention for homeless adolescents. *Addiction Research and Theory* 12:317–34.

Becker, G. 1964. *Human capital: A theoretical and empirical analysis, with special reference to education.* New York: National Bureau of Economic Research.

———. 1968. Crime and punishment: An economic approach. *Journal of Political Economy* 76:169–217.

Bray, J., G. Zarkin, C. Ringwalt, and J. Qi. 2000. The relationship between marijuana initiation and dropping out of high school. *Health Economics* 9 (1): 9–18.

Botvin, G., E. Baker, L. Dusenbury, E. Botvin, and T. Diaz. 1995. Long-term follow-up results of a randomized drug abuse prevention trial in a white middle-class population. *Journal of the American Medical Association* 273:1106–12.

Botvin, G., K. Griffin, T. Diaz, and M. Ifill-Williams. 2001. Drug abuse prevention among minority adolescents: Posttest and one-year follow-up of a school based preventive intervention. *Prevention Science* 2:1–13.

Burgess, S., and C. Propper. 1998. Early health-related behaviors and their impact on later life chances: Evidence from the US. *Health Economics* 7:381–99.

Catalano, R., R. Gainey, C. Fleming, and K. Haggerty. 1999. An experimental intervention with families of substance abusers. *Addiction* 94 (2): 241–54.

Caulkins, J., R. Pacula, S. Paddock, and J. Chiesa. 2002. *School-based drug prevention: What kind of drug use does it prevent?* Santa Monica: RAND.

Chatterji, P. 2006. Illicit drug use and educational attainment. *Health Economics* 15:489–511.

Chatterji, P., and E. Meara. 2007. Health and labor market consequences of eliminating federal disability benefits for substance abusers. NBER Working Paper no. 13407. Cambridge, MA: National Bureau of Economic Research, September.

Chen, K., and D. Kandel. 1995. The natural history of drug use from adolescence to the mid-thirties in a general population sample. *American Journal of Public Health* 85:41–7.

Coffey, C., J. Carlin, M. Lynskey, N. Li, and G. Patton. 2003. Adolescent precursors of cannabis dependence: Findings from the Victorian Adolescent Health Cohort Study. *British Journal of Psychiatry* 182:330–36.

Cook, P., and M. Moore. 1993. Drinking and schooling. *Journal of Health Economics* 12 (4): 411–29.

D'Amico, E., and M. Edelen-Orlando. 2007. Pilot test of Project CHOICE: A voluntary after school intervention for middle school youth. *Psychology of Addictive Behaviors* 21 (4): 592–98.

D'Amico, E., and S. A. Stern. 2008. Alcohol and drug use among youth: Advances in prevention. In *Best practices in the behavioral management of health from preconception to adolescence, volume III,* ed. J. Trafton and W. Gordon. Los Altos, CA: Institute for Disease Management.

Dee, T., and W. Evans. 2003. Teen drinking and educational attainment: Evidence from two-sample instrumental variables estimates. *Journal of Labor Economics* 21 (1): 178–209.

DeSimone, J. 2002. Illegal drug use and employment. *Journal of Labor Economics* 20 (4): 952–77.

Douglas, S. 1998. The duration of the smoking habit. *Economic Inquiry* 36:49–64.

Eckhardt, L., S. Woodruff, and J. Elder. 1997. Related effectiveness of continued, lapsed, and delayed smoking prevention intervention in senior high school students. *American Journal of Health Promotion* 11 (6): 418.

Elder, J., M. Wildey, C. de Moor, J. Sallis, L. Eckhardt, C. Edwards, A. Erickson, et al. 1993. The long-term prevention of tobacco use among junior high school students: Classroom and telephone interventions. *American Journal of Public Health* 83 (9): 1239–44.

Ellickson, P., R. Bell, and K. McGuigan. 1993. Preventing adolescent drug use: Long-term results of a junior high program. *American Journal of Public Health* 83 (6): 856–61.

Ellickson, P., D. McCaffrey, B. Ghosh-Dastidar, and D. Longshore. 2003. New inroads in preventing adolescent drug use: Results from a large-scale trial of project ALERT in middle schools. *American Journal of Public Health* 93: 1830–36.

Ellickson, P., J. Tucker, and D. Klein. 2003. Ten-year prospective study of public health problems associated with early drinking. *Pediatrics* 111 (5): 949–55.

Faggiano, F., F. Vigna-Taglianti, E. Zambon, A. Borraccino, and P. Lemma. 2005. School-based prevention for illicit drugs use. *Cochrane Database of Systematic Reviews,* Issue 2.

Fergusson, D., and L. Horwood. 1997. Early onset cannabis use and psychosocial adjustment in young adults. *Addiction* 92:279–96.

Fergusson, D., L. Horwood, and A. Beautrais. 2003. Cannabis and educational achievement. *Addiction* 98 (12): 1681–92.

Fergusson, D., L. Horword, and N. Swain-Campbell. 2002. Cannabis use and psychosocial adjustment in adolescence and young adulthood. *Addiction* 97:1123–35.

Flay, B. R. 2000. "Approaches to substance use prevention utilizing school curriculum plus social environment change. *Addictive Behaviors* 25 (6): 861–85.

Flynn, B. S., J. K. Worden, R. H. Secker-Walker, P. L. Pirie, G. J. Badger, and J. H. Carpenter. 1997. Long-term responses of higher and lower risk youths to smoking prevention interventions. *Preventive Medicine* 26:389–94.

Flynn, B. S., J. K. Worden, R. H. Secker-Walker, P. L. Pirie, G. J. Badger, J. H. Carpenter, and B. M. Geller. 1994. Mass media and school interventions for cigarette smoking prevention: Effects two years after completion. *American Journal of Public Health* 84 (7): 1148–50.

Foxcroft, D., D. Ireland, D. Lister-Sharp, G. Lowe, and R. Breen. 2003. Longer-term primary prevention for alcohol misuse in young people: A systematic review. *Addiction* 98 (4): 397–411.

French, M., and G. Zarkin. 1995. Is moderate alcohol use related to wages? Evidence from four worksites. *Journal of Health Economics* 14 (3): 319–44.

French, M., G. Zarkin, and L. Dunlap. 1998. Illicit drug use, absenteeism, and earnings at six U.S. worksites. *Contemporary Economic Policy* 16 (3): 334–46.

Gates, S., J. McCambridge, L. Smith, and D. Foxcroft. 2006. Interventions for prevention of drug use by young people delivered in non-school settings. *Cochrane Database Systematic Reviews,* Issue 1.

Gill, A., and R. Michaels. 1992. Does drug use lower wages? *Industrial and Labor Relations Review* 45 (3): 419–34.

Goldberg, L., D. Elliot, D. MacKinnon, E. Moe, and K. Kuehl. 2007. Outcomes of a prospective trial of student-athlete drug testing: The student athlete testing using random notification (SATURN) study. *Journal of Adolescent Health* 41 (5): 421–9.

Gottfredson, D., and D. Wilson. 2003. Characteristics of effective school-based substance abuse prevention. *Prevention Science* 4:27–38.

Greene, J., S. Ennett, and C. Ringwalt. 1997. Substance use among runaway and homeless youth in three national samples. *American Journal of Public Health* 87 (2): 229–35.

Grossman, J., and J. Tierney. 1998. Does mentoring work? An impact study of the Big Brothers Big Sisters program. *Evaluation Review* 22 (3): 403–26.

Haapanen, R., and L. Britton. 2002. Drug testing for youthful offenders on parole: An experimental evaluation. *Criminology and Public Policy* 1:217–44.

Hansen, W., and J. Graham. 1991. Preventing alcohol, marijuana, and cigarette use among adolescents: Peer pressure resistance training versus establishing conservative norms. *Preventive Medicine* 20:414–30.

Hawkins D., R. Catalano, and J. Miller. 1992. Risk and protective factors for alcohol and other drug problems in adolescence and early adulthood: Implications for substance abuse prevention. *Psychological Bulletin* 112:64–105.

Hawkins, D., R. Kosterman, R. Catalano, K. Hill, and R. Abbott. 2005. Promoting positive adult functioning through social development intervention in childhood: Long-term effects from the Seattle Social Development Project. *Archives of Pediatrics & Adolescent Medicine* 159 (1): 25–31.

Hecht, M., F. Marsiglia, E. Elek, D. Wagstaff, S. Kulis, P. Dustman, and M. Miller-Day. 2003. Culturally grounded substance use prevention: An evaluation of the keepin' it R.E.A.L. curriculum. *Preventative Science* 4 (4): 233–48.

Herrera, C., J. Grossman, T. Kauh, A. Feldman, J. McMaken, and L. Jucovy. 2007. *Making a difference in schools: The Big Brothers Big Sisters school-based mentoring impact study.* New York: Public/Private Ventures.

Hornik, R., D. Maklan, D. Cadell, C. Barmada, L. Jacobsohn, and V. Hendersen. 2003. *Evaluation of the National Youth Anti-Drug media campaign: 2003 report of findings executive summary (evaluation of the National Youth Anti-Drug media campaign executive summary).* Rockville, MD: Westat.

Hornik, R., D. Maklan, D. Cadell, C. Barmada, L. Jacobsohn, and A. Prado. 2003. *Evaluation of the National Youth Anti-Drug media campaign: Fifth semi-annual report of findings.* Rockville, MD: Westat.

Jayakody, R., S. Danziger, and H. Pollack. 2000. Mental health problems, substance abuse and welfare reform. *Journal of Health Politics, Policy and Law* 25 (4): 623–51.

Johnson, R., and D. Gerstein. 1998. Initiation of alcohol, cigarettes, marijuana, cocaine and other substances in U.S. birth cohorts since 1919. *American Journal of Public Health* 88:27–33.

Johnson, R., and C. Herring. 1989. Labor market participation among young adults. *Youth and Society* 21 (1): 3–31.

Johnston, L., P. O'Malley, J. Bachman, and J. Schulenberg. 2005. *Monitoring the future national survey results on drug use, 1975–2004. Volume II: College students and adults ages 19–45.* Bethesda, MD: National Institute on Drug Abuse.

Kaestner, R. 1991. The effect of illicit drug use on the wages of young adults. *Journal of Labor Economics* 9 (4): 381–412.

———. 1994a. New estimates of the effect of marijuana and cocaine use on wages. *Industrial and Labor Relations Review* 47 (3): 454–70.

———. 1994b. The effects of illicit drug use on the labor supply of young adults. *Journal of Human Resources* 29 (1): 126–55.

———. 1998. Drug use and AFDC participation: Is there a connection? *Journal of Policy Analysis and Management* 17 (3): 495–520.

———. 1999. Does drug use cause poverty? In *The economic analysis of substance use and abuse,* ed. F. Chaloupka, M. Grossman, W. Bickel, and H. Saffer, 327–54. Chicago: University of Chicago Press.

Kandel, D., K. Chen, and A. Gill. 1995. The impact of drug use on earnings: A lifespan perspective. *Social Forces* 74 (1): 243–70.

Kandel, D., and M. Davies. 1990. Labor force experiences of a national sample of young adult men. *Youth and Society* 21 (4): 411–45.

Kandel, D., M. Davies, D. Karus, and K. Yamaguchi. 1986. The consequences in young adulthood of adolescent drug involvement: An overview Archives of General Psychiatry. *Archives of General Psychiatry* 43 (8): 746–54.

Kandel, D., and J. Logan. 1984. Patterns of drug use from adolescence to young adulthood, I: Periods of risk for initiation, continued use and discontinuation. *American Journal of Public Health* 74:660–66.

Kandel, D., and K. Yamaguchi. 1987. Job mobility and drug use: An event history analysis. *American Journal of Sociology* 92 (4): 836–78.

Kenkel, D., and D. Ribar. 1994. Alcohol consumption and young adults Socioeconomic status. *Brookings Paper on Economic Activity: Microeconomics:* 119–61.

Kenkel, D., and P. Wang. 1998. Are alcoholics in bad jobs? NBER Working Paper no. 6401. Cambridge, MA: National Bureau of Economic Research, February.

Kilmer, B. 2008. Does parolee drug testing influence employment and education outcomes? Evidence from a randomized experiment with noncompliance. *Journal of Quantitative Criminology* 24:93–123.

Levy, S. 2009. Drug testing of adolescents in schools. *Robert Wood Johnson Foundation's Substance Abuse Policy Research Program Knowledge Asset.* Available at: http://saprp.org/knowledgeassets/knowledge_detail.cfm?KAID=16.

Longshore, D., B. Ghosh-Dastidar, and P. L. Ellickson. 2006. National Youth Anti-Drug media campaign and school drug prevention: Evidence for a synergistic effect in ALERT Plus. *Addictive Behaviors* 31:496–508.

MacCoun, R. 2007. Testing drugs vs. testing users: Private risk management in the shadow of the criminal law. *DePaul Law Review* 56:507–38.

Manski, C., J. Pepper, and C. Petrie. 2001. *Informing America's policy on illegal drugs: What we don't know keeps hurting us.* Washington, DC: National Academy of Sciences.

McCaffrey, D., R. Pacula, B. Han, and P. Ellickson. Forthcoming. Marijuana use and high school dropout: The influence of unobservables. *Health Economics.*

Mincer, J. 1970. The distribution of labor incomes: A survey with special reference to the human capital approach. *Journal of Economic Literature* 8 (1): 1–26.

Mullahy, J., and J. Sindelar. 1993. Alcoholism, work, and income. *Journal of Labor Economics* 11:494–520.

———. 1994. Alcoholism and income: The role of indirect effects. *Milbank Quarterly* 72 (2): 359–75.

———. 1996. Employment, unemployment and problem drinking. *Journal of Health Economics* 15:409–34.

National Institute on Drug Abuse. 2009. *Principles of drug addiction treatment: A research based guide* (2nd edition). Available at: http://www.nida.nih.gov/PDF/PODAT/PODAT.pdf.

Newcomb, M. D., and P. M. Bentler. 1988. Impact of adolescent drug use and social support on problems of young adults: A longitudinal study. *Journal of Abnormal Psychology* 97 64–75.

Patton, G., C. Coffey, J. Carlin, L. Degenhardt, M. Lynskey, and W. Hall. 2002. Cannabis use and mental health in young people: Cohort study. *British Medical Journal* 325:1195–98.

Patton, G., C. Coffey, M. Lynskey, S. Reid, S. Hemphill, J. Carlin, and W. Hall. 2007. Trajectories of adolescent alcohol and cannabis use into young adulthood. *Addiction* 102 (4): 607–15.

Pentz, M. 2003. Evidence-based prevention: Characteristics, impact, and future direction. *Journal of Psychoactive Drugs* 35 (Suppl 1): 143–52.

Perry, C., K. Komro, S. Veblen-Mortenson, L. Bosma, K. Farbakhsh, K. Munson, M. Stigler, and L. Lytle. 2003. A randomized controlled trial of the middle and junior high school D.A.R.E. and D.A.R.E. Plus programs. *Archives of Pediatrics and Adolescent Medicine* 157 (2): 178–84.

Peterson, A., K. Kealey, S. Mann, P. Marek, and I. Sarason. 2000. Hutchinson smoking prevention project: Long-term randomized trial in school-based tobacco use prevention—Results on smoking. *Journal of the National Cancer Institute* 92 (24): 1979–91.

Phillips, D., N. Christenfeld, and N. Ryan. 1999. An increase in the number of deaths in the United States in the first week of the month: An association with substance abuse and other causes of death. *New England Journal of Medicine* 341:93–98.

Pollack, H., S. Danziger, K. Seefeldt, and R. Jayakody. 2002. Substance use among welfare recipients: Trends and policy responses. *Social Service Review* 76:256–74.

Pudney, S. 2004. Keeping off the grass? An econometric model of cannabis consumption in Britain. *Journal of Applied Econometrics* 19:434–53.

Register, C., and D. Williams. 1992. Labor market effects of marijuana and cocaine use among young men. *Industrial and Labor Relations Review* 45 (3): 435–51.

Rhodes, J. 2008. Improving youth mentoring interventions through research-based practice. *American Journal of Community Psychology* 41:35–42.

Ringel, J., P. Ellickson, and R. Collins. 2006. The relationship between high school marijuana use and annual earnings. *Contemporary Economic Policy* 24 (1): 52–63.

Roebuck, M., M. French, and M. Dennis. 2004. Adolescent marijuana use and school attendance. *Economics of Education Review* 23 (2): 133–41.

Rosen, M., T. McMahon, H. Lin, and R. Rosenheck. 2006. Effect of social security payments on substance abuse in a homeless mentally ill cohort. *Health Services Research* 41 (1): 173–91.

Schulenberg, J., P. O'Malley, J. Bachman, K. Wadsworth, and L. Johnston. 1996. Getting drunk and growing up: Trajectories of frequent binge drinking during the transition to young adulthood. *J. Stud. Alcohol* 57 289–304.

Shaner, A., T. Eckman, L. Roberts, J. Wilkins, D. Tucker, J. Tsuang, and J. Mintz. 1995. Disability income, cocaine use, and repeated hospitalization among schizophrenic cocaine abusers. *New England Journal of Medicine* 333 (12): 777–83.

Skara, S., and S. Sussman. 2003. A review of 25 long-term adolescent tobacco and other drug use prevention program evaluations. *Preventive Medicine* 37:451–74.

Spoth, R., C. Redmond, C. Shin, and K. Azevedo. 2004. Brief family intervention effects on adolescent substance use initiation: School-level growth curve analyses 6 years following baseline. *Journal of Consulting and Clinical Psychology* 72: 535–42.

St. Pierre, T., D. Osgood, C. Mincemoyer, D. Kaltreider, and T. Kauh. 2005. Results of an independent evaluation of Project ALERT delivered in schools by cooperative extension. *Prevention Science* 6 (4): 305–17.

Substance Abuse and Mental Health Services Administration (SAMHSA), Office of Applied Studies. 2008. *Results from the 2007 National Survey on Drug Use and Health: National findings.* Rockville, MD: Department of Health and Human Services.

Sun, W., S. Skara, P. Sun, C. W. Dent, and S. Sussman. 2006. Project towards no drug abuse: Long-term substance use outcomes evaluation. *Preventative Medicine* 42 (3): 188–92.

Taylor, B., J. Graham, P. Cumsille, and W. Hansen. 2000. Modeling prevention program effects on growth in substance use: Analysis of five years of data from the adolescent alcohol prevention trial. *Prevention Science* 1 (4): 183–97.

Tevyaw, T., and P. Monti. 2004. Motivational enhancement and other brief interventions for adolescent substance abuse: Foundations, applications, and evaluations. *Addiction* 99:63–75.

van Ours, J. 2006. Dynamics of the use of drugs. *Health Economics* 15 (12): 1283–94.

van Ours, J., and J. Williams. 2007. Cannabis prices and dynamics of cannabis use. *Journal of Health Economics* 26:578–96.

Walter, H., R. Vaughan, and E. Wynder. 1989. Primary prevention of cancer among children: Changes in cigarette smoking and diet after six years of intervention. *Journal of the National Cancer Institute* 81 (13): 995–9.

Wells, J., L. Horwood, and D. Fergusson. 2004. Drinking patterns in mid-adolescence and psychosocial outcomes in late adolescence and early adulthood. *Addiction* 99:1529–41.

Wenzel, S., J. Tucker, M. Elliott, K. Hambarsoomians, J. Perlman, K. Becker, C. Kollross, and D. Golinelli. 2004. Prevalence and co-occurrence of violence, substance use and disorder, and HIV risk behavior: A comparison of sheltered and low-income housed women in Los Angeles County. *Preventive Medicine* 39 (3): 617–24.

Werch, C., D. Owen, J. Carlson, C. DiClemente, P. Edgemon, and M. Moore. 2003. One-year follow-up results of the STARS for families alcohol prevention program. *Health Education Research* 18:74–87.

Willis, R., and S. Rosen. 1979. Education and self-selection. *Journal of Political Economy* 87 (5): S7–S36.

Yamaguchi, R., L. Johnston, and P. O'Malley. 2003. Relationship between student illicit drug use and school drug-testing policies. *Journal of School Health* 73 (4): 159–64.

Zarkin, G., T. Mroz, J. Bray, and M. French. 1998. The relationship between drug use and labor supply for young men. *Labour Economics* 5 (4): 385–409.

8

Teen Pregnancy Prevention

Melissa Schettini Kearney

8.1 Introduction

Teen childbearing is widely considered to be a major social problem in the United States. There are currently more than 400,000 teen births per year. Births to teen mothers account for roughly one-quarter of the nearly 1.5 million births per to unmarried women in the United States each year.[1] Women who give birth during their teenage years experience negative economic and social outcomes, both in the immediate years and during early adulthood. They are more likely than other women to drop out of high school, to remain unmarried, and to live in poverty. The children of teenage mothers fare worse than other children on economic, social, and cognitive dimensions.[2]

In the year 2004, roughly seventy-two of every 1,000 girls age fifteen to nineteen in the United States became pregnant, and forty-one out of 1,000 gave birth. Cumulatively, nearly 30 percent of females become pregnant before age twenty and more than 20 percent give birth before age twenty. There is large variation in rates of teen pregnancy and childbearing across racial and ethnic groups, as shown in table 8.1. In 2004, the pregnancy rate among black and Hispanic teens was more than twice as high as among white teens. The birth rate among Hispanic teens was 82.6 per 1,000, compared to 63.1 among black teens and 26.7 among white teens.[3]

The good news is that in 2004, the U.S. teen pregnancy rate was at its lowest level in thirty years, 38 percent lower than its peak in 1990. The

Melissa Schettini Kearney is an assistant professor of economics at the University of Maryland and a research associate of the National Bureau of Economic Research.

1. U.S. Department of Health and Human Services (2005, Table 18).
2. The award-winning book *Kids Having Kids,* edited by Rebecca Maynard (2007), is a widely-cited consideration of the issue. An updated version is forthcoming from the Urban Institute.
3. Guttmacher Institute (2006).

Table 8.1   Teen pregnancy and birth rates in the United States

	1990	1995	2002
All teens			
Pregnancy rate	116.9	99.0	75.4
Birth rate	60.3	56.0	43.0
White teens			
Pregnancy rate	98.8	84.9	65.0
Birth rate	51.2	49.5	39.4
Black teens			
Pregnancy rate	222.3	181.4	134.2
Birth rate	112.9	94.4	66.6
Hispanic teens			
Pregnancy rate	162.2	158.5	131.5
Birth rate	99.5	99.3	83.4

Source: Guttmacher Institute (2006).

decline appears to reflect both a decrease in sexual activity and an increase in contraception (Santelli et al. 2004). Between 1988 and 2000, teen pregnancy declined in every state and the District of Columbia. But there is bad news as well. First, rates of teen pregnancy and childbearing in the United States remain substantially higher than in other industrialized nations.[4] Second, the rate of decline was only half as large for Hispanic teens as for white and black teens.[5] And third, teen birth rates increased between 2005 and 2006, the first year-to-year increase since 1991. Perhaps these facts should be taken as a challenge, in that they reveal there is still much room for improvement.

The past two decades have seen numerous and varied efforts from a wide set of actors—community groups, schools, nonprofits, and all levels of government—to bring down rates of teen pregnancy and childbearing in this country. Youth advocates, social scientists, and policymakers are all keenly interested in determining what caused the rise in teen childbearing in the 1980s and the subsequent decline in the 1990s. Unfortunately the research and policy community is far from being able to offer a conclusive answer to the question of what drove the rise and subsequent decline. If we could pinpoint the causes, we could confidently say what we need to continue doing in the years ahead. Unfortunately, the best we can do with any real

4. Because so many factors differ across countries—including economic institutions; inequality levels; cultural practices and norms; welfare, abortion, and contraception policies; as well as family and living arrangements—it is not well understood among researchers which factors in particular drive cross-country differences in teen pregnancy, abortion, and birth rates. In general, the particularly high rate among U.S. teens remains even if one considers only non-minority teens.

5. Guttmacher Institute (2006).

confidence is to review what careful research reveals about the effectiveness of particular interventions in reducing rates of unprotected sex and teen pregnancy among targeted youth. This chapter focuses on program interventions, but it also includes a brief discussion of the potential impacts of relevant public policies.

The effectiveness of teen pregnancy prevention as an antipoverty strategy depends on two key elements: (a) the effectiveness of teen pregnancy prevention interventions in preventing teen pregnancies and births, and (b) the effectiveness of reducing teen childbearing in driving down rates of poverty. The bottom line of this review is that there is a lack of evidence demonstrating the effectiveness of many program interventions, but there is some cause for optimism that the best programs may work in the right settings. The most rigorous study of representative abstinence education programs fail to provide evidence that these programs are effective at reducing rates of sexual behavior. There are a few studies finding that select contraceptive-focused sexual education programs are potentially effective at reducing risky sexual behavior for targeted youth. The evidence regarding the effectiveness of multicomponent, expensive interventions (such as the Carrera program in New York City) is the most encouraging, but these programs can be quite expensive and difficult to replicate.

The latter part of the chapter reviews the evidence on the link between teen childbearing and subsequent economic outcomes, including rates of poverty, among teen mothers. On this second link, the evidence is weak that driving down rates of teen childbearing per se will lead to measurable reductions in poverty.

8.2   Factors Driving Teen Pregnancy

There is a vast literature exploring the antecedents and determinants of teenage pregnancy and childbearing. Study approaches and perspectives vary widely across academic disciplines. Noneconomists typically attribute early childbearing to be the result of myriad influences that affect a youth's development and fall outside the control of a rational decision-making process. Brooks-Gunn and Furstenberg (1989) identify five perspectives on adolescent sexual behavior: biological perspectives, parental influences, peer influences, academic perspectives, and social cognitive perspectives. Brooks-Gunn and Paikoff (1997) add to this list the importance of adolescent feelings in driving their behaviors. They propose four key topics that need to be explored in order to understand adolescent sexuality: sexual well-being and developmental transitions, the gendered nature of sexuality, decision making and sexuality, and the meaning of sexuality to youth. Many of the program interventions designed to educate teenagers about reproductive health and to reduce sexual activity and pregnancy risk have been developed with these broad theoretical perspectives in mind.

Economists tend to model teen childbearing using a rational choice framework, positing that teens make decisions regarding sexual activity use and contraception in a cost-benefits framework. Cultural and peer influences are understood to affect that decision-making process, but they are not modeled explicitly. Public policies that alter the cost-benefit calculation are prime candidates for interventions affecting rates of teen childbearing. These include, but are not limited to, policies making welfare more or less attractive, policies making abortion more or less readily available, and policies increasing access to low-cost contraception.[6]

8.3   Teen Pregnancy Prevention Programs

8.3.1   Overview

Teen pregnancy prevention programs can be usefully categorized into three types: (a) sex education programs with an abstinence focus; (b) sex education with a contraception focus; and (c) multicomponent youth development programs that include sex education as one of many features. Some programs are based in schools and are compulsory, others are school-based but voluntary, and others are run through community centers and groups. There is substantial variation across programs in terms of the types of populations served, including racial and ethnic differences as well as age makeup of the teenagers involved.

There is disagreement among those who work in this field about whether sex education should be abstinence-focused. As helpfully explained by Scher, Maynard, and Stagner (2006), nearly all sex education programs explicitly mention that abstinence is the safest method for avoiding unwanted pregnancies and sexually transmitted infections (STIs). However, the difference between programs with an abstinence focus and a contraception focus is that programs of the latter type explicitly encourage the use of contraception among those who choose to become or remain sexually active. But there is large variation across these programs in the extent of their contraception component.

There have been a number of reviews of teenage pregnancy prevention programs. Scher, Maynard, and Stagner (2006) list twenty large-scale reviews published between 1994 and 2002. These reviews differ across one another in the methodological standards imposed on reviewed studies. They therefore include different studies in their reviews and meta-analyses (where applied) and often reach different conclusions about the effectiveness of

---

6. Moffitt (1998) provides a review of the evidence on the link between welfare and nonmarital childbearing; Grogger and Karoly (2005) provide a comprehensive review of the economic research on the impacts of welfare reform, including on nonmarital and teen childbearing; and Levine (2004) reviews the economic evidence on the link between abortion policy and fertility outcomes.

particular types of interventions. Scher, Maynard, and Stagner (2006) only consider evaluations based on randomized control trials, yielding a sample of thirty-one evaluations conducted between 1981 and 2006. They further limit their sample to evaluations of programs with a primary goal of reducing heterosexual risk-taking behavior and that include measures of sexual experience, pregnancy risk, and/or pregnancy as outcomes. Note that many program evaluations have only short-term follow-up periods and focus on measures of attitude and knowledge, as opposed to actual risk-taking behavior.

Around the same time as the Scher, Maynard, and Stagner review, the National Campaign to Prevent Teen Pregnancy released *Emerging Answers 2007,* completed by Douglas Kirby. This report is a follow-up project to the widely-cited and popular 2001 publication by the same name. *Emerging Answers 2007* reviews the evaluations of more than 115 teen pregnancy prevention programs in the United States published between 1990 and 2007. Kirby includes both random control trials and evaluations with quasi-experimental designs.

8.3.2   Sex Education Programs with an Abstinence Focus

The review by Scher, Maynard, and Stagner (2006) identifies only three abstinence-focused programs with evaluations that meet their criteria. These include the review of Education Now and Babies Later (ENABL) by Kirby et al. (1995); the review of Project Taking Charge by Jorgensen, Potts, and Camp (1993); and the review of McMaster Teen Program by Thomas et al. (1992). Their overall assessment of these reviews is that they provide no evidence that these particular programs changed the likelihood of sexual initiation or unprotected sex. But, the reviewers note that these somewhat outdated programs are not representative of the newer abstinence programs widely implemented today. Kirby's review of abstinence-focused programs also concludes that there is no convincing evidence that abstinence programs have the intended effect.

In April 2007, Mathematica Policy Research (MPR) issued a highly anticipated experimental design evaluation of four Title V, Section 510 Abstinence Education Programs. Section 510 of the 1996 Personal Responsibility and Work Opportunity Act (PRWORA) (welfare reform) legislation significantly increased funding for abstinence education. Since fiscal year (FY) 1998, the Title V, Section 10 program has allocated $50 million annually in federal funding for programs that teach abstinence from sexual activity outside of marriage as the expected standard for school-age children. Under the matching block grant program administered by the Department of Health and Human Services, states must match this federal funding at 75 percent, resulting in annual expenditures of $87.5 million for these programs. With the Balanced Budget Amendment of 1997 Congress authorized an evaluation of these programs, resulting in the Mathematica report.

The Mathematica evaluation is a multiyear impact study of four programs: My Choice, My Future in Powhatan, Virginia; ReCapturing the Vision in Miami, Florida; Families United to Prevent Teen Pregnancy (FUPTP) in Milwaukee, Wisconsin; and Teens in Control in Clarksdale, Mississippi. The Miami and Milwaukee programs served a mix of urban communities and the Virginia and Mississippi programs served rural areas. The demographic make-up of the populations served by the four programs also varied, ranging from poor, single-parent minority families to middle-class, two-parent white households.

The four evaluated programs offered a range of implementation settings. All four programs were implemented in school settings, but the FUPTP program was an after-school program. Two of the programs (ReCapturing the Vision and FUPTP) were elective classes in school and the other two were nonelective. Three of the programs had mandatory attendance. None of the programs served high school students; two were in middle schools and two were in upper elementary grades. All programs offered more than fifty contact hours, making them among the more intense of Title V, Section 510 programs. ReCapturing the Vision and FUPTP were particularly intensive, meeting every day of the school year. Table 8.2 reports details of the programs and analysis samples.

The Mathematica evaluation was carried out with a "gold standard" randomized trial design. The final report presents estimated program impacts on youth behavior from a follow-up survey administered to 2,057 adolescents. By the time of the follow-up survey, youth in the study sample had all completed their programs. Though there are some positive differences in reported rates of knowledge about sexually transmitted disease (STD) identification and risks, there are no measured differences in key behavioral outcomes. About half of both program and control groups report remaining abstinent. When asked about the prior twelve months, 23 percent of both groups report having sex and always using a condom; 17 percent of both groups report having sex and only sometimes using a condom; and 4 percent of both groups report having had sex and never using a condom. Program and control groups also did not differ in the number of partners with whom they had sex. About one-quarter of all youth in both groups had sex with three or more partners. The findings of the Mathematica (2007) evaluation are quite sobering. The authors state in stark terms the challenge facing those who would design and implement teen pregnancy prevention programs: "The evaluation highlights the challenges faced by programs aiming to reduce adolescent sexual activity and its consequences. Nationally, rates of teen sexual activity have declined over the past 15 years, yet even so, about half of all high school youth report having had sex, and more than one in five report having had four or more partners by the time they graduate from high school" (xxiii).

Table 8.2   Title V, Section X abstinence education programs, studied by Mathematica Policy Research

Study	Intervention	Program components	Evaluation design	Sample	Reported effects on sexual behavior outcomes
Trenholm et al. (1997), Mathematica Policy Research Inc.	Teens in Control Clarksdale, MS (rural setting)	5th graders Mandatory class; met once per week during school day; 2-year program	Experimental design; youth were randomly assigned to intervention or control; control program was district-wide health, family life, and sex education curricula.	Evaluation sample: 715 Program: 341 Control: 371	4–6 years after program: No observable impact on sexual initiation, frequency of sex, unprotected sex, or pregnancy rates.
	My Choice, My Future! Powhattan, VA (semirural setting)	8th graders Mandatory class at school; 3-year program	Experimental design; youth were randomly assigned to intervention or control; control program was 9-week health and physical education class.	Evaluation sample: 448 Program: 286 Control: 162	4–6 years after program: No observable impact on sexual initiation, frequency of sex, unprotected sex, or pregnancy rates.
	ReCapturing the Vision Miami, FL (urban setting)	6th–8th graders Mandatory class at school; 1-year program	Experimental design; youth were randomly assigned to intervention or control; control program was mandated health and family life school curriculum.	Evaluation sample: 480 Program: 275 Control: 205	4–6 years after program: No observable impact on sexual initiation, frequency of sex, unprotected sex, or pregnancy rates.
	Families United to Prevent Teen Pregnancy (FUPTP) Milwaukee, WI (urban setting)	3rd–8th graders Elective after-school program operating daily for 2.5 hours; students could attend for up to 4 years.	Experimental design; youth were randomly assigned to intervention or control; control program was mandatory family life curricula.	Evaluation sample: 414 Program: 271 Control: 140	4–6 years after program: No observable impact on sexual initiation, frequency of sex, unprotected sex, or pregnancy rates.

8.3.3   Sex Education Programs with a Contraception Focus

The evidence on the effectiveness of sex education programs with a contraception focus is somewhat more encouraging, though still limited. Kirby (2007) reviews forty-eight studies of comprehensive sex and STD/HIV education programs. Kirby reports that about two-thirds of the evaluations show a reduction in unprotected sex among program participants, but the large number of studies included means that there is variation in the rigor across the full set of studies. Scher, Maynard, and Stagner (2006) identify eighteen studies of programs of this type that meet their inclusion criteria, including four from 1990 or earlier and some with sample sizes of fewer than 100 observations. They conclude from these reviews that "there is no consistent evidence that sex education programs altered the likelihood that youth would initiate sex, would have unprotected sex, or would become (or get someone) pregnant" (37). However, they report that a number of individual studies found positive program effects, particularly related to increased contraception use.[7] These include the evaluations by DiClemente, Wingood, and Harrington (2004) of an untitled HIV prevention serving African American females between ages fourteen and eighteen and the evaluation by St. Lawrence et al. (1995) of Becoming a Responsible Teen (BART). These programs are both summarized in table 8.3.

An important issue in determining the effectiveness of programs is whether positive results found for one implementation can be replicated in other communities, a point made by Kirby (2001). The program Be Proud! Be Responsible! and curricula derived from it have been evaluated a number of times. This program was designed to be implemented outside school, often on Saturdays. Original evaluations of three- and six-month implementations suggested positive results (Jemmott, Jemmott, and Fong 1992; and Jemmott, Jemmott, Fong, and McCaffree 1999). The program was modified, lengthened, implemented under the name Making Proud Choices! A Safer Sex Curriculum. A related abstinence curriculum was developed and named Making a Difference! A Sexual Abstinence Curriculum. Jemmott, Jemmott, and Fong (1998) evaluated the implementation of these programs in three middle schools in Philadelphia in the early 1990s.

The programs were run over the course of two Saturdays. Recruited participants—sixth- and seventh-grade boys and girls—were randomly assigned to one of three intervention groups: the safer sex intervention that included lesson modules about condom use and negotiation; the abstinence intervention; and a control intervention that consisted of a health promotion

---

7. Only five of these evaluations even measure pregnancy as an outcome and none of these are able to detect statistically significant effects. This could reflect either a lack of a true effect or merely statistical limitations. The number of pregnancies that are observed in any given year among a sample of a few hundred teens is quite small, making it difficult for evaluations of this kind to detect statistically meaningful changes.

workshop. There were initially 659 sample adolescents; at the twelve-month follow-up there were 610 adolescents. At the twelve-month follow-up, for the full sample of youth, there were no statistically significant differences between participants in either treatment program relative to the control program in the likelihood of sexual intercourse or in the percent reporting unprotected sex. However, among the 102 adolescents who were sexually experienced at baseline, those in the safer sex program reported a lower frequency of unprotected sex as compared to control program participants and abstinence program participants.

This curriculum was adapted for Latino adolescents and named *Cuidate!* (translation: Take care of yourself!). A randomized implementation of this program from April 2000 through March 2003 was evaluated by Villar-ruel, Jemmott, and Jemmott (2006). Latino adolescents ages thirteen to eighteen were recruited from three northeast Philadelphia high schools and community-based organizations within these neighborhoods. The adapted program incorporated "salient aspects of Latino culture, specifically famil-ialism, or the importance of family, and gender-role expectations. Absti-nence and condom use were presented as culturally accepted and effective ways to prevent sexually transmitted diseases" (Villarruel, Jemmott, and Jemmott 2006, 773). The analysis found that adolescents in the program intervention were less likely to report sexual intercourse (odds ratio of 0.66) and more likely to report consistent condom use (odds ratio of 1.91). The positive results were driven by Spanish speakers.[8]

The program Becoming a Responsible Teen was evaluated in randomized trials in three settings. As described by Kirby (1997), first it was implemented in a community setting in urban Jackson, Mississippi. The program con-sisted of eight 90- to 120-minute meetings. The evaluation of this program by St. Lawrence et al. (1995) found that at a fourteen-month follow-up, program participants had delayed sexual initiation, reduced frequency of sex among sexually active youth, increased condom use, and reduced rates of unprotected sex. Second, the program was implemented in two drug reha-bilitation centers in Mississippi. St. Lawrence et al. (2002) report that at a thirteen-month follow-up, program participants had increased abstinence, reduced number of sexual partners, increased condom use, and decreased rates of unprotected sex. But the total sample size for the evaluation sample was 142, which raises questions about the power of the analysis to find statis-tically significant differences. And third, the program was shortened by more

8. A look at the evaluation data reveals that, in fact, the proportion of treatment respon-dents who reported consistent condom use actually decreased and the proportion of treatment respondents who reported sexual intercourse in the past three months increased, as compared to baseline reports; the evaluators' finding of program success is because these rates of decrease and increase are lower than the corresponding rates among control group members. While this is arguably a reasonable evaluation approach, the lack of finding an absolute improvement among program participants is potentially a cause for caution in interpreting the program as successful.

Table 8.3   **Sex education programs with contraception component**

Study	Intervention	Program components	Evaluation design	Sample	Reported effects on sexual behavior outcomes
DiClemente, Wingood, and Harrington (2004)	Untitled HIV Prevention Intervention 1995–2002 Alabama; four community health agencies 14–18 year old African American females who were seeking services and reported having intercourse in past six months.	Four 4-hour sessions on consecutive Saturdays. Trained African American peer educators and a trained African American health educator delivered program to small groups of 10–12 participants. Program included modeling and creating supportive group norms; focused on ethnic and gender pride; discussed abstinence and condom use; included role-plays, refusal skills development, and discussed health relationships.	Adolescents were randomly assigned to the HIV prevention intervention or to control program consisting of a 16-hour general health class focusing on nutrition and exercise.	Baseline evaluation sample: 522 girls 12-month evaluation sample: 460	6- and 12-months follow-up. Intervention group members were more likely to use contraception consistently, had reduced sexual activity rates, no evidence of reductions in pregnancy rates. Reexamination of data by Scher, Maynard, and Stagner (2006) finds results consistent with the original study author's findings.
Jemmott, Jemmott, and Fong (1998)	Be Proud! Be Responsible! Two Interventions: "Making a Difference! A Sexual Abstinence Curriculum" and "Making Proud Choices! A Safer Sex Curriculum" Three middle schools in Philadelphia, PA; 6th and 7th grade boys girls, primarily African American, low income, 25% had initiated sex at baseline.	Two Saturdays; total of approximately 8 hours. Peer and adult facilitators provided interventions based on social cognitive theory, the theory of reasoned action, and theory of planned behavior. Both interventions were highly structured, culturally sensitive, and encouraged adolescents to be proud and responsible for themselves and their communities and to consider future goals. Abstinence curricula focused on abstinence to prevent STD and pregnancy; Safe Sex curricula included lessons on condom use and negotiation. Both included small group discussions and skill-building exercises.	Experimental design; recruited adolescents were randomly assigned to one of three groups (Abstinence, Safer Sex, or Control). Control group program was a health promotion workshop.	Baseline: 659 12-month follow-up: 610	At 12-month follow-up, for the full sample of youth, no statistically significant differences between participants in either treatment program relative to the control program in the likelihood of sexual intercourse or in the percent reporting unprotected sex. Among those sexually experienced at baseline, those in the safer sex program reported a lower frequency of unprotected sex as compared to other two programs.

St. Lawrence et al. (1995)	Project BART (Becoming a Responsible Teen) Early 1990s Jackson, MS; (comprehensive health center) Adolescents ages 14–18; primarily African American, low income; approximately half were sexually experienced at baseline.	8-week program; weekly 90–120 minute sessions. Trained male and female cofacilitators provided this HIV prevention program based on social learning theory that contained the following components: (1) AIDS education (stressing abstinence and contraception use); (2) group discussion and video regarding decision making and values; (3) condom demonstration and practice; (4) role plays and discussions focusing on social competency and communication skills; (5) discussions with HIV-positive youth, focus on cognitive competency; (6) peer coping models focusing on social support and empowerment.	Adolescents were randomized to the behavioral skills training intervention or the control program. The control program consisted of a one-time 2-hour educational intervention that provided standard HIV/AIDS information and was less sexually explicit than intervention program.	Baseline: 246 12 month follow-up: 225	At one year post-program, program participants report lower rates of sexual initiation, fewer partners, and lower frequency of unprotected sex. Reduction in unprotected sex found for both boys and girls. (Pregnancy not measured.)
Villarruel, Jemmott, and Jemmott (2006)	Cuídate! (an adaptation of Be Proud! Be Responsible! for Latino adolescents) Philadelphia, PA 2000–2003 8th–11th graders	16 hrs. of instruction; Saturday meetings. Modules delivered by trained, bilingual facilitators to small, mixed-gender groups. The HIV-risk reduction curriculum was an adaptation of Be Proud! Be Responsible!, based on social cognitive theory and the theories of reasoned action and planned behavior. It incorporated salient aspects of Latino culture.	Recruited youth randomly assigned to program or control intervention. Control intervention consisted of a health promotion curriculum.	Evaluation sample: 550 Latino adolescents Program: 263 Control: 287	At 12-month follow-up, program participants significantly less likely to have had sex and to have had multiple partners; significantly more likely to use condoms; differences driven by Spanish-speakers. (Pregnancy outcome not measured.)

than half and implemented in a state juvenile reform center in Mississippi. In this instance of the program, the evaluation (St. Lawrence et al. 1999) did not detect any program effects on observed outcomes.

8.3.4   Multi-Component Programs

It is generally understood that many factors influence the process by which teenagers engage in sexual risk-taking behaviors and find themselves in the situation of being pregnant. A teenager's decision to be sexually active and the level of precaution taken against pregnancy are determined only in part—and arguably only in small part—by her knowledge about pregnancy risk and contraception. A teen's sense of self-confidence, her academic goals, her career aspirations, her relationship with her family, all of these are among the many other factors determining a teen's likelihood of engaging in risky sexual behaviors. In recognition of this, some advocates favor a more comprehensive youth development approach to teen pregnancy prevention.

The evidence from multicomponent programs serving disadvantaged youth is the most promising. Scher, Maynard, and Stagner (2006) review the evaluations of seven multicomponent programs, including the two described below. Compared to the other types of interventions reviewed, the authors view these as showing the most promising impacts, in particular for girls. However, even this small set of seven evaluated programs includes at least one program with a questionable randomized design and some that are now quite dated. The body of evidence is therefore not very solid and the reviewers caution that "there is a paucity of rigorous evaluations of such programs" (37). I highlight here two programs that have received a good amount of attention for having produced evaluations with favorable results: The Children's Aid Society-Carrera Program in New York City and the Teen Outreach Program (TOP), a service learning program that has been implemented in various sites throughout the country. Table 8.4 reports details.

The Carrera program aims to address the underlying factors associated with teenage pregnancy and childbearing, such as poverty, school failure, unemployment, and inadequate health care. It is an intensive, multiyear after-school program for high-risk high school students. The program is year-round, offered five to six days each week, and it serves teens until they complete high school. During the school year, program activities were scheduled after school each day for approximately three hours. During the summer, the program provided employment, academic assistance, and sex education for approximately three hours a day.[9] The program has been evaluated

---

9. The cost of the program in New York City sites is reported to be approximately $4,000 per teen per year, or an average of $16 a day per teen. These costs included staffing, medical and dental care, stipends, and wages for teens to work in part-time or full-time jobs. The program has been funded privately through foundations and donors. In New York City, the Robin Hood Foundation provides principal support.

Table 8.4 Evidence from two multicomponent programs

Study	Intervention	Program components	Evaluation design	Sample	Reported effects on sexual behavior outcomes
Philliber et al. (2002)	Children's Aid Society—Carrera Program 1997–2000 New York City Adolescents age 13–15, followed through high school. Predominantly African American and Hispanic teens from low-income, single-parent families.	Intervention group adolescents participated, on average, in 242 hours of activities in New York City sites. The program had five main components: (1) work experience and support through a "job club;" (2) educational component (tutoring, SAT prep, college entrance assistance); (3) family life and sex education; (4) self-expression through the arts; and (5) lifetime individual sports. In addition, adolescents were provided with comprehensive medical services including reproductive counseling/contraceptive services, year-round support services, and social/recreational/cultural field trips.	Adolescents were randomized to treatment or control conditions. Control conditions typically meant an alternative program of recreation, homework help, and arts and crafts. Evaluated intention-to-treat, regardless of attendance.	Baseline: 565 Follow-up: 484	At the end of the 3-year program: Girls in treatment group significantly less likely to have had sex; more likely to use dual methods of contraception at last sex. Preg. rates 55% lower: 10% among program participants compared to 22% among controls; Birth rate of 3% among program participants versus 10% among controls. No behavioral effect for boys.
Allen, et al. (1997)	Teen Outreach Program (TOP), 1991–1995 Schools and communities in 25 sites throughout U.S. High school aged, primarily girls (85%), majority African-American (67%), baseline sexual experience information not available.	Approximately 71 hours of program participation, including an average of 46 hours of volunteer service plus 25 hours of classroom discussions. The stated program goals are: (1) to reduce incidences of school failure and (2) to reduce incidences of teen pregnancies. Intervention included: (1) supervised community volunteer services (minimum of 20 hours); (2) classroom-based discussions about service experiences; and (3) classroom-based related to "social-development tasks." Classroom lessons were taught by trained facilitators and included group exercises, role-plays, guest speakers, informational presentations. Less than 15% of written curriculum focused on sexuality.	Randomization at either student or classroom level.	Baseline: 695 Follow-up: 560 (female only)	At 9-mo. follow-up: reductions in incidences of pregnancies, school failure, and academic suspensions. Scher, Maynard, and Stagner (2006) note the following methodological concerns: (1) unclear numbers of adolescents randomized at the classroom level (and no adjustment for this clustering) and (2) unclear information on control group experiences.

by Philliber et al. (2002) and its evaluation favorably reviewed by both Kirby (2007) and Scher, Maynard, and Stagner (2006).

The description of the program that follows is based on its operation from 1997 to 2000, the years of basis for the Philliber et al. (2002) evaluation.[10] The program operated five days a week and provided services in a wide range of areas. It had five main components: (a) work experience and support through a "job club;" (b) educational component (tutoring, SAT prep, college entrance assistance); (c) family life and sex education; (d) self-expression through the arts; and (e) lifetime individual sports. In addition, adolescents were provided with comprehensive medical services including reproductive counseling and contraceptive services. The program's message was meant to unambiguously promote avoiding unprotected sex and pregnancy. The program had a full-time coordinator, a full-time community organizer, and part-time employees.

Teens were recruited from age thirteen to fifteen and encouraged to participate throughout high school. Teens spent an average of sixteen hours per month in the program during the first three years. The population served was primarily African American and/or Latino and low income. The evaluation of the New York City site involved six agencies in New York City, each randomly assigning 100 disadvantaged youths to their usual youth program or to the Carrera program. The control group experience typically involved an alternative program that included recreational activities and homework help. Both program and control youth were followed for three years; 79 percent of participants remained in the program for three full years.

Philliber et al. (2002) find no effects on the behavior of males. However, the analysis finds that female participants had significantly lower odds of being sexually active and, conditional on sexual activity, of using a condom and a hormonal method at last intercourse. There is a statistically significant reduction in the likelihood of having experienced a pregnancy. This important finding has been demonstrated in replication sites as well.[11]

The service-learning program Teen Outreach Program (TOP) has also been promoted as an effective teen pregnancy prevention program. This program was created in St. Louis in the 1970s and is currently found in more than four hundred schools and organizations across the country (Isaacs 2007). These programs involve both volunteer work, such as tutoring or park

---

10. The original program sample for this program was based in New York City. Replications took place in Baltimore, MD; Broward County, FL; Houston, TX; Portland, OR; Rochester, NY; and Seattle, WA.

11. The multicomponent Aban Aya Youth Project has also been found to have positive effects on recent sexual activity and condom use, but only for boys. This program was designed for African American youth in grades five through eight and was developed to address multiple problem behaviors such as violence, substance abuse, delinquency, and sexual activity. It is based on an Afrocentric Social Development curriculum instructed over a four-year period. The evaluation is based on self-reported behavior and does not include a measure of teen pregnancy as an outcome. See Flay et al. (2004).

cleanup, and structured time for preparation and reflection. These programs often link the voluntary work to academic instruction in the classroom. Less than 15 percent of the written curriculum addresses issues of sexuality. Allen et al. (1997) evaluate the impact of TOP in twenty-five sites across the country in the mid-1990s. The evaluation finds a statistically significant reduction in teen pregnancy rates among female participants. However, these results should be viewed with caution, as the level of randomization did not always occur at the student level and the statistical analysis makes no adjustment for this (Scher, Maynard, and Stagner 2006). Furthermore, it is not clear what the comparison intervention constituted.

8.3.5   Summary

The majority of evaluations of teen pregnancy prevention programs fail to provide evidence of effectiveness. But that does not imply that such programs can *never* work. The state of the evidence on teen pregnancy prevention programs does not permit a general conclusion about whether one type of program unambiguously works and another unambiguously does not.

The most compelling research on representative abstinence-focused programs (Trenholm et al. 1997) finds no difference in the rates of sexual activity among students in these programs compared to sexual education courses. But, contrary to critics' claims, this empirical research also rejects the hypothesis that the abstinence-focused programs increase rates of unprotected sex. Furthermore, the evaluated programs were implemented in middle schools, and might have different impacts if implemented at the high school level, when students are more likely to be making decisions regarding sexual activity and contraception.

With regard to contraceptive-focused curriculum-based programs, it appears to be the case that in general, these programs also fail to produce noticeable changes in sexual behavior and teen pregnancy rates. But, as highlighted in the previous discussion, there are a few noteworthy curriculum-based programs that may show signs of effectiveness. Still, the effectiveness of these programs and others derived from them will depend on the particular implementation and the appropriate pairing of setting, staff, and targeted population.

There are two widely-heralded multicomponent programs that appear to have had success in bringing down rates of sexual activity and teen pregnancy. But the success of similarly designed programs will also depend crucially on the particular implementation in a particular community setting. Furthermore, the costs will vary widely. Estimates for the TOP program put the costs at around $600 a year per student, compared to $4,000 a year per student served by Carrera. There are two caveats to interpreting these dollar figures. On the one hand, the cost per teen pregnancy averted by these programs would be orders of magnitude higher than these per student figures, since there is nowhere near a one-to-one correspondence between the number of students served and the number of teen pregnancies averted.[12] On the other hand, there are likely to be other benefits to the participants of these programs beyond those captured with sexual outcome measures.

8.3.6 Simulating Pregnancy Impacts from Program Effects

It is instructive to consider how program findings regarding delayed sexual initiation and increased use of contraception can be expected to translate into reductions in teen birth rates. Given that pregnancy is not deterministic, only some acts of unprotected sex will result in pregnancy. The rate of pregnancy resulting from unprotected sex will vary across women and couples and across the timing of the menstrual cycle in which the act occurs. Furthermore, given the imperfect nature of contraception and its use in practice, some women who use contraception, either always or sometimes, will experience a pregnancy anyway. This will depend on method used and consistency and faithfulness of use. So, even if a program has been demonstrated to increase contraceptive use among program teens, it is not entirely straightforward to predict what this will mean for rates of pregnancy. And finally, projecting impacts on birth rates from changes in predicted pregnancy rates will depend on the fraction of affected teens who would have carried the pregnancy to term and given birth.

Amato and Maynard (2007) simulate the effect of reduced sexual activity and increased contraception use on the number of teen births. Their simulations are based on population data from 2004 and information about sexual behavior and contraceptive use among teenagers from the National Survey of Family Growth (NSFG). They find that other things being equal, delaying first intercourse for one year would lower the share of twelve- to fifteen-year-olds at risk for pregnancy and birth by about 9 percentage points. The delay would reduce the number of teen births, at present rates, by about 81,000 a year, a proportional decline of 24 percent. If half of those who do not use contraception were to become consistent users of condoms, the pill, an injectable form of contraception, or an implant, the number of unintended teen births would fall another 60,000 a year, or 14 percent.

8.4   Other Types of Interventions

This section briefly reviews two of the major policy interventions relevant to teen pregnancy and childbearing. These include policies to expand access to affordable contraception and welfare reform. Advocates often call for increased access to contraception as a way to combat high rates of pregnancy among teens and unmarried young women. The presumption is that expanded access to (subsidized) contraception will necessarily lead to

12. Kane and Sawhill (2003) and Isaacs (2007) argue for the cost-effectiveness of such programs.

lower rates of unprotected sex. But this need not be true. If teenagers who get pregnant are by and large not committed to avoiding pregnancy, then a policy of increased access to contraception will not have much impact. Put differently, if teens who are committed to avoiding pregnancy take the necessary measures, then those who take up the newly provided (or subsidized) services might well be those who were already using contraception, or abstaining from sex, before the policy or program change.

8.4.1   Expanded Provision of Contraception

What are the contraceptive practices of teens? Data from the 2002 National Survey of Family Growth (NSFG), tabulated in Kearney and Levine (2009b), reveal that 36 percent of teens were sexually active in the past three months. Of those, 17 percent did not use contraception at their last intercourse, implying that 6 percent of teenage girls had unprotected sex in the past three months. Black and Hispanic teens are significantly less likely than their white counterparts to use contraception. Compared to a rate of 11 percent among white teenage girls, 26 percent of black teenage girls and 37 percent of Hispanic teenage girls report not using contraception at their last intercourse. The most common form of primary contraception among teens in the NSFG is the pill (44.6 percent), followed closely by condoms (40.9 percent). The trends are encouraging. In the 1995 NSFG survey data, 32 percent of teens did not use contraception at last intercourse, yielding a rate of pregnancy risk of 12 percent.

The very limited evidence from school-based contraception-availability programs is not favorable. According to Kirby (2007), the experience of such programs is that they do not appear to increase sexual activity. But unless the clinic focuses on pregnancy reduction in addition to providing contraception, they do not increase the overall use of contraceptives markedly or decrease overall rates of pregnancy or childbirth (17).

Beyond schools, policymakers in Congress are calling for expanded coverage of contraception under the public Medicaid program as a way to reduce rates of unintended pregnancy. Medicaid is now the largest source of public funding for family planning services in the country. Kearney and Levine (2009b) have evaluated the experience of states that have expanded Medicaid family planning coverage. Their analysis provides robust evidence that such expansion policies can lead to sizable reductions in teen birth rates. The results indicate that expanding eligibility to women at higher levels of income (above the traditional Medicaid eligibility level) reduced overall birth rates among teens age fifteen to seventeen by 1.2 percent and teens age eighteen to nineteen by 6.8 percent; birth rates to women age twenty to twenty-four decrease by 5.1 percent. There are no statistically significant decreases in birth rates to older women. Kearney and Levine calculate that as a result of the expansion policy, there is one birth averted for every thirty-six additional Medicaid family planning clients. This suggests program costs on the order of $6,800 per averted birth, though this number cannot be calculated separately for teens.

8.4.2   Welfare Policy

Some scholars have argued that teen and nonmarital childbearing are facilitated and to some extent encouraged by welfare programs that enable a teen mother to financially support her own family. In response to this concern, the 1996 PRWORA legislation explicitly stated as a goal reductions in teen and nonmarital childbearing and included relevant provisions. A key provision aimed at this goal was the requirement of "family caps," which capped the monthly benefit for a family on welfare, regardless of whether the mother gave birth to an additional child. There were also requirements that teen mothers continue to live with their parents in order to qualify for benefits.

The research consensus on welfare policies is that the link between the generosity of cash welfare programs and rates of nonmarital and teen births is at best quite modest. Moffitt (1998) reviews the broad literature on welfare and concludes that the wide range of point estimates across studies suggests some (small) positive causal relationship between welfare benefits and the likelihood of female headship. Kearney (2004) and Levine (2002) find that family cap policies implemented as part of welfare reform were not effective at reducing birth rates among targeted women. Grogger and Karoly (2005) provide extensive review of welfare reform studies and conclude that "there is little evidence that welfare reform as a whole lowers childbearing" (196).[13]

8.5   The Consequences of Teen Pregnancy

It is well-documented that women who give birth as teenagers have inferior later life outcomes than women who give birth at a later age. On average they are less likely to graduate high school, they are more likely to be single mothers, they have lower wages, they have lower family income, and they are more likely to live in poverty, as are their children. These observations drive much of the common perception that teen childbearing has large adverse consequences for girls who become teen mothers. It is also these observed correlations that are behind claims about how much overall poverty has increased or decreased as a result of movements in teen childbearing rates.[14]

Empirical research by economists focuses on identifying the causal link

13. Abortion availability is another policy that is obviously related to teen childbearing. Phillip Levine estimates that abortion legalization in the 1970s led to a 12 percent relative decrease in teen childbearing. However, with regard to pregnancy, expanded access to abortion could lead women and teens to take more risks with regard to getting pregnant (since abortion essentially provides a way to avoid an unwanted birth, should the woman become pregnant). Empirical examinations by economists have confirmed this prediction. For a thorough treatment of the issue, see Levine's 2004 book, *Sex and Consequences*.

14. For example, U.S. Congress (2004).

between teen childbearing (or teen pregnancy) and subsequent poverty. We know that teen mothers are more likely than other mothers to live with their children in poverty, but to what extent would their subsequent poverty rates be different if they delayed childbearing into their twenties? To answer this question, we cannot merely take the lower poverty rate among women who did actually delay childbearing into their twenties. Economists talk about "selection effects" when considering such possibilities. The idea is that teenage girls who select into becoming pregnant and subsequently giving birth (as opposed to choosing abortion) are different in terms of both background characteristics and potential future outcomes than those girls who delay childbearing, either through avoiding pregnancy or choosing abortion. This is a crucial issue to resolve when trying to determine what the realized benefits would be to a program that successfully reduced teen pregnancy or teen childbearing.

To determine the costs of teen pregnancy in terms of reduced earnings and increased poverty, the key question that needs to be answered is to what extent the inferior outcomes of teen mothers are driven by the event of having given birth as a teenager, as opposed to other related factors, such as growing up in disadvantaged circumstances. For example, it is well known that girls who grow up in poverty are more likely to get pregnant and give birth as teenagers. In tabulations of data from the 2003 Panel Study of Income Dynamics (PSID), Kearney and Levine (2009a) report that among the full sample of women age twenty to thirty-five, 24 percent give birth before age twenty. But among the subsample of women age twenty to thirty-five who were born into poverty, 49 percent give birth before age twenty. It is also understood that children who grow up in poverty are more likely to have low family income as adults. So it is almost certainly the case that at least some of the relationship between giving birth as a teen and having lower family income as an adult is due to having grown up in poverty. In other words, a girl who grows up in poverty is relatively more likely to have lower income as an adult whether or not she gives birth as a teen. This is true for other observable family characteristics such as growing up in a female-headed household or being born to a teen mother.

There have been a number of recent studies in which the authors have tried to carefully identify the causal effect of teenage childbearing on subsequent outcomes while holding constant family background characteristics. In one of the first studies in this line of research, Geronimus and Korenman (1992) noted that the prevailing view of teen childbearing as a cause of persistent poverty and poverty transmitted across generations was drawn from cross-sectional studies comparing teen mothers to women who had their first birth at later ages. They point to a review of this early literature conducted by Hayes (1987) that linked teen childbearing to elevated high school dropout rates, rising numbers of female-headed households, and excessive rates of low birth weight and infant mortality among U.S. blacks. To isolate the effect of teen childbearing from the effect of family background, Geronimus and Korenman employ a "within-family" estimation approach that compares differences in subsequent socioeconomic status of sisters who experienced their first births at different ages. They analyze samples from three data sets: the National Longitudinal Survey Young Women's Sample (NLSYW), the Panel Study of Income Dynamics (PSID), and the National Longitudinal Survey Youth Sample (NLSY).

The main findings of Geronimus and Korenman (1992) are that cross-sectional comparisons that do not control for detailed family background greatly overstate the costs of teen childbearing. These main findings were replicated by Hoffman, Foster, and Furstenberg (1993), but this set of authors argues in favor of larger estimated costs found among the PSID sample. In a 1993 reply piece, Geronimus and Korenman argue that even the fairly modest differences in outcomes observed in the PSID sample probably overstate the costs of teen childbearing, since sisters who give birth as teens are potentially on different (and lower) education, earnings, and income trajectories than their sisters who give birth at older ages.

This last point raises the issue that in addition to potential differences in observed and unobserved family background characteristics, girls who are more committed to achieving higher levels of educational attainment and economic success may be more committed to preventing a pregnancy from occurring during their teenage years. Such girls may also be more inclined to choose abortion if they do get pregnant. To the extent that the girls who become teen mothers expect beforehand to be on lower educational and earnings trajectories, we would have observed lower levels of educational attainment and earnings among them later in life even if they had delayed giving birth. From a research perspective, to isolate the effect of the teen birth on later outcomes, we would want to observe a sample of women who have the same potential outcomes and the same inclination to get pregnant and give birth, but by random chance, some do and some do not become teen mothers. Hotz, McElroy, and Sanders make use of a clever research strategy that arguably achieves exactly this.

Hotz, McElroy, and Sanders (2005, 1997) exploit the fact that some women who become pregnant as teenagers experience a miscarriage and thus do not have a birth. They carry out this empirical analysis using data from the National Longitudinal Survey of Youth (NLSY79) on women who were aged thirteen to seventeen between 1971 and 1982. Before describing the results of their analysis, it is informative to consider the descriptive statistics they report from the NLSY79. First, the data reveal that among women who become pregnant before age eighteen, there is no statistical difference in family background characteristics between those who experience a miscarriage and those who give birth. This validates their empirical approach. Second, among women who become pregnant before age eighteen, those who choose to end their pregnancy in abortion on average have family incomes that are 40 percent higher than those who give birth. This supports the claim that among pregnant teens, there are important selection effects driving the decision to become a teen mother.

The consequences of teen childbearing measured by Hotz, McElroy, and Sanders (2005) can be interpreted as the effect of not delaying childbearing for women who become pregnant as teenagers. Importantly, this is the group that is of interest from a policy or program point of view since these are the girls who are targeted by teen pregnancy prevention programs. The authors begin by replicating previous findings of adverse consequences, using straightforward regression techniques that compare outcomes for teen mothers and those who delay childbearing. But when they employ their miscarriages experiment, and thereby avoid confounding selection effects, none of the differences are statistically significant, and some are even reversed in sign, suggesting potentially beneficial effects of teen childbearing for these women. A recent reexamination of this data and approach by Saul Hoffman (2008) finds that the estimated impacts of a teen birth are more negative for teen mothers who had births in the early 1980s relative to 1970s. Looking separately at these two groups of teen mothers suggests that the consequences of teen motherhood may be more negative for more recent cohorts of women.

A recent study by Ashcraft and Lang (2006) builds directly on the Hotz, McElroy, and Sanders study. Their analysis is based on data from the 1995 wave of the National Survey of Family Growth (NSFG), which they claim is better suited for measuring pregnancy outcomes than the NLSY. They argue that the miscarriage experiment approach taken by Hotz and colleagues provides an unbiased estimate of the effects of teen childbearing under two conditions: (a) miscarriages are (conditionally) random across pregnant teens and (b) all miscarriages occur before teenagers can obtain abortions. But as Ashcraft and Lang argue, some girls choose to abort their pregnancies before a potential miscarriage (spontaneous abortion) occurs. They confirm in their data that pregnant teens who obtain an abortion are more likely to come from advantaged backgrounds. Thus, the sample of teens who delay childbearing due to a miscarriage are more likely to be teens who would have chosen to give birth, meaning that they might have had less to lose in terms of educational attainment or earnings from teen childbearing then those who did not. Ashcraft and Lang replicate the Hotz, McElroy, and Sanders approach and confirm that when the analysis sample is limited to pregnant teens who either give birth or miscarry (by excluding girls who obtain an abortion), the estimated effects of teen childbearing move from slightly positive to slightly negative.

Ashcraft and Lang (2006) convincingly demonstrate that the two approaches provide upper and lower bounds on the consequences of teen childbearing. They combine the bounds from the two approaches with some additional information about abortion and miscarriage likelihoods to produce statistically consistent estimates of the effect of teen childbearing on those teenagers who would choose to give birth (as opposed to have an abortion). They report the following estimated effects for the sample of women who were at least twenty years old at the time of the survey and who had their first pregnancy before age eighteen: (a) the likelihood of being currently married is reduced by about 3 percentage points; (b) total number of children is increased on average by 0.8; (c) completed education is reduced by about 0.15 years; (d) the probability of working is reduced by about 5 percentage points, earnings conditional on working are not affected; (e) family income is unaffected. The conclusion of their work is that while teen childbearing might not be as benign as suggested by the results of Hotz, McElroy, and Sanders (2005), any adverse consequences on socioeconomic outcomes that exist are quite small in magnitude.

8.5.1 Reconciling the Research with the Perception

The collective results of these careful studies call into question the view that postponing childbearing will substantially improve the socioeconomic attainment of teen mothers. And if there are not observable improvements in outcomes for the teen mothers themselves, there are not likely to be observable improvements in outcomes for the children of these mothers. How should one reconcile the finding that teen childbearing is not very costly for teen mothers (and potentially their children) with the common perception of substantial consequences? I offer a few observations on this point. The first is the interpretation of the results offered by Hotz, McElroy, and Sanders (2005). The authors note that women who begin motherhood as teens come from less advantaged backgrounds, are less likely to be successful in school, and as such, are less likely to end up in occupations that require higher education compared with women who postpone childbearing. This would explain the absence of adverse, or very large adverse, effects on subsequent work probabilities, earnings, and family income.

A second important observation is that the estimated effects are for teens who choose to carry their pregnancy to term. If abortion were not available as an option, it is likely that the observed effects of teen childbearing would be different because women who would prefer to avoid teen childbearing—presumably because they expect it to have negative consequences—would not have that choice. Tabulations from the 1995 NSFG presented in Ashcraft and Lang (2006) reveal that among first pregnancies to teens under age eighteen, 10 percent are resolved in a miscarriage, 25 percent end in abortion, and 65 percent result in a live birth.[15] In terms of background characteristics, pregnant teens who obtain an abortion are more likely to come from families with higher levels of parental education and are more likely to be

---

15. As a side note, if reducing abortion were the goal, as opposed to reducing poverty, then teen pregnancy prevention could very well be an effective investment.

white. Among the pregnant teens who give birth, 41 percent receive a high school diploma, as compared to 73 percent among those who obtain abortions. From these unadjusted comparisons, we might suspect that part of that difference reflects the negative consequence of giving birth. But among those who miscarry, only 45 percent earn a high school diploma. These numbers reveal that pregnant teens who delay childbearing due to nature (miscarriage) rather than their own choice (abortion) do not complete high school at noticeably higher rates. This fact strongly suggests that teenage girls who intend to achieve higher levels of education, and presumably labor market career outcomes, are more likely to avoid teen childbearing, even if they become pregnant.

Third, we need to think about what avoiding teen childbearing or teen pregnancy means in terms of subsequent childbearing. Among the sample of pregnant teens in Ashcraft and Lang's 1995 NSFG sample, the average age of next pregnancy is 19.6. That suggests that even if programs are successful at getting teens to avoid becoming pregnant in any given year, there is a fairly sizable chance that they will initiate childbearing before their late twenties. And it seems reasonable to speculate that the chances of them waiting until they are in a stable marriage are even smaller. This is potentially what is needed to observe improvements not just for the teen mothers themselves, but also for their children.

It is potentially the case that a longer delay of childbearing initiation, to older ages or a more stable economic or relationship situation, is what is needed in order to see a real positive change in the life course of these teen moms, and perhaps in the lives of their children. Importantly, this might be why the Hotz, McElroy, and Sanders and Ashcraft and Lang papers fail to find large consequences of teen childbearing. The miscarriage "intervention" studied by those papers is only about delaying childbearing past teenage years. If a teen pregnancy prevention program affects more than just the fact of a pregnancy in a given year, say by achieving a longer delay in childbearing initiation or the formation of life-improving skills and aspirations, then larger, more positive effects on subsequent life outcomes could potentially be achieved.

This final point, related to the previous observation, is that perhaps it is not teen childbearing in particular that is consequential, but nonmarital childbearing. In other words, even if these teen mothers were to avoid childbearing until they were in their twenties, if they were still to become single mothers, their rates of poverty would be unaffected. It is well-known that single mothers have the highest rates of poverty. According to 2006 Census figures, 5.7 percent of people living in married couple families live below the federal poverty threshold, as compared to 30.5 percent of people living in female-headed households.[16] Amato and Maynard (2007) argue that school

16. Source: U.S. Census Bureau (2007).

and community programs to help prevent nonmarital births would reduce poverty.

Furthermore, while this piece has focused on the outcomes of teen mothers themselves, much of the public concern about teen pregnancy is driven by concern for the children of these teen mothers. Though there is a lack of compelling evidence suggesting that delaying teen childbearing would noticeably improve outcomes for children, there is overwhelming evidence that children raised in a family with two biological parents fare much better in terms of economic and cognitive outcomes than children raised in single-mother households.

8.6   Final Discussion

The research reviewed in this chapter suggests that the socioeconomic consequences of teen childbearing for teen mothers are at worst only modestly adverse. The most methodologically compelling studies demonstrate that the lower rates of high school completion, lower rates of marriage, lower family income, and higher rates of poverty observed among women who were teen mothers reflect selection effects as opposed to the consequences of teen childbearing itself. It appears to be the case that girls who become pregnant and give birth tend to be headed for lower levels of educational attainment and family income even before the event of the teen birth. A pessimistic reading of these results might lead one to conclude that teen pregnancy prevention programs are therefore not effective investments if the goal is to reduce poverty.

A more ambitious take-away is that the previous discussion makes the case that in order to reduce poverty and improve adult outcomes, programs designed to reduce teen pregnancy need to focus on a much broader set of outcomes. Successful programs would steer teenage girls away from whatever sense of disadvantage it is that is leading them to become teen mothers. This could mean equipping these girls with skills that would facilitate educational and labor market success. It could mean helping reshape their life vision and ambitions. In their ethnographic study of single mothers in a poor urban setting, Edin and Kafalas (2006) observe that many of the women in their sample became mothers because they saw it as something positive they could achieve. They observe that "the daily stresses of an impoverished adolescence . . . breed a deep sense of need for something positive to 'look to'" (205). If teen childbearing is not costly for teen mothers because these girls were not aiming for education or labor market success, then arguably the best investment would be to successfully change their goals and aspirations and put them on the path to a better life. And in fact, as the review of the aforementioned program interventions suggests, this is just the kind of program that is showing signs of success in reducing teen pregnancy.

References

Allen, J. P., S. Philliber, S. Herrling, and G. P. Kupermine. 1997. Preventing teen pregnancy and academic failure: Experimental evaluation of a developmentally based approach. *Child Development* 64 (4): 729–42.

Amato, P. R., and R. A. Maynard. 2007. Decreasing nonmarital births and strengthening marriage to reduce poverty. *Future of Children* 17 (2): 117–41.

Ashcraft, A., and K. Lang. 2006. The consequences of teenage childbearing. NBER Working Paper no. 12485. Cambridge, MA: National Bureau of Economic Research, August.

Brooks-Gunn, J., and F. F. Furstenberg, Jr. 1989. Adolescent sexual behavior. *American Psychologist* 44 (2): 249–57.

Brooks-Gunn, J., and R. Paikoff. 1997. Sexuality and developmental transitions during adolescence. In *Health risks and developmental transitions during adolescence,* ed. J. Schulenberg, J. L. Maggs, and K. Hurrelmann, Cambridge: Cambridge University Press.

DiClemente, R. J., G. M. Wingood, and K. F. Harrington. 2004. Efficacy of an HIV prevention intervention for African American adolescent girls. *Journal of the American Medical Association* 292 (2): 171–79.

Edin, K., and M. Kefalas. 2005. *Promises I can keep: Why poor women put motherhood before marriage.* Berkeley, CA: University of California Press.

Flay, B. R., S. Graumlich, E. Segawa, J. L. Burns, and M. Y. Holliday. 2004. Effects of 2 prevention programs on high-risk behaviors among African American youth: A randomized trial. *Pediatric Adolescent Medicine* 158 (April): 377–84.

Geronimus, A. T., and S. Korenman. 1992. The socioeconomic consequences of teen childbearing reconsidered. *Quarterly Journal of Economics* 107 (4): 1187–214.

———. 1993. The socioeconomic costs of teen childbearing: Evidence and interpretation. *Demography* 30 (2): 281–90.

Geronimus, A. T., S. Korenman, and M. M. Hillemeier. 1994. Does young maternal age affect child development? Evidence from cousin comparisons in the United States. *Population and Development Review* 20 (3): 585–609.

Grogger, J., and L. A. Karoly. 2005. *Welfare reform: Effects of a decade of change.* Cambridge, MA: Harvard University Press.

Guttmacher Institute. 2006. *U.S. teenage pregnancy statistics: National and State trends and trends by race and ethnicity.* New York: Guttmacher Institute.

Hayes, C. D. 1987. Adolescent pregnancy and childbearing: An emerging research focus. In *Risking the future,* volume 2, ed. S. L. Hofferth and C. D. Hayes, 1–6. Washington, DC: National Academy Press.

Hoffman, S. D. 2008. Updating the teen miscarriage experiment: Are the effects of a teen birth becoming more negative? Working Paper no. 08-08. University of Delaware, Department of Economics.

Hoffman, S., M. Foster, and F. F. Furstenberg, Jr. 1993. Reevaluating the costs of teen childbearing. *Demography* 30:1–13.

Hotz, V. J., S. W. McElroy, and S. Sanders. 2005. Teenage childbearing and its life cycle consequences: Exploiting a natural experiment. *Journal of Human Resources* 40 (3): 683–715.

Hotz, V. J., C. Mullin, and S. Sanders. 1997. Bounding causal effect using data from a contaminated natural experiment: Analyzing the effects of teenage childbearing. *Review of Economic Studies* 64 (4): 575–603.

Isaacs, J. B. 2007. Cost-effective investments in children. Budgeting for National Priorities Paper. Washington, DC: Brookings Institution, January.

Jemmott, J., III, L. Jemmott, and G. Fong. 1992. Reductions in HIV risk-associated

sexual behaviors among black male adolescents: Effects of an AIDS prevention intervention. *American Journal of Public Health* 82 (3): 372–77.
———. 1998. Abstinence and safer sex HIV risk-reduction interventions for African American adolescents: A randomized controlled trial. *Journal of the American Medical Association* 279 (19): 1529–36.
Jemmott, J., III, L. Jemmott, G. Fong, and K. McCaffree. 1999. Reducing HIV risk-associated sexual behaviors among African American adolescents: Testing the generality of intervention effects. *American Journal of Community Psychology* 27 (2): 161–87.
Jorgensen, S. R., V. Potts, and B. Camp. 1993. Project taking charge: Six-month follow-up of a pregnancy prevention program for early adolescents. *Family Relations* 42 (4): 401–06.
Kane, A., and I. Sawhill. 2003. Preventing early childbearing. In *One percent for the kids*, ed. I. Sawhill, 56–75. Washington, DC: Brookings Institution.
Kearney, M. S. 2004. Is there an effect of incremental welfare benefits on fertility behavior? A look at the family cap. *Journal of Human Resources* 39 (2): 295–325.
Kearney, M. S., and P. B. Levine. 2009a. Socioeconomic disadvantage and early childbearing. In *An economic perspective on the problems of disadvantaged youth*, ed. J. Gruber, 181–209. Chicago: University of Chicago Press.
———. 2009b. Subsidized contraception, fertility, and sexual behavior. *Review of Economics and Statistics* 91(1): 137–51.
Kirby, D. 1997. *No easy answers: Research findings on programs to reduce teen pregnancy*. Washington, DC: National Campaign to Prevent Teen Pregnancy.
———. 2001. *Emerging answers: Research findings on programs to reduce teen pregnancy*. Washington, DC: National Campaign to Prevent Teen Pregnancy.
———. 2007. *Emerging answers 2007: Research findings on programs to reduce teen pregnancy and sexually transmitted disease*. Washington, DC: National Campaign to Prevent Teen Pregnancy.
Kirby, D., M. Korpi, C. Adivi, and J. Weissman. 1997. An impact evaluation of Project SNAPP: An AIDS and pregnancy prevention middle school program. *AIDS Education and Prevention* 9 (A): 44–61.
Kirby, D., M. Korpi, R. Barth, and H. Cagampang. 1995. *Evaluation of education now and babies later (ENABL): Final report*. Berkeley, CA: University of California, School of Social Welfare.
Levine, P. B. 2002. The impact of social policy and economic activity throughout the fertility decision tree. NBER Working Paper no. 9021. Cambridge, MA: National Bureau of Economic Research, June.
———. 2004. *Sex and consequences: Abortion, public policy, and the economics of fertility*. Princeton, NJ: Princeton University Press.
Maynard, R. A., ed. 1997. *Kids having kids: Economic costs and social consequences of teen pregnancy*. Washington, DC: The Urban Institute Press.
Moffitt, R. 1998. The effect of welfare on marriage and fertility: What do we know and what do we need to know? In *Welfare, the family, and reproductive behavior*, ed. R. Moffitt, 50–97. Washington, DC: National Research Council, National Academy of Sciences Press.
Philliber, S., J. W. Kaye, S. Herrling, and E. West. 2002. Preventing pregnancy and improving health care access among teenagers: An evaluation of the Children's Aid Society-Carrera Program. *Perspectives on Sexual and Reproductive Health* 34 (5): 244–51.
Ribar, D.C. 1994. Teenage fertility and high school completion. *Review of Economics and Statistics* 76 (3): 413–24.
Santelli, J. S., J. Abma, S. Ventura, L. Lindberg, B. Morrow, J. Anderson, S. Lyss,

and B. Hamilton. 2004. Can changes in sexual behaviors among high school students explain the decline in teen pregnancy rates in the 1990s? *Journal of Adolescent Health* 35 (2): 89–90.

Scher, L., R. Maynard, and M. Stagner. 2006. *Interventions to reduce pregnancy-related outcomes among teenagers.* Social Welfare Review Groups: Campbell Collaboration. Available at: http://www.campbellcollaboration.org/doc-pdf/teenpregreviewdec2006.pdf.

Schinke, S. P., B. J. Blythe, L. D. Gilchrist, and G. A. Burt. 1981. Primary prevention of adolescent pregnancy. *Social Work With Groups* 4 (1–2): 121–35.

St. Lawrence, J., R. Crosby, L. Belcher, N. Yazdani, and T. Brasfield. 1999. Sexual risk reduction and anger management interventions for incarcerated male adolescents: A randomized controlled trial of two interventions. *Journal of Sex Education and Therapy* 24 (1–2): 9–17.

St. Lawrence, J., R. Crosby, T. Brasfield, and R. O'Bannon, III. 2002. Reducing STD and HIV risk behavior of substance-dependent adolescents: A randomized controlled trial. *Journal of Consulting and Clinical Psychology* 70 (4): 1010–21.

St. Lawrence, J., K. Jefferson, E. Alleyne, T. Brasfield, R. O'Bannon, and A. Shirley. 1995. Cognitive-behavioral intervention to reduce African American adolescents' risk for HIV infection. *Journal of Consulting and Clinical Psychology* 63 (2): 221–37.

Thomas, B. H., A. Mitchell, M. C. Devlin, C. Goldsmith, J. Singer, and D. Watters. 1992. Small group sex education at school: The McMaster Teen Program. In *Preventing adolescent pregnancy: Model programs and evaluations,* ed. B. C. Miller, J. C. Card, R. L. Paikoff, and J. L. Peterson, 28–52. Newbury Park, CA: Sage Publications, Inc.

Thomas, M. H. 2000. Abstinence-based programs for prevention of adolescent pregnancies. *Journal of Adolescent Health* 26 (1): 5–17.

Trenholm, C., B. Devaney, K. Fortson, L. Quay, J. Wheeler, and M. Clark. 2007. *Impacts of four Title V, Section 510 abstinence education programs: Final report.* Mathematica Policy Research Inc., April.

U.S. Census Bureau. 2007. *Current population survey, 2007 annual social and economic supplement.* Washington, DC: U.S. Census Bureau.

U.S. Congress, Ways and Means Committee-Democrats. 2004. Steep decline in teen birth rate: Significantly responsible for reducing child poverty and single-parent families. Committee Issue Brief, Washington, DC.

U.S. Department of Health and Human Services. 2005. National Center for Health Statistics, National Vital Statistics Report 55 (1). Available at: www.cdc.gov/nchs/data/nvsr/nvsr55_01.pdf.

Villarruel, A. M., J. B. Jemmott, III, and L. S. Jemmott. 2006. A randomized controlled trial testing an HIV prevention intervention for Latino youth. *Pediatric Adolescent Medicine* 160 (August): 772–7.

Dropout Prevention and College Prep

Bridget Terry Long

9.1 Introduction

The benefits of education are substantial in terms of both monetary and nonmonetary returns. However, the pathway to obtaining a bachelor's degree involves many milestones, and along the education pipeline, two decision points have proven critical hurdles: obtaining a high school degree and successfully transitioning to a postsecondary institution. In 2007, nearly 7,000 students dropped out of high school each day with 1.2 million students not graduating from high school as scheduled (Editorial Projects in Education EPE Research Center [EPE] 2008). While some may eventually complete a General Educational Development (GED) certificate or other high school equivalent, analysis suggests high school dropouts face a tough labor market and are more likely to need government support and become entangled in the criminal justice system. Meanwhile, of the students who do graduate high school, about two-thirds subsequently enroll in higher education within two years, but there are huge disparities by income, race, ethnicity, and gender (Advisory Committee on Student Financial Assistance 2001). Once arriving at a college or university, many of these students are not prepared for college-level work, and over one-third are therefore forced to first complete remedial or developmental courses before starting to accumulate credits towards postsecondary degree (Bettinger and Long 2007).

Investments in high school dropout prevention and college preparatory programs could greatly reduce poverty by addressing these major leaks in the educational pipeline. Improving these critical transition points would bolster a student's chances for gaining the skills necessary to thrive in the labor

Bridget Terry Long is a professor of economics and education at Harvard University and a faculty research fellow of the National Bureau of Economic Research.

market as well as have numerous nonmonetary benefits on the quality of the student's life. This chapter reviews the literature on high school dropout prevention and college preparatory programs with the goal of summarizing the available research. I review studies on a number of the larger programs geared at improving these transition points and extrapolate on the likelihood that investments in such programs would be an effective antipoverty effort.

The chapter continues by giving additional background on the problems: the considerable number who drop out of high school, the low college entry rates among some groups, and the insufficient postsecondary preparation of many high school graduates. I then elaborate on the underlying reasons for these problems and outline the approaches that have been taken to address these problems. Following this, I describe the major initiatives and programs that target high school dropout prevention and college preparation. Section 9.4 discusses the key evidence on the effectiveness of these programs and considers the implications of this research. Section 9.5 concludes and offers suggestions about future lines of research.

9.2   Background

9.2.1   Problem no. 1: High School Dropout Rates

To understand the prevalence of students dropping out of high school, one must first settle on a definition of the term. High school dropout rates are often not measured uniformly with school districts, states, and researchers using a variety of definitions. Until recently, many definitions were used without discussion about the underlying assumptions of each statistic and the comparability of numbers across sources. Different assumptions are often made about the grade levels or age of student who should be classified as dropouts. For example, some measures include the ninth through twelfth grades while other only count students who dropout within their last (twelfth) year. There is also variation in the length of time that a student is required to miss school before they are considered a dropout (this can range from fifteen to forty-five days of unexcused absence), which students are included in the calculation (e.g., some may exclude students who receive special education services), and which programs count toward enrollment (some count students enrolled in GED programs or night schools while others only include those enrolled in traditional day schools). Finally, the flow of students who transfer in or out of the school can complicate the process of determining an accurate dropout rate (Lehr et al. 2004).

Noting these issues in measurement, there has been a recent push to establish a consistent set of indicators across time and school district. In terms of the educational pipeline, the most useful measures track a cohort of students over time to determine whether and how they progress through school. Greene and Winters (2005) and the Editorial Projects in Education

(EPE) Research Center (2008) attempt to approximate the percentage of ninth graders who earn a regular diploma four years later.[1] Although not a true longitudinal measure, they both find that about 70 percent of students graduate high school on time.[2] Similarly, in a 2008 study using a slightly different measure but intending to reflect the same type of longitudinal measure, the National Center for Education Statistics (NCES) found the high school graduation rate for the 2005 to 2006 school year to be 73.4 percent (Stillwell and Hoffman 2008).[3]

All of the studies found high school dropout rates to differ by demographics, background, and region. For instance, EPE's *Diploma Counts 2008* study found that only about 57.8 percent of Hispanic students, 55.3 percent of black students, and 50.6 percent of Native American students graduated on time with a regular diploma compared to 81.3 percent of Asian students and 77.6 percent of white students. Stillwell and Hoffman (2008) found similar differences by racial group although the percentages for each group were slightly higher. There were also differences by gender with women graduating at a much higher rate than men.

While freshmen graduation rates four years later give some sense of the students left behind without a degree, another way to measure the prevalence of dropping out of high school is to use direct estimates. Stillwell and Hoffman (2008) provide an event dropout rate, which is the proportion of students who drop out in a single year.[4] During the 2005 to 2006 school year, they find that there were more than 579,000 dropouts from high school (grades nine through twelve) among forty-eight reporting states. The overall annual event dropout rate was 4.0 percent but ranged from 3.2 percent in grade nine to 5.5 percent in grade twelve. It also differed greatly by state from 1.6 percent in New Jersey to 8.9 percent in Alabama. As with the

1. According to Greene and Winters (2005), there are several reasons why GED recipients should not be included in the high school graduation rates. They point to research that has found that the returns to a GED are far less than that of a regular diploma (see Cameron and Heckman 1993; Murnane, Willett, and Boudett 1995). Further, EPE (2008) notes that the No Child Left Behind Act counts only students receiving standard high school diplomas as graduates.

2. The Greene method estimates the number of students who enter the ninth grade, makes some adjustments for changes in population, and then divides the resulting number into the number of students who actually graduated with a regular diploma; while EPE uses the Cumulative Promotion Index (CPI) method, in which they multiply grade-specific promotion ratios (i.e., the ninth to tenth-grade promotion rate times the tenth to eleventh-grade rate, etc.). This takes into account the schooling conditions prevailing during a particular school year.

3. An averaged freshman graduation rate (AFGR) was calculated by NCES, and divides an estimate of an incoming freshman class with the number of diplomas awarded four years later. The incoming freshman class size is estimated as the summation of the enrollment in eighth grade in one year, ninth grade for the next year, and tenth grade for the year after, and then dividing by three.

4. A dropout is defined as a student who was enrolled at any time during the previous school year but who did not enroll at the beginning of the next school year and had not completed school. The following are not considered dropouts: students who have transferred to another school, died, moved to another country, or who are out of school due to illness.

aforementioned measure, there were differences in dropout rates by race. The high school event dropout rates were highest for Native American (7.4 percent), black, non-Hispanic (6.1 percent), and Hispanic (6.0 percent) students; and lowest for white, non-Hispanic (2.7 percent) and Asian (2.4 percent) students.

A third (and broader) way to measure high school degree attainment is to examine at one point in time the proportion of students who have not completed a high school degree and are not enrolled in school. The U.S. Department of Education tracks this information over time to produce a status dropout rate, which includes any sixteen- to twenty-four-year-old student without a high school credential (i.e., diploma or equivalent, such as GED) regardless of when they dropped out of school. Table 9.1 summarizes the trends from 1972 to 2006. Over this time period, the status dropout rate fell from 14.6 percent to 9.3 percent. Most of the decline occurred prior to 1992 and the rate stagnated in the late 1990s and early 2000s. Although the rate has decreased over time, the total number of dropouts remains above 3.4 million students due to the growing numbers of individuals age sixteen to twenty-four years old.

There are several reasons why the status dropout rate differs from the high school graduation rate reported above, which is about 70 percent. First, the high school graduation rate only includes students who finish on time, while the status rate includes anyone who eventually completes a high school degree by the time surveyed (up to age twenty-four). In addition, the status rate includes individuals who eventually complete an alternative degree, such as a GED. Finally, it is worth noting that the status rate is based on self-reported data rather than school records, and so some individuals may inflate their actual attainment level. This could particularly be a concern for students who attended high school during their senior year but did not actually complete the requirements for a diploma.

Table 9.2 gives a more detailed snapshot of the status dropout rate for sixteen- to twenty-four-year-olds in October of 2006. As noted above in other studies, this measure of the dropout rate also highlights differences by race and gender. While only 3.6 and 5.8 percent of Asian and white students age sixteen to twenty-four did not have a high school credential, respectively, the rates were 10.7 percent for black, and 22.1 percent for Hispanic students. Given such differences, even though the white population is much larger than the Hispanic population, there are more Hispanic dropouts than white dropouts. In terms of gender, men are more likely to drop out, and the dropout rate increases with age. The dropout rate was also very high among Hispanic students born outside of the United States (36.2 percent).

While the above measures document differences in the propensity to drop out of high school by race/ethnicity, gender, and age, other studies have also found a connection between family income and the likelihood of graduating high school on time. Graduation rates are significantly lower in districts

Table 9.1   **Status high school dropout rates for sixteen- to twenty-four-year-olds, 1972–2006**

Year	Status dropout rate (%)	Number of dropouts (thousands)	Population (thousands)
1972	14.6	4,769	32,643
1977	14.1	5,031	35,658
1982	13.9	5,056	36,452
1987	12.7	4,252	33,452
1992	11.0	3,410	30,944
1997	11.0	3,624	32,960
1998	11.8	3,942	33,445
1999	11.2	3,829	34,173
2000	10.9	3,776	34,568
2001	10.7	3,774	35,195
2002	10.5	3,721	35,495
2003	9.9	3,552	36,017
2004	10.3	3,766	36,504
2005	9.4	3,458	36,761
2006	9.3	3,462	37,047

Sources: Laird et al. (2008, table 7). U.S. Department of Commerce, Census Bureau, Current Population Survey (CPS), October (1972–2006).

Notes: The status dropout rate indicates the percentage of sixteen- through twenty-four-year-olds who are not enrolled in high school and who lack a high school credential. High school credentials include high school diplomas and equivalent credentials, such as a General Educational Development (GED) certificate. Estimates beginning in 1987 reflect new editing procedures for cases with missing data on school enrollment items. Estimates beginning in 1992 reflect new wording of the educational attainment item. Estimates beginning in 1994 reflect changes due to newly instituted computer-assisted interviewing.

with higher percentages of students who are eligible for free or reduced-price lunches (Swanson 2004). Moreover, Lehr et al. (2004) found that low-income students as well as non-native English speakers, disabled students, and children of single or unemployed parents are more likely to drop out of high school than other students. For example, high school students living in low-income families drop out of school at six times the rate of their peers from high-income families (NCES 2004). Achievement in high school is also an important factor as Carnevale (2001) found that the lowest achieving quarter of students were twenty times more likely to drop out of high school than students in the highest achievement quartile.

9.2.2   Problem no. 2: College Access and Preparation

While obtaining a high school degree is an accomplishment, it is not sufficient enough to grant a student the opportunities necessary for a middle class standard of living. Unfortunately, the likelihood of attending college varies substantially by family income. Among high school graduates in 2004, only 43 percent of students from families who made less than $30,000 immediately entered a postsecondary institution. In contrast, 75 percent

Table 9.2   Status dropout rates for sixteen- to twenty-four-year-olds, October 2006

Characteristic	Status dropout rate (%)	Number of dropouts (thousands)	Population (thousands)
Total	9.3	3,462	37,047
Race/ethnicity			
White, non-Hispanic	5.8	1,337	22,863
Black, non-Hispanic	10.7	565	5,260
Hispanic	22.1	1,421	6,439
Asian, non-Hispanic	3.6	56	1,549
More than one race	7.0	49	703
Gender			
Male	10.3	1,935	18,707
Female	8.3	1,527	18,340
Age			
16	2.8	124	4,462
17	5.0	210	4,212
18	8.6	356	4,120
19	9.7	386	3,982
20–24	11.8	2,385	20,270
Born outside the United States			
Hispanic	36.2	959	2,648
Non-Hispanic	6.6	126	1,898

Sources: Laird (2008, table 6). U.S. Department of Commerce, Census Bureau, Current Population Survey (CPS), October 2006.

Notes: The status dropout rate indicates the percentage of sixteen- through twenty-four-year-olds who are not enrolled in high school and who lack a high school credential. High school credentials include high school diplomas and equivalent credentials, such as a General Educational Development (GED) certificate. Due to small sample size, American Indians/Alaska Natives are included in the total but are not shown separately. Detail may not sum to totals because of rounding.

of students from families who made more than $50,000 did so.[5] Even after accounting for differences in academic preparation and achievement, substantial gaps in college access still exist by income. Low-income high school graduates in the top academic quartile attended college only at the same rate as high-income high school graduates in the bottom quartile of achievement (Advisory Committee on Student Financial Assistance 2001).

Even if students are able to access higher education, a high school degree also does not guarantee that they are prepared to undertake postsecondary level courses. Greene and Foster (2003) estimate that only 34 percent of high school graduates in 2002 were academically prepared for college.[6] College

5. Authors' computations using 2004 October Current Population Survey.
6. They measured college readiness by trying to reproduce the minimum standards of the least selective four-year colleges. To meet the criteria, students must have graduated with a regular high school diploma (i.e., not a GED), have completed a minimum set of course requirements, and been able to read at a basic level.

readiness rates were lowest for African American and Hispanic students (23 and 20 percent, respectively), with 40 percent of white students being found prepared. Although it is debatable whether this is the most accurate method of determining the proportion who are college-ready, most accept that many students finish high school below grade-level competency and certainly below the level expected for college.

Sometimes academic deficiencies are so severe that colleges choose to expel the students. For instance, during the fall of 2001, the California State University system "kicked out more than 2,200 students—nearly 7 percent of the freshman class—for failing to master basic English and math skills" (Trounson 2002). However, the most common response of institutions has been to test and place ill-prepared students in college remedial or developmental courses.[7] In 2001, colleges required nearly one-third of first-year students to take remedial courses in reading, writing, or mathematics (NCES 2003). Moreover, there is some evidence that the proportion of students in need of college remediation has been growing. According to the NCES (1996), 39 percent of colleges surveyed reported that remedial enrollments had increased during the last five years. At some colleges and universities, over two-thirds of the entering class is placed into remedial courses (Bettinger and Long 2007).

9.2.3   The Consequences of High Dropout Rates and Low College Access and Preparation

The repercussions of these two leaks in the educational pipeline are evident in many ways. High school dropouts earn less; in 2006, the annual income of persons age eighteen to sixty-five who did not have a high school degree was $21,000 compared to over $31,400 for those with a high school degree or GED. (U.S. Bureau of the Census 2007). Rouse (2005) concludes that "over a lifetime, an eighteen-year-old who does not complete high school earns approximately $260,000 less than an individual with a high school diploma." Combined with contributing less in federal and state taxes, she finds that the total losses to the country for not having a person graduate from high school amount to $192 billion for one cohort of students. High school dropouts are also more likely to rely on government support programs, such as welfare and food stamps, suffer from health ailments, and be incarcerated (College Board 2004, 2007). According to 1997 and 1998 data from the U.S. Department of Justice (2000, 2002), approximately 30 percent of federal inmates, 40 percent of state prison inmates, and 50 percent of persons on death row are high school dropouts. As Rouse summarizes,

---

7. Most scholars define "remediation" as courses students need to retake while defining courses that are new material as "developmental." In this chapter, I will refer to both types of courses as being remedial.

having a high school diploma is a "necessary (but not sufficient)" condition for being successful in America.

However, earning a high school degree is also not sufficient to enabling students to reach a middle class standard of living. Higher education plays an increasingly important role in helping individuals attain social and economic success. According to the U.S. Census Bureau, individuals with a college degree made 62 percent more than those with only a high school degree in 2005 (College Board 2007). The monetary rewards to a college degree are so great that many in the field have begun to summarize the college attendance decision as the "million dollar question." On average, people with a bachelor's degree will earn $1 million more over the course their lifetimes than those with only a high school diploma. Additionally, as noted above, there are many nonmonetary benefits associated with attaining more education such as lower rates of government dependency and incarceration and better health.

9.3   Possible Solutions: An Overview

The need to target investments to reduce the number of high school dropouts and better prepare students for college is evident. However, the first key to determining the best way to invest resources is to understand why students drop out of high school or fail to prepare and enter college. This section first reviews the research on why these problems exist and then introduces the general approaches that have been taken to address these issues. The following section focuses on particular programs and evaluations, but first I summarize some of the challenges in conducting convincing and useful evaluations.

9.3.1   Understanding High School Dropout
Behavior and Potential Solutions

Certain behaviors are associated with dropping out that could be addressed and altered using interventions. The Northwest Regional Educational Laboratory (NREL) (1995) summarizes these behaviors as fitting them into four main categories. The first is school-related factors such as poor academic performance, repeating a grade, poor attendance (truancy, absenteeism, tardiness, suspension), and other disruptive behaviors and disciplinary infractions. Student-related factors are the second category and include personal problems that are separate from social or family background. Among these factors could be substance abuse, pregnancy, and legal problems. Third are family related factors such as an unstable or stressful home life, socioeconomic status, and the education level of the parents. Lehr et al. (2004) also note that the families of dropouts have permissive parenting styles and few educational supports. Finally, community-related factors like poverty are also associated with dropout behavior. Whether these behaviors and factors are the actual causes of dropping out or things that are correlated with the true root cause remains to be determined.

In an effort to improve the preparation of high school students, educational reforms may have also inadvertently increased dropout rates. During the last thirty years, nearly every state has increased their high school graduation requirements in response to concerns about educational quality and the declining value of the high school, especially following the *A National at Risk* report. However, several studies suggest that increasing high school graduation requirements adversely affected graduation rates. For instance, Bishop and Mane (2001) find higher course graduation requirements are associated lower high school graduation rates. Lillard and DeCicca (2001) find similar results. Another effort to improve academic preparation has come in the form of high school exit exams. However, similar to the above results concerning graduation requirements, Dee and Jacob (2007) find that exit exams increase the probability of high school dropout, particularly among twelfth grade students.

Meanwhile, the growth of alternative ways to get a high school credential may have also increased dropout behavior. Heckman (1993) highlights the growth in exam-certified high school equivalents, such as the GED. He notes that government funding for adult education programs that feature such certification has grown along with increasing numbers of postsecondary programs that require the GED or a similar credential in order for students to qualify for benefits. Such development could have a role in encouraging high school dropout behavior as students may believe that the GED is a good substitute for a regular degree (Tyler 2003). In fact, Heckman, LaFontaine, and Rodriguez (2008) found that raising the difficulty of the GED exam caused more students to finish high school rather than dropping out.

To reduce dropout rates, efforts have typically focused on interventions within schools. High schools have tried to provide adequate financing for programming that meets the needs of dropouts and improve connections with postsecondary education, particularly community colleges (Steinberg and Almeida 2004). Many have also implemented early warning systems to target interventions for at-risk students (Kennelly and Monrad 2007). Reforms have also focused on altering school structures to improve educational outcomes. For example, some have tried implementing schools within a school, redefining the role of the homeroom teacher, reducing class size, and creating an alternative school (NREL 1995).

Other interventions work outside of the typical school setting. NREL (1995) categorizes several types of interventions. The first is called personal or affective and refers to programs that involve individual counseling or target self esteem. The second type of intervention is academic and includes the provision of special academic courses, individualized methods of instruction, and tutoring. Family outreach, or programs that include increased feedback to parents or home visits, is another type of intervention. Finally, interventions that work outside of schools may be work related and consist of vocational training or participation in volunteer or service programs. While the main focus of this chapter is on these "add on" interventions (i.e., programs that work either outside of or in partnership with schools), I also include several important interventions that are school-based.

9.3.2   Understanding Gaps in College Enrollment and Preparation and Potential Solutions

Focusing on the transition to higher education, there are three main barriers to enrollment. The first is cost, and that issue is being addressed by another chapter in this volume. A second major barrier is academic preparation. Numerous studies link the types of courses students take in high school to their entry into and performance in higher education. For example, in descriptive work, Adelman (1999) finds that a student's academic background, defined by measures of academic content and performance in secondary school such as high school curriculum intensity, class rank and GPA, are highly correlated with college enrollment and success. In an update, Adelman (2006) finds curriculum to be even more strongly correlated with degree completion. Not surprisingly, studies also identify academic preparation to be related to the need for college developmental or remedial courses. A 2002 study by the Ohio Board of Regents (OBR) found that students who had completed an academic core curriculum in high school were half as likely to need remediation in college when compared to students without this core curriculum.

Even students who complete the recommended high school courses often are still placed into postsecondary remediation. In the OBR study, 25 percent of those with a core high school curriculum still required remediation in either math or English. As a result, many officials interpret the increasing role of remediation as a signal of the ineffectiveness of secondary school systems. While many reforms attempt to improve the quality of teaching and rigor of high school classes, even these efforts may not be sufficient. Several researchers also note the large disconnect between what high schools aspire to achieve and the competencies that colleges require (McCabe 2001). Venezia, Kirst, and Antonio (2003) detail how the coursework in high schools is designed according to standards that are entirely different in college. Moreover, assessments in high school often emphasize different knowledge and skills than those that are tested in college entrance and placement. This points the possible role of inventions that work outside of regular high schools.

The above point about the disconnect between high schools and colleges also underscores a third major barrier to college enrollment and success: information. Lack of good information about how to access, pay for, and succeed in college is a major concern. In terms of financial aid, the Commission on the Future of Higher Education, assembled by Secretary of Education Spellings, concluded that some students "don't enter college because of inadequate information and rising costs, combined with a confusing financial aid system." The Commission further emphasized that "our financial aid system is confusing, complex, inefficient, [and] duplicative" (2006). Perhaps due to the complexity of the system and the lack of information about the availability of aid, 850,000 students who would have been eligible for federal financial aid in 2000 did not complete the necessary forms to receive such aid (King 2004).

Lack of information also results in students not performing the steps necessary to gain admissions into college or taking the proper courses to adequately prepare for higher education. College attendance is the culmination of a series of steps and benchmarks, and this current landscape is too complex and difficult for many families to decipher and navigate. First, students must aspire to attend college or derive aspirations from their parents, teachers, and/or mentors. Additionally, students must prepare academically for college by taking the proper classes and getting a sufficiently high grade point average, particularly if they wish to attend selective schools. To gain entry into a four-year college, students must also register for a college admissions exam (i.e., the SAT or ACT). Finally, students must fulfill the requirements for high school graduation. Research by Kane and Avery (2004) showed that low-income high school students possess little understanding of how to handle this admissions process or knowledge about actual college tuition levels. Other work has also found a significant lack of information among prospective college students in general (Ikenberry and Hartle 1998; Horn, Chen, and Chapman 2003).

9.3.3   Addressing the Problems: An Overview of Programs and Research Issues

Programs targeting students at risk of dropping out or not continuing to college often have multiple components (Gándara and Bial 2001). The programs usually include some combination of academic enrichment, counseling, mentoring, and personal enrichment along with possible college and/or financial aid advising and scholarship support. However, while most programs choose to target high school students, others begin to target children in elementary or middle school. Some programs work directly with schools or adopt an entire cohort of students, but others instead choose to work with individual students. Figure 9.1 summarizes the goals of outreach programs, while figure 9.2 gives a sense of the range of services offered by such programs. The information was collected by the College Board in the National Survey of Outreach Programs.[8]

8. This survey was conducted in association with the Education Resources Institute and the Council for Opportunity in Education during the 1999 to 2000 school year with the intent of collecting detailed information about all types of early intervention programs. Figures 9.1 and 9.2 were reported in Swail (2000).

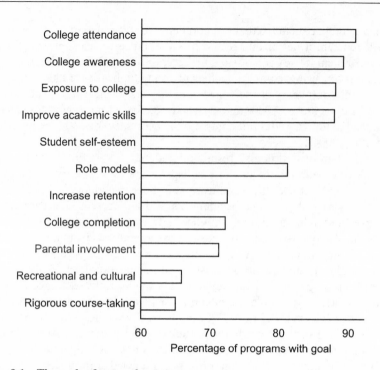

Fig. 9.1   The goals of outreach programs
Source: College Board (2000); reported in Swail (2000).

The following section reviews the evidence on some of these programs to comment on their effectiveness. While there have been a number of evaluations of the programs that aim to reduce the number of high school dropouts and increase college access and success, most have faced a number of difficulties. Lack of good data is a major problem, and for this reason, conclusions about programs are often reduced to statistics on the dropout or college entry rate of participants without much additional detail. Other issues make it difficult to establish the causal effect of the interventions.

The first major problem of many of these evaluations is lack of an appropriate comparison group. In order to determine the effects of a program, one must consider what would have happened otherwise, and so a control group is necessary to provide that baseline. However, few programs collect information on such a comparison group, and using a group of students with similar characteristics may not give unbiased results. This is because participation in an intervention is often not random and so there are unobservable differences between the students who do and do not choose to participate in a program. As a solution, several studies try to identify peer schools with similar student body characteristics as the focal school, but who were not offered the intervention. The quality of this research approach

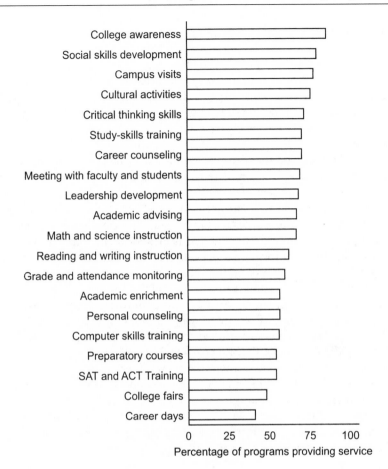

Fig. 9.2   The services offered by outreach programs (by percentage)
Source: College Board (2000); reported in Swail (2000).

depends greatly on the amount of information the researcher has to make the matches. Still, the local environments and trends of each matched pair may differ in ways that could affect the analysis, and so one must be cautious in interpreting the results of such analyses.

Many evaluations are also unable to isolate which components of a program are successful or not successful in helping students. For instance, as part of Upward Bound, students could participate in an intensive instructional program as well as receive counseling. However, when examining the outcomes of students in the program, it may not be possible to know if the instructional program was the reason for the effect, or the counseling was the reason instead (or perhaps both services are needed to produce a result). Related to the issue of isolating the effect of a particular component of an intervention is the fact that students often have the opportunity to participate in several support programs at the same time. In other words, a focal intervention does not operate in a vacuum. Detailed information on services received, whether they be from the focal intervention or some other program, is needed to properly interpret the results, but these data are not usual available. One may also be unable to determine the relative effectiveness of one program or component versus another. However, such information could be extremely valuable in determining how to invest limited resources.

Researchers face another complication when trying to evaluate large programs with many sites. Often there is a great deal of variation across sites in which students are recruited to participate and how, the supports they receive, the leadership, and the information collected from students and the comparison group. Sometimes the lack of standardization is advantageous so that programs can adjust to the needs of a local environment, but this makes evaluating multiple programs difficult. For example, the large federal programs require grantees to follow basic principles to accomplish a common goal, but each program can vary in exactly how they choose to offer and implement an intervention. Evaluations of the overall program are then complicated by the fact of this underlying variation by program site.

Keeping all of the aforementioned complications in mind, the following review highlights some of the best research that has been done on the major programs that target reducing high school dropout rates and increasing college access and success. Unfortunately, the previous concerns call into question the interpretation of many of the results. Therefore, it is difficult to draw steadfast conclusions about what exactly works. Also, most studies report little on costs, and so one is unable to do a proper cost-benefit analysis to determine the most effective investments.

9.4   Specific Interventions and Evaluations

This section summarizes and reviews the evaluations of programs that attempt to reduce high school dropout rates and increase college access and success. I discuss the key evidence on the effectiveness of the programs and consider the implications of this research. Special attention is paid to what has been learned about how to best target investments with the goal of reducing poverty by increasing educational attainment. However, instead of directly measuring the effects of programs on degree completion, many of the studies focus on intermediate outcomes that might be positively associated with eventual attainment and skill acquisition. For example, outcomes such as parental knowledge and involvement, course-taking patterns, and college application behavior are common. As mounting evidence indicates that a student's decision to finish high school and go to college is the result of a complex web and series of decisions and influences that begin long before high school, many of the programs profiled provide multiple services over a period of time, and the evaluations look at how these interventions influence outcomes that occur long before high school graduation or college entry. Many of the key programs combine the multiple goals of high school preparation and graduation and postsecondary enrollment, and so I do not separate the discussion of the programs into two groups. Table 9.3 summarizes the characteristics of the major programs, while table 9.4 highlights the major studies on their effectiveness.

9.4.1   GEAR UP

The October 1998 reauthorization of the Higher Education Act created the Gaining Early Awareness and Readiness for Undergraduate Programs (GEAR UP). The federal program is a comprehensive intervention program and is tasked with equalizing access to higher education for low-income students. The GEAR UP grantees are charged with establishing partnerships among school districts, colleges and other organizations to operate the projects; and states and partnerships are awarded six-year grants to provide the services at high-poverty middle and high schools. There is a great deal of variation in how the funds are used, but as mandated by legislation, the programs must promote giving college information to students and parents and providing individualized academic and social support to students; the funds may also be used to provide college scholarships (Westat 2003). With 185,602 participants in its first year (2000 to 2001), the program grew quickly to 305,888 participants in its second year. The typical partnership served an average of 1,264 students between 2001 and 2002 (Terenzini et al. 2005).[9]

Westat (2003) did some initial descriptive analysis on the early implementation of GEAR UP. They followed a group of GEAR UP participants in twenty partnership programs who had entered the program in seventh grade during the 2000 to 2001 school year. The services received included tutoring, college planning activities, summer programs, and professional development activities for teachers. Given that the analysis was only on the first two years of the program, the participants had not reached the age of high school graduation or college entry.

After the initial analysis, the researchers chose eighteen middle schools and matched them with eighteen similar schools as a comparison group (Westat 2008). The schools chosen were not done so randomly, and there were limits to the researchers' ability to find good match schools, and so this should be considered a nonexperimental design. The small sample size of schools also limits that analysis of school-level outcomes. However, the researchers also randomly selected 140 seventh graders from each school to survey along with their parents. In their analysis, they concluded that

---

9. As noted by the authors, these figures may differ somewhat from those of other sources due to the fact that GEAR UP participants tend to be highly mobile, and the count will vary depending on the time taken. The figures here are from the GEAR UP Annual Performance Reports.

Table 9.3   **Overview of major interventions**

Program name	Location(s)	Participant characteristics	Approach and program components
GEAR UP (Gaining Early Awareness and Readiness for Undergraduate Programs)	242 Partnerships nationwide in 2001–2002	Low-income students	Comprehensive intervention program tasked with equalizing access to higher education for low-income students. Program promotes giving college information to students and parents, providing individualized academic and social support to students, and college scholarships. Grantees are also charged with establishing partnerships among school districts, colleges, and other organizations.
Upward Bound	In 2004, about 52,000 students in 727 projects nationally	Economically disadvantaged students At least two-thirds participants must be both low-income and potential first-generation college students	Provides a variety of services; including instruction, tutoring, and counseling, throughout the school year. Also offers an intensive instructional program that meets daily for about six weeks during the summer. Majority of projects are hosted by four-year colleges. Students typically enter the program while in ninth or tenth grade and may participate through the summer following twelfth grade (most typically remain in Upward Bound for about 21 months).
Talent Search	382,500 students in 470 projects nationally (FY2004)	Low-income, potentially first-generation college students	Designed to help students prepare for and gain access to college. Provides information on the types of high school courses students should take to prepare for college and on the financial aid available to pay for college. Helps students complete financial aid applications and navigate the college application process.

Program	Location	Target Population	Description
Project GRAD (Graduation Really Achieves Dreams)	Houston, TX Atlanta, GA Columbus, OH (nationally, serves more than 121,900 youth in 205 public schools)	Low-income students in economically disadvantaged communities	Goal is to see at least 80 percent of students graduate from high school and 50 percent of these graduates enter and graduate from college. Aims to reduce dropping out and increase rates of college enrollment and graduation by increasing reading and math skills and improving behavior in school. Provides services in those elementary and middle schools that feed in to the participating high schools. At the high school level, students are required to take an academic program, attend college campus–based summer academic institutes, participate in career exploration activities, and they can earn scholarships for college. The scholarship program is available to all graduates with 2.5 GPA.
AVID (Advancement Via Individual Determination Program)	3,500 schools in 45 states and 15 countries (2007)	Students capable of completing a rigorous curriculum	Attempts to enroll students in more challenging classes, including honors and AP courses. Students also enroll in the AVID elective, in which they learn organizational and study skills, work on critical thinking, and get academic help from peers and college tutors.
Puente Project	California	Services all kinds of students but targets nonimmigrant Latino students	Goal of increasing the number of educationally disadvantaged students who enroll in four-year institutions, earn degrees, and return to the community as mentors. Program includes a rigorous counseling component in which participants meet with trained community members. Student must also meet at least monthly with teachers and advisors to discuss challenges and life choices. Parents must also sign a statement agreeing to support the student and attend meetings.

Table 9.4   Overview of major evaluations

Intervention and study	Data and sample	Research design	Outcome
GEAR UP Westat (2008)	18 middle schools and matched them with 18 similar schools Randomly selected 140 seventh graders from each school to survey along with their parents	Comparisons between matched schools Analysis of the student and parent surveys	Positively associated with the student's and parents' college knowledge Likelihood of parents being involved in their children's education Rigorous courses taken during middle school
GEAR UP Terenzini et al. (2005)	Annual Performance Reports and school-level data on 47 GEAR UP schools to 133 peer schools	Examined how the outcomes of cohorts changed over time Compared schools with GEAR UP to their similar peers	Students' college plans Students' math scaled scores on the Stanford-9 test (accounting for students' previous test scores and school characteristics)
Upward Bound Myers and Schirm (1999) Myers et al. (2004) Mathematica Policy Research, Inc.	Nationally representative sample of eligible applicants Data from surveys, transcripts, and staff reports	Longitudinal evaluation Applicants were randomly assigned to Upward Bound or a control group	Number of high school math credits earned and other measures of high school academic preparation. Course-taking: honors and AP courses Enrollment at four-year institutions
Talent Search Constantine et al. (2006)	Florida, Indiana, and Texas	State administrative records Compared the outcomes of participants to similar students	Apply for financial aid Enroll in a public institution Graduate from high school (Florida and Texas only)
Project GRAD Snipes et al. (2006).	Houston, TX: ninth-grade students from thirteen high schools (three Project GRAD schools and ten comparison schools) Atlanta and Columbus (in each, one Project GRAD school and one comparison school)	Interrupted time series analysis and comparisons with similar schools Outcomes were tracked from the implementation at each site (ranging from the mid-1990s to the early 2000s) until the 2002 to 2003 school year	Proportion of students who completed a core academic curriculum on time Attendance and promotion to tenth grade (Atlanta and Columbus sites where it is too soon to examine the impact on high school graduation)
AVID Guthrie and Guthrie (2000, 2001)	Initial cohort of 435 students; Increased sample to 1,100 later	Compared the high school outcomes of students who took AVID in middle school to students who did not	High School GPA High school credit accumulation
Puente Gándara (1998) Moreno (2002)	Small sample of 144 students	Matched participants with students in the control group that had similar characteristics	Admission Test Completion SAT by twelfth grade Attend a four-year college Attend a two-year college College persistence after three years

Effect size	Cost
Positively associated with college knowledge. Used various measures. Ranged from 6 to 19 percent point differences. Parents reported attending meetings about college preparatory curricula: 17 percent versus 9 percent (GEAR UP program vs. not). African American students from GEAR UP schools averaged one-half more rigorous courses as compared to those from non-GEAR UP schools.	DOE awarded $75 million to 164 partnership grantees and $42 million to 21 state grantees in 1999 No information on specific programs or services within partnerships
Positively affected (strongest effects with parent-focused activities). By the end of the seventh grade (one year later), growth favored CIP schools by 2.05 mean scaled math score. By the end of the eighth grade, CIP schools outperformed their counterparts by 1.2 mean scaled math score (marginally insignificant).	
Raised the average number of high school credits earned from nineteen credits to twenty-one credits. Much of the increase from additional credits in core academic subjects); however, the effects were statistically significant only for math (0.2 credits) Increased the number of honors and AP courses completed by lower-expectation students by 0.7 credits (70 percent of the treatment group completed one more course than they would have otherwise). Increased likelihood of four-year college enrollment by 6 percentage points; larger for students with lower educational expectations.	Upward Bound is an intensive program and so considered expensive On average, cost per student served was about $4,800 per year, and these expenditures provided a variety of services (FY2001)
17, 14, and 28 percentage points more likely to apply, respectively, for Florida, Indiana, and Texas. Enrollment was higher by 14, 6, and 18 percentage points, respectively, for Florida, Indiana, and Texas. Increased graduation 9 and 14 percentage points, respectively, for Florida and Texas, but these results may be biased upward.	Received $144 million to serve 382,500 students in 470 projects nationally in fiscal year 2004 (averaged $375 per participant served)
At the initiative's flagship school, program had a statistically significant positive effect of nearly 7 percentage points (no effects found at the two other Houston high schools). Consistently finds positive effects but they are only sometimes statistically significant.	Difficult to price the individual components as much is done within schools (implementing a specific curricula, academic counseling summer academic enrichment, and a scholarship)
Higher GPAs the longer the exposure to AVID in middle school (effects not sustained in high school). Positively influenced credit accumulation but the difference appears small (around 2 credits).	No information
36 percent points higher among Puente students. 7 percentage points higher among Puente students. 13 percentage points higher among Puente students. 19 percentage points higher among Puente students.	Budget of $1,501,000 in 2004 serving 3,799 students (average around $395/person)

attending a GEAR UP school (measured near the end of eighth grade) was positively associated with several intermediate outcomes that could in turn improve educational attainment. Students and parents at GEAR UP schools knew more about the opportunities and benefits of postsecondary education (ranging from gains of 6 to 19 percentage points), there was an increased likelihood of parents attending meetings about college preparatory curricula (17 percent for GEAR UP program participants versus 9 percent among nonparticipants), and parental expectations were higher. On the other hand, there was no evidence that GEAR UP influenced academic performance, school behavior, nor students' aspirations to attend college. African American students also seemed to be positively impacted by GEAR UP to take 0.5 more rigorous courses during middle school than students at non-GEAR UP schools (Westat 2008). The lack of information on the costs associated with GEAR UP schools precludes a clear cost-benefit analysis of these outcomes.

Terenzini et al. (2005) also analyzed the effects of GEAR UP using two data sources on the first two years of the program. The first data source was the GEAR UP Annual Performance Report for Partnerships (APR) database, which contains information at the partnership level of 265 GEAR UP programs. This information includes partnership enrollments, activities, programs, staffing, and selected outcomes as reported in student and parent surveys. The researchers did not have a separate comparison group and instead examined how the outcomes of cohorts changed over time with more exposure to GEAR UP-based activities. For example, they tracked how the percentages of students performing academically at specified levels or who knew certain kinds of information changed over time.

The second data source of Terenzini et al. (2005) was information on all California public elementary schools from the Policy and Evaluation Division of the California Department of Education. Although this part of the research did not focus on GEAR UP exclusively, the researchers focused on schools offering GEAR UP programs to analyze "the outcomes associated with the structural concepts and kinds of activities and programs that GEAR UP embodies" (11). The researchers compared the outcomes of these schools to similar peer schools also in the state. In total, the study compared 47 GEAR UP schools to 133 peer schools by examining academic performance as measured by the Stanford-9 tests.

The results of Terenzini et al. (2005) are somewhat limited by their use of data aggregated to the partnership or school level (in comparison to the more nuanced analysis possible with individual student data). However, they did find that GEAR UP was positively associated students' college plans with the parent-focused activities having a stronger effect than those directed at students. Because the effects were more pronounced in the second year, the researchers suggest that the impact of GEAR UP on college aspirations and plans may be cumulative. Focusing on college-readiness levels, the researchers found that GEAR UP schools had higher Stanford-9 math scores in grade seven (the mean scaled math score was 2.05 points higher) even after accounting for students' previous test scores and school characteristics. However, there was no statistical difference by grade eight, and the analysis did not find statistically significant differences in reading scores.[10] Based on the nonexperimental research design, these results should be considered only suggestive of the possible effects of GEAR UP. Due to the age of the students in the sample, no direct statements were made about how GEAR UP did or did not affect eventual attainment.

9.4.2   Upward Bound

One of the largest and longest running federal programs, Upward Bound is "designed to generate skills and motivation necessary for success in education beyond high school among young people from low-income backgrounds and inadequate secondary school preparation" (Public Law 90-222, December 23, 1967). In 2004, about 52,000 students participated in 727 regular Upward Bound projects around the country (Myers et al. 2004). At least two-thirds of each project's participants must be both low-income and potential first-generation college students. Students typically enter the program while in ninth or tenth grade and may participate through the summer following twelfth grade (most typically remain in Upward Bound for about twenty-one months). Projects provide students with a variety of services, including instruction, tutoring and counseling. In addition to regularly scheduled meetings throughout the school year, projects also offer an intensive instructional program that meets daily for about six weeks during the summer. The vast majority of projects are hosted by four-year colleges (Myers et al. 2004).

Mathematica Policy Research, Inc., (MPR) has been conducting a national evaluation of Upward Bound for the Department of Education since December 1991. The effects of Upward Bound on high school outcomes were presented in Myers and Schirm (1999), and Myers et al. (2004) presents results based on the national evaluation's third follow-up data collection (completed in 2000). The latter report updates the findings from the former and examines the impact of Upward Bound on students' postsecondary experiences. These are longitudinal evaluations in which eligible applicants were randomly assigned into an Upward Bound program or to a control group. In deciding which Upward Bound programs to study, the researchers formed a nationally representative sample of Upward Bound projects.

For the analysis, the researchers used data from surveys (a baseline survey conducted from 1992 to 1994, and follow-up surveys conducted from 1994 to 1995, 1996 to 1997, and 1998 to 2000), high school and postsecondary

---

10. These results are reported in more detail in Cabrera et al. (2006).

transcripts, and reports on participation from Upward Bound project staff. In comparison to many other evaluations, the research design of these studies is experimental and quite strong.

The analysis suggests that for the average student, Upward Bound increased the number of high school math credits earned but did not affect other measures of high school academic preparation. Upward Bound may have also increased enrollment at four-year institutions, particularly for students with lower educational expectations, but "the evidence is not conclusive" (xvii). The evidence is more definitive in establishing that students with lower expectations who participated in Upward Bound did earn more credits at four-year colleges. The number of credits completed on average doubled from eleven to twenty-two credits thereby suggesting Upward Bound may have an impact on educational attainment for some students. However, students with higher expectation did not experience similar gains, and there was no overall effect on enrollment or total credits earned (Myers et al. 2004). Both reports suggest that Upward Bound would have had larger effects if students had remained in the program for longer periods of time as many left after during the first year of participation (Myers and Schirm 1999; Myers et al. 2004).

The earlier report also emphasized the fact that Upward Bound appeared to have differential effects for different kinds of students. The found impacts were larger for boys in comparison to girls, for Hispanic and white students in comparison to African American students, and for students who were low-income only or low-income and potential first-generation college students in comparison to students who qualified for the program only as potential first-generation students. Poorer performing students were also found to benefit substantially more than their better performing peers (Myers and Schirm 1999).

Because it is a relatively intensive program, Upward Bound is considerably more expensive than most other precollege programs. In fiscal year 2001, the cost per student served was about $4,800 per year (Myers et al. 2004), or $5,620 in 2007 dollars. While the MPR evaluations establish the relative outcomes of Upward Bound participants and nonparticipants using an experimental design with random assignment, the reports do not provide precise cost information for the sites they evaluated nor a full cost-benefit analysis making it difficult to compare these results with alternative interventions.

There is also a math and science initiative within Upward Bound. In 1990, the U.S. Department of Education created this initiative with the goal of addressing the relatively low levels of academic achievement by economically disadvantaged students in math and science courses. Upward Bound Math-Science (UBMS) awards grants to institutions to provide instruction to students, including hands-on experience in laboratories, computer facilities, and at field sites. They also offer a six-week summer program providing intensive instruction in laboratory science and mathematics through precalculus. As such, the program provides intense instruction and support. The costs of UBMS are similar to Upward Bound.

To do their evaluation, which was nonexperimental, MPR randomly selected a sample of students who were participating in UBMS and compared them to students who had applied to enroll in regular Upward Bound but who had never participated in UBMS. They found that the program improved high school grades in math (from an average of 2.7 to 2.8) and science (from 2.7 to 2.9) and overall, increased the likelihood of taking chemistry and physics in high school (from 78 to 88 percent and 43 to 58 percent, respectively), and increased the likelihood of enrolling in more selective four-year institutions from 23 to 33 percent (Olsen et al. 2007). However, it is important to note that these results are based on a less rigorous research design than the Upward Bound evaluations discussed before.

9.4.3   Talent Search

The Talent Search program was created in 1965 as one of the original federal TRIO programs, which also includes Upward Bound (discussed in the previous section). The program is designed to help low-income, first-generation college students prepare for and gain access to college by providing information on the types of high school courses students should take to prepare for college and on the financial aid available to pay for college. The program also helps students complete financial aid applications and navigate the college application process. According to Constantine et al. (2006), Talent Search received approximately $144 million to serve 382,500 students in 470 projects nationally in fiscal year 2004, or $158 in 2007 dollars. This averaged to approximately $375 per participant served that year, or $412 in 2007 dollars.

Constantine et al. (2006) collected administrative records from multiple sources to evaluate the effectiveness of Talent Search in Florida, Indiana, and Texas. They compared the outcomes of participants to similar students at the same schools or other schools who did not participate. As noted before, this nonexperimental approach may not be sufficient in establishing a causal relationship if there are important differences in the nonobservable characteristics of participants and the matched control group. To enable them to study the impact of Talent Search on high school completion and postsecondary enrollment, the analysis focuses on the cohort of students who were in ninth grade during the 1995 to 1996 school year. Students may have received services at any point from grades six until the end of high school.

The researchers found that Talent Search participants were more likely to apply for financial aid and enroll in a public institution, especially a two-year college, than the comparison students. The differences in initial enrollment in a postsecondary institution was 14, 6, and 18 percentage points higher for Talent Search participants in Florida, Indiana, and Texas, respectively. In Florida and Texas, where they had good data about high school completion, they also found differences between the outcomes participants and nonparticipants: those in Talent Search graduated high school at rates 9 and 14 percentage points higher in Florida and Texas, respectively. However, the authors are less confident about this finding due to the possibility that program staff may have chosen to serve students they deemed more likely to complete high school. In summary, although this is not a randomized study, the use of detailed individual student data makes this a stronger analysis than other studies with certain caveats previously noted and by the researchers.

Brewer and McMahan Landers (2005) conducted another study of Talent Search. This paper focuses on the program at the University of Tennessee-Knoxville and compares the enrollment rates of 758 participants to a control group of 450. However, because the control group is made up of students who were eligible for Talent Search services but elected not to receive them, it is likely that there are unobservable differences between the two groups. If motivation and aspirations affected the likelihood of participating in Talent Search, and these factors are also related to the outcomes of interest (i.e., postsecondary attendance), then the results will be biased upward. There were also observable differences between the groups as the nonparticipants' parents had lower average educational attainment. The researchers indeed find that the participants were significantly more likely to attend college, but it is unclear how large the bias might be, and so the contributions of this study are limited.

9.4.4   Project GRAD

First launched in Houston, Texas, Project Graduation Really Achieves Dreams (Project GRAD) is designed to improve academic achievement, high school graduation rates, and rates of college attendance for low-income students. It does this by first trying to help students arrive at high school better prepared academically by implementing a specific reading and math curricula, along with enhanced professional development for teachers, at the elementary and middle school levels. At the high school level, Project GRAD offers special academic counseling and summer academic enrichment and a college scholarship (Partee 2000). The scholarship typically provides a minimum of $1,000 per year for four years, and students must meet eligibility requirements that are formalized in a contract designed to motivate students to stay in school and focus on college preparation (Project GRAD n.d.)

The nonprofit, nonpartisan MDRC research organization conducted an evaluation of Project GRAD to determine its effects on high school course-taking, academic performance, and graduation rates. The researchers used a nonexperimental research design by comparing the changes in student outcomes at Project GRAD schools with changes at similar, non-Project GRAD schools in the same districts. Outcomes were tracked from the implementation of the first components of the model at each site (ranging from the mid-1990s to the early 2000s) until the 2002 to 2003 school year. However, due to the fact that many Project GRAD students did not benefit from exposure to the model in elementary or middle school, many did not enter high school at the appropriate level of preparation as originally intended, and this affected the implementation of the program at the high school level and the overall evaluation of its effects (Snipes et al. 2006).

For the study of the Houston sites, Snipes et al. (2006) focused on three Houston high schools that implemented Project GRAD from 1998 to 2004 and compared their outcomes to ten high schools in the district that did not implement the program but had similar student body characteristics. The researchers concluded that Project GRAD had a statistically significant positive impact on the proportion of students who completed a core academic curriculum on time and graduated from high school within four years at the initiative's flagship school in Houston (which improved 12 percentage points to 21 percent) relative to the control group (which improved 6 percentage points to 17 percent). However, at the two other Houston high schools, they did not find positive effects on students' academic preparation. Improvements in graduation rates at the three Project GRAD Houston high schools were generally matched by improvements in graduation rates at the comparison schools suggesting Project GRAD did not have an effect on the likelihood of high school graduation. Project GRAD high schools in Columbus and Atlanta showed improvements in attendance and promotion to tenth grade that appear to have outpaced improvements at the comparison schools. However, the differences are only sometimes statistically significant. Moreover, due to the limited amount of follow-up in the expanded program sites, the researchers suggest that the results for sites other than Houston should be treated as more provisional.

The researchers conclude that Project GRAD had limited effects most likely due to the fact that it does not intervene directly in classroom instruction at the high school level. However, they do point out that the program's "focus on the full span of grades, the connection to postsecondary education, and the need to work above the level of individual schools are now appreciated as important aspects of many district-level reforms" (Snipes et al. 2006). Although the Project GRAD materials and website tout much more positive research results, other studies of Project GRAD only examine changes overtime within the Project GRAD schools (e.g., Opuni 1999; Opuni and Ochoa 2002). They do not utilize comparison groups to establish a counterfactual and determine a more accurate measure of the effects of the program.

9.4.5   AVID

The Advancement Via Individual Determination (AVID) Program targets students in fifth through twelfth grade with the hope of helping students who are capable of completing a rigorous curriculum but currently fall short of their potential. Many of AVID's students are from low-income or minority families. To improve outcomes, AVID attempts to enroll students in more challenging classes, including honors and advanced placement (AP) courses. Students also enroll in the AVID elective, in which they learn organizational and study skills, work on critical thinking, and get academic help from peers and college tutors. According to its website, in fall 2007, AVID was in 3,500 schools in forty-five states and fifteen countries.

Guthrie and Guthrie (2000, 2001) conducted longitudinal studies of the program designed to examine the impact of AVID on middle school students as they transition to high school. The research tracked an initial cohort of 435 students and added of new cohort of ninth graders during year three of the study for a study sample of about 1,100 students. The nonexperimental study then compared the high school outcomes of students who took AVID in middle school to students who did not. The early results suggested that students with two years of AVID in middle school had a significantly higher GPA than those with only one year of AVID or no AVID experience. However, this pattern was not sustained in high school. The researchers did find that AVID appeared to positively influence credit accumulation. While the accumulation of credits put the AVID students on track for acceptance into a public university, their standardized reading test scores were below the national average.

Another study of AVID focused on ten high schools in Texas (Watt, Powell, and Mendiola 2004). The researchers collected data on nearly 1,300 participants and found that all of the AVID schools improved their accountability ratings during the first three years of AVID implementation. In comparison to their classmates, AVID students did better on standardized tests and attended school more often. Finally, the study concludes that enrollment in AP courses at AVID schools is increasing, suggesting that more underrepresented students are being prepared for college. However, little is known about the exact research design to comment on the strengths versus weaknesses of this study, which appears to have used a nonexperimental design.

9.4.6   Puente Project

The Puente Project is an outreach program with the goal of increasing the number of educationally disadvantaged students who enroll in four-year institutions, earn degrees, and return to the community as mentors. Although it services all kinds of students, Puente targets nonimmigrant Latino students in particular as an original goal was to increase the number of Latino students attending the University of California. (Gándara 1998). In 2004, it served nearly 3,800 students (Gándara 2005). The program includes a rigorous counseling component in which participants meet with trained community members. Student must also meet at least monthly with teachers and advisors to discuss challenges and life choices. Their parents must also sign a statement agreeing to support the student and attend necessary meetings.

Gándara (1998) and Moreno (2002) are two studies of Puente. Gándara (1998) focused on college going rates, admissions test trends, and high school course-taking and performance. Her nonexperimental study compared participants with students who had similar characteristics (e.g., by achievement level and grades). Gándara found that Puente was associated with positive effects on the outcomes of students participating in the program, including increasing the likelihood of applying to a University of California campus and taking a precollege admissions exam. Slightly more Puente students took honors courses and participated in the SAT II subject exams. The study by Moreno (2002) of long-term outcomes further support claims about the positive effects of Puente. In the long-term, Puente students were more likely to have both gone and persisted in college. However, both studies are based on a very small sample of students; the Gándara (1998) study has a population of 144 students in both the treatment and control groups. Also, many of the outcomes are self-reported.

9.4.7   Other Programs and Evaluations

The profiles and discussion of research on the above programs gives a basic sense of the types of programs implemented to address the dropout and college access problems. There have been other studies that have reviewed additional programs. For example, Dynarski, Gleason, Rangarajan, and Wood (1998) is an evaluation of sixteen dropout prevention programs that were supported by grants from the U.S. Department of Education from 1991 to 1995. The programs of the study ranged from those located middle versus high schools but all were designed to help students perform better and stay in school. The services of the programs included intensive instruction, attendance monitoring, counseling, small school settings, mentoring, and links with social service providers. To determine the effectiveness of the programs, the researchers used an experimental design by randomly assigned students to treatment or control groups and tracked their outcomes with surveys and school records. Students assigned to treatment groups could participate in one of the programs while those in the control group could attend school as they normally would, and could participate in other available education programs.

The analysis resulted in two sets of conclusions. Of the middle school program, the authors concluded that intensive programs can improve grade promotion and reduce the rate of dropping out while low-intensity middle school programs did not improve outcomes. At the high school level, the research suggests that the GED programs were successful helping students obtain GED certificates. However, alternative high school programs did not reduce dropping out or improve other outcomes. The high school programs also did not affect personal and social outcomes (Dynarski et al. 1998).

To the question of whether programs for at-risk high school students can impact outcomes, the authors conclude that such interventions "can affect high school completion mostly in the form of GED attainment" (56). They also cite an evaluation by Hayward and Tallmadge (1995) of dropout prevention programs that found that four of the ten programs reduced the dropout rate but not other outcomes.

Gándara and Bial (2001) also try to identify the most effective practices of programs "capable of at least doubling the college-going rate of participants." They conclude that the best programs provided mentors who would guide a student over a long period of time, high-quality instruction through access to the most challenging courses offered by the school, and financial assistance and incentives. The most effective programs also focused on long-term investments (rather than shorter-term investments), paid attention to the cultural background of students, and provided a peer group that supported a student's academic aspirations as well as social and emotional support. However, the authors underscore the limitations of much of the underlying research on which they base their conclusions. Supplementing my previous list of research difficulties, they point to program attrition, incomplete records on program contact, little information on long-term outcomes as problems of the research, and note that there was limited evidence that the programs raised academic achievement.

9.4.8   Mandatory Schooling Laws: Dropout Prevention?

In addition to the intervention programs reviewed before, compulsory schooling laws are another form of dropout prevention. By requiring students to remain in school until a certain age, they have effectively set a minimum for educational attainment, which was an increase from what some students would have otherwise completed. Angrist and Krueger (1991) established this fact by documenting the fact that laws were binding for some students. They estimate that compulsory schooling laws required as many as 25 percent of potential high school dropouts to remain in school thereby increasing their educational attainment. Their estimates apply to men who were high school-age by at least 1980, so it is unclear whether the results accurately describe the effects of compulsory schooling laws for current cohorts. Goldin and Katz (2003) examine an earlier period using 1960 census data and conclude that the expansion of state compulsory schooling and child labor laws from 1910 to 1939 explains about 5 percent of the increase in the educational attainment. Lleras-Muney (2001) also finds that the laws had a positive effect on individuals age fourteen between 1915 and 1939.

Similar results in terms of the effects of compulsory schooling laws have also been found in other countries (Oreopoulos 2003). Beyond educational attainment, the research suggests these laws are also connected to lower crime rates (Lochner and Moretti 2004) and lower mortality (Lleras-Muney

2001). However, these outcomes are likely indirectly related to the laws and instead the result of increased educational levels.

9.5   Summary and Conclusions

The objective of this chapter was to review the literature on high school dropout prevention and college preparatory programs with the goal of determining the likelihood that investment in such programs would be an effective antipoverty effort. As documented by many sources, substantial numbers of students do not graduate from high school. Among high school graduates, many do not enroll in college or find themselves underprepared for college-level coursework. These are significant problems that cost society dearly in terms of the reliance on expensive government programs and lost tax revenue, but more importantly, individuals suffer in multiple ways as a result of low educational attainment.

While there are many programs that attempt to address these problems, as my review demonstrates, it is difficult to draw strong conclusions about what are the most effective approaches. The research literature is plagued by poor data, inadequate comparison groups, and complications when trying to determine the relative impact of multiple services. Additionally, there is little information about cost to extrapolate a cost-benefit analysis.

Ultimately, the key question is whether any of these interventions show promise in terms of increasing educational attainment. Several of the studies focus on outcomes such as credit accumulation, high school graduation, and college entry, and the results suggest that more intensive interventions (e.g., Upward Bound) can have positive effects but perhaps only for certain subgroups of students (e.g., students with low expectations). Still, much of the evidence is not conclusive nor are many estimates that large. Other studies look more at intermediate steps that might lead to greater educational attainment, such as taking a more challenging curriculum, getting a higher GPA, or applying to college. There is more supportive evidence on these outcomes, but clearer connections need to be made with educational attainment.

While the research literature does not provide clear and definitive answers on this topic, a few general points can be taken away from the aforementioned studies. Several of the evaluations concluded that more systemic, longitudinal interventions were more successful with the effects increasing with prolonged involvement in a program. Interventions providing a variety of services, including instruction, counseling, and intensive summer activities were also found to have more positive effects. However, starting early (i.e., in middle school) and continuing to work with students until the end of high school can be quite expensive. Also, while some results suggest the effects of early investments are sustaining, other studies did not find that early positive effects still remained as the students got older and farther away from the intervention.

9.5.1 Suggestions for Future Research

Looking forward, future analyses should follow the example of some of the more in-depth studies and implement random assignment to determine who gets the intervention (e.g., Dynarski et al. 1998). This would create the best possible comparison group for causal analysis, but a great deal of planning is necessary to accomplish this. However, with limited resources and the great need for such programs, oversubscribed programs could use a lottery to determine who gets the benefits, and as long as the researchers continue to track the applicants who did not get into the program, they should be able to establish a rigorous study.

The availability of new data sources should also greatly help future analyses. Similar to Constantine et al. (2006), researchers should tap into the state and district administrative databases that now include kindergarten through twelfth grade, and postsecondary data on students. Supplemented by surveys and program information, one might be able to do more comprehensive research on the effects of programs. Special attention should also be paid to collecting information on program costs to enable full cost-benefit analyses in the future.

There is also a great need to distinguish the effects of one particular service versus another or how different combinations of services impact student outcomes. To address this, researchers should carefully consider research designs that will allow them to estimate separately the effects of different parts of an intervention. This may involve larger sample sizes and more complex randomization plans, but the result would be more specific information about exactly what types of services to include in the most effective program. Finally, with careful research design and larger sample sizes, future evaluations should attempt to estimate how the effects of an intervention differ by type of student, as research suggests that one size fits all is not the best way to try to address these problems.

References

Adelman, C. 1999. *Answers in the tool box: Academic intensity, attendance patterns, and bachelor's degree attainment* (short web-based version). Washington, DC: U.S. Department of Education. Available at: http://www.ed.gov/pubs/Toolbox/toolbox.html.

———. 2006. *The toolbox revisited: Paths to degree completion from high school through college. Executive summary.* Washington, D.C.: U.S. Department of Education. Available at: http://www.ed.gov/print/rschstat/research/pubs/toolbox revisit/index.html.

Advisory Committee on Student Financial Assistance. 2001. *Access denied: Restoring the nation's commitment to equal educational opportunity.* Washington, DC: U.S. Department of Education.

Alliance for Excellent Education. 2008. *The high cost of high school dropouts: What the nation pays for inadequate high schools.* Issue Brief. Washington, DC: Author. Available at: http://www.all4ed.org/files/HighCost.pdf.

Angrist, J., and A. Krueger. 1991. Does compulsory school attendance affect schooling and earnings? *Quarterly Journal of Economics* 106:979–1014.

Bettinger, E., and B. T. Long. 2007. Institutional responses to reduce inequalities in college outcomes: Remedial and developmental courses in higher education. In *Economic inequality and higher education: Access, persistence, and success,* ed. S. Dickert-Conlin and R. Rubenstein, 69–100. New York: Russell Sage Foundation.

Bishop, J. H., and F. Mane. 2001. The impacts of minimum competency exam graduation requirements on high school graduation, college attendance and early labor market success. *Labour Economics* 8:203–222.

Brewer, E. W., and J. M. Landers. 2005. A longitudinal study of the talent search program. *Journal of Career Development* 31 (3): 195–208.

Cabrera, A. F., R. J. Deil-Amen, R. Prabhu, P. T. Terenzini, C. Lee, and R. E. Franklin. 2006. Increasing the college preparedness of at-risk students. *Journal of Latinos and Education* 5 (2): 79–97.

Carmeron, S. V., and J. J. Heckman. 1993. The nonequivalence of high school equivalents. *Journal of Labor Economics* 11 (1): 1–47.

Carnevale, A. P. 2001. *Help wanted . . . College required.* Washington, DC: Educational Testing Service, Office for Public Leadership.

College Board. 2000. *National survey of outreach programs directory.* Washington, DC: College Board.

———. 2004. *Education pays.* New York: Sandy Baum and Kathleen Payea.

———. 2007. *Education pays.* New York: Sandy Baum and Jennifer Ma.

Commission on the Future of Higher Education. 2006. Commission Report 08/09/06. Available at: http://www.ed.gov/about/bdscomm/list/hiedfuture/reports/0809-draft.pdf.

Constantine, J. M., N. S. Seftor, E. S. Martin, T. Silva, and D. Myers. 2006. *A study of the effect of the talent search program on secondary and postsecondary outcomes in Florida, Indiana and Texas: Final report from phase II of the National Evaluation.* Washington, DC: U.S. Department of Education. (Prepared for: U.S. Department of Education, Office of Planning, Evaluation and Policy Development, Policy and Program Studies Service under contract Number ED98-CO-0073 with Mathematica Policy Research, Inc.)

Dee, T. S., and B. A. Jacob. 2007. Do high school exit exams influence educational attainment or labor market performance? In *Standards-based reform and children in poverty: Lessons for "No Child Left Behind,"* ed. A. Gamoran, 154–199. Washington, DC: Brookings Institution Press.

Dynarski, M., P. Gleason, A. Rangarajan, and R. Wood. 1998. *Impacts of dropout prevention programs.* Princeton: Mathematica Policy Research, Inc.

Editorial Projects in Education Research Center. 2008. Diplomas count 2008: School to college. *Education Week* 27 (40).

Gándara, P. 1998. Raising minority academic achievement: Final report of the evaluation of high school Puente: 1994–1998. *American Youth Policy Forum.*

———. 2002. A study of high school Puente: What we have learned about preparing Latino youth for post-secondary education. *The Journal of Education Policy* 16 (4): 474–95.

Gándara, P., with D. Bial. 2001. *Paving the way to postsecondary education: K–12 intervention programs for underrepresented youth.* Report of the National Postsecondary Education Cooperative Working Group on Access to Postsecondary Education under the sponsorship of the National Center for Education Statistics (NCES), U.S. Department of Education.

Goldin, C., and L. F. Katz. 2003. Mass secondary schooling and the state: The role of state compulsion in the high school movement. NBER Working Paper no. 10075. Cambridge, MA: National Bureau of Economic Research, November.

Greene, J. P., and G. Foster. 2003. *Public high school graduation and college readiness rates in the United States.* New York: The Manhattan Institute for Policy Research.

Greene, J. P., and M. A. Winters. 2005. Public high school graduation and college-readiness rates: 1991–2002. Manhattan Institute for Policy Research, Education Working Paper no. 8. Available at: http://www.manhattan-institute.org/html/ewp_08.htm.

Guthrie, L. F., and G. P. Guthrie. 2000 and 2001. *Longitudinal research on AVID, 1999–2000; 2000–2001.* Center for Research, Evaluation and Training in Education.

Hayward, B., and G. Tallmadge. 1995. *Strategies for keeping kids in school: Evaluation of dropout prevention and reentry projects in vocational education.* Raleigh, NC: Research Triangle Institute, June.

Heckman, J. 1993. The nonequivalence of high school equivalents. *Journal of Labor Economics* 11 (1): 1–47.

Heckman, J. J., P. A. LaFontaine, and P. L. Rodriguez. 2008. Taking the easy way out: How the GED testing program induces students to drop out. NBER Working Paper no. 14044. Cambridge, MA: National Bureau of Economic Research, May.

Horn, L. J., X. Chen, and C. Chapman. 2003. *Getting ready to pay for college: What students and their parents know about the cost of college tuition and what they are doing to find out* (no. 2003030). Washington, DC: National Center for Education Statistics, U.S. Department of Education.

Hoyt, J. E., and C. T. Sorensen. 1999. *Promoting academic standards?: The link between remedial education in college and student preparation in high school.* A report of the Department of Institutional Research and Management Studies, Utah Valley State College, Orem, UT, May.

Ikenberry, S. O., and T. W. Hartle. 1998. *Too little knowledge is a dangerous thing: What the public thinks about paying for college.* Washington, DC: American Council on Education.

Kane, T. J., and C. Avery. 2004. Student perceptions of college opportunities: The Boston COACH program. In *College decisions: The new economics of choosing, attending and completing college,* ed. C. Hoxby, Chicago: University of Chicago Press.

Kennelly, L., and M. Monrad. 2007. *Approaches to dropout prevention: Heeding early warning signs with appropriate interventions.* National High School Center at the American Institutes for Research.

King, J. E. 2004. Missed opportunities: Students who do not apply for financial aid. American Council on Education Issue Brief.

Laird, J., E. F. Cataldi, R. A. Kewal, and C. Chapman. 2008. *Dropout and completion rates in the United States: 2006* (NCES 2008-053). Washington, DC: National Center for Education Statistics, Institute of Education Sciences, U.S. Department of Education. Available at: http://nces.ed.gov/pubsearch/pubsinfo.asp?pubid=2008053.

Lehr, C. A., D. R. Johnson, C. D. Bremer, A. Cosio, and M. Thompson. 2004. *Essential tools: Increasing rates of school completion: Moving from policy and research to practice.* Minneapolis, MN: University of Minnesota, Institute on Community Integration, National Center on Secondary Education and Transition.

Lillard, D. R., and P. P. DeCicca. 2001. Higher standards, more dropouts? Evidence within and across time. *Economics of Education Review* 20:459–73.

Lleras-Muney, A. 2002. Were compulsory attendance and child labor laws effective: An analysis from 1915 to 1939. *Journal of Law and Economics* 45:401–35.

Lochner, L., and E. Moretti. 2004. The effects of education on crime: Evidence from prison inmates, arrests, and self-reports. *American Economic Review* 94.

McCabe, R. H. 2001. Developmental education: A policy primer. *League for Innovation in the Community College* 14 (1): 1–4.

MDRC. 2006. MDRC's evaluation of Project GRAD. New York: MDRC. Available at: http://www.mdrc.org/publications/431/summary.html.

Moreno, J. 2002. The long-term outcomes of Puente. *Educational Policy* 16 (4): 572–87.

Murnane, R. J., J. B. Willett, and K. P. Boudett. 1995. Do high school dropouts benefit from obtaining a GED? *Educational Evaluation and Policy Analysis* 17 (2): 133–47.

Myers, D., R. Olsen, N. Seftor, J. Young, and C. Tuttle. 2004. The impacts of regular upward bound: Results from the third follow-up data collection. Document no. PR04-30. Washington, DC: Mathematica Policy Research, Inc.

Myers, D., and A. Schirm. 1999. The impacts for upward bound: Final report for phase I of the national evaluation. Document no. PR99-51. Washington, DC: Mathematica Policy Research, Inc., April.

National Center for Education Statistics. 1996. *Remedial education at higher education institutions in Fall 1995.* Washington, DC: Office or Educational Research and Improvement.

———. 2003. *Remedial education at degree-granting postsecondary institutions in Fall 2000.* Washington, DC: Department of Education.

———. 2004. *The condition of education 2004.* Washington, DC: U.S. Department of Education, Indicator 16:61.

———. 2007. *The condition of education 2007* (NCES 2007-064). Washington, DC: U.S. Department of Education.

Northwest Regional Educational Laboratory. (1995). *Reducing the dropout rate.* Available at: http://www.nwrel.org/scpd/sirs/9/c017.html.

Ohio Board of Regents. 2002. *Making the transition from high school to college in Ohio 2002.* Columbus, OH: Ohio Board of Regents.

Olsen, R., N. Seftor, T. Silva, D. Myers, D. DesRoches, and J. Young. 2007. Upward bound math-science: Program description and interim impact estimates. Document no. PR07-18. Washington, DC: Mathematica Policy Research, Inc., April.

Opuni, K. 1999. *Project GRAD: Graduation really achieves dreams. 1998–99 program evaluation report.* Houston, TX: University of Houston.

Opuni, K., and M. Ochoa. 2002. *Project GRAD: A comprehensive school reform model.* Houston, TX: University of Houston.

Oreopoulos, P. 2003. Do dropouts drop out too soon? International evidence from changes in school-leaving laws. NBER Working Paper no. 10155. Cambridge, MA: National Bureau of Economic Research, July.

Partee, G. 2000. *Project GRAD—Graduation really achieves dreams: A multi-intervention approach in urban schools shows success.* American Youth Policy Forum.

Project GRAD. (n.d.). Our model. Available at: http://www.projectgrad.org/site/pp.asp?c=fuLTJeMUKrH&b=487653.

Rouse, C. E. 2005. Labor market consequences of an inadequate education. Paper prepared for the symposium on the Social Costs of Inadequate Education, Teachers College Columbia University, October.

Snipes, J. C., G. I. Holton, F. Doolittle, and L. Sztejnberg. 2006. *Striving for student success: The effect of Project GRAD on high school student outcomes in three urban school districts.* New York: MDRC.

Steinberg, A., and C. Almeida. 2004. *The dropout crisis: Promising approaches in prevention and recovery.* Jobs for the Future.

Stillwell, R., and L. Hoffman. 2008. *Public school graduates and dropouts from the common core of data: School year 2005–06* (NCES 2008-353). National Center for Education Statistics, Institute of Education Sciences, U.S. Department of Education. Washington, DC. Available at: http://nces.ed.gov/pubsearch/pubsinfo .asp?pubid=2008353.

Swail, W. S. 2000. Preparing America's disadvantaged for college: Programs that increase college opportunity. *New Directions in Institutional Research* 27 (3): 85–101.

Swanson, C. 2004. *Who graduates? Who doesn't? A statistical portrait of public high school graduation, class of 2001.* Washington, DC: The Urban Institute, Education Policy Center.

Terenzini, P. T., A. F. Cabrera, R. Deil-Amen, and A. Lambert. 2005. *The dream deferred: Increasing the college preparedness of at-risk students.* Washington, DC: U.S. Department of Education, Year 4: Final Report Grant no. R305T010167.

Trounson, R. 2002. Cal State ouster rate rises slightly. *Los Angeles Times,* January 31.

Tyler, J. 2003. Economic benefits of the GED: Lessons from recent research. *Review of Educational Research* 73 (3): 369–403.

U.S. Census Bureau. 2007. *Educational attainment—People 18 years old and over, by total money earnings in 2006, age, race, Hispanic origin, and sex.* Washington, DC: Author. Available at: http://pubdb3.census.gov/macro/032007/perinc/new04_001 .htm.

U.S. Department of Justice, Bureau of Justice Statistics. 2000. *Correctional populations in the United States, 1997* (NCJ-177613). Washington, DC: U.S. Government Printing Office.

———. 2002. *Correctional populations in the United States, 1998* (NCJ-192929). Washington, DC: U.S. Government Printing Office.

Venezia, A., M. Kirst, and A. Antonio. 2003. *Betraying the college dream: How disconnected K-12 and postsecondary education systems undermine student aspirations.* Stanford, CA: Stanford Bridge Project.

Watt, K. M., C. A. Powell, and I. D. Mendiola. 2004. Implications of one comprehensive school reform model for secondary school students underrepresented in higher education. *Journal of Education for Students Placed at Risk* 9 (3): 241–59.

Westat. 2003. *National evaluation of GEAR UP: A summary of the first two years.* Rockville, MD: Author. Report to the U.S. Department of Education, Office of the Under Secretary, Policy and Program Studies Service.

———. 2008. *Early outcomes of the GEAR UP program: Final report.* Rockville, MD: Author. Report to the U.S. Department of Education, Office of Planning, Evaluation and Policy Development, Policy and Program Studies Service.

What Works Clearinghouse. 2007. *Project GRAD: What works clearinghouse intervention report.* Washington, DC: U.S. Department of Education, Institute of Education Sciences.

10

College Aid

David Deming and Susan Dynarski

10.1 Introduction

College-going has risen substantially over the past forty years. In 1968, 36 percent of twenty-three-year-olds had gone to college, while by 2005, that figure had grown to 58 percent.[1] But these gains have been uneven. African Americans are about half as likely as non-Hispanic whites to earn a bachelor's degree (19 percent versus 37 percent) and Hispanics less than one-third as likely (11 percent).[2] Females are about 12 percentage points more likely than males to have attended college by age twenty-three (64 versus 52 percent), and about 7 percentage points more likely to have completed a Bachelor of Arts degree (BA) (32 versus 25 percent).

Some of these differences trace back to performance gaps in elementary school and high school. But even among those who do well on achievement tests, socioeconomic inequalities remain: 74 percent of high scorers who grew up in upper-income families complete college, compared to only 29 percent of those who grew up in low-income families (College Board 2005).

While thirty years ago a high school degree was sufficient for financial security, it is now a college degree that is the key to a middle-class lifestyle. Since the 1970s, high school dropouts and graduates have lost ground, with their real earnings dropping substantially (figures 10.1 and 10.2, from College Board [2005]). Typical earnings for a full-time, male high school graduate in 1972 were $45,000 (in constant 2003 dollars). That figure had dropped

David Deming is a doctoral candidate in public policy at Harvard University. Susan Dynarski is an associate professor of education and public policy at the University of Michigan and a research associate of the National Bureau of Economic Research.

1. Authors' calculations from the October Current Population Survey.
2. Authors' calculation of BA completion rates for twenty-five- to twenty-six-year-olds in the 2005 CPS.

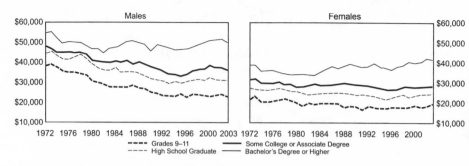

Fig. 10.1   Median annual earnings of males and females ages 25–34 by education level, 1972–2003 (constant 2003 dollars)

Sources: Figure is from College Board (2005) and is based on data from the National Center for Education Statistics (NCES), 2005a, Indicator 14 (based on U.S. Census Bureau, *Current Population Survey,* March Supplement, 1972–2003 and unpublished data).

Note: Includes full-time, full-year workers.

2004	15%	32%	25%		28%
2000	16%	33%	25%		26%
1990	22%	38%	18%		21%
1980	31%	37%	15%		17%
1970	45%	34%	10%		11%
1960	59%	25%	9%		8%
1950	66%	20%	7%		6%
1940	76%	14%	5%		5%

☒ Not a High School Graduate   ☐ Some College or Associate Degree
▨ High School Graduate   ▨ Bachelor's Degree or Higher

Fig. 10.2   Years of schooling completed by people 25 and older, 1940–2004
Sources: Figure is from the College Board (2005) and is based on data from the U.S. Census Bureau, 2005, Table A-1.
Note: Percents may not sum to 100 percent due to rounding.

by a third ($30,000) by 2005.[3] By contrast, real earnings for the college-educated have held steady; among women, they have risen.

These two sets of trends—steady earnings for those with a college education, plunging earnings for those without—mean that college is increasingly important to financial well-being. In 1972, men with a bachelor's degree typically earned 22 percent more than those with a high school degree. By 2003, this return had nearly tripled, up to 60 percent.

In light of the rising importance of a college degree, policymakers have

3. Over the same period, earnings among male high school dropouts plunged from $40,000 to $22,000.

focused on increasing college enrollment as an important tool for mitigating poverty. This chapter reviews the evidence on a key tool available to policy-makers—reducing college costs. Section 10.2 briefly outlines the policy context; section 10.3 reviews the evidence from experimental and high-quality quasi-experimental studies of college cost reduction; section 10.4 discusses the broad lessons derived from these studies and concludes.

10.2 Policy Context

Colleges, state and federal government, and private organizations spend billions to subsidize college costs. In this section, we briefly describe the major programs.

Two federal programs provide the bulk of aid to college students: the Pell Grant and the Stafford Loan. Pell Grants flow almost exclusively to families with incomes below $40,000 (Stedman 2003). During the 2004 to 2005 academic year, $13.6 billion in Pell Grants was delivered to over five million students (College Board 2005). During the same year, $55 billion in loans was delivered to undergraduates through the Stafford Loan program.

States hold down college costs by subsidizing public universities, which in turn charge lower tuition prices than their private counterparts. The vast majority of students attend public colleges, so this is an important channel through which government subsidizes college costs. In addition to charging artificially low prices to all students, states also offer scholarships to individual students. Most of these are small-scale programs, but beginning in the early 1990s, more than a dozen states established broad-based merit aid programs. These programs typically award full tuition and fees at state public universities (or in some cases, an equivalent voucher to attend a private school) to residents who maintain a minimum high school grade point average. Many require a grade point average of 3.0, not a particularly high threshold—Dynarski (2004) calculates that in 1999, 40 percent of high school seniors met this standard.

In recent years, the federal and state tax codes have also been used as a vehicle for subsidizing college costs. The Hope and Lifetime Learning tax credits and the deduction for college tuition and fees help families pay for current college costs. Parents can also claim children under twenty-four as dependents if they are enrolled in college. The federal Coverdell Education Savings Account and the state 529 savings plans help families pay for college in the future by increasing their after-tax returns on savings. With a total cost of $10.5 billion, these education tax incentives approach spending on the Pell Grant, historically the cornerstone of federal aid for college students (College Board 2005). But, as they are currently configured, these programs almost exclusively benefit upper-income families (Dynarski 2004; Dynarski and Scott-Clayton 2006a) and so are not candidate instruments for reducing poverty.

Foundations and colleges are additional sources of student aid. Programs such as the Gates Millenium Scholars, the I Have a Dream foundation, and Kalamazoo Promise fully sponsor college attendance (or "top up" the difference between government grants and estimated need) for low-income and/or minority students. Although these programs are small in scale compared to the federal and state aid programs discussed previously, they are highly visible and intended to increase college attendance, and so we will discuss them in the chapter.

We will not examine the new and widely-discussed scholarship programs of elite colleges (such as Harvard and Princeton) which offer a free ride for low-income students (Pallais and Turner 2007; Avery et al. 2006; Linsenmeier, Rosen, and Rouse 2006; Rothstein and Rouse 2007, van der Klaauw 2002). Helping low-income students make the leap from high school into *any* college is the critical task if the goal is poverty reduction, and these programs do not serve this function. The low-income student who takes up Princeton's offer of a free ride would likely have gone to Harvard (or Berkeley) had Princeton not been so generous. Convincing more nonwhite and low-income students to attend Princeton instead of Berkeley may serve important social goals, such as diversifying our political leadership (Bok and Bowen 2000), but poverty reduction is not among them.

Most evaluations of the programs we have mentioned focus on the enrollment margin. However, while enrollment has risen substantially over the past forty years, degree receipt has barely budged (Turner 2007). Thus retention and graduation of college enrollees has also become an important policy issue. We review evidence from several recent experimental evaluations that provide scholarships and services to existing college enrollees. These programs are of particular interest since they focus on marginal students, for whom retention rates are lowest.

10.3   Evidence

Economic theory (and common sense) predicts that lowering the price of college will increase attendance. While the theoretical prediction is clear, students' marginal responsiveness to additional dollars of aid is an empirical question. Answering this question is a challenge, since eligibility for subsidies is certainly not random and is likely correlated with unobserved determinants of schooling. As a result, estimates based on the cross-sectional correlation of aid with schooling are subject to multiple sources of bias.

A long empirical literature examines the effect of college costs on schooling decisions. Leslie and Brinkman (1988) review more than seventy of these studies.[4] With few exceptions, discussed later in this chapter, this long literature suffers from a key limitation: the response of schooling to price is

---

4. Heller (1997) updates this review with studies done after Leslie and Brinkman (1988).

poorly identified. That is, the variation in schooling prices used to estimate the parameter of interest is likely to be correlated with the unobserved determinants of schooling.

More formally, the relationship between financial aid and schooling decisions can be expressed with the following equation:

(1) $$S_i = \alpha + \beta \, Aid_i + \varepsilon_i.$$

Here, S_i is some measure of an individual's schooling, such as college attendance or completed years of college, Aid_i is the amount of student aid (expressed in dollars) for which an individual is eligible, and the error term ε_i represents the unobserved determinants of schooling. If aid is uncorrelated with ε_i, then β can be interpreted as the effect of an additional dollar of aid on college attendance or completed education.

If financial aid is randomly assigned in an experimental setting, Aid_i is uncorrelated with ε_i. In nearly all nonexperimental studies, however, aid is offered to students on the basis of characteristics that independently affect the probability of college attendance. For example, the federal government uses the Pell Grant to increase the college attendance of low-income youth. If such students are relatively unlikely to attend college, perhaps because of low levels of parental education or poor secondary schooling, then estimates of β based on this source of variation in aid will be biased downward. Conversely, since many colleges use merit scholarships to attract high-achieving students, β could be biased upward if such scholarships are included in the analysis.

One can attempt to correct for this bias by controlling for observed determinants of schooling (such as parental income or academic achievement) in a vector of regressors X_i:

(2) $$S_i = \alpha + \beta \, Aid_i + \delta \, X_i + \varepsilon_i.$$

If X_i is sufficiently rich that it captures all other sources of variation in individual schooling decisions and schooling costs, then β will be unbiased. However, under plausible conditions this approach will fail, for two reasons:

- Complete data on relevant characteristics is rarely available. For example, parental wealth affects schooling decisions, both directly and through eligibility for aid, but comprehensive measures of parental (and extended family) wealth are rarely present in survey data, especially among adults who have completed their education.
- Even if all relevant variables are available, their role in the schooling decision may not be properly modeled. Theory provides little guidance as to which attributes should be held constant in estimating equation (2). This is particularly problematic because point estimates in this literature are often quite fragile, even changing sign with small changes in specification. As a practical example, the effect of income on Pell

Grant eligibility is highly nonlinear, and unless the functional form of the underlying relationship between income and schooling is perfectly specified, the resulting estimate will be biased.

10.3.1   Quasi-Experimental Studies

We now discuss analyses of natural (or quasi-) experiments, in which a discrete shift in aid policy affects one group of individuals but not others. Beginning with Hansen (1983), who examined the introduction of the Pell Grant in the early 1970s, a small but growing number of studies has used this approach to estimate the effect of schooling costs on college-going. We summarize the main results of these studies in table 10.1.

Federal Programs

Most of these studies examine the effect of grant aid. Studies that examine the Pell Grant, currently the largest source of federal grant aid, produce mixed results: Hansen (1983) and Kane (1995) found no effect of the introduction of the Pell on the college enrollment rate of low-income recent high school graduates. Seftor and Turner (2002) use a differences-in-differences framework to examine the effect of changing Pell Grant eligibility rules, and find that "nontraditional" students are about 4 percentage points more likely to attend college once they are considered eligible. Bettinger (2004) uses a regression-discontinuity approach to look at the effect of the Pell Grant on persistence using a sample of college students; his estimates are extremely sensitive to specification.

Veterans' educational benefits have historically been one of the largest sources of grant aid for college in the United States. Since children from poor families are more likely than others to enroll in the military, programs that increase veterans' education have the potential to reduce poverty. Multiple studies of the post-World War II GI Bills (Angrist 1993; Stanley 2003; Turner and Bound 2003; Bound and Turner 2003) have found these benefits to have raised schooling levels substantially.

Evaluating another federal program, Dynarski (2003) concludes that an additional $1,000 in aid increases college attendance by about 4 percentage points. She examines the elimination of the Social Security student benefit program, which paid the college costs of the children of deceased, disabled, or retired Social Security beneficiaries. Eligible students were disproportionately poor, nonwhite, and from single-parent families, so these estimates are quite relevant. Dynarski uses the death of a parent during a person's childhood as a proxy for Social Security beneficiary status, and finds that college attendance of the affected group dropped by more than a third, and schooling by two-thirds of a year.

While loans are the dominant form of federal aid today, we unfortunately know little about how they affect behavior. Reyes (1995) examines the effect of relative changes in loan eligibility across income groups in the early eighties, and concludes that loan access increases attendance and completed schooling. Dynarski (2005) addresses this question using variation in loan eligibility induced by the Higher Education Amendments of 1992, which removed home equity from the set of assets taxed by the federal aid formula. She finds a small effect of loan eligibility on college attendance and a larger effect on the choice of college.

State Programs

Subsidized public tuitions, which vary considerably by state, are one of the largest sources of education subsidies. Estimates based on cross-sectional variation in tuition may be biased, since states with a preference for education may have both low tuition prices and high college attendance rates. The solution of Kane (1995) is to use state fixed effects; his identifying assumption is that within-state changes in tuition prices are uncorrelated with changes in a state's taste for college. He concludes that a $1,000 drop in public tuition produces about a 4 percentage point increase in college attendance rates of recent high school graduates.

Several studies have used the introduction of state merit scholarship programs as a source of variation in schooling costs. Dynarski (2000) and Cornwell, Mustard, and Sridhar (2006) conclude that the Georgia HOPE scholarship increases college attendance by 4 to 6 percentage points per $1,000 in grant aid. Dynarski (2004) finds that a dozen states' scholarship programs have had similar, but slightly smaller effects, and that their positive effects on college attendance are greater for nonwhites. Kane (2003) uses a regression discontinuity approach to examine the CalGrant, and finds substantial impacts on college entry for students who had already applied for financial aid. Abraham and Clark (2006) and Kane (2007) evaluate the DC Tuition Assistance Grant program, which allowed DC residents to pay in-state tuition at public schools across the country. They find that the fraction of DC residents that attended Maryland and Virginia schools more than doubled, and estimate an impact on overall enrollment of 3 to 4 percentage points per $1,000 of effective tuition reduction. Goodman (2008) examines a program in Massachusetts that assigns aid on the basis of a standardized test score, and finds that the scholarship induced 6 percent of winners to switch from private to public four-year colleges. He also finds that low-income (and low test score) students are more price sensitive. However, there was no impact on overall enrollment.

Dynarski (2008) finds that the Georgia and Arkansas merit scholarship programs have also increased degree completion, by around 3 to 4 percentage points. She estimates that the scholarships increases persistence by 5 to 11 percent for those who would have entered college anyway. This suggests that the positive effect of lower cost on retention outweighs any negative effect of enrolling marginally weaker students who are less likely to persist.

Finally, a recent paper by Scott-Clayton (2009) examines the impact

Table 10.1   Summary of studies

Study	Sample	Intervention/method	Financial award	Evaluation design	Outcomes	Effects
			Experimental studies			
STAR—Canada (Angrist et al. 2009)	~1,600 entering freshman at a public university in Canada, satellite campus	3 treatment groups— 1) peer advising and organized study group; 2) a merit scholarship for above-avg. grades; 3) both	Yes—$5,000 for a 3.0 avg., $1,000 for a 2.3 avg.	Randomized experiment	Grades, retention	Largest effect for combined group: 0.1–0.2 SD increase in grades; 4–5 percentage point decrease in probation. No effect on retention for any group. Weak/no effects for groups 1 and 2; no effect for males in any group.
Opening Doors— New York (Bloom and Sommo 2005; Scrivener et al. 2008)	~750 Community College Attendees, mixed races, mostly immigrant	Learning Communities— organized cohort of entering students into same classes; improved counseling and monitoring; instructors work together	No—(except textbook voucher)	Randomized experiment	Credits taken and earned; pass rate and GPA; retention	8 percentage points less likely to withdraw and 10 point increase in pass rate; cumulative impact of 2.4 credits and 0.1 semesters; 5 percentage point increase in enrollment post-program.
Opening Doors— Louisiana (Brock and Richburg-Hayes 2006)	~500 Community college attendees, mostly female and African American	Financial aid; improved counseling and monitoring	Yes—$1,000 per semester for half-time enrollment and 2.0 GPA	Randomized experiment	Credits taken and earned; pass rate and GPA; retention	7 percentage points less likely to withdraw and 12 point increase in pass rate; cumulative increase of 3.3 credits and 0.3 semesters; 11 percentage point increase in post-program enrollment.
Opening Doors— Ohio (Scrivener and Au 2007; Scrivener and Pih 2007)	~1,000 community college attendees, mostly female and mixed race	Multiple mandatory meetings with counselors; aid award given for attendance	Yes—$150 per semester	Randomized experiment	Credits taken and earned; pass rate and GPA; retention	No effect on withdrawal or pass rate; cumulative increase of 0.8/1.0 credits and 0.1/0.2 semesters; 5.6/10.5 percentage point increase in post-program enrollment.

Quasi-experimental studies

Study	Data	Identification strategy	Price variation	Method	Outcome	Effect
Introduction of Pell Grant Program (Hansen 1983; Kane 1995)	October Current Population Survey; 1970–1977	Compare enrollment of eligible to noneligible population, before and after 1973 when the Pell Grant was established	Yes—maximum of $3,544 in 1991 dollars	Differences-in-differences	College enrollment and type	No effect
Change/discontinuity in Pell Grant eligibility (Seftor and Turner 2002; Bettinger 2004)	October Current Population Survey; 1969–1977 and 1984–1990—"nontraditional" older students only	Same as Kane (1995), plus a before/after comparison when independent student definition changed; Student Aid Index that determines eligibility is estimated directly from data	Yes—maximum of $3,544 in 1991 dollars	Differences-in-differences	Enrollment	~1.5 percentage point increase for initial Pell introduction; ~4 percentage points for 2nd change.
Tuition changes (Kane 1995)	CPS; NLSY-79; High School and Beyond	Between and within-state variation in public subsidization of college	Changes in tuition sticker price	State fixed effects	Enrollment	~4 percentage points per $1,000 drop in tuition.
Expansion of Stafford Loan eligibility (Reyes 1995; Dynarski 2005)	October CPS 1984-2000 and the Survey of Income and Program Participation (SIPP) 1986–1996	Before/after 1992 legal change—home equity no longer taxed in the federal student aid formula	Yes—reduced expected contribution by $2,400 for family with median equity	Differences-in-differences	Enrollment	5.1 percentage points per $1,000 of loan subsidy in the CPS; imprecise/no effect in SIPP; Reyes: 1.5 percentage points per $1,000.
GI Bill (Angrist 1993; Stanley 2003; Bound and Turner 2003; Turner and Bound 2003)	Survey of Occupational Change in a Generation, 1973; U.S. Census	Compare enrollment of military enlistees before/during/after eligibility periods	Yes—fully subsidized college attendance plus living stipend	Between/with-in cohorts	Total years of educational attainment	~0.25 years of education, or a 5–6 percentage point increase in attendance due to Korean War and World War II GI Bills.
Social Security Student Benefits (Dynarski 2003)	National Longitudinal Survey of Youth–1979	Elimination of the program in 1981—compared those with deceased father before and after	Yes—average annual payment was $6,700 in 1980 dollars	Differences-in-differences	Enrollment	3.6 percentage points per $1,000 of grant aid.

(continued)

Table 10.1 (continued)

Study	Sample	Intervention/method	Financial award	Evaluation design	Outcomes	Effects
State Merit Aid Programs—Georgia HOPE scholarship (Dynarski 2000; Cornwell, Mustard, and Sridhar 2006)	CPS and Integrated Postsecondary Education Data System (IPEDS) 1988–1997	Before/after institution of a statewide merit (3.0 GPA minimum) scholarship in 1993	Yes—tuition and required fees at public institutions in GA	Differences-in-differences	Enrollment; college choice	4–6 percentage points per $1,000 of grant aid; increase in enrollment in GA schools.
State Merit Aid Program—CAL Grant (Kane 2003)	Administrative Data from California and the National Student Clearinghouse	Discontinuous changes in the eligibility formula for CAL Grants	Yes—tuition and required fees at public institutions or a private school grant of ~9,000	Regression discontinuity	Enrollment	3–4 percentage point increase (among those who applied for financial aid) for those eligible for CAL Grant A.
State Merit Aid Program—Adams Scholarship (Goodman 2008)	Administrative Data from Massachusetts Department of Education	Discontinuous change in eligibility based on test score cutoff; before/after institution of merit aid program	Yes—tuition waiver at MA public schools; ~$1,575 per year at 4 yrs.	Regression discontinuity; differences-in-differences	Enrollment	6% of winners switched from private to public four-year colleges; no impact on overall enrollment.
DC Tuition Assistance Grant (Kane 2004; Abraham and Clark 2006)	IPEDS; Department of Ed. FAFSA data; DCTAG administrative records; SAT data	Allowed DC residents to attend public schools in other states and pay in-state tuition	Yes—difference between out- and in-state tuition (up to $10,000)	Differences-in-differences	Enrollment; college location and type	~3–4 percentage point increase per $1,000 effective tuition reduction; fraction of DC residents at MA and VA colleges more than doubled.

Current Population Survey; WV State Administrative Data	Merit Aid programs in GA and other states— before/after creation of each program; West Virginia PROMISE scholarship	Varies—usually tuition and fees at a state public school or equivalent voucher for private	Differences-in-differences; regression discontinuity	Enrollment; college type; completion	~5–7 average percentage point increase in enrollment due to state programs; shift away from two-year and toward four-year schools; ~3–4 percentage point increase in degree completion (6 percentage point increase in on-time graduation for PROMISE recipients—linked to credit requirements).
Administrative data from anonymous colleges, 1989–1993 and 1998	Discontinuous changes in the formula for aid allocation; before/after shift from loan/grant mix to grants only	Merit grants for students of higher ability ~$2,000 on average; full tuition	Regression discontinuity; differences-in-differences	Enrollment	~4 percentage points per $1,000 in grant aid; no impact on enrollment overall, but 8–10 percentage points for minorities.
National Opinion Research Center survey of program participants	Discontinuous change in eligibility based on an application cut score	"Tops up" diff. between need-based aid and price of college	Regression discontinuity	Retention; loan debt; hours worked	No impact on retention; 60% less debt; 35% fewer hours worked.

State Merit Aid Program—multiple/ other (Dynarski 2004; Dynarski 2008; Scott-Clayton 2009)

Effect of school aid on yield rate (van der Klaauw 2002; Linsenmeier, Rosen, and Rouse 2006)

Gates Millenium Scholars (DesJardins and McCall 2007)

of the PROMISE scholarship, a merit aid program in West Virginia. The PROMISE scholarship was similar to other state merit programs in its initial eligibility requirements and the amount of aid it offered. But it was unique in requiring students to complete at least thirty credits per year in order to keep their scholarships, a rate which would put them on track to graduate in four years. She finds that PROMISE increased eventual graduation rates by almost 4 percentage points, while the percentage of students graduating on time increased by about 7 percentage points from a baseline of just 27 percent. The impacts on year-by-year credit completion were concentrated around the annual renewal threshold in the freshman through junior years, but disappeared in the senior year when students were still receiving their scholarships but no longer faced any renewal requirements (scholarships could not be renewed for a fifth year in any case). This finding suggests that a combination of cost reduction and performance incentives may have a greater impact than financial aid alone.

Other Programs

DesJardins and McCall (2007) study the impact of the Gates Millenium Scholarship (GMS) using a regression discontinuity design. The GMS tops up the difference between need-based grants and unmet financial need for eligible minority applicants. Scholars are selected on the basis of high school record and a scored application process, which generates discontinuous changes in the probability of receiving an award. Although the evaluation is still ongoing, they find weak impacts on overall retention but strong evidence of decreased loan debt and work hours.

Table 10.1 summarizes the findings from the quasi-experimental studies discussed earlier. The studies in this table are those that we consider as estimating causal impacts of the effect of schooling costs on schooling decisions. The best estimates suggest that eligibility for $1,000 of subsidy increases college attendance rates by roughly 4 percentage points. Aid eligibility also appears to increase completed schooling and shift students from community colleges toward four-year schools.

10.3.2   Experimental Evaluations

One straightforward way to assess the causal impact of financial aid on college enrollment and persistence is to randomly allocate scarce scholarship funds to an eligible population. Several experimental studies have examined the effect of scholarships when they are combined with mentoring or other services. A key unresolved question in these studies is the extent to which services, and the cost of providing them, are more effective than the scholarships.

Most randomized trials in higher education examine the effect of aid or services on grades, credit accumulation and/or persistence past the first year, *conditional on enrollment*. The reasons for this are largely practical—school-based interventions are more administratively feasible than tracking high school students to their chosen colleges around the country. To our knowledge, only one randomized trial looks directly at the enrollment margin.

Upward Bound

Upward Bound is a federal and nationwide program that provides comprehensive precollege services to participants, including supplemental college preparatory coursework in math, science, and English; tutoring; counseling; and activities such as attendance at museums and plays. Mathematica Policy Research conducted a randomized trial of Upward Bound from 1992 to 1994, following participants for several years. They found weak impacts of Upward Bound on performance in high school courses (Myers and Schirm 1999.) A more recent evaluation finds no statistically significant impact on college enrollment (Myers et al. 2004) though there is some evidence of substitution from two- to four-year colleges.[5] There is no impact on total college credits earned.[6] See the chapter by Long (chap. 9 in this volume) for more detail on the administration and evaluation of Upward Bound.

Experimental Effects of College Persistence Programs

About 20 percent of students who enroll at a four-year college leave within one year. About 40 percent fail to obtain a degree within six years (College Board 2005.) Attrition is even higher at nonselective schools, where the majority of students commute from home and work part- or full-time. Since these students are more weakly attached to their institutions, policies have focused on creating a stronger connection with the college experience via more extensive mentoring, counseling, and collaborative "learning communities" (Bloom and Sommo 2005). Two randomized trials have evaluated the effect of such programs; we discuss them in the sections that follow.

Student Achievement and Retention Project

The Student Achievement and Retention Project (STAR) was a large-scale randomized trial launched in 2005 at the urban campus of a major Canadian public university (Angrist, Lang, and Oreopoulos 2009). Participants in the STAR experiment are similar to students at nonselective universities in the United States. About 80 percent of the sample lived with their parents and

5. The treatment group was 5 to 6 percentage points *more* likely to have attended a four-year college, and 3 to 5 percentage points *less* likely to have attended a two-year college than the control group.

6. The evaluation does report much larger results for students with low (versus high) "educational expectations." Among students who did not expect to earn a bachelor's degree, the treatment group was about 20 percentage points more likely to attend a four-year college than the control group, although the overall enrollment effect was still not significant. However, since this evaluation does not actually measure degree receipt, this result is difficult to interpret. Other results by subgroup are available in Myers et al (2004).

commuted to school, and the majority planned to work part-time while enrolled. Many of the students were first- or second-generation immigrants. Incoming freshman were randomly assigned to one of four groups. The first was offered enhanced services, in the form of peer advising and organized study groups. The second was offered a financial incentive of $5,000 to complete a full course load with a grade point average of 3.0 or higher (the payment was $1,000 for a GPA of at least 2.3). A third group was offered both services and a financial incentive, while a fourth group formed a control group and was offered the college's typical services.

Overall, the effect of STAR was modest. The largest impacts were found for the group offered both services and a financial incentive. First-year grade point average increased between 0.1 and 0.2 standard deviations, and the combined group was about 5 percentage points less likely to be placed on academic probation. Significant effects of STAR were driven entirely by female participants—there was no effect of the program on males in any group. There was also no effect of the program for the services or scholarship-only groups.

Opening Doors

Opening Doors is a large-scale randomized trial at six community colleges in four states run by MDRC. Preliminary results are currently available for five of the six sites. The interventions varied by site, but were some combination of "learning communities" (in which entering students take blocks of classes together and are offered extra tutoring); supplementary financial aid; and enhanced student services (extra counseling and monitoring).

The first Opening Doors evaluation occurred at Kingsborough Community College in Brooklyn, New York in the fall of 2003 (Bloom and Sommo 2005). The intervention targeted approximately 750 entering freshman, who were ethnically and racially diverse; many were recent immigrants who needed training in remedial English. Treatment group members were placed in learning communities of about twenty-five students each and received textbook vouchers.

Three semesters after the program at Kingsborough Community College, the treatment group was 5.6 percentage points more likely to be enrolled in any college (Scrivener et al. 2008). Treatment group members earned an average of 2.4 more credits and were in school about 0.1 more semesters. They were more likely to attempt and pass standardized reading and writing assessments. The effect sizes for these various assessments were around 0.1 standard deviations (SDs), but were closer to 0.2 SDs for students whose initial English skills were worse at baseline.[7]

A second set of Opening Doors demonstrations took place in northern Ohio (Scrivener and Au 2007; Scrivener and Pih 2007.) Students were given

---

7. For more detail on the assessments and subgroup effect sizes, see Scrivener et al (2008).

regular appointments with an Opening Doors counselor and given a $150 per semester scholarship if they attended these meetings. Results were weak. There was no increase in credits attempted or earned in the initial semester, nor any impact on pass rate or grade point average. However, there was an effect on retention of 5 to 10 percentage points and a small effect on earned credits.

Two Opening Doors demonstrations also took place at community colleges in New Orleans in 2004 (Brock and Ritchburg-Hayes 2006.) The treatment group was offered $1,000 per semester for half-time enrollment and a C average. First year impacts were substantial. Opening Doors participants were about 9 percentage points more likely to be enrolled full-time, and earned on average 1.1 additional credits in the first semester. They were about 12 percentage points more likely to pass and about 7 percentage points less likely to withdraw from an attempted course. These effects persisted into the second and third semesters. The treatment group was about 18 percentage points more likely to remain enrolled into the second semester and about 11 percentage points more likely to enroll for a third semester. The pass rate for enrolled courses also remained significantly higher, and there was some evidence of small grade point average increases as well. The cumulative effect of the program was a large and statistically significant increase of 3.3 credits earned, and an average gain of 0.3 semesters worth of enrollment.

Overall, the results from Opening Doors are very encouraging. While cost estimates were unavailable in MDRC's preliminary report, the financial incentives offered were modest and the cost of providing services was likely to be relatively low as well (especially to the extent that they were integrated into the colleges' existing programs). Opening Doors had effects that were at least as large as the state merit aid programs reviewed earlier. Still, sample sizes in the evaluations were relatively small, and caution is warranted until the results can be scaled up and replicated. Further research is needed on these promising programs.

Several themes emerge from these experimental evaluations. First, the effect of aid appears to be greater than that of services. Interventions that offered services alone generally had weak impacts, whereas aid typically generated positive effects on enrollment and persistence. Second, aid has a larger impact when combined with services. In the STAR experiment, the only sustained gains were found in the treatment group that combined aid and services. The impact of Opening Doors (which combined aid and services) was proportionally larger than quasi-experimental estimates of aid alone from the studies reviewed in section 10.3.1.

10.4   Discussion

The effects of the financial aid programs we have discussed appear to depend critically on the form taken by the intervention. Program design matters. In particular, there appears to be an important trade-off between targeting and program effectiveness. Highly-targeted programs such as the Pell focus their dollars on poorer students, but impose substantial paperwork burdens in order to identify the neediest. If targeted students are deterred by administrative hurdles, these programs will not work as well as intended. This is consistent with the pattern in table 10.1, in which the Pell and Stafford have small to zero effects while simpler, less-targeted programs have substantial effects.

The paperwork requirements of the federal, need-based aid programs are high. For the typical household, the aid application (the Free Application for Federal Student Aid, or FAFSA) is longer and more complicated than the federal tax return. The aid process is also highly uncertain, with definitive information about freshman-year aid not revealed until the spring of the senior year in high school (Dynarski and Scott-Clayton 2006b). This process may be particularly daunting for low-income families. Parents in these families have typically not gone to college themselves, so cannot draw from their own experiences to help their children. Low-income high school students have few guidance counselors to guide them through the process. They are unlikely to have Internet access at home and frequently speak English as a second language. As a result, need-based aid—which requires gathering extensive information about income and expenses—may have a smaller effect on this population than less-targeted forms of subsidy with fewer application requirements and lower transaction costs.

By contrast, Georgia's HOPE scholarship requires only that high school students maintain a 3.0 GPA in order to have their tuition and fees paid at any public college in Georgia. High schools proactively send transcript data to the state in order to identify scholarship winners. For most students, the HOPE application consists of a half page of basic biographical information. High school students are knowledgeable about HOPE. More than 70 percent of Georgia high school freshmen surveyed were able to name the program without prompting; and, when asked to list some requirements of HOPE, 59 percent volunteered that a high school GPA of 3.0 is necessary (Bugler and Henry 1998). The compliance costs of the Social Security student benefit program were also minimal.

Promising recent evidence on the benefits of simplification comes from a randomized trial of assisted Free Application for Federal Student Aid (FAFSA) completion conducted in partnership with H&R Block, an accounting firm that provides tax preparation assistance (Bettinger et al. 2009). Tax professionals prepopulated the FAFSA with income and asset information and assisted families with completion and filing of the form. The treatment group was also provided with an immediate estimate of aid eligibility and information about local postsecondary options and costs. Early results from the program suggest that assistance increased college enrollment substantially, both for recent high school graduates and for older, independent students with no college experience (Bettinger et al. 2009). The results suggest that simplification may be a highly cost-effective way to improve college access. In contrast, there was no effect for a second treatment group that received only information, with no assistance. This implies that compliance costs, rather than lack of information, may be the more important barrier. The results suggest that increases in educational attainment could be achieved at virtually no cost by making existing aid programs simpler and more transparent.

In sum, the best evidence for effective financial aid on educational attainment comes from simple, broad-based programs. Given that many students in these programs would have gone to college anyway, the benefits of simplicity versus targeting are an empirical question. The evidence suggests that even broad-based programs may pass a social cost-benefit test. Dynarski (2008) estimates that state merit aid programs in Georgia and Arkansas pass a cost-benefit test if the return to schooling is between 5 and 9 percent. This is on the low end of instrumental variable rates of return to schooling, and is well below the rate of return estimated for recent cohorts (Angrist and Krueger 1991; Kane and Rouse 1995; Oreopoulos 2007). Thus it appears that even with a low effective increase in enrollment due to subsidization of inframarginal students, a simple, broad-based aid program can increase social welfare.

Students who enter college but drop out without a degree are an important target for those who wish to increase educational attainment. Dropout rates are especially high at community colleges, where poor students are concentrated. Interventions that increase persistence in community colleges are therefore a sensible focus if the goal is to increase the educational attainment of the poor. The Opening Doors demonstration projects provide strong evidence that pairing financial incentives with support services can increase college persistence among low-income students attending community colleges. Testing the efficacy of these programs at scale is an important next step for researchers.

References

Abraham, K., and M. Clark. 2006. Financial aid and students' college decisions: Evidence from the District of Columbia Tuition Assistance Grant Program. *Journal of Human Resources* 41 (Summer): 578–610.

Angrist, J. D. 1993. The effect of veterans benefits on education and earnings. *Industrial and Labor Relations Review* 46 (4): 637–52.

Angrist, J. D., and A. B. Krueger. 1991. Does compulsory school attendance affect schooling and earnings? *Quarterly Journal of Economics* 106 (4): 979–1014.

Angrist, J. D., D. Lang, and P. Oreopoulos. 2009. Incentives and services for college achievement: Evidence from a randomized trial. *American Economic Journal: Applied Economics* 1 (1): 136–63.

Avery, C., C. Hoxby, C. Jackson, K. Burek, G. Poppe, and M. Raman. 2006. Cost should be no barrier: An evaluation of the first year of Harvard's financial aid initiative. NBER Working Paper no. 12029. Cambridge, MA: National Bureau of Economic Research, February.

Avery, C., and T. J. Kane. 2004. Student perceptions of college opportunities: The Boston COACH program. In *College choices: The economics of where to go, when to go, and how to pay for it*, ed. C. Hoxby, 355–94. Chicago: University of Chicago Press.

Bettinger, E. 2004. How financial aid affects persistence. In *College choices: The economics of where to go, when to go, and how to pay for it*, ed. C. Hoxby, 207–38. Chicago: University of Chicago Press.

Bettinger, E., B. T. Long, P. Oreopoulos, and L. Sanbonmatsu. 2009. The role of information and simplification in college decisions: Results from the H&R Block FAFSA Experiment. NBER Working Paper no. 15361. Cambridge, MA: National Bureau of Economic Research, September.

Bloom, D., and C. Sommo. 2005. Building learning communities: Early results from the opening doors demonstration at Kingsborough Community College. Manpower Development Research Corp., New York.

Bok, D., and W. G. Bowen. 2000. *The shape of the river: Long-term consequences of considering race in college and university admissions*. Princeton, NJ: Princeton University Press.

Bound, J., and S. Turner. 2002. Going to war and going to college: Did World War II and the G.I. Bill increase educational attainment for returning veterans? *Journal of Labor Economics* 20 (4): 784–815.

Brock, T., and L. Richburg-Hayes. 2006. Paying for persistence: Early results of a Louisiana scholarship program for low-income parents attending community college. Manpower Development Research Corp., New York.

Bugler, D. T., and G. T. Henry. 1998. An evaluation of Georgia's HOPE Scholarship Program: Impact on college attendance and performance. Council for School Performance, Georgia State University.

College Board. 2005. *Education pays 2005*. New York: The College Board.

Cornwell, C., D. Mustard, and D. Sridhar. 2006. The enrollment effects of merit-based financial aid: Evidence from Georgia's HOPE Scholarship. *Journal of Labor Economics* 24: 761–86.

DesJardins, S. L., and B. P. McCall. 2007. The impact of the Gates Millenium Scholars Program on selected outcomes of low-income minority students: A regression discontinuity analysis. Working Paper. University of Michigan.

Dynarski, S. 2000. Hope for whom? Financial aid for the middle class and its impact on college attendance. *National Tax Journal* 53 (3): 629–61.

———. 2003. Does aid matter? Measuring the effect of student aid on college attendance and completion. *American Economic Review* 93 (1): 279–88.

———. 2004. Who benefits from the college saving incentives? Income, educational expectations, and the value of the 529 and Coverdell. *National Tax Journal* (September): 359–83.

———. 2005. Loans, liquidity, and schooling decisions. Working Paper. Harvard University.

———. 2008. Building the stock of college-educated labor. *Journal of Human Resources* 43 (3): 576–610.

Dynarski, S., and J. Scott-Clayton. 2006a. Simplify and focus the education tax incentives. *Tax Notes* (June): 1290–92.

—————. 2006b. The cost of complexity in Federal Student Aid: Lessons from optimal tax theory and behavioral economics. *NBER Working Paper* no. 12227. Cambridge, MA: National Bureau of Economic Research, May.

Goodman, J. 2008. Who merits financial aid?: Massachusetts' Adams Scholarship, *Journal of Public Economics*, 92 (10–11): 2121–31.

Hansen, W. L. 1983. The impact of student financial aid on access. In *The crisis in higher education*, ed. J. Froomkin, 84–96. New York: Academy of Political Science.

Heller, D. E. 1997. Student price response in higher education: An update to Leslie and Brinkman. *Journal of Higher Education* 68 (6): 624–59.

Kane, T. J. 1995. Rising public college tuition and college entry: How well do public subsidies promote access to college? NBER Working Paper no. 5164. Cambridge, MA: National Bureau of Economic Research, July.

—————. 2003. A quasi-experimental estimate of the impact of financial aid on college-going. NBER Working Paper no. 9703. Cambridge, MA: National Bureau of Economic Research, May.

—————. 2004. Evaluating the impact of the D.C. tuition assistance grant program. NBER Working Paper no. 10658. Cambridge, MA: National Bureau of Economic Research, July.

—————. 2007. Evaluating the impact of the D.C. tuition assistance grant program. *Journal of Human Resources* XLII (3): 555–82.

Kane, T. J., and C. E. Rouse. 1995. Labor market returns to two- and four-year college. *American Economic Review* 85 (3): 600–14.

Leslie, L., and P. Brinkman. 1988. *The economic value of higher education.* New York: Macmillan.

Linsenmeier, D. M., H. S. Rosen, and C. E. Rouse. 2006. Financial aid packages and college enrollment decisions: An econometric case study. *Review of Economics and Statistics* 88 (1): 126–45.

Myers, D., R. Olsen, N. Seftor, J. Young, and C. Tuttle. 2004. *The impacts of regular Upward Bound: Results from the third follow-up data collection.* Washington, DC: Mathematica Policy Research.

Myers, D., and A. Schirm. 1999. *The impacts of Upward Bound: Final report for phase I of the National Evaluation.* Washington, DC: Mathematica Policy Research.

Oreopoulos, P. 2007. Do dropouts drop out too soon? Wealth, health and happiness from compulsory schooling. *Journal of Public Economics* 91 (11–12): 2213–29.

Pallais, A., and S. E. Turner. 2007. Access to elites. In *Economic inequality and higher education: Access, persistence and success,* ed. S. Dickert-Conlin and R. H. Rubenstein, 128–56. New York: Russell Sage Foundation.

Reyes, S. L. 1995. Educational opportunities and outcomes: The role of the guaranteed student loan. Working Paper. Harvard University.

Rothstein, J., and C. E. Rouse. 2007. Constrained after college: Student loans and early career occupational choices. NBER Working Paper no. 13117. Cambridge, MA: National Bureau of Economic Research, May.

Scott-Clayton, J. 2009. On money and motivation: A quasi-experimental analysis of financial incentives for college achievement. Working Paper. Harvard University.

Scrivener, S., and J. Au. 2007. *Enhancing student services at Lorain County Community College: Early results from the opening doors demonstration in Ohio.* New York: Manpower Development Research Corp.

Scrivener, S., D. Bloom, A. LeBlanc, C. Paxson, C. E. Rouse, C. Sommo, et al. 2008. *A good start: Two-year effects of a freshman learning community program at Kingsborough Community College.* New York: Manpower Development Research Corp.

Scrivener, S., and M. Pih. 2007. *Enhancing student services at Owens Community*

College: Early results from the opening doors demonstration in Ohio. New York: Manpower Development Research Corp.

Seftor, N., and S. Turner. 2002. Back to school: Federal student aid policy and adult college enrollment. *Journal of Human Resources* 37 (2): 336–52.

Stanley, M. 2003. College education and the mid-century G.I. Bills. *Quarterly Journal of Economics* 118 (2): 671–708.

Stedman, J. B. 2003. *Federal Pell Grant Program of the Higher Education Act: Background and reauthorization.* Washington, DC: Congressional Research Service.

Turner, S. 2007. Higher education: Policies generating the 21st century workforce. In *Workforce policies for a changing economy,* ed. H. Holzer and D. Nightingale, 91–118. Washington, DC: Urban Institute Press.

Turner, S., and J. Bound. 2003. Closing the gap or widening the divide: The effects of the G.I. Bill and World War II on the educational outcomes of black Americans. *Journal of Economic History* 63 (1): 145–77.

van der Klaauw, W. 2002. Estimating the effect of financial aid offers on college enrollment: A regression-discontinuity approach. *International Economic Review* 43 (4): 1249–88.

11
Neighborhood and Community Initiatives

Julia Burdick-Will and Jens Ludwig

11.1 Introduction

Educational outcomes vary dramatically across neighborhoods in America. For example, in the Chicago North-shore suburb of Wilmette, where the median home value is $441,000 and only 2 percent of residents live below the poverty line, almost everyone graduates from high school and a majority go on to attend—and even complete—college. In contrast, the dropout rate in the Chicago Public Schools is well over 40 percent (Allensworth and Easton 2001), and is even higher in some of Chicago's most disadvantaged neighborhoods on the South and West Sides.

Why are children who grow up in disadvantaged areas at such elevated risk for educational problems, even beyond what we would predict based on their own family circumstances? The answer is important in part because of the persistence of concentrated urban poverty in America. Residential segregation by income has been increasing since 1970 (Watson 2009); in 2000 there were 8 million people living in high-poverty Census tracts (≥ 40 percent), nearly twice the number as in 1970 (Jargowsky 2003). Because blacks are much more likely than whites to live in high-poverty neighborhoods, even controlling for family poverty status (Jargowsky [1996, 2003]; see also Massey and Denton [1993] and Massey [1996]), there is concern that

Julia Burdick-Will is a doctoral candidate in sociology at the University of Chicago. Jens Ludwig is the McCormick Foundation Professor of Social Service Administration, Law, and Public Policy at the University of Chicago, a Non-resident Senior Fellow in Economic Studies at the Brookings Institution, and a research associate and co-director of the working group on the Economics of Crime at the National Bureau of Economic Research.

Thanks to Jeffrey Kling, Phillip Levine, Stephen Raudenbush, Robert Sampson, Lisa Sanbonmatsu, Patrick Sharkey, David Zimmerman, and an anonymous referee for useful comments. Any errors and all opinions are our own.

"neighborhood effects" contribute to the overall test score disparities observed between rich and poor children or between blacks and whites (see, for example, Wilson [1998]).

One reason that neighborhood residence might impact children's achievement outcomes is because of variation across areas in the quality of local public schools. Another possible explanation focuses on the influence of peers and other neighborhood residents. Distinguishing between these two competing explanations is important for the design of antipoverty policies. If social context influences children's life chances, then education policies that break the link between neighborhood residence and school assignments, or housing policies that help poor families move to lower-poverty areas, may be an important strategy for improving the achievement outcomes of low-income children. On the other hand, if neighborhood effects on children's outcomes are driven mainly by the quality of local institutions, then in principle it may be possible to design community-level interventions that improve achievement without having to re-sort poor children across social environments.

Empirical claims for the powerful effect of neighborhood context on children's schooling outcomes dates back at least to the landmark Coleman Report, which argued that "attributes of other students account for far more variation in the achievement of minority group children than do any attributes of school facilities and slightly more than do attributes of staff" (Coleman 1966, 302). These findings, if taken at face value, would seem to imply the existence of powerful neighborhood effects on children's learning, given school composition is determined in large part by neighborhood composition. However, drawing causal inferences from this type of nonexperimental research on peer or neighborhood effects is complicated by the fact that most families have at least some degree of choice over where they live. These studies may confound the causal effects of social context with those of unmeasured family attributes that affect both educational outcomes and residential location.

This chapter will review the available evidence about neighborhood effects on children's achievement outcomes, and the degree to which "place-based" policies might help improve outcomes for poor children and reduce disparities across race and class lines. Our study focuses mostly on those studies that exploit the substantial excess demand for means-tested housing subsidies, and in particular housing vouchers, which provide a source of identifying variation in neighborhood environments across observably similar low-income families that helps overcome the self-selection concerns with previous research in this area. There is a large literature that examines the effects of community development interventions such as urban enterprise zones (see, for example, Ladd [1994], or Busso and Kline [2007]) or policing interventions (Sherman 2001), but almost none of this literature examines impacts on children's outcomes.[1] In discussing the policy value of the housing voucher research literature, Heymann and Fischer (2003, 344) noted that "the best solution-oriented research to date has been conducted on moving people out of hard-hit neighborhoods."

Previous research suggests that offering housing vouchers to low-income families who already live in private-market housing does not lead these families to move to substantially different types of neighborhoods (see Olsen [2003]; Jacob and Ludwig [2009]). On the other hand, housing vouchers do enable families living in public housing to move to less disadvantaged, dangerous, and socially disorganized neighborhoods. Historically, public housing units have been disproportionately likely to be located in high-poverty urban neighborhoods (Jencks and Mayer 1990; Massey and Denton 1993; Wilson 1987). In order to receive help with their housing needs, low-income families have to live in the neighborhoods in which public housing projects have been developed. Housing vouchers instead provide low-income families with some additional choice over where they live. We focus our attention mostly on studies of a single, clearly defined, and quite important policy question—what happens to the academic outcomes of poor children in public housing when their families are offered the chance to move somewhere else with a housing voucher.

The existing research paints a somewhat complicated picture of what "vouchering out" public housing might do to the academic outcomes of low-income children. There is some evidence that voucher-induced moves to lower-poverty neighborhoods may improve the academic achievement outcomes of African American children in some cities, but not in others. Why impacts vary across cities remains unclear. On the other hand, the research is more clear that using housing vouchers to help public housing families move to less distressed areas can improve other key outcomes such as mental health and criminal behavior, which may in turn improve labor market outcomes and are of course also key contributors to well-being in their own right as well.

The remainder of our chapter is organized as follows. The next section discusses the different behavioral mechanisms through which voucher-induced neighborhood moves might affect the academic outcomes of poor children. The third section provides some additional discussion of the housing voucher program rules, and notes that the government monetary costs of vouchering out public housing may be negative—that is, most housing economists believe that housing vouchers cost less than public housing in providing a given level of housing unit quality to a family. Section four reviews the available empirical evidence, the fifth section discusses potential

---

1. One recent exception is Dobbie and Fryer's (2009) study of the effects of the Harlem Children's Zone on children's academic achievement test scores.

voucher effects on other outcomes that are relevant for social welfare, while the sixth section concludes.

11.2   Conceptual Framework

Since the early days of the "Chicago School," sociologists have theorized about the ways in which neighborhood environments may impact child development. Early theories emphasized the role of social disorder and the ecological competition for resources. These early scholars viewed the city in terms of an urban ecology in which different ethnic groups, in various stages of assimilation and economic integration, compete for vital resources and niches in neighborhoods, in the same way that species compete in the natural world. Therefore, the most disadvantaged populations naturally end up in the least desirable locations and disproportionately are exposed to high crime, limited institutional resources, and the physical dangers and health risks of the zones closest to industry (Park, Burgess, and McKenzie 1967).

Furthermore, the early sociological literature saw the urban environment as a place where the density and heterogeneity of the population contributed to the disruption of strong social ties that may help maintain order and deter deviant behavior, such as crime and poor school performance, in small towns (Simmel 1997; Wirth 1997). This was especially true in the "slums," where high residential mobility and large numbers of family-less individuals further contributed to the deterioration of the social and moral order (Zorbough 1983). While current research has largely abandoned these relatively deterministic models of human ecology, there remains a great deal of interest in the potential relationship between neighborhood environments and children's life chances.

In their 2002 review of neighborhood effects, Harvard sociologist Robert Sampson and his colleagues identify four general social processes through which neighborhood characteristics are currently thought to affect those who live in them (Sampson, Morenoff, and Gannon-Rowley [2002, 457–8]; see also Jencks and Mayer [1990]). First, the social ties and interpersonal interactions with coresidents in a neighborhood provide different opportunities to accumulate social capital. In terms of school outcomes, children living in poor neighborhoods may have diminished access to well-educated adults to help them with homework or act as pro-academic role models (Wilson 1987, 1996). Parents in poor neighborhoods may also be less involved in their children's schools and less able to activate the social capital necessary to advocate for school improvement (Coleman 1991). Moreover, children's peer groups often come overwhelmingly from their neighborhood. Prosocial and antisocial neighborhood peer groups may influence student achievement either directly by affecting the level of instruction in the classroom (Hoxby 2000; Zimmer and Toma 2000), or indirectly by shaping the social rewards to pro- versus antisocial behavior (Gavaria and Raphael 2001).

Second, neighborhoods may influence school outcomes not through the direct ties of the residents, but through their social norms and capacity for informal social control (Sampson, Morenoff, and Earls 1999). In other words, it may not be who the local children know directly, but rather the general levels of trust and expectations for behavior that prevail in the neighborhoods. For example, children may be less likely to get into trouble that would interfere with school when their neighbors are willing to intervene and keep an eye out for them. High expectations about overall educational attainment and achievement may also lead students to be more willing to work hard in school.

Third, the quantity and quality of neighborhood institutional resources may matter. When it comes to academic achievement, neighborhood schools are probably the most important—but not the only relevant—local institutions. Resources ranging from adequate medical care facilities, child care centers, parental employment opportunities, and after-school social and academic organizations could all influence children's academic performance in potentially important ways (Jencks and Meyer 1990; Brooks-Gunn et al. 1993).

Finally, children's routine activities and those of their neighbors are shaped by the geography of neighborhoods, and may also have a direct influence on student achievement. Land use, such as the presence of bars, parks, or highrise versus single-family homes, may shape the type of people that children interact with and the types of places in which they can interact with their peers (Sampson, Sharkey, and Raudenbush 2008). These ecological factors may also have a direct impact on the safety level of the neighborhood by, for instance, affecting the degree to which public spaces can be easily monitored by police or community residents (Jacobs 1997). Furthermore, the patterns of adult activity that children experience on a daily basis may also affect their own behavior in and outside of school, which may indirectly impact their achievement levels. For example, children who observe their parents and neighbors coming and going regularly to work and attend formally organized activities during the standard workday may more quickly learn the value of routine and punctuality needed to excel in school. They may also learn how to navigate the world of formal interactions and organizations, such as schools, better than children who spend their time playing informally in the street (Lareau 2003).

Implicit in most of the aforementioned mechanisms is the assumption that "better" (i.e., less poor or otherwise disadvantaged or distressed) neighborhoods should always lead to improvements in child achievement. However, especially when considering housing voucher programs, it is important to note that this need not necessarily be the case. For example, Small and Stark (2005) find that poor neighborhoods often have more vital resources appropriate to low-income households, such as affordable child care centers, than more affluent neighborhoods. It is possible that, just like child care centers, the after-school resources available for children in poor neighborhoods may be more affordable and accessible than those in their new more affluent neighborhoods. Furthermore, feelings of relative deprivation and low social and academic standing with respect to their new neighbors and classmates may be discouraging to students and reduce the effort they make in school, or make them less happy with potentially adverse consequences for their schooling engagement and outcomes (Jencks and Meyer 1990; Luttmer 2005).

In sum, there are many reasons to theorize that moving children out of poor neighborhoods may improve their test scores and school outcomes. But there are also reasons to hypothesize that voucher-assisted moves to less distressed areas may not produce the desired outcomes. This means that the actual impact of moving children to less disadvantaged areas is ultimately an empirical question.

11.3   The Housing Voucher Program

Housing vouchers subsidize low-income families to live in private-market housing.[2] Eligibility limits for housing programs are a function of family size and income, and have been changing over time. Since 1975 an increasing share of housing assistance has been devoted to what the U.S. Department of Housing and Urban Development (HUD) terms "very low-income households," with incomes for a family of four that would be not more than 50 percent of the local median. (The federal poverty line is usually around 30 percent of the local median.) The maximum subsidy available to families is governed by the Fair Market Rent (FMR), which equaled the forty-fifth percentile of the local private-market rent distribution through 1995, was lowered to the fortieth percentile in 1995, and then in 2001 selected metropolitan areas, including Chicago, have been allowed to set FMR equal to the fiftieth percentile. For example, the FMR for a two-bedroom apartment in the Chicago area was equal to $699 in 1994, $732 in 1997, and $762 in 2000.

Families receiving vouchers are required to pay 30 percent of their adjusted income toward rent. Adjusted income is calculated by subtracting from a family's (reported) gross income deductions of $480 per child, $400 per disabled member of the household, child care expenses, and medical care expenses over 3 percent of annual income. Temporary Assistance for Needy Families (TANF) is counted toward the calculation of gross income, but Earned Income Tax Credit (EITC) benefits and the value of Food Stamps, Medicaid, and other in-kind benefits are not counted. The voucher covers the difference between the family's rent contribution and the lesser of the FMR or the unit rent. Starting in 1987, the government made these tenant-

2. This discussion is based on the excellent, detailed and highly readable summary in Olsen (2003).

based subsidies "portable," meaning that families could use them to live in a municipality different from the one that issued them the subsidy.

As noted before, housing assistance is not an entitlement. In Chicago, as in other big cities, there are generally extremely long waiting lists to receive housing assistance, especially for housing vouchers. Once a family receives a housing voucher they can keep the subsidy for as long as they meet the program's income and other eligibility requirements.

Despite the excess demand for housing vouchers, not all families offered vouchers wind up using them. Many apartments have rents above the FMR limit, some landlords may avoid renting to voucher families,[3] and families offered vouchers have a limited time (usually three to six months) to use the voucher to lease up a unit. Mobility outcomes in voucher programs are affected by family preferences as well as housing market constraints—that is, both the demand and supply sides of the housing market are relevant. Relatively little is known at present about what sorts of information families have available to them about different neighborhood options, or what types of neighborhood attributes factor most importantly into the mobility decisions of voucher families.

There are currently around 1.95 million households receiving housing vouchers to rent privately-owned units, 1.1 million households living in public housing, and an additional 1.4 million or so households living in other project-based housing units.[4] Just under two-thirds of housing voucher recipients are families with children, about twice the number of families with children living in public housing.[5]

Olsen's (2003) review of the available housing research argues that the costs to the government of providing low-income families with a housing unit of given quality is lower with the housing voucher program than with project-based programs such as public housing or Section 8 project-based housing (basically privately-operated public housing), perhaps by as much as 20 percent or more. Among the potential explanations include the potentially greater efficiency with which private-market landlords may operate housing units compared to project-based units. If this view is correct,[6] then

3. Some landlords may avoid renting to voucher families because of the paperwork requirements, the program's minimum housing quality standards (which must be verified by an inspection, although failed units can be modified and re-inspected), and a previous rule that has since been abolished that limited the ability of landlords to turn away future voucher applicants ("take one, take all").

4. Housing voucher figures are for early 2007 calculated by the Center on Budget and Policy Priorities (www.centeronbudget.org/5-15-03hous.htm, accessed 1/12/09). Data on public housing figures are from www.cbpp.org/10-11-06hous.htm, accessed on 1/12/09, while figures on other project-based housing comes from www.gao.gov/new.items/d07290.pdf, p. 14, accessed on 1/12/09.

5. Counts of families receiving vouchers have been estimated using the total number of units available and the percent of those units occupied by different family types. Source: A Picture of Subsidized Housing—2000, http://www.huduser.org/picture2000/.

6. There does remain some debate in the literature on this point; see for example McClure (1998) versus Shroder and Reiger (2000).

the budget cost to the government of vouchering out public housing may be negative—that is, this policy may wind up saving government money.

It is important to recognize, however, that some of the most important costs of vouchering out public housing may be nonmonetary. Specifically, if housing vouchers help public housing children by exposing them to more affluent and prosocial peers, then in principle, vouchering out public housing could have some adverse impact on the academic outcomes of children in destination neighborhoods. In the next section we discuss these sorts of peer mechanisms in more detail, and return in the conclusion to this chapter to what is known about any adverse peer impacts on children living in areas that experience an influx of vouchered-out public housing families.

What would it cost to move the other (nonpublic housing) children from high-poverty areas into less economically disadvantaged neighborhoods? The answer is that we currently do not know. As noted in the introduction, previous research has found that giving housing vouchers to low-income families who are already living in private-market housing does not lead them to move into different types of neighborhoods. These housing voucher subsidies typically represent a very large share of the family's total income—for example, on the order of 75 percent among all families applying for housing vouchers in Chicago in the late 1990s (Jacob and Ludwig 2009). It is possible that "super vouchers" that provide families with intensive extra supports to negotiate the housing market or incentives to move into particular types of neighborhoods could lead to more pronounced effects of vouchers on mobility outcomes. While these types of "super vouchers" have been offered in the past to public housing families (as part of the Moving to Opportunity [MTO] experiment discussed following), we know of no study that has offered these types of enhanced vouchers to families who were already living in private-market housing. The question of what it would take to help move low-income private-market families from high- to low-poverty neighborhoods is an important one for public policy, given that the majority of low-income children (and even of low-income children living in high-poverty areas) do not live in public housing.

11.4   Empirical Evidence

Measuring the causal effect of neighborhood environments on children's school outcomes is complicated by the fact that most families have at least some degree of choice over where they live. This raises the possibility that observational studies may confound the causal effects of neighborhood environments on children with those of hard-to-measure family attributes that are associated with residential sorting. As a result of this concern about neighborhood selection, much of the evidence for neighborhood effects on academic achievement has come from a few key natural or randomized experiments and a few unusually rich observational data sets.

The first quasi-experimental study of the effects of neighborhoods on school outcomes arose out of a 1966 lawsuit filed by a Chicago public housing resident named Dorothy Gautreaux (see table 11.1). Her lawsuit claimed that the Chicago Housing Authority (CHA) and U.S. Department of Housing and Urban Development (HUD) did not provide adequate opportunities for public housing residents in Chicago to live in racially integrated neighborhoods. The case eventually reached the U.S. Supreme Court, which in 1976 ruled in her favor.

As a result of the Supreme Court's ruling, what came to be known as the Gautreaux program began offering public housing residents the opportunity to use housing vouchers in racially integrated neighborhoods (less than 30 percent black) in the city and suburbs. Participants who volunteered for the program were assigned housing based on where there happened to be openings. Once the program was fully established in the 1980s, around 1,700 to 2,000 families a year signed up to participate, out of whom about 19 percent of those, or 300 families a year, were placed in racially and economically integrated, mostly suburban, neighborhoods using the vouchers (Rubinowitz and Rosenbaum 2000, 67). Many of the remaining families wound up being placed in neighborhoods that were still poor and segregated, but judged to be improving, which were usually located within the Chicago city limits (Mendenhall, DeLuca, and Duncan 2006). While in theory, participants could choose not to accept the housing units assigned to them, most families reportedly accepted the first available apartment (Kaufman and Rosenbaum 1992).

In 1988, a random sample of 342 Gautreaux participants was surveyed in an attempt to compare the suburban movers with those who had stayed in the city of Chicago. The surveyed families had enrolled in the Gautreaux program between 1976 and 1981, and so were surveyed from seven to twelve years after their Gautreaux-assisted neighborhood moves. Compared to the surveyed students who remained in the city of Chicago, suburban movers were four times less likely to have dropped out of school (20 percent versus 5 percent); more likely to be in a college track in high school (24 versus 40 percent); twice as likely to attend any college (21 percent versus 54 percent); and almost seven times as likely to attend a four-year college (4 percent versus 27 percent). The only educational attainment measure for which the suburban students did not appear to be doing significantly better than the city students was their grade point average, which could simply reflect higher grading standards in suburban schools (Rubinowitz and Rosenbaum 2000, 134–6).

While the Gautreaux program results were quite encouraging, there necessarily remains some question about whether the Gautreaux families surveyed in the suburbs were comparable in all respects to the surveyed city movers. For example, there is now some evidence that the initial residential placements of Gautreaux families is systematically correlated with the characteristics of families and their neighborhoods at baseline (Mendenhall,

Table 11.1   Neighborhood effects studies and their results for educational achievement

Study	Intervention	Design	Sample	Outcomes measured	Findings
Rubinowitz and Rosenbaum (2000)	Gautreaux	Comparison of Suburban and City Movers	African American, Chicago	Dropout Rate, College Track, College Attendance, Grades	15% point TOT decrease in drop outs 16% point TOT increase in college track placement 33% point TOT increase in any college attendance 13% point TOT increase in four-year college attendance No change in grades
Sanbonmatsu (2006)	Moving to Opportunity	Randomized Controlled Experiment	2/3 African American, 1/3 Hispanic, Five cities	Woodcock-Johnson-Revised Reading and Math Scores	Zero main effects Do not vary by age or gender For African American children, ITT of .084 sd on reading scores (TOT .14sd), driven by African American children in the Baltimore and Chicago sites
Jacob et al. (2008)	Chicago CHAC vouchers	Quasi-Experiment: Randomized Voucher Wait-list	African American, Chicago	Iowa Test of Basic Skills Reading and Math Scores	0.1sd TOT gain in reading, 0.16sd TOT gain in math
Sampson, Sharkey, and Raudenbush (2008)	Project on Human Development in Chicago Neighborhoods	Longitudinal Observational Study	African American, Chicago	Factor analysis of Wechsler Intelligence Scale vocab., and Wide Range Achievement test, reading	0.25sd gain in verbal ability, equivalent to TOT estimates

Note: TOT = effects of treatment on the treated (i.e., effects of relocating with a voucher).

DeLuca, and Duncan 2006; Votruba and Kling 2009). It is possible that at least part of the differences in schooling outcomes observed between city and suburban movers in Gautreaux are due to differences in the background attributes of the families who are being compared.

In response to the apparent success of the Gautreaux program, federal funding was allocated for a true housing voucher experiment designed to test the effects of neighborhood poverty called Moving to Opportunity (MTO). Between 1994 and 1998, a total of 4,600 low-income, mostly minority public housing residents in five U.S. cities (Chicago, New York, Boston, Baltimore, and Los Angeles) signed up to participate in the MTO program. Through a random lottery, families who signed up for MTO were assigned to one of three different residential mobility groups. Families assigned to the *Experimental group* were awarded a housing voucher that could be used for private housing only in a low-poverty area (census tracts with 1990 poverty rates of less than 10 percent), and were also given counseling and assistance in finding their new apartment. Families assigned to the *Section 8-only group* were given a standard Section 8 housing voucher that could be used in any census tract in which the family wished to live and could find a suitable unit to lease. Families assigned to the *Control group* did not receive a voucher of any kind, but maintained their current project-based housing and their eligibility for whatever other social programs they were receiving (Orr 2003).

Of the families assigned to the experimental group, around 47 percent relocated with a housing voucher through MTO while 62 percent of those assigned to the Section 8-only group relocated through MTO. Many of the families who moved through the MTO experimental group to a low-poverty tract eventually moved again and returned to higher-poverty neighborhoods, while some families in the control group relocated on their own, even without MTO assistance. Nevertheless, random assignment to the MTO experimental rather than control group generates large differences in residential neighborhood characteristics, with differences in tract poverty rates equal to 25 to 30 percent of the control mean one year after random assignment and around 20 to 25 percent over the six years after assignment. The MTO generates similarly large changes in other measures of neighborhood socioeconomic composition, safety, social disorder, and social cohesion, but leads to more modest changes in neighborhood racial composition.

Data on children's outcomes collected on average five years after random assignment found that on average there is no statistically significant effect of MTO-induced moves on children's scores on the Woodcock-Johnson-Revised reading or math achievement tests (Sanbonmatsu 2006). The estimates do not seem to be any larger for children who were relatively younger at the time of baseline. However, it is important to keep in mind that these achievement test scores were recorded just five years after baseline, and so many of those children who were very young at the time of random assignment (and so could potentially benefit the most from MTO moves; see, for example, Shonkoff and Phillips [2000] and Knudsen et al. [2006]) were still too young to be tested at the time of the interim MTO evaluation.

Additional subgroup analyses find that there might be some effect of being assigned to the experimental rather than control group on the reading test scores of African American children, with an intent to treat effect (ITT) equal to around 0.1 standard deviations so that the effect of actually using a voucher is more like 0.2 standard deviations (Sanbonmatsu 2006, Web Appendix). However, these impacts seem to be driven by African American children in just two of the five MTO sites—Baltimore and Chicago, where almost all of the MTO program population is African-American, although only the Baltimore results are statistically significant.[7] In the other three MTO cities (Boston, Los Angeles, and New York) the program sample is split between African American and Hispanic children, and separate subgroup analyses reveal no statistically significant gains in test scores for either black or Hispanic children.[8]

Given the large number of subgroup estimates generated with the MTO achievement test analysis, it is possible that the hints of reading score gains for African American children in the Baltimore and Chicago MTO sites could be "false positives"—that is, if we simply generate enough estimates, at least one may be significant at the 5 percent cutoff just by chance alone. Some support for the idea that African American children in Baltimore and Chicago MTO might really have improved reading scores comes from a more recent study, which analyzes data on every public housing family in Chicago who applied to the city's regular housing voucher program when the program's wait-list was opened in 1997 for the first time in a dozen years (see Jacob et al. 2009b).

In total, 82,607 eligible families applied, far more than the number of vouchers that were available, with around 10 percent of all applicants living in public housing at the time they applied. The firm running the city's housing voucher program at the time, CHAC Inc., randomly assigned all families who applied for a voucher to a position on the voucher wait-list. Given the random assignment of families to the voucher program wait list, the causal effects of vouchering out public housing can be estimated with this larger

7. Ludwig, Ladd, and Duncan (2001) analyzed short-term achievement test scores measured two to three years after random assignment for children in the Baltimore MTO site and found very sizable gains in test scores for children who relocated through the MTO demonstration. The site-specific analyses in the interim (five year) MTO study, which examined data from all five MTO sites, suggest the way to reconcile the short-term and interim results is site heterogeneity in MTO impacts rather than "fade out" of MTO test gains.

8. While the estimated experimental treatment impact on reading scores is not statistically significant in either the Baltimore or Chicago site when analyzed separately, the impact is significant when data from those two sites are pooled together. In contrast the estimated impacts of MTO experimental group assignment on reading or math scores are very small both absolutely and relative to the standard errors when data from the other three MTO sites (Boston, Los Angeles, and New York) are pooled together and analyzed overall or analyzing African American and Hispanic children separately. Thanks to Jeffrey Kling for his helpful discussions on this point.

Chicago housing voucher sample in the same way as in the randomized MTO experiment, by basically comparing the outcomes of those children whose families were assigned good versus bad wait-list positions. As in the MTO experiment, families in Chicago who lived in public housing at baseline and were offered vouchers wound up moving to neighborhoods that were less economically segregated than those of families who were not offered vouchers, but these areas were not less racially segregated. Children in the families who relocated with a voucher experienced gains on their Iowa Test of Basic Skills (ITBS) reading and math assessments equal to 0.16 standard deviations relative to their control group counterparts (Jacob et al. 2009a).

Similar evidence comes from nonexperimental analyses of data from the Project on Human Development in Chicago Neighborhoods (PHDCN). While the PHDCN is an observational, not experimental study, the longitudinal structure of the data and the rich set of observable covariates help generate correlational estimates that are a useful complement to those from MTO and CHAC. The PHDCN is a longitudinal study of a random sample of approximately 3,000 children ages zero to eighteen at wave one, in randomly selected Chicago neighborhoods. The children are followed for three waves over seven years to wherever they moved in the United States. Sampson and his colleagues exploit the longitudinal nature of the data and the rich set of covariates to predict selection into and out of disadvantaged neighborhoods and then use those predicted probabilities to estimate the effect of moving out of a disadvantaged neighborhood (Sampson, Sharkey, and Raudenbush 2008).

The explanatory variable of interest in their analysis is a measure of "concentrated disadvantage" that comes from a factor analysis of the concentration of welfare receipt, poverty, unemployment, female-headed households, African Americans, and children under eighteen years old (Sampson, Sharkey, and Raudenbush 2008, 848). In Chicago, the only ethnic group in the sample living in neighborhoods with the most extreme levels of concentrated disadvantage (the bottom quartile of the Chicago distribution) is African Americans. Therefore, Sampson, Sharkey, and Raudenbush restrict their analysis only to African American children, and find that children who leave severely disadvantaged neighborhoods experience a 0.25 standard deviation increase in their later verbal test scores (a combination of the Wechsler Intelligence Scale vocabulary test and the Wide Range Achievement reading test) compared to other African American children in the PHDCN (Sampson, Sharkey, and Raudenbush 2008).

11.5   Other Effects of Housing Voucher Programs

Regardless of the direct effect of housing vouchers on test scores, a number of other social benefits seem to arise from providing public housing families with housing vouchers to move to less disadvantaged neighborhoods. One of the most robust findings from MTO was that program moves substantially improved the mental health of females, with impacts on parent depression that are about as large as current best-practice antidepressant drug treatment and even larger gains in mental health for female youth (Kling, Liebman, and Katz 2007).[9] These reductions in mental health problems appear to be linearly related to the poverty level of the neighborhood that the women move to; that is, the greater the reduction in neighborhood percent poor, the greater the impact of the move on the mental health of female adults and youth. Interestingly, MTO moves did not seem to generate similar improvements in mental health for male youth. It is still unclear exactly why there are such stark gender differences, but it may have to do with the different ways in which male and female youth adjusted to their new environments and peers (Kling, Ludwig, and Katz 2005; Clampet-Lundquist et al. 2006).

The MTO moves have also been demonstrated to reduce the social costs of criminal activity by program youth (Kling, Ludwig, and Katz 2005). Female youth experience large reductions in arrest rates for all types of offenses. Female youth who moved with the voucher, were on average approximately 85 percent less likely to be arrested for any kind of crime than were controls. The relative declines in violent and property crime arrests specifically were equal to 76 and 85 percent. The results for males are mixed, with declines in violent crime arrests but large increases (equal to 76 percent of the control mean) in property crime arrests. Because the costs to society from violent crimes are far larger than those from property offenses, the net effect of relocating with a MTO experimental group voucher is to reduce the social costs of crime from around $3,000 to $25,000 per youth, depending on the age of the sample and the measure of the costs of crime that is used (Kling, Ludwig, and Katz 2005).

11.6   Conclusion

Taken together, the available evidence seems to suggest that using housing vouchers to move African American public housing children into less distressed areas can improve their achievement test scores, at least in some cities. In different Baltimore and Chicago samples the Treatment on the Treated (TOT) impacts of voucher utilization is on the order of .1 to .2 standard deviations, which is in the same ballpark as the famous Tennessee Student Teacher Achievement Ratio (STAR) class-size reduction experiment (Krueger 1999). Why housing voucher moves should help boost the test scores of African American children in Chicago, and perhaps Baltimore,

---

9. Mothers in experimental group who moved were 13 percent more likely to report feeling calm and peaceful and 0.2 standard deviations lower on a scale of psychological distress than the mothers in the control group. On average, young females who moved were a full 0.59 standard deviations lower on the psychological distress scale than those who were not offered a voucher and 13 percent less likely to have symptoms of generalized anxiety disorder.

but not for either black or Hispanic children in the other MTO cities remains a mystery.

On the other hand, voucher-induced moves into less distressed areas improves other outcomes such as mental health, crime victimization, and socially costly criminal behavior that may influence labor market outcomes. Of course, since the ultimate goal of social policy is to improve the well-being of families rather than simply change their incomes relative to the federal poverty line, impacts on health and crime are important outcomes in their own right as well.

Unfortunately relatively little is currently known about what specific mechanisms underlie the observed impacts of voucher-assisted neighborhood moves. The MTO treatment group assignment improves neighborhood socioeconomic composition, generates relatively modest changes in neighborhood racial composition or school quality, and large changes in safety. Because MTO randomization generates large changes in multiple candidate mechanisms simultaneously, it is not possible to determine the independent causal contribution of each potential behavioral pathway. There is some evidence that criminal behavior among MTO participants may have declined the most in demonstration sites where MTO families experienced the largest changes in neighborhood racial segregation (Ludwig and Kling 2007), but this does not seem to be the case for achievement test scores.

The other key question that remains with vouchering out public housing has to do with the costs. Our reading of the housing economics literature suggests that housing vouchers are probably more cost-effective than project-based housing programs, at least with respect to the government financial costs. But perhaps the most important costs associated with vouchering out public housing could be nonmonetary, in the form of potential adverse peer effects on children who are living in the destination neighborhoods to which voucher families relocate. If relocating from a high-poverty to a low-poverty neighborhood might generate positive impacts on the poor children who move, then it must be logically possible that such moves could adversely impact the children in the receiving low-poverty areas. How vouchering out effects overall aggregate test scores will depend on whether any peer influences on achievement vary linearly or nonlinearly with neighborhood poverty, and on whether different types of children respond similarly or differently to the same types of neighborhood environments. To date, almost nothing is known about this important question since the voucher mobility work is largely dominated by studies of just those children who move.[10]

10. Some indirect evidence on this question comes from studies of what happens to property values in neighborhoods into which housing voucher families move. For example, in a case study of Philadelphia, Lee, Culhune, and Wachter (1999) find that concentrations of voucher recipients in a neighborhood lead to small property value reductions, which are much smaller than those predicted by the construction of new public housing projects. Whether these property value impacts reflect actual adverse peer influences on children, or instead, a form of statistical discrimination is currently not known.

Most parents probably believe that neighborhood environments matter to some degree for how their children turn out, and certainly few parents who could avoid it would wish their children to grow up in the housing projects found in some of our nation's most disadvantaged and dangerous urban neighborhoods. Existing research suggests that, not surprisingly, helping families move out of dangerous, high-poverty housing projects improves the safety and well-being of parents and children, and even reduces the net social costs of criminal activity committed by children in these families. But whether vouchering out housing projects across the country would generate large changes in children's achievement test scores, and subsequently help them earn enough to avoid poverty during adulthood, remains unclear.

References

Allensworth, E., and J. Q. Easton. 2001. *Calculating a cohort dropout rate for the Chicago public schools: A technical research report.* Chicago, IL: Consortium on Chicago School Research, June.

Brooks-Gunn, J., G. J. Duncan, P. K. Klebanov, and N. Sealand. 1993. Do neighborhoods influence child and adolescent development? *American Journal of Sociology* 99 (2): 353–95.

Busso, M., and P. Kline. 2007. Do local economic development programs work? Evidence from the Federal Empowerment Zone program. University of California at Berkeley. Working Paper.

Coleman, J. S. 1966. *Equality of educational opportunity: The Coleman Study.* Washington, DC: U.S. Department of Health, Education and Welfare.

———. 1991. *Parental involvement in education.* Washington, DC: U.S. Department of Education, Office of Educational Research and Improvement, Programs for the Improvement of Practice. Opinion Paper.

Clampet-Lundquist, S., G. J. Duncan, K. Edin, and J. R. Kling. 2006. Moving at risk teenagers out of high-risk neighborhoods: Why girls fare better than boys. Princeton, NJ: Princeton University, Industrial Relations Section Working Paper 509.

Clampet-Lundquist, S., and D. Massey. 2008. Neighborhood effects on economic self-sufficiency: A reconsideration of the Moving to Opportunity experiment. *American Journal of Sociology* 114 (1): 107–43.

Dobbie, W., and R. G. Fryer, Jr. 2009. Are high-quality schools enough to close the achievement gap? Evidence from a bold social experiment in Harlem. NBER Working Paper no. 15473. Cambridge, MA: National Bureau of Economic Research, November.

Gaviria, A., and S. Raphael. 2001. School-based peer effects and juvenile behavior. *The Review of Economics and Statistics* 83 (2): 257–68.

Heymann, J., and A. Fischer. 2003. Neighborhoods, health research, and its relevance to public policy. In *Neighborhoods and health,* ed. I. Kawachi and L. F. Berkman, 335–48. New York: Oxford University Press.

Hoxby, C. 2000. Peer effects in the classroom: Learning from gender and race variation. NBER Working Paper no. W7867. Cambridge, MA: National Bureau of Economic Research, August.

Jacob, B. A., J. Ludwig, G. J. Duncan, J. Rosenbaum, and M. Johnson. 2009a. The effects of providing housing vouchers to public housing families. University of Michigan, Department of Economics. Working Paper.

———. 2009b. Neighborhood effects on low income families: Evidence from a randomized housing voucher in Chicago. University of Michigan, Department of Economics. Working Paper.

Jacobs, J. 1997. The use of sidewalks. In *Metropolis: Center and symbol of our times,* ed. P. Kasinitz, 30–45. New York: New York University Press.

Jargowsky, P. A. 1996. Poverty and place: Ghettos, barrios, and the American city. New York: Russell Sage Foundation.

———. 2003. Stunning progress, hidden problems: The dramatic decline of concentrated poverty in the 1990s. Living cities census series. Washington, DC: Brookings Institution.

Jencks, C., and S. E. Mayer. 1990. The social consequences of growing up in a poor neighborhood. In *Inner-city poverty in the United States,* ed. L. E. Lynn, Jr. and M. G. H. McGeary, 111–86. Washington, DC: National Academies Press.

Kaufman, J. E., and J. E. Rosenbaum. 1992. The education and employment of low-income black youth in white suburbs. *Educational Evaluation and Policy Analysis* 14 (3): 229–40.

Kling, J. R., J. B. Liebman, and L. F. Katz. 2007. Experimental analysis of neighborhood effects. *Econometrica* 75 (1): 83–119.

Kling, J. R., J. Ludwig, and L. F. Katz. 2005. Neighborhood effects on crime for female and male youth: Evidence from a randomized housing voucher experiment. *Quarterly Journal of Economics* 120 (1): 87–130.

Knudson, E. I., J. J. Heckman, J. L. Cameron, and J. P. Shonkoff. 2006. Economic, neurobiological, and behavioral perspectives on building America's future workforce. *Proceedings of the National Academy of Sciences of the United States of America* 103 (27): 10155–62.

Krueger, A. B. 1999. Experimental estimates of education production functions. *Quarterly Journal of Economics* 114 2: 497–532.

Ladd, H. F. 1994. Spatially targeted economic development strategies: Do they work? *Cityscape: A Journal of Policy Development and Research* 1.1 (August): 193–218.

Lareau, A. 2003. *Unequal childhoods: Class, race, and family life.* Berkeley: University of California Press.

Lee, C.-M., D. P. Culhune, and S. M. Wachter. 1999. The differential impacts of federally assisted housing programs on nearby property values: A Philadelphia case study. *Housing Policy Debate* 10 (2): 75–93.

Ludwig, J., and J. Kling. 2007. Is crime contagious? *Journal of Law and Economics* 50 (3): 491–518.

Ludwig, J., J. Liebman, J. Kling, G. Duncan, L. Katz, R. Kessler, and L. Sanbonmatsu. 2008. What can we learn about neighborhood effects from the Moving to Opportunity experiment? *American Journal of Sociology* 114 (1): 144–88.

Ludwig, J., H. F. Ladd, and G. J. Duncan. 2001. Urban poverty and educational outcomes. In *Brookings-Wharton papers on urban affairs,* ed. W. Gale and J. Rothenberg Pack. 147–201. Washington, DC: Brookings Institution.

Luttmer, E. F. P. 2005. Neighbors as negatives: Relative earnings and well-being. *The Quarterly Journal of Economics* 120 (3): 963–1002.

Massey, D. 1996. The age of extremes: Concentrated affluence and poverty in the twenty-first century. *Demography* 33 (4): 395–412.

Massey, D. S., and N. A. Denton. 1993. *American apartheid: Segregation and the making of the underclass.* Cambridge, MA: Harvard University Press.

McClure, K. 1998. Housing vouchers versus housing production: Assessing long-term costs. *Housing Policy Debate* 9 (2): 355–71.

Mendenhall, R., S. DeLuca, and G. Duncan. 2006. Neighborhood resources, racial segregation, and economic mobility: Results from the Gautreaux program. *Social Science Research* 35 (4): 892–923.

Olsen, E. 2003. Housing programs for low-income households. In *Means-Tested Transfer Programs in the United States*. A National Bureau of Economic Research Conference Report, ed. R. Moffitt, 365–442. Chicago: University of Chicago Press.

Orr, L. L., J. D. Feins, R. Jacob, E. Beecrof, L. Sanbonmatsu, L. Katz, J. Liebman, and J. Kling. 2003. *Moving to Opportunity Interim impacts evaluation.* Washington, DC: U.S. Department of Housing and Urban Development, Office of Policy Development and Research.

Park, R. E., E. W. Burgess, and R. D. McKenzie. 1967. *The city [by] Robert E. Park, Ernest W. Burgess [and] Roderick D. McKenzie.* (With an introduction by Morris Janowitz). Chicago: University of Chicago Press.

Rubinowitz, L. S., and J. E. Rosenbaum. 2000. *Crossing the class and color lines: From public housing to white suburbia.* Marketing Department, University of Chicago Press.

Sampson, R. J. 2008. Moving to inequality: Neighborhood effects and experiments meet social structure. *The American Journal of Sociology* 114 (1): 189–231.

Sampson, R. J., J. D. Morenoff, and F. Earls. 1999. Beyond social capital: Spatial dynamics of collective efficacy for children. *American Sociological Review* 64 (5): 633–60.

Sampson, R. J., J. D. Morenoff, and T. Gannon-Rowley. 2002. Assessing neighborhood effects: Social processes and new directions in research. *Annual Review of Sociology* 28 (August): 443–78.

Sampson, R., P. Sharkey, and S. Raudenbush. 2008. Durable effects of concentrated disadvantage on verbal ability among African-American children. *Proceedings of the National Academy of Sciences* 105 (3): 845–52.

Sanbonmatsu, L. 2006. Neighborhoods and academic achievement: Results from the Moving to Opportunity experiment. NBER Working Paper no. 11909. Cambridge, MA: National Bureau of Economic Research, January.

Sherman, L. W. 2001. Fair and effective policing. In *Crime: Public policies for crime control*, ed. J. Q. Wilson and J. Petersilia, 383–412. Oakland, CA: Institute for Contemporary Studies Press.

Shonkoff, J. P., and D. Phillips. 2000. *From neurons to neighborhoods: The science of early childhood development.* Washington, DC: National Academy Press.

Shroder, M., and A. Reiger. 2000. Vouchers versus production revisited. *Journal of Housing Research* 11 (1): 91–108.

Simmel, G. 1997. Metropolis and mental life. In *Metropolis: Center and symbol of our times,* ed. P. Kasinitz, 30–45. New York: New York University Press.

Small, M. L., and L. Stark. 2005. Are poor neighborhoods resource deprived? A case study of childcare centers in New York. *Social Science Quarterly* 86 (5): 1013–36.

Votruba, M. E., and J. R. Kling. 2008. Effects of neighborhood characteristics on the mortality of black male youth: Evidence from Gautreaux, Chicago. *Social Science and Medicine* 68 (5): 814–23.

Watson, T. 2009. Inequality and the measurement of residential segregation by income in American neighborhoods. NBER Working Paper no. 14908. Cambridge, MA: National Bureau of Economic Research, April.

Wilson, W. J. 1987. *The truly disadvantaged: The inner city, the underclass, and public policy.* Chicago: The University of Chicago Press.
———. 1996. *When work disappears: The world of the new urban poor.* New York: Knopf.
———. 1998. The role of the environment in the black-white test score gap. In *The black-white test score gap,* ed. C. Jencks and M. Phillips, 501–10. Washington, DC: Brookings Institution Press.
Wirth, L. 1997. Urbanism as a way of life. In *Metropolis: Center and symbol of our times,* ed. P. Kasinitz, 58–84. New York: New York University Press.
Zimmer, R. W., and E. F. Toma. 2000. Peer effects in private and public schools across countries. *Journal of Policy Analysis and Management.* 19 (1): 75.
Zorbaugh, H. W. 1983. *The Gold Coast and the slum: A sociological study of Chicago's Near North Side.* Chicago: The University of Chicago Press.

12

Vocational Training

Robert LaLonde and Daniel Sullivan

12.1 Introduction

It is well-documented that public investments in secondary and postsecondary schooling greatly benefit both the youths who receive the investments and the societies in which they live. Indeed, rates of return from investments in both academic and vocational schooling have been found to be on par with, if not larger than, the returns on physical capital.[1] In the United States, where the returns to education are among the highest in the developed world, researchers and policymakers have sought to understand why youths do not invest more in schooling, given that such investments have clear benefits and that labor market opportunities for the unskilled have steadily deteriorated for more than a quarter of a century.[2]

Although overall educational attainment in the United States remains relatively high, even compared with other Organization for Economic Cooperation and Development (OECD) countries, for those in the bottom one-third of the distribution, especially young males, the picture is quite different. The economic position of high school dropout youths, a group long targeted by government workforce development initiatives, has

Robert LaLonde is a professor in the Harris School of Public Policy of the University of Chicago. Daniel Sullivan is a senior vice-president and director of research at the Federal Reserve Bank of Chicago, and an adjunct faculty member at the Harris School of Public Policy of the University of Chicago.

The opinions expressed in the paper are those of the authors and not official positions of the Federal Reserve Bank of Chicago or the Federal Reserve System.

1. See Heckman, Lochner, and Todd (2006). They report that the real internal social rate of return from investments in public schooling have been about 7 percent; private internal rates of return are higher. Returns to human capital investment also may be less variable, as recent events in the financial markets highlight.
2. See French, Mazumder, and Taber (2006).

deteriorated precipitously since the 1960s. At the same time as the demand for such workers' skills has fallen, this group's skills have remained stagnant. Recent studies document that for the last forty years, roughly 30 percent of male birth cohorts do not graduate from high school.[3] By comparison, in the world's second largest economy, Japan, high school dropout rates remain in the 1 to 2 percent range. There is, moreover, mounting evidence that many low-skilled U.S. workers not only lack the preparation necessary for the jobs of the twenty-first century economy, but also the skills necessary to take advantage of the many subsidized post-high school training opportunities that currently exist for them.

To address this group's failure to thrive in mainstream educational and vocational tracks, the federal government (starting in the mid-1960s) has established a variety of employment and vocational training initiatives. Current programs and strategies include vocational training opportunities with private employers, programs that focus on basic education and general life skills, employment and job readiness training, subsidized work experience, school-to-work transition programs, and more expensive comprehensive strategies that attempt to combine several strategies.

The purpose of this chapter is to assess the success of these public sector-sponsored vocational and training programs in augmenting the skills of youths and young adults and, subsequently, reducing adult poverty. We proceed in two steps. First, we survey the range of existing programs and initiatives and review what the evaluations of these programs tell us about the likelihood that youth or young adult participants will be poor when they reach adulthood.[4] We do not summarize the evidence from all evaluations or treat the evidence from those that we do summarize equally. Clearly some evaluations are better than others. Our survey places more weight on those evaluations we believe to be methodologically stronger. Second, we link the results of the evaluation literature on the impacts and outcomes associated with these youth programs and initiatives to adult poverty. The key question here is whether these programs—some of which could be cost effective from society's perspective—raise the earnings of participants by enough to significantly reduce their risk of poverty in adulthood.

We conclude, as have others before us, that most employment and training programs targeting economically disadvantaged youths have failed to raise the skills of their participants by enough to meaningfully improve their well-being as adults. There are several reasons for this outcome. First, the resources invested in this group have been trivial compared to the size of the challenge that these disadvantaged youths face in order to escape poverty as adults. Several studies document that, on a per capita basis, public

---

3. Heckman, Lochner, and Todd (2006).
4. There have been many surveys during the last twenty years of evaluations of government-sponsored training for youths. These include Barnow (1987); Foster (1995); LaLonde (1995); Friedlander, Greenberg, and Robins (1997); Lerman (2000); and Lerman (2005).

investments in the skills of high school dropouts between the ages of sixteen and twenty-four are less than one-tenth of those made in the skills of their college-bound peers.[5] Second, even though these public expenditures in training are concentrated on the relatively few youths who participate in these programs, the investment per participant is still usually too small to make a detectable difference in their economic outcomes. This result follows from a well-known result from the human capital literature that can be summarized as "big earnings gains require big investments." Third, we find that, when they are evaluated carefully, a majority of program strategies are simply ineffective. Often they generate zero earnings gains; other times when they do generate earnings gains, they are not cost-effective.

In the near term, the current crop of vocational and employment training initiatives for out-of-school youths offers scant promise for improving these individuals' economic well-being as adults. This is not to say that the programs necessarily are poorly designed or ineffectively implemented. There is plenty of evidence that similar strategies can cost-effectively raise the earnings of economically disadvantaged adult women who are in their thirties. Low-intensity employment and vocational training programs that have repeatedly "worked" for adult women have just as consistently "not worked" for economically disadvantaged youths. More research is needed to understand the developmental barriers that prevent these youths from acquiring skills both in classroom and in on-the-job settings.

The future success of training strategies for many economically disadvantaged youths will depend on the progress we make in understanding and implementing on a larger scale those programs that appear to "work," but whose efficacy right now appears to be idiosyncratic and hard to replicate. One reason youth training is not as effective as it could be today is that policymakers and those in the training community have been slow to acknowledge that these programs have performed poorly.[6] As a result they have not sought to distinguish systematically and rigorously the components that "work" from those that "do not work," or to identify to what extent success depends on the characteristics of participants and the environments in which they live.

In the next section, we describe the characteristics of economically

---

5. See Katz (1994); Lerman (1996, 186, Table 1). Note Table 1 in Lerman's paper is limited to a comparison of federal expenditures on education and training programs and does not include state subsidies for secondary and postsecondary education.

6. In the late 1990s Congress slashed funding for Youth Activities under the Job Training Partnership Act. This decision was in response to the findings from the National JTPA Study and twenty years of previous studies indicating that these initiatives produced little if any earnings gains for their participants. One rationale for taking so long to recognize these programs' failures is that because of the uncertainty associated with these impacts that policymakers should consider that the decision to end a program that does not work should be taken only after a lot of evidence is compiled compared with what would be required when deciding whether to continue funding for a program that appears to work (Stafford 1979).

disadvantaged youths targeted for these programs. Then we describe in more detail the different elements of these programs and the skill deficiencies that policymakers intend for them to address. We next discuss the policy implications of prior evaluations of employment and training programs for youths.

12.2   Vocational and Training Programs for Youths

12.2.1   Background: The Returns from General Life Skills, Work Experience, and Employment Services

Studies show that there are long-term economic benefits associated with early work experience. Returns to on-the-job training measured from the shapes of age-earnings profiles indicate that, on average, young workers acquire valuable skills that greatly raise their long-term earnings (Mincer 1962; Ben Porath 1967). Even work experience acquired as a teenager has been consistently shown to be associated with increased wages in adulthood. These findings do not depend very much on workers' education levels, at least among noncollege educated workers.[7] For such men, wages rise by about 45 percent between the ages of eighteen and twenty-eight. Thus, labor market experience allows young workers, even poorly educated workers, to acquire new skills that increase their productivity by more than enough to move these individuals out of poverty.[8]

By contrast to this compelling evidence on the returns to work experience in regular jobs, government employment and training programs that provide work experience for youths and young adults who have had difficulty finding jobs on their own have been remarkably unsuccessful at improving either the short- or the long-term earnings of their participants. These initiatives include those subsidized under the Comprehensive Employment and Training Act (1973), the National Supported Work Demonstration (1975 to 1977) (NSW) and programs funded under the Youth Employment and Demonstration Projects Act (1977) (YEDPA) or the National and Community Service Act (1990). In addition to these work experience initiatives, policymakers have had about forty years of experience with subsidized public sector summer jobs programs, starting with the Neighborhood Youth Corps created during the 1960s to provide summer jobs for unemployed urban youths.[9]

---

7. Tricia Gladden and Christopher Taber (2000, 2009).

8. See Heckman, Lochner, and Todd (2006). Wage growth for these workers is very sensitive to the business cycle, so that during the last twenty years wage growth has been twice as high during economic expansions as during recessions. This finding underscores the importance of sound fiscal and monetary polices for reducing poverty.

9. See Manpower Report, 1969. The program enrolled nearly 1.6 million youths from low-income families from its beginning in 1964 through the end of FY68. The summer program employed nearly 700,000 boys and girls. In addition, about 500,000 were in-school youths who were given paid, part-time jobs to help them stay in school; and nearly 400,000 were out-of-school youths who were provided with jobs and other needed services to help them either return to school or find regular jobs. For a discussion of the Work Experience programs of the late 1970s, see Farkas et al. (1982).

The findings from the National Support Work (NSW) Demonstration that operated in the mid-1970s illustrate the typical results from programs designed to provide economically disadvantaged youths between sixteen and twenty-one years old with guaranteed job experience. Participants typically were allowed to hold these guaranteed jobs for up to one year. The average age of the participants was 18.3 years, they had completed on average 9.6 years of school, and 88 percent were male. Moreover, previously 54 percent had been arrested and 28 percent had been incarcerated. In this social experiment, part of the program was to raise productivity standards (relative to a control group) during the year that members of the treatment group were eligible for these jobs. After one year, participants were expected to find regular jobs on their own. Program designers intended that this work experience would help make participants more reliable employees, so that they would be able to hold on to a job longer when they found work.

To be sure, during the time treatment group members were eligible to work in subsidized jobs, their employment rates were much higher than those of the control group. As a result, exposure to the program raised participants' work experience (Kemper, Long, and Thornton 1981). In the end, however, more than seven years of follow-up data indicate that this subsidized work experience had no effect on the disadvantaged high school dropouts' employment rates or earnings (Couch 1992).

The NSW results for youths were largely replicated by an early 1980s experimental study of employment and training initiatives targeting youths at risk for criminal activity by Vera Institute, the same organization that had originally devised and tested NSW for ex-offenders. Although during the eight- to twelve-month follow-up period, youth participants were more likely to find jobs—a result largely generated by low employment rates for the control group in one site—there was no evidence that these youths found better paying jobs or held them especially long (Sadd, Kotkin, and Freidman 1983). The positive employment effects resulted largely from program participants being more likely to find a first job after exiting the program.

These disappointing results for high-risk youths contrast with those for another group targeted by the Supported Work design: long-term welfare recipients who also happened to be mostly high school dropouts with poor employment histories, but who were on average more than ten years older than the youths. These women from the same sites benefited for at least eight years from similar types of work experience (Maynard 1980; Couch 1992). So it was not that the treatment could not work, but that for some reason it did not work for young high school dropouts.

The federal government has also subsidized on-the-job training (OJT) with private employers, which in many cases also amounts to subsidized work experience. The distinction between OJT and work experience is with the former it is expected that employers will provide formal or informal skill training to young trainees, whereas with the latter it is understood that recipients are learning about the world of work and how to hold on to a job. These initiatives have been part of the federal government's menu of employment services for the poor for more than four decades, and currently include OJT under the Workforce Investment Act (1998) (WIA) and the Work Opportunity Tax Credit (WOTC).

Programs to provide OJT were created during the 1960s specifically to address the possibility that classroom training did not work because the skills taught did not match those demanded by the private sector. Although rules have differed over time and across OJT programs, they typically offer employers who are willing to participate—and take-up rates historically have been low—a wage subsidy of approximately 40 percent for the first six months to one year that an eligible employee is on the job.[10] Nonetheless, there is little evidence that these initiatives improve youths' outcomes, except during the period when they are in subsidized jobs during which their employment rates are above expected levels.

Private employers' low rates of participation in OJT programs for youths suggests that they perceive that the productivity of participating workers is about one-half of the minimum wage or less. In other words, even though employers can effectively pay these workers only one-half the minimum wage, this incentive is still insufficient to entice most of them to participate in such programs. An alternative possibility is that many employers are unaware of the program and are, therefore, "leaving money on the table."[11] At least one organization, Employ America, attempts to arbitrage these public resources to encourage employers to take advantage of these underused subsidies.[12] However, one study that employed an experimental design, the Dayton, Ohio Targeted Jobs Tax Credit, indicates that the prospects for arbitrage by itself to expand training or work experience opportunities for youths are limited. When employers know about the program and can identify that an applicant would make them eligible to receive a wage subsidy, they are less likely to hire this applicant. Employers behave not as if they do not know about the program, but that they do not believe the targeted applicants are worth it even if they effectively are paid a subminimum wage.

Another approach to providing youths and other economically disadvantaged people with work experience is based on the idea that youths do not live near jobs where their skills are in demand. This "spatial mismatch" hypothesis has led to programs that provide information about and trans-

---

10. Under the Work Opportunity Tax Credit (reauthorized in 2007), employers who hire "Designated Community Residents," eighteen through thirty-nine years of age, can receive $2,400 for each new adult hire, $1,200 for each new summer youth hire, and up to $9,000 for each new "long-term family assistance recipient" hired over a two-year period. In 2007, the Welfare-to-Work (WtW) Tax Credit was merged with the WOTC. Eligible summer youth hires are sixteen- to seventeen-year-old Enterprise Zone, Enterprise Community, Renewal Community residents hired between May 1 and September 15 who work at least for ninety days. See USDOL Employment and Training website: http://www.doleta.gov/business/incentives/opptax.

11. Burtless (1985).

12. See http://www.employamerica.org/.

portation to jobs in the suburbs for economically disadvantaged youths who reside in the central city. Careful analysis, including at least one social experiment, known as Bridges to Work, has shown this strategy to be largely ineffective (Roder and Scrivner 2005). These results suggest that the job market hurdle these young people face has more to do with their lack of marketable skills than with their geographical location.

12.2.2   Formal Training Opportunities for Economically Disadvantaged Youths

Since the passage of the Economic Opportunity Act of 1964, economically disadvantaged youths have been targeted for various low-intensity public sector-sponsored employment and training initiatives that seek (a) fuller utilization of participants' existing skills and abilities and (b) the development of new occupational skills and abilities.[13] Since the mid-1960s, these initiatives have been incorporated into successive legislation governing the provision of basic skills, job search assistance, work experience, and occupational training in a classroom or on-the-job setting to young people fourteen to twenty-one years old (and more recently sixteen to twenty-four year olds) with very poor job histories or prospects for employment.[14]

Perhaps the most ambitious government job training program for youths is Job Corps. This program provides a comprehensive set of services to low-income youths in a "structured residential environment for learning and development" for up to two years. This strategy was originally advocated by Senator Hubert Humphrey during the 1950s and, along with Head Start, became one of the most enduring Great Society programs after it was established during the mid-1960s (LaLonde 2003).

Job Corps has four features that distinguish it from other government-sponsored employment and training services. First, the federal government continues to administer and operate the program, whereas programs under WIA are administered by the states through Workforce Investment Boards. Second, Job Corps provides a comprehensive array of services. Participants receive counseling, education, training, work experience, health care, and job placement services. The assumption underlying Job Corps is that economically disadvantaged youths need to address a range of deficiencies before

---

13. Manpower Report (1963, 10–11). The 1966 amendments to MDTA further focused training policy on the skill deficiencies of the economically disadvantaged. See Manpower Report (1967, 47).

14. The Manpower Development and Training Act (1962) (MDTA), the Comprehensive Employment and Training Act (1973), the Job Training Partnership Act (1982), the Workforce Investment Act (1998). The MDTA began by addressing policymakers' concerns about "technological displacement." As unemployment declined during the 1960s, concerns about persistent youth unemployment and the transition from school to work led to the development of special youth programs. The 1964 and 1966 amendments to MDTA reoriented the program away from retraining displaced workers toward providing employment and training for the economically disadvantaged.

they can become "job ready," and that these services can only be effective when participants are removed from their home environment. Third, Job Corps usually provides these services in residential training centers. Job Corps centers usually house sixteen- to twenty-one-year-old participants away from their neighborhoods, sometimes in remote rural settings. They receive most of their education and vocational training on site, and these services are not often integrated with the existing educational establishment.[15] Finally, a fourth unique feature of Job Corps is its cost. It is by far the most expensive public-sector training program and constitutes a significant investment in participants' skills, with expenditures exceeding $20,000 per participant year.[16]

12.2.3   Who are the Youths Targeted for Government Training Programs?

Government job training programs for youths are designed mostly for those who are not "job ready." By providing them with skills, policy makers expect to make them employable and give them the ability to acquire new skills on-the-job just as other workers do. The United States Department of Labor, which administers these "Youth Activities" under the Workforce Investment Act (WIA), provides the following description of the youths it targets:

WIA Youth programs serve eligible low-income youth ages 14–21 that face barriers to employment. These include youth who have deficiencies in basic skills or meet one or more qualifying criteria: homeless, runaway, pregnant, parenting, an offender, school dropout or a foster child. The programs also serve youth with disabilities and others who may require additional assistance to complete an educational program or to secure employment.[17]

The WIA administrative data indicate the program has attempted to address basic skill deficiencies among youths who do not appear to be job ready. The vast majority of WIA's youth participants were lacking basic skills, had not graduated from high school, and were jobless when they entered the program. About 70 percent of both younger (fourteen to eigh-

---

15. By contrast, the program's twenty-two to twenty-four-year-old participants and young female participants with children are usually trained in nonresidential settings located close to where they live.

16. These expenditures are scaled down from the late 1960s, when outlays per participant averaged roughly $8,000 per participant in 1967 dollars. Adjusting for inflation this amount totals nearly $50,000 in 2007 dollars. No surprise then that at the time, the cost of Job Corps was compared to the cost of a Harvard education! Another program that provides comprehensive services to youth in a residential setting is the National Guards' Youth ChalleNGe Program. This program includes a 20 week residential component often at a military facility followed by a year long mentoring component. Its costs have averaged $10,000 to $15,000 per participant (National Guard 2006). It has shown enough promise that several prominent foundations are funding an evaluation that uses an experimental design (Bloom, Gardenhire-Crooks, and Mandsager 2009).

17. Employment and Training Administration (2008, 29).

Table 12.1 Characteristics of WIA youth participants[a] and outcomes at program exit

	Younger youth, ages 14 to 18 years, Exiters from April 2006 to March 2007			Older youth, ages 19 to 21 years, Exiters from April 2005 to March 2006		
	Number of exiters	Percentage of exiters (%)	Diploma attainment rate (%)	Number of exiters	Percentage of exiters (%)	Employment retention 3rd quarter after exit (%)
All younger/older youth	88,539	100	67.1	33,149	100	82.5
Male	40,872	46	65	13,018	39	82
Female	47,628	54	68.9	20,124	61	82.7
Black or African American	30,635	35	62.3	12,945	39	80
White (only)	25,478	29	70.8	10,608	32	84.2
Hispanic	26,111	29	69	7,696	23	83.8
Offender	7,234	8	47.4	3,738	11	76.7
Ever in foster care	4,190	5	61.2	437	1	78.7
Individual with a disability	14,770	17	75.2	3,020	9	82.9
Pregnant or parenting youth	5,942	7	54.2	10,189	31	82.3
Highest grade completed						
8th or less	18,338	21	52.9	1,159	3	76.7
Some high school	62,422	71	69.5	13,727	41	78.2
High school graduate	5,237	6	0	13,443	41	85.7
High school equivalency	847	1	0	1,696	5	82.1
Some postsecondary, no degree	355	0	0	2,109	6	89.1
Attending school	67,392	76	77.4	5,332	16	86.8
Not attending school	21,048	24	45.3	27,531	83	81.6
Basic literacy skills deficiency	56,397	64	64.2	17,350	52	81.2
Limited English-language proficiency	8,542	10	80.4	1,458	4	85.9
Employed at registration	5,815	7	71	5,162	15	88.7
Public assistance recipient	19,633	22	65.2	7,809	16	65.2

Sources: PY 2006 WIA Performance Measures for Demographic and Service Groups—Younger Youth (derived from PY 2006 WIASRD Records), February 4, 2008. PY 2006 WIA Performance Measures for Demographic and Service Groups—Older Youth (derived from PY 2006 WIASRD Records), February 4, 2008.

[a]Excludes younger youth who were high school graduates or the equivalent at registration and younger youth who were still attending high school at exit.

teen years old) and older (nineteen to twenty-one years old) participants have been from low-income households. However, as shown by the figures in table 12.1 indicating the percentage receiving public assistance, not all trainees have been low-income youths. One reason for this is that the program also serves disabled youths (about one-fifth of younger participants, as shown in the table), whether they are from low-income households or not.

Nearly all participants were not employed when they entered the program. Whether they were unemployed or making the transition from out of the laborforce often is unclear, though prior research indicates that it is informative to distinguish between these distinct labor market states. That these youths often are not employed at the time that they enter the program is not surprising, because they are apparently not job ready to begin with and the younger ones include many who were still in school. Although children can work, it also is the case that teenage labor force participation has dropped markedly during the present decade. If, as some have argued, there are longer term benefits from such teenage work experience in regular jobs, this development should be considered to constitute an additional challenge that policy makers face when they design employment-related interventions for teenaged at-risk youths.[18]

Besides the lack of recent, or possibly any, prior employment experience, another barrier to employment faced by economically disadvantaged youths is their low levels of literacy. About 64 percent of the younger youths and more than 80 percent of the older youths were designated by program administrators as having a "basic literacy skills deficiency." As shown by table 12.1, participants' limited English proficiency can not explain much of this high percentage of participants who lack basic skills. Although it is not surprising that many younger youths are not high school graduates, more than one-fifth had not completed eighth grade. Among the older youths, 45 percent were high school dropouts. But the low rate of literacy for this older group indicates that even many of the high school graduates also lack high school graduate skills. For youths targeted by government employment and training initiatives, years of schooling is a misleading indicator of their actual level of basic skills. These individuals likely perform much worse on standard instruments that measure these skills than comparably educated peers who are job ready.

Among older out-of-school youths, post-program employment is a "performance standard" used by officials to assess the effectiveness of their services and service providers. As shown by table 12.1, 82 percent of these older participants were employed during the third quarter following the quarter that they exited from the program. These employment retention rates vary by participants' prior skill levels. Among participants who had completed

18. Well-known contributions to the literature on the value of working while in school include Ruhm (1997) and Stinebrickner and Stinebrickner (2003).

the eighth grade or less prior to entering the program, 76.7 percent were employed during the third quarter after exiting from training; among participants who had attended some college, this percentage was 89.1 percent. This finding is expected and has little to do with the effectiveness of training. It has been shown not to imply that more skilled participants benefit more from these programs. Instead, these figures indicate that more skilled participants—at least in the short-term—would have had better employment outcomes whether or not these programs raised their earnings.[19] Although schooling can be a misleading indicator of basic skill levels, among this population it is still the case that more years of schooling are associated with increased employment rates even in the absence of training.

To recruit youths for these government programs, operators have relied on private recruiters, local community organizations, and the state Employment Service. One-Stop Centers also identify participants and sometimes offer programs that provide youths with career development, job search, and basic and leadership skills, while at the same time referring youths to vocational or basic skills training. In addition to these standard services, the centers sometimes provide training in a range of general life skills that enhance participants' employability, financial knowledge, time management, citizenship, and etiquette. Some centers and community organizations also provide or refer participants to teen pregnancy prevention programs and mentoring activities, such as Big Brothers Big Sisters, that provide companionship and assistance with homework and preparation for standardized assessment examinations.[20] Some One-Stop Centers also establish "mini one-stops" at local high schools to target younger at-risk youths fourteen to eighteen years of age.

12.2.4   High School Vocational Programs

The characteristics of WIA participants observed in the previous subsection underscore the point that a major challenge in providing economically disadvantaged youths with occupational training is their lack of basic skills. This observation implies that primary and secondary schools—especially the public schools—have large roles to play in improving the vocational skills of this portion of the U.S. workforce. Policymakers have long recognized this problem. As a part of its mandate to improve access to vocational training for individuals lacking basic skills, the Carl D. Perkins Vocational and Technical Education Act of 1984 stipulated that if these individuals required additional programming to make them eligible to participate in vocational education, federal vocational funds may pay up to 50 percent of the cost of these supplemental programs' services.

19. See, for example, LaLonde (1986); Heckman, LaLonde, and Smith (1999).
20. See, for example, http://www.onestopahead.com/onestop/youth/. For a description of Big Brothers, Big Sisters programs and their effectiveness, see, for example, Tierney, Grossman, and Resch (2000).

The important role of the public schools in preparing future workers for the labor market and for vocational training was the theme of the U.S. Department Of Labor's Secretary's Commission On Achieving Necessary Skills (SCANS) Commission Report released in June 1991. This Commission was established to address the problem that "more than half of our young people leave school without the knowledge or foundation required to find and hold a good job" (i). (Another report, published a few years later, that highlighted some of the same concerns as the SCANS report is that of the Carnegie Council on Competitiveness [1996].) In response to this deficiency, the Commission made three recommendations:

1. All American high school students must develop a new set of competencies and foundation skills if they are to enjoy a productive, full, and satisfying life.

2. The qualities of high performance that today characterize our most competitive companies must become the standard for the vast majority of our companies, large and small, local and global.

3. The nation's schools must be transformed into high-performance organizations in their own right.

To implement these recommendations the SCANS Commission identified "eight areas that represent essential preparation for all students, both those going directly to work and those planning further education" (SCANS 1991, ii). Among these areas, basic skills, critical thinking, and developing personal qualities, such as "sociability, self-management, and integrity" were deemed essential for preparing students for the world of work and the opportunity to acquire high-paying jobs. Policymakers recognize the central role that public schools must play in order to address these broadly defined skill deficiencies of the workforce.

One model developed to provide both basic skills and vocational training within high schools is the Career Academy (CA). These institutions are set up inside public schools and offer participating high school aged students a mixture of academic and vocational courses. Participating students also are exposed to various career development interventions, including resume writing and exposure to potential employers.

The evaluation of Career Academies by MDRC offers perhaps the most promising evidence of an effective strategy for enhancing the skills of disadvantaged male youths.[21] This experimental evaluation indicates that substituting vocational courses for academic courses does not affect standardized test scores and, among high risk students, it increases graduation rates and numbers of completed courses. These findings on test scores imply that there is no loss in basic skill acquisition associated with attending a Career Acad-

---

21. Career Academies have been around for at least thirty-five years. They usually have been organized around cohorts of thirty to sixty high school students who take career-related classes together. Earlier nonexperimental evaluations are found in Stern et al. (1989) and Stern, Raby, and Dayton (1992).

emy program. Consequently, high school vocational programs likely do not create a "road not taken" dilemma, where in the future participants are less likely to qualify for other training opportunities, such as those offered in community colleges, because they sacrificed their basic skills in order to acquire vocational skills when in high school.

Attrition rates from these vocational training programs are considered high. However, they are not out of line with those of government-sponsored training programs or community colleges and nonselective public four year universities. For instance, MDRC's Career Academy evaluation found that 15 percent of candidates were no-shows, and an additional 30 percent dropped out prior to the end of high school. The evaluation is unclear about the number of participants who left the Career Academy program because they found a job related to the skills that they learned when in school. This pattern of dropping out of vocational programs is common in community colleges, which serve a similar function for older youths and adults as Career Academies do for those in high school.

As with community college dropout rates, there is concern that high dropout rates from Career Academies result from program flaws rather than from productive experimentation by students. These dropout rates from CA programs may simply mimic the practice of young people sampling college majors or jobs looking for opportunities that match their interests and skills. Indeed, when surveyed, most dropouts reported that they voluntarily left the program for another high school or for the academic track within their high school. After trying the vocational course work, they decided that these skills were not for them. In an uncertain world, this behavior can be thought of as a form of job shopping. Workers sample different jobs early in their career in order to find occupations that match their skills and their tastes. Such job shopping early in young workers' careers is often thought to contribute to a significant share of their wage growth. Therefore, by analogy it seems likely that some attrition from CA programs is desirable. As a result, program performance measures based on completion rates are likely to be counterproductive and lead to a misallocation of resources.

An eight year follow-up report by MDRC indicated that the Career Academy model generated large impacts on men's earnings, but small impacts on women's earnings. Among males, the treatment group's earnings were about $500 per month, or nearly 20 percent greater than those of the control group during the eighth year following their scheduled graduation. This is a very large impact—likely larger than we would expect for these youths had they stayed and completed two years of high school. By contrast, among women, the gap was about $100 per month, or less than 5 percent of expected monthly earnings.[22] The difference between the long-term earnings impacts for young men and women is puzzling as it appears that both the training and academic experiences that women received were similar to those received

22. See Kemple (2008, Exhibit 5, 21).

by men. Possibly, the training received is more suitable for the typical labor market experiences of men than women.[23]

The gender gap in program impacts results entirely from CA apparent impact on hours worked during the year rather than on wages. Among men the program raised the number of months employed by about 7.3 percent (i.e., 2.8 months divided by 38.2 months worked by the control group) during year five through eight of the follow-up period, it raised weekly hours worked by 12.3 percent (i.e., 4.1 divided by 33.3 the average weekly hours worked by the control group). By contrast, the program had no effect on hours worked for female participants.[24]

The CA program was associated with nearly identical and statistically insignificant gains in hourly wages for both male and female participants. During years five through eight the experimental impacts of CA on earnings per hour were $0.59 for males and $0.65 for females.[25] Although these impacts are statistically insignificant, they still might be potentially economically meaningful. These figures imply a 3.7 percent and a 4.9 percent impact on the hourly wages of males and females, respectively. As we will subsequently explain in the section on cost-benefit analyses, given the small incremental costs of the CA program, if these percentage impacts were to persist throughout individuals' working lives, they would constitute very large gains per dollar spent. At the same time, these modest percentages underscore the point that despite the large gender differences in earnings impacts, the impacts of the CA program on the productivity of young adults are modest in size and similar for males and females.

The earnings history of the Career Academy control group reveals that advocates of this promising approach should be cautious about the efficacy of this strategy for the most disadvantaged out-of-school youths long targeted by government job training programs under WIA. In the eighth year following random assignment, the control group's earnings averaged more than $26,000, or a few percentage points greater than the earnings of their peers who attended urban public high schools at the same time. Although such urban students may be disadvantaged relative to the general population of high school students, Career Academy students are not disadvantaged relative to the population of urban high school students. The same cannot be said for participants in WIA's youth activities or Job Corps.

12.2.5 Subsidized Investments in Job Training Programs: WIA Youth Activities and Job Corps

An important shortcoming of subsidized job training programs for youths is that they have provided participants with too little training to

23. See Kemple (2008, Exhibits 3.7, 4.7-YM, and 4.7-YW, 51, 67, 81–82).
24. See Kemple (2008, Exhibits 3 and 4, 18–19).
25. See Kemple (2008). Adjusted for inflation between 2006 and 2007, these figures become $0.61 and $0.67, respectively.

meaningfully increase their skills. In the National JTPA Study, evaluators reported that youth participants received on average 180 hours of employment and training services. For comparison, consider that had these youths not dropped out of school, they would have spent more than 1,000 hours in school over a nine to ten month period.

As previously indicated, studies show that much additional schooling is associated with approximately a 10 percent rise in annual earnings during their subsequent careers. As a result, because training amounts to about only about one-fifth of a year of schooling, we might reasonably expect these programs (if effective) to generate an approximately 2 percent increase in earnings. There are many reasons why the actual impacts might differ, but our main point is that we should be surprised if the impact of a small investment were to raise earnings by, say, 10 percent, because it would imply that government investment in low intensity WIA-type training is dramatically more cost-effective than formal schooling. Therefore, when evaluating these programs, it is reasonable to expect that even if they are cost effective—as they have been repeatedly shown to be for adult women—their impacts will be small (LaLonde 1995, 2003).

The foregoing analysis highlights one problem with youth training initiatives: even if they are effective, the interventions are too small. This shortcoming has been shared by many programs targeted toward youths, including the Department of Labor's YouthBuild program.[26] The Department advertises this program as having allocated "more than $700 million in federal funds since 1994 to low income communities for 226 YouthBuild programs." At approximately $3 million per program, this approach is best thought of an "incubator" program designed to foster innovation of new strategies to improve the skills of out-of-school youths, rather than as a program that directly contributes to this group's skill development.

12.2.6   Earnings Impacts of Job Corps

Job Corps stands in contrast to most government training programs, because it is designed to make a meaningful investment in skills. Are the benefits from this investment worth the cost? One reason Job Corps is so expensive is that it includes residential centers. How important are these centers to the efficacy of the program? The evidence on this point is mixed. The National Job Corps Study reported that by far the largest earnings impacts were for older participants who usually are not assigned to the residential centers. As a result, this finding may signify instead that Job Corps is more effective for older participants, no matter whether they receive services in a residential center or in their communities.

---

26. YouthBuild is a community-based program that provides participants with job skills through renovating abandoned buildings, counseling, academic instruction and test preparation, and leadership skills. See http://www.huduser.org/Publications/PDF/YouthBuild.pdf. See also Jastzrab et al. (1996) YouthBuild evaluation.

On balance the evaluations of Job Corp indicate the program can raise participants' future earnings. In the recent National Job Corps Study, during the fourth year following random assignment, the program raised the earnings of male youths by $1,695 per year and the earnings of female youths by $1,466 per year.[27] These gains for young men were about one-half the size reported nearly a generation earlier in a well-known and influential nonexperimental evaluation also by Mathematica Policy Research, Inc. (Mallar et al. 1982). The impacts reported for the recent cohort of young women were nearly the same as those reported a generation earlier.

These earnings gains associated with an expensive program such as Job Corps demonstrate that public-sector programs can improve labor market outcomes. Unfortunately, these earnings increases by themselves do not make the program cost-effective. The original cost-benefit analysis for the National Job Corps Study reported substantial net benefits for society from this program. However, the reason for this finding was that the evaluation assumed that the fourth-year earnings impacts would persist through these youths' careers. Although this assumption may prove to be true, early indications are that these earnings impacts have dissipated with time. Without them, and because Job Corps does not appear to have the same large impact on male youths' use of the criminal justice system as it did a generation earlier, Job Corps—though it does raise earnings—does not appear to be a cost-effective intervention.

The earnings impacts of Job Corps are even more discouraging when the impacts from the National Job Corps study are analyzed by age and ethnic group. As shown by table 12.2, the large positive earnings impacts we previously reported for the program result in large part from the extraordinarily large impacts reported for white and black twenty- to twenty-four-year-old participants. The fourth-year impacts were $7,333 and $4,271, respectively. By contrast, the program did not raise the earnings of Hispanic participants, and the impacts for African American sixteen- to seventeen- and eighteen-to nineteen-year-old youths were $712 and $926, respectively. Neither of these impacts for African American teens was statistically significant. Consequently, the results from the rigorous National Job Corps Study are consistent with the view that the Job Corps program is not an effective strategy for improving labor market outcomes of minority youths.

12.2.7   When Considering Replications of the Job Corps and Career Academy Models

When considering whether to fund Job Corps at its current levels or even to expand it, policymakers should consider whether these resources would be better spent increasing training opportunities for prime-aged workers,

---

27. These figures are expressed in 2007 dollars; the original figures from the Mathematica report were $1,362 and $1,178, respectively. See Burghardt and Glazerman (2000).

Table 12.2   Taking apart the earnings impacts from the National Job Corps Study (annualized impacts during the 4th year after the baseline, by ethnicity, age, and Latino center)

	Ethnicity		
Participant Age/center type	Whites	Blacks	Latinos
16–17	$3,915*	$712	–$925
18–19	–$712	$926	$0
20–24	$7,333*	$4,271*	$2,421
Latino center	–$427	$926	–$1,742

Source: Schochet, Brughardt, and Glazerman (2001).
Notes: Impacts have been converted from 1999 to 2007 dollars. Annual earnings equal estimated impact on weekly earnings times 52.
*Significant at the 10 percent level.

especially economically disadvantaged women. As indicated previously, evaluations of low-cost programs for adult women have consistently shown cost-effective earnings gains (LaLonde 1995, 2003; Heckman, LaLonde, and Smith 1999). For these adult women, these gains, measured in terms of gains per hour of training, are arguably larger than those expected from completing an additional year of schooling. As a result, policymakers currently contemplating new employment and training initiatives are faced with the choice of whether to appropriate scarce workforce development resources to unproven new or existing programs for youths or to proven strategies for mothers, many of whom are parenting the children who are targeted by the other programs and initiatives discussed in this volume.

Additional concerns about the Job Corps program include the cost of recruiting applicants and its relatively high turnover rates. From the start, state employment services received a per capita bounty for each Job Corps applicant. On the one hand, it is not surprising that even a well-known program such as Job Corps has to recruit eligible applicants whom its operators believe would likely benefit from the program. After all, these operators must meet performance standards to fulfill their contractual obligations to serve this population. Accordingly, Job Corps performance standards suggest that the program's operators have an incentive to create a desirable pool of applicants. Early on operators screened out younger applicants and applicants prone to behavioral problems. On the other hand, that such a well-known comprehensive program is not oversubscribed and operators must recruit is consistent with the contention that the target population expects on average small (private) net benefits from these services.

Another indication that participants do not expect to benefit economically from a program that provides both basic skills and essentially entry-level vocational training is high program turnover. As shown by table 12.3, roughly one-fourth of the treatment group in the National Job Corps Study

Table 12.3   Participation in Job Corps by program group in the National Job Corps Study

	Males (%)	Females w/ children (%)	Age 16–17 (%)	Age 18–19 (%)	Age 20–24 (%)	All (%)
% of program group that did not enroll	24.7	36.4	21.4	29.8	32.5	27.1
% of program group that dropped out						
Within 1 month	6.9	5.2	6.8	6.7	5.6	6.4
After 1 to 3 months	15.1	12.8	17.1	12.6	10.5	13.9
After 3 to 9 months	27.0	23.7	29.2	25.3	22.4	26.2
After 9 months	26.4	21.9	25.5	25.6	28.9	26.5
	100	100	100	100	100	100
% of program group that enrolled in academic classes and vocational training for						
500–1,000 hours	15.6	12.7	17.2	15.0	11.9	15.1
> 1,000 hours	30.9	23.9	30.5	28.5	31.3	30.1
% of program group that enrolled in academic classes for						
500 to 1,000 hours	13.0	10.2	15.6	11.2	9.2	12.5
> 1,000 hours	8.6	7.4	9.6	7.4	8.7	8.7
% of program group that enrolled in vocational training for						
500–1,000 hours	16.3	12.7	17.1	14.7	14.6	15.6
> 1,000 hours	18.6	13.7	15.8	18.5	21.0	18.1

Sources: Schochet, Burghards, and Glazemen (2001)—Tables IV.1–IV.4 Table iv.1, enrollment in job corps, timing of enrollment, and month of participation for the program group, p. 55; table iv.2 combined academic and vocational training participation measures for program group enrollees, p. 61; table iv.3, academic experiences in job corps for program group enrollees, p. 63; table iv.4 vocational training experiences in job corps for program group enrollees, p. 64–65.

were no-shows and did not enroll in the program, one-fourth of the treatment group dropped out within the first three months, and another one-fourth dropped out between three and nine months after enrolling. Only about one-fourth of the program group remained enrolled for at least nine months and received the program's comprehensive services as intended by the program's design. Although it is tempting to contend that this pattern of turnover reflects the same kind of job shopping behavior identified previously in the chapter, this is a less compelling explanation for a more homogenous long-running program like Job Corps that, among other things, provides its participants with a range of essential basic and life skills.

As a result of this turnover, only about 40 percent of Job Corps enrollees and 30 percent of the treatment group received at least 1,000 hours—the equivalent of one academic year—of instruction in academic or vocational skills. Male participants received roughly two-thirds of this instruction in vocational skills. Among the youngest Job Corps participants, this fraction was closer to one-half. One implication of these patterns of training is that Job Corps instruction resembles somewhat the training provided by a Career Academy, although Job Corps targets a much harder to serve, more economically disadvantaged population.

To appreciate the difference in the populations served by Job Corps and those likely to be served by Career Academies, it is instructive to compare the characteristics of the control groups from the National Job Corps Study and from the Career Academy Demonstration. Although the Career Academy Demonstration control group is younger than the Job Corps control group, it is more skilled. Among these controls, 73.3 percent graduated on time, and an additional 10.3 percent graduated late. These percentages do not include those controls who received a GED, a qualification whose market value (at least for males) is questionable.[28] Further, during the four years after their scheduled graduation dates, these controls earned on average about $1,235 per month.[29] By contrast, only 14.8 percent of the control group in the National Job Corps Study received a high school diploma or higher degree. On average, the Job Corps control group completed only 10.7 years of schooling. Further, by the tenth quarter following random assignment, the Job Corps control group participants, despite being older, earned about $1,125 per month—or about 8 percent less—than those in the Career Academy control group.[30] These differences between Job Corps and Career Academy

28. See Heckman et al. (1993), which shows that the earnings of male GED recipients closely track those of male high school dropouts.

29. See Kemple and Willner (2008, 18, 19, and 28, Exhibits 3, 4, and 7).

30. See Schochet, Burghardt, and Glazerman (2000, 96, and 122, Tables V.7 and VI.4. Table VI.4), who report that during the tenth quarter after random assignment, the controls earned $213.3 per week (or $167.7 per week in 1998 dollars). To convert this figure to monthly 2007 dollars, we multiplied 167.7 dollars times 4.35 weeks per month times 1.27 to account for inflation in the Consumer Price Index (CPI) between 1998 and 2007. See also http://data.bls.gov/cgi-bin/surveymost for CPI statistics.

participants suggest that one reason for the differences in outcomes between the two programs is that they serve different people, and these youths "self-selected" to be different: Career Academy participants stayed in high school; Job Corps participants had dropped out of high school.

The Career Academy evaluation conducted by MDRC shows that a vocationally-oriented high school curriculum can effectively transition economically disadvantaged male youths into the labor market. Further, these impacts were larger for the high- and median-risk youths and smaller for youths deemed to have been at low risk for dropping out of school. At first, these observations suggest that perhaps the Job Corps and Career Academy groups are not all that different. But even the controls in the high-risk Career Academy control group graduated from high school at a rate more than 55 percentage points above the rate for the Job Corps controls.[31]

As prior research indicates, graduating from high school, as opposed to obtaining a GED, is associated with improved labor market and other socially desirable outcomes throughout a person's life. This observation is important for policies that target idle youth dropouts. Career Academies, like the initiatives launched and supported as part of the School-to-Work Act of 1989, target in-school youths and, apparently, as we observed from the characteristics of the control group in the Career Academy Demonstration, youths who have a good chance of finishing high school. It is still unclear to what extent these initiatives work by encouraging kids to stay in school who might otherwise drop out or by leading to better labor market outcomes later in life among those likely to graduate anyway.[32]

12.3   Required Investments in Public Sector-Sponsored Training for Economically Disadvantaged Youths

12.3.1   Comparing Previous Program Costs to Program Benefits

As discussed in the previous section, over the last four decades it has proven difficult to identify and to replicate strategies that improve labor outcomes much less reduce the risk of poverty for economically disadvantaged youths. The Career Academy Demonstration's success demonstrates the potential benefits of blending academic and vocational education within public high schools for young at-risk males. A study by MDRC indicates that the incremental cost of moving a child from regular high school to a Career Academy model is approximately $700 per year of high school. During the first eight years, members of the CA treatment group earned about $17,000 more than their counterparts in the control group. With real interest

---

31. See Kemple and Willner (2008, Exhibit 5.4 HR, 94).
32. See studies by Joyce and Neumark (2001); Neumark and Joyce (2001); Neumark and Allen (2003).

rates at about 2 percent, discounting will not shave off much off this gross benefit of CA.

As we indicated previously, the CA impact evaluation revealed economically different earnings impacts for male and females. During the first eight years after scheduled graduation, CA raised males' earnings by about $30,000, but raised females' earnings by only about one-third as much.[33] This means that the cost-benefit calculations differ substantially for male and female CA participants. However, given the relatively small direct and indirect cost associated with this intervention, the cost-benefit ratios are potentially still impressive even for female participants.

Successes such as we have seen with the MDRC's Career Academy model have been the exception rather than the rule for economically disadvantaged youths. The exception largely centers the cost-benefit studies of the Job Corps. Mathematica Policy Research's nonexperimental evaluation of the 1977 Job Corps cohort reported that for every $1 spent on youths in Job Corps, society gained $1.48. This substantial gain resulted from participants' increased earnings and from their reduced criminal activity. The more recent National Job Corps Study also reported a similar—if not a more impressive—cost-benefit ratio. In contrast to the earlier study, these gains resulted almost entirely from participants' increased earnings. For the 1995 Job Corps cohort, the program's impacts on criminal activity were small.

A closer look at the National Job Corps Study's cost-benefit analysis reveals that about 95 percent of the earnings gains used in the cost-benefit analysis were based on projected out-of-sample impacts. During the first four years, Job Corps treatments earned in total about $1,500 more than Job Corps controls. The program cost about $17,000 per participant. The large benefit attributed to the program results because the study assumed that the earnings gains during the fourth year after the baseline would persist for the remainder of participants' working lives. The present discounted value of these projected gains were estimated to be roughly $35,000. In addition, given the concentration of the four-year gains among the older participants who were over twenty years old, and the relatively meager gains reported for most of the teenage demographic groups, there is scant evidence from the National Job Corps Study that economically disadvantaged high school dropout teens benefit from Job Corps enough to justify the high costs of the program. The results of the rigorous National Job Corps Study suggest that this model would be more cost-effective if it focused more of its resources

---

33. A hard to quantify but potentially important social benefit of CA was from the 33 percent rise (i.e., 27 percent compared to 36 percent) in the percentage of men who were married and living with their spouses. This increase was nearly matched by a corresponding decline in the percentage of men who were divorced or separated. These changes resulted because those men who had children were much more likely to be living with their children than were men in the control group. Men in the treatment group were a little less likely to have had children during the study period. By contrast to the young men, the program had no apparent effects on family formation for young women (Kemple 2008, 35–38).

on serving participants over twenty years old who are not in the program's residential centers. The JOBSTART Demonstration from the early 1990s found no effect of Job Corps-like services when provided to youths under twenty-one years old in their communities. (See Cave et al. 1993.)

12.3.2   Grounding Expectations about Program Impacts

One problem raised in the previous section is that policymakers have had unrealistic expectations about the impact of their youth employment and training initiatives (Heckman, Roselius, and Smith 1994). To understand this point it is helpful to consider the size of the investment required by society in order to raise the skills of the some five million at-risk youth, such that they would be capable of earning $10.00 per hour, or $20,000 as a full-time worker. We assume conservatively that each of these youths would be capable of securing a full-time job at the current federal minimum wage of $7.25 per hour.[34] This estimate is conservative because in fact many of these youths' skills are such that they are unlikely to be employed full time at the minimum wage. Indeed, as we discussed previously, government training programs target these youths largely because they are not "job ready."

The goal just described is to raise the skills of at-risk economically disadvantaged youths by roughly $2.75 per hour, or $5,500 per year.[35] This desired impact is on par with those reported for 20- to 24-year-old African American and white participants in the National Job Corps Study. Given conventional estimates of the return to investments in formal schooling, we expect an effective employment and training or education program to generate a real rate of return of 10 percent per year. Accordingly, we should expect a program that permanently increases young participants' earnings by this amount to cost roughly $55,000 per participant. Such a program might require participants' full-time participation for eighteen months at a direct cost of $34,000 and indirect costs of $19,000 associated with lost time from work while in training.

How much would government expenditures on training have to be in order to achieve the foregoing objective of raising the skills levels of economically disadvantaged 14- to 24-year-olds? We estimate that it would require approximately $160 billion dollars (i.e., $34,000 times 5 million youths) or more than 1 percent of our national gross domestic product (GDP). This figure is our estimate of required government expenditures. It does not include our estimate of trainee's forgone earnings while they participate in such intensive training; we estimate this cost could be as much as an additional $100 billion (i.e., $19,000 times 5 million youths). In any case, the combined total could amount to nearly 2 percent of GDP.

34. The current federal minimum wage of $6.55 per hour was effective July 24, 2008; see www.dol.gov/esa/whd/flsa.

35. We arrive at $2.65 as the difference between $9.00 and $6.55 times 1.075, accounting for employers' additional contributions to Social Security and Medicare.

There are two caveats to keep in mind when interpreting these figures. First, these calculations assume that policymakers have identified and implemented programs that generate standard returns to human capital—an assumption that for this population appears to be exceedingly optimistic. Second, this total only addresses the skill deficiencies of the existing cohort of youths. Unless other interventions such as those discussed elsewhere in this volume are successful for younger children, these expenditures and costs would have to be repeated with successive cohorts of fourteen- to twenty-four-year-old youths.

12.4   Concluding Remarks

Most youths graduate from high school, and a majority of these acquire some postsecondary schooling or training either immediately after high school or later on as adults. Many studies document that both youths and society benefits from these investments. The existing array of community colleges, private vocational schools, and private and public colleges and universities, on balance, successfully augment the human capital of this segment of the U.S. population.

By contrast, we conclude, as have other surveys, that employment and training initiatives that target economically disadvantaged youths who are at risk of dropping out of school or have already dropped out of high school have not usually been effective. Not only have they not been cost-effective, but also their impacts on youths' short- or long-term earnings often have been nil. As currently configured, nearly all of these programs—including Job Corps—offer no promise of reducing adult poverty. Therefore, despite the enormous social problems associated with this group's daunting skill deficiencies, it will be difficult to make a case for expanding intervention until policymakers can identify effective strategies.

To this end, we recommend that increased attention be given to carefully designed demonstrations. After the process analyses of these demonstration programs indicate that they have been implemented as intended, they then can be subjected to a rigorous impact evaluation. Unfortunately, at this point there are not many compelling designs that are ready for such evaluation, much less ready to be brought to scale. Instead, if training strategies are to have any impact on adult poverty, policymakers need to return to the drawing board and devise strategies that account for the many challenges posed by this population segment over the last four decades. One element that appears to need more attention is these youths' developmental delays. Perhaps one way to understand the failures of these programs is to ask a simple rhetorical question: does anyone think we can address problems that such a youth has accumulated over a lifetime with a $3,000 program?

The lessons to date underscore the importance of the public schools. Once a student has dropped out of school, policymakers have no ready answers to address his or her skill deficiencies, other than to wait until the person is older and, when existing programs appear, to generate modest benefits, at least for adult women. In the meantime, improving basic skill levels in primary schools and keeping kids in secondary school through a range of options from Career Academies to athletic programs appears—at least for now—to be the most effective strategy for reducing the risk of adult poverty among at-risk youths.

References

Andersson, F., H. Holzer, and J. Lane. 2005. *Moving up or moving on: Who advances in the low-wage labor market?* New York: Russell Sage Foundation.
Barnow, B. S., and C. T. King. 2000. *Improving the odds, increasing the effectiveness of publicly funded training.* Washington, DC: Urban Institute.
Ben Porath, Y. 1967. The production of human capital and the life cycle of earnings. *Journal of Political Economy* 75 (August): 352–65.
Barnow, B. S. 1987. The impact of CETA programs on earnings: A review of the literature. *Journal of Human Resources* 22 (2): 157–93.
———. 1999. Exploring the relationships between performance management and program impact: A case study of the Job Training Partnership Act. *Journal of Policy Analysis and Management* 18 (4): 744.
Bloom, D., L. Gardenshire-Crooks, and C. Mandsager. 2009. *Reengaging high school dropouts: Early results of the National Guard Youth ChalleNGe Program Evaluation.* New York: MDRC.
Bloom, H. S., L. Orr, S. H. Bell, G. Cave, F. Doolittle, W. Lin, and M. B. Johannes. 1997. The benefits and cost of JTPA Title II-A program: Key findings from the national JTPA study. *Journal of Human Resources* 32 (3): 549–76.
Burghardt, J., and S. Glazerman. 2000. *National job corps study: The short-term impacts of job corps on participants' employment and related Outcomes, Final Report.* Princeton, NJ: Mathematica Policy Research, Inc., February.
Burtless, G. 1985. Are targeted wage subsidies harmful? Evidence from a wage voucher experiment. *Industrial and Labor Relations Review* 39 (1): 105–14.
Cameron, S. V., and J. J. Heckman. 1993. The nonequivalence of high school equivalents. *Journal of Labor Economics* 11 (1): 1–47.
Cave, G., H. Bos, F. Doolittle, and C. Toussaint. 1993. *JOB-START: Final report on a program for school dropouts.* New York: Manpower Demonstration Research Corporation, October.
Carnegie Council on Adolescent Development. 1996. *Great transitions.* Washington, DC: Carnegie Council on Adolescent Development.
Couch, K. A. 1992. New evidence on the long-term effects of employment training programs. *Journal of Labor Economics* 10 (4): 380–88.
Edelman, P., H. J. Holzer, and P. Offner. 2005. *Reconnecting young men: Improving education and employment outcomes.* Washington, DC: Urban Institute Press.
Employment and Training Administration. 2008. *Workforce system results, second quarter fiscal year 2008.* Washington, DC: U.S. Department of Labor.
Farkas, G., D. A. Smith, E. Stromsdorfer, G. Trask, and R. Jerrett, III. 1982. *Impacts from the youth incentive entitlement pilot projects: Participation, work, and school-*

ing over the full program period. New York: Manpower Demonstration Research Corporation, June.

Foster, E. M. 1995. Why teens do not benefit from work experience programs: Evidence from brother comparisons. *Journal of Policy Analysis and Management* 14 (3): 393–414.

French, E., B. Mazumder, and C. Taber. 2006. *The changing pattern of wage growth for low skilled workers.* Unpublished Working Paper, the Federal Reserve Bank of Chicago.

Friedlander, D., D. H. Greenberg, and P. K. Robins. 1997. Evaluating government training programs for the economically disadvantaged. *Journal of Economic Literature* 35 (4): 1809–55.

Gladden, T., and C. Taber. 2000. Wage progression among low skilled workers. In *Finding jobs: Work and welfare reform,* ed. D. Card and R. Blank, 160–92. New York: Russell Sage Foundation.

———. 2009. The relationship between wage growth and wage levels. *Journal of Applied Econometrics* 24 (6): 914–32.

Heckman, J., R. LaLonde, and J. Smith. 1999. The economics and econometrics of active labor market policies. In *The handbook of labor economics,* ed. O. Ashenfelter and D. Card, 1865–2097. Amsterdam: North-Holland.

Heckman, J. J., L. J. Lochner, and P. E. Todd. 2006. Earnings functions, rates of return, and treatment effects: The Mincer Equation and beyond. In *Handbook of the economics of education,* ed. E. Hanushek and F. Welch, 307–458. Oxford: Elsevier.

Heckman, J. J., R. L. Roselius, and J. A. Smith. 1994. U.S. education and training policy: A re-evaluation of the underlying assumptions behind the "new consensus." In *Labor markets, employment policy and job creation,* ed. L. C. Solomon and A. B. Levenson, 83–121. Boulder, CO: Westview Press.

Holzer, H., and R. LaLonde. 2000. Job stability and job change among less skilled workers. In *Labor markets and less-skilled workers,* ed. D. Card and R. Blank, 125–59. New York: Russell Sage Foundation.

Jastrzab, J., J. Masker, J. Bloomiquist, and L. Orr. 1996. *Impacts of service: Final report on the evaluation of American conservation and youth service corps.* Cambridge, MA: Abt Associates.

Joyce, M., and D. Neumark. 2001. School-to-work programs: Information from two surveys. *Monthly Labor Review* August: 38–50.

Katz, L. 1994. Active labor market policies to expand employment and opportunity. Presented at Proceedings of Conference on Reducing Unemployment: Current Issues and Policy Options. Federal Reserve Bank of Kansas City, August 25–27.

Katz, L., A. Krueger, and M. Stanley. 1998. *Impacts of employment and training programs: The American experience.* Background paper prepared for British Chancellor of the Exchequer for 1998 G-8 Meeting.

Kemper, P., D. A. Long, and C. Thornton. 1981. *The supported work evaluation: Final benefit-cost analysis.* New York: Manpower Demonstration Research Corporation, September.

Kemple, J. J. (with C. Willner). 2008. *Career academies: Long-term impacts on labor market outcomes, educational attainment, and transitions to adulthood.* New York: MDRC, June.

LaLonde, R. 1986. Evaluating the econometric evaluations of training programs with experimental data. *American Economic Review* 76 (5): 604–20.

———. 1995. The promise of U.S. employment and training programs. *Journal of Economic Perspectives* 9 (2): 149–68.

———. 2003. Employment and training programs. In *Means tested transfer programs in the U.S.,* ed. M. Feldstien and R. Moffitt, 517–86. Chicago: University of Chicago Press.

Lerman, R. 1996. Helping disconnected youth by disconnected youth by improving linkages between high school and careers. Washington, DC: Urban Institute.

———. 2000. Are teens in low-income and welfare families working too much? Washington, DC: Urban Institute.

———. 2005. Career focused education and training for youth. In *Reconnecting young men: Improving education and employment outcomes,* ed. P. Edelman, H. J. Holzer, and P. Offner, 41–90. Washington, DC: Urban Institute Press.

Mallar, C., S. Kerachasky, C. Thornton, and D. Long. 1982. *Evaluation of the economic impact of the job corps program.* Third follow-up report. Princeton, NJ: Mathematica Policy Research. September.

Manpower Administration. 1963. *Manpower report.* Washington, DC: U.S. Department of Labor and U.S. Department of Health, Education, and Welfare.

———. 1967. *Manpower report.* Washington, DC: U.S. Department of Labor and U.S. Department of Health, Education, and Welfare.

Maynard, R. 1980. *The impact of supported work on young school dropouts.* New York: Manpower Demonstration Research Corporation, September.

Mincer, J. 1962. On-the-job training: Costs, returns and some implications. *Journal of Political Economy* 70:50–79.

National Guard. 2006. Youth ChalleNGe Program: 2006 Performance and accountability highlights. Washington, DC: GPO.

Neumark, D., and A. Allen. 2003. What do we know about the effects of school-to-work? A case study of Michigan. *Journal of Vocational Education Research* 1:59–84.

Neumark, D., and M. Joyce. 2001. Evaluating school-to-work programs using the new NLSY. *Journal of Human Resources* Fall: 666–702.

Roder, A., and S. Scrivner. 2005. *Seeking a sustainable journey to work: Findings from the national bridges to work demonstration.* Philadelphia: Public Private Ventures, July.

Ruhm, C. 1997. Is high school employment consumption or investment? *Journal of Labor Economics* October: 735–76.

Sadd, S., M. Kotkin, and S. R. Friedman. 1983. *Alternative youth employment strategies project: Final report.* Report prepared by the Vera Institute for the U.S. Department of Education, Contract Number 28-36-78-05, August.

Secretary's Commission on Achieving Necessary Skills. 1991. *What work requires of schools.* A SCANS Report of America 2000. Washington, DC: U.S. Department of Labor.

Schochet, P. J. 2000. *National job corps study: Methodological appendixes on the short-term impact analysis: Final report, February 9, 2000.* Princeton, NJ: Mathematica Policy Research, Inc., Contract No. K4279-3-00-80-30.

Schochet, P., J. Brughardt, and S. Glazerman. 2001. *National Job Corps Study: The impacts of Job Corps on participants' employment and related outcomes.* Princeton, NJ: Mathematica Policy Research, Inc.

Stafford, F. P. 1979. A Decision theoretic approach to the evaluation of training programs. *Research in Labor Economics* Supplement 1:9–55.

Stinebrickner, R., and T. Stinebrickner. 2003. Working during school and academic performance. *Journal of Labor Economics* 21 (2): 449–72.

Stern, D., C. Dayton, I.-W. Paik, and A. Weisberg. 1989. Benefits and costs of dropout prevention in a high school program combining academic and vocational education: Third-year results from replications of the California Peninsula Academies. *Educational Evaluation and Policy Analysis* 11 (4): 405–16.

Stern, D., M. Raby, and C. Dayton. 1992. *Career academies: Partnerships for reconstructing American high schools.* New York: Jossey-Bass Publishers.

Tierney, J., J. B. Grossman, and N. L. Resch. 2000. *Making a difference: An impact study of big brothers big sisters.* Available at: http://www.ppv.org/ppv/publications/assets/111_publication.pdf.

U.S. General Accounting Office. 1996. *Job training act: Long-term earnings and employment outcomes.* GAO/HEHS-96-40. Washington, DC: GAO, March.

V

Epilogue

Synthesizing the Results

Phillip B. Levine and David J. Zimmerman

13.1 Introduction

The preceding twelve chapters reviewed the evidence regarding the effectiveness of programs that could alter the subsequent poverty status of children who are poor today. These programs ranged from those that affect very young children to those who are bordering on adulthood. Each review highlighted the impact of these interventions on children's outcomes, emphasizing those that may alter economic well-being in adulthood. In some cases, the reviews indicated that the programs were not found to significantly alter children's outcomes. In others, they did seem to have an effect, but perhaps not in ways that would affect children's earnings later in life. Still others did have some promising findings, suggesting that there are ways to intervene in a child's life and potentially make a difference in reducing poverty.

Our initial goal in this chapter is to summarize all of this evidence. For those programs that are not found to alter children's outcomes in any way, any further discussion would require an investigation into the content of the program, the quality of the methodology employed in its review, or other topics that are not the focus of our analysis. Similarly, it is beyond the scope of this exercise to further consider those programs that appear to have an impact on children's outcomes in ways that may not alter their subsequent poverty status. These programs may be well-positioned to satisfy other social goals and worthy of further study or even broader implementation, but that is not the exercise we are seeking to conduct.

Phillip B. Levine is the Class of 1919 Professor and chair of department of economics at Wellesley College, and a research associate of the National Bureau of Economic Research. David J. Zimmerman is a professor of economics and Orrin Sage Professor of Political Economy at Williams College, and a research associate of the National Bureau of Economic Research.

Our goal is to evaluate the poverty-reducing impact of these interventions and it is in this dimension that we pursue additional analysis of those programs that would appear to help accomplish that task. Among those programs, the question then becomes which of these policies works the best. Since different interventions target different outcomes, a direct comparison of their benefits is difficult. The ultimate goal of this chapter is to undertake this task.

13.2   Summary of Program Effectiveness

The lessons to be learned from the dozens of programs described in the preceding twelve chapters of this volume may be difficult to decipher by the sheer volume of information presented. In this section, we will boldly attempt to summarize all of this evidence. The attempt is bold because there are many nuances involved in different specific interventions that may make some effective and others not. Labeling entire categories as successful or otherwise in some dimension requires overlooking those nuances. In each case, we use our best judgment in providing our interpretation of the big picture, but it is important to recognize that our black and white interpretations may overlook some of the relevant grays.

Tables 13.1 through 13.3 provide our summary of the effectiveness of the types of interventions reviewed in this volume. The three tables are distinguished by the child's developmental level at the time of the intervention—early childhood, middle childhood, and adolescence. The tables indicate the types of interventions attempted at each developmental stage and then summarize the outcomes studied and their overall impact. In many, if not all, of these cases, the results of several individual studies are being aggregated in our description of the impact. Any specific estimates are ballpark midpoint estimates across studies.

The summaries we provide suggest that interventions can be categorized into three groups: (a) those that do not seem to have an any impact on children's outcomes; (b) those that seem to have an impact on children's outcomes, but not in any way that may lead to subsequent poverty reduction; and (c) those that may reduce the likelihood that the child is poor later in life. The programs that fit into each category were listed earlier in the introduction to this volume. For our purposes, an outcome that can alter subsequent poverty status is one that has an impact on some dimension of human capital. Outcomes like improving test scores and increasing the likelihood of graduating from high school are measures of human capital and they are well known to improve subsequent earnings. There are some limitations of distinguishing outcomes in this way and we will discuss those in more detail later, but for now this is how we will make this distinction.

When we categorize interventions in this way, we find a variety of interventions that show promise and many that do not. Investments targeted at high-quality center-based preschool programs have been shown to raise both short- and long-term cognitive test scores as well as to improve adult labor market outcomes. These programs are reviewed in chapter 2 by Duncan, Ludwig, and Magnuson. Model preschool programs such as the Abecedarian Program and the Perry Preschool Project, for example, show significant impacts on participating children's IQ scores. Gains of around a standard deviation are apparent for children during their participation in the program. These gains are cut roughly in half by age twelve and by another quarter by age twenty-one. Still, the Abecedarian Program reports gains of .38 standard deviations for these young adults. In addition, participants in the Perry Preschool Program were 17 percentage points more likely to graduate from high school than their counterparts in the control group. These effects were generated in an experimental setting and, while based on small samples, give credible evidence of the potential effectiveness of high quality preschool care. These programs are, however, expensive. Total per-student costs for the Abecedarian Program reached $85,000.[1] The Perry Preschool Program devoted $15,705 per student. Not surprisingly, the less expensive and less intensive Head Start and state universal pre-k programs showed smaller effects or found improvements in outcomes that are only distantly connected to labor market effects.

Given the promise of these results, it might be expected that investments in high-quality day care or after-school programs would offer similarly impressive results. That, however, was not the case, as reported by Anderson in chapter 3 and Levine and Zimmerman in chapter 5. While high-quality day care may offer some benefits, the statistical evidence is not yet compelling. Similarly, the best evidence on the efficacy of after-school programs shows no reliable evidence on improvements in test scores or graduation rates.

Investments targeted at the parents of young children yielded mixed results, also reported in chapter 2 by Duncan, Ludwig, and Magnuson. Prenatal programs such as the Elmira Nurse Family Partnership show some evidence of gains in IQ scores, but these gains are not statistically significant at the long term follow-up when the children are four years old. Children in the "at-risk" sample were, however, less likely to have been arrested or subject to alcohol or drug impairment at age fifteen. Programs targeted at improving parenting techniques similarly show gains in children's problem behavior, but do not register improvements easily linked to the child's human capital.

While programs targeted at improving parental care have shown limited success in raising a child's productive attributes, mentoring programs such as those provided by the Big Brothers Big Sisters Program have shown positive effects on participants' academic performance (Levine and Zimmerman,

---

1. All dollar amounts reported in this chapter refer to 2008 dollars. The value of the Consumer Price Index was 219.1 in August of 2008 (the most recent available at the time this chapter was written) on a base of 100 in 1982–1984.

Table 13.1 Summary of early childhood intervention effects

Intervention	Intervention/outcomes	Effect
	Child development	
Parental Education Programs	Programs seek to boost parent's general knowledge about parenting and child development. Outcomes: IQ, health, crime, child abuse, emergency room visits, alcohol and drug use.	Generally modest and statistically insignificant effects on longer-term measures of child development.
Parent Management Programs	Programs designed to teach strategies to improve children's problem behavior. Outcomes: Negative parenting, parenting stress, problem behavior.	Reduced problem behavior.
Early Education (Perry Pre-School, Abecedarian, Head Start)	Center-based early childhood intervention programs. Outcomes: IQ, test scores, behavior problems, crime, teen parent, drug use, high school graduation, college entry.	Model programs show improvements at age 3 or 4 in IQ ($+1$ sd), reading ($+.7$ sd), math ($+.7$ sd). IQ gains decline with age (.5 sd at age 12 and .38 sd at age 21). Also improvements in high school graduation rates in Perry ($+17$ pp). Earnings higher by \$5,500 in Perry Pre-School (\$2000). State programs show average gains of .14 sd for PPVT and .29 sd for math effects at age 4. Most effects smaller and often ns in Head Start at age 4. Head Start shows high school graduation $+21$ pp at age 23.
	Child care	
Day care provision	Provision of child care for preschool aged children. Outcomes: Behavioral and cognitive outcomes of child, family incomes impact on child.	High-quality care may be beneficial, though no good experimental evidence. No causal link in outcomes with family income.

Child health

Medicaid/SCHIP Expansion	Provision of health insurance. Outcomes: Probability child uninsured, probability of child visits doctor, birth weight.	Insurance increases prenatal care but no measured effect on child health. Birth weight is linked to education, but not to interventions.
WIC	Provision of food and nutrition education for mothers. Outcomes: birth weight, gestational length.	Little evidence linking WIC to birth weight.
ADHD Drug Treatment	Treatment for Attention Deficit Hyperactivity Disorder. Outcomes: Test scores, grade retention, special education placement.	ADHD linked to GPA and test scores, but no credible evidence on long-term or short-term effects from treatment.
Asthma treatment	Treatment for asthma. Outcomes: doctor visits, school days missed, academic performance.	Little evidence linking asthma to academic achievement or income.
Dental health	Provision of fluoridation, dental sealants, or dental insurance. Outcomes: tooth loss, income.	Little evidence linking dental health to income.
Obesity	Obesity prevention programs. Outcomes: Family Income, probability of marriage, wages.	Obesity linked to outcomes, but no effective intervention.
Environmental toxins	Improvements in air quality and lead exposure. Outcomes: Absenteeism, asthma, pneumonia, infant mortality.	Links established, but interventions not evaluated.

Note: SCHIP = State Children's Health Insurance Program; WIC = Women, Infants, and Children.

Table 13.2   Summary of middle childhood intervention effects

Intervention	Intervention/outcomes	Effect
	After-school programs	
After-school care	Provision of after-school programs for school-aged children.	No statistically significant effect.
	Outcomes: Self-care. Maternal employment, reading test-score (SAT-9), English grade, math grade, science and social science grades, TV viewing time, homework completion, attendance.	
QOP	Intensive intervention in high-risk adolescents.	No statistically significant effect.
	Outcomes: High-school graduation rates, attend postsecondary institution, achievement test scores, behavioral issues.	
Mentoring	Mentoring programs.	+ .08 grade points (Big Brother Big Sister)
	Outcomes: drug abuse, crime, academic performance.	Smaller or insignificant effects from School-Based Programs.
		Basal word recognition and spelling show statistically significant gains (Howard Street).
	Education reforms	
Direct dollar investments	Policies changing per-pupil expenditures in schools.	Mixed. Mostly no effect.
	Outcomes: test scores.	

Class size reduction	Policies reducing school class size. Outcomes: Third- and eighth-grade test scores, taking college entrance exam.	+.15 sd on composite test. +.02 probability took college entrance test.
Curriculum and instructional programs	Curricular innovations. Outcomes: Test scores.	Limited evidence. "Success for All" program increased reading test scores by .21–.36 sd.
Computer aided instruction	Integrating computers into schools' instruction programs. Outcomes: Math and reading test scores.	Mixed results. Some programs have very large effects and others find nothing statistically significant.
Teacher wages, recruitment, professional development	Policies aimed at improving teacher quality. High school graduation, college enrollment, reading, math, and science tests.	10% increase in teachers wages yields 3–4% fall in dropout rates and 1–2% increase in college enrollment. "Teach for America": +.07–.15 sd in math versus not traditionally trained teachers.
Vouchers and charter schools	Vouchers that can be used for tuition at a private school. Public funding of charter schools. Outcomes: Test scores.	Insignificant or negative effects.

Note: QOP = Quantum Opportunities Program.

Table 13.3   Summary of adolescent intervention effects

Intervention	Intervention/outcomes	Effect
	Substance abuse prevention	
School-based	School-based training providing information, skill building, and normative education. Outcomes: Use of drugs, alcohol, and tobacco, wages, employment, educational outcomes.	Limited evidence on the effects of drug, alcohol, and tobacco use.
Family-based	Programs aimed at families where a parent or child is at high risk. Outcomes: Time to initiation of drug, alcohol, and tobacco use.	Mixed results.
Community-based	Programs include targeted mentoring programs, drug treatment, and criminal justice interventions. Outcomes: Time to initiation of drug, alcohol, and tobacco use, educational outcomes.	Improved educational outcomes (see after-school care), delayed initiation of drug and alcohol use.
Drug and alcohol testing	Drug testing by schools, employers, or criminal justice agencies. Outcomes: drug and alcohol use.	Mixed results.
	Pregnancy prevention	
Sex education (abstinence focus)	Education programs emphasizing abstinence. Outcomes: sexual initiation, frequency of sex, unprotected sex, pregnancy.	No observable impact.
Sex education (contraception focus)	Education programs emphasizing contraception. Outcomes: sexual initiation, frequency of sex, unprotected sex, pregnancy.	Mixed. Some evidence of delayed sexual initiation, increased condom use.
Multicomponent approaches	Comprehensive approach to teen pregnancy prevention. Outcomes: sexual initiation, frequency of sex, unprotected sex, pregnancy, academic and social behaviors.	Reduced pregnancy rates, increased condom use (Carrera Program).

Dropout prevention and college preparatory programs

Gear up	Comprehensive federal program tasked at equalizing access to higher education for low-income students. Outcomes: college plans, math and reading scores.	Positive effect on college plans. Mixed results on math skills. No effect on reading scores.
Upward bound	Comprehensive federal program offering a variety of services including instruction, tutoring, and counseling. Outcomes: various measures of high school academic preparation.	Increase in high school math credits (+ .2 credits). No effect on other measures of high school academic preparation. Increased likelihood of four-year college enrollment (+ 6 pp).
Talent search	Federal program providing information to low-income students on high school curricular choices and on financial aid and the college application process. Outcomes: college attendance, high school graduation, apply for financial aid.	Participants more likely (+ 12 pp) to enroll in public postsecondary institution.
Project grad	Implements math and reading curricula along with professional development for teachers. Outcomes: complete core curriculum, promoted to 10th grade.	Mixed or insignificant effects.
AVID	Attempts to enroll capable students in 5th–12th grades in rigorous curriculum. Outcomes: high school GPA, high school credit accumulation.	Higher GPA in middle school, effects not sustained in high school. Small positive effect on core credits accumulation.
Puente	Program targeted at Latino students, includes counseling designed to increase college enrollment. Outcomes: complete SAT, attend two- or four-year college, remain in college 3 + years.	Increased college attendance and persistence, through self-reports and small samples.
College aid		
College financial aid	$1,000 increase in college financial aid. Outcomes: college attendance.	4 pp increase in college attendance.

(continued)

Table 13.3   (continued)

Intervention	Intervention/outcomes	Effect
STAR project	Incoming students received either peer advising and organized study groups or financial incentives based on academic performance, both of these, or neither of these. Outcomes: Grades, retention.	Modest effects. GPA increased (+ .1–.2 sigma) for first-year grades. Effect for females only with the strongest effects from services combined with incentives.
Opening doors	Entering students take blocks of classes together, receive extra tutoring, supplementary financial aid, and enhanced student services. Outcomes: credits taken and earned, pass rates, GPA, retention	Increased retention (7–8 pp). Increased pass rate (10–12 pp), more credits taken (2–3).
	Neighborhood and community initiatives	
Housing vouchers	Low-income families in public housing receive a voucher to move elsewhere. Outcomes: dropping out of high school, reading and math test scores, grades, college attendance.	Mixed results. Increases in reading and math scores in Chicago (+ .2 sd) and Baltimore. Statistically insignificant effects in Boston, Los Angeles, and New York.
	Vocational training	
Job Corps	Intensive and expensive program targeting economically challenged youth with counseling, education, training, health care, and job placement services. Residential training centers used. Outcomes: employment, earnings.	Increases in both male and female earnings. Impact largest for 22- to 24-year-olds. No significant impact for youths.
Career Academy	Provides basic skills and vocational training within high schools. Substitutes vocational courses for academic courses. Outcomes: earnings.	Increased earnings for males (+ 20%). Decreased earnings for women (–5%). Population treated less disadvantaged than Job Corps participants.

chapter 5). Participants in this program register grades that are .08 grade points higher than nonparticipants. Costs in this program are modest at about $1,500.

The evidence on investments in children's health is problematic, as reviewed by Shore-Sheppard in chapter 4. While there is good evidence that policy can be initiated that can expand health care insurance opportunities, the evidence is weaker that this improves child health. Further, the links between child health and adult labor market outcomes are not well-established. For example, effective interventions targeted at dental health, asthma, and exposure to environmental toxins have been developed, but the evidence linking these improvements to adult poverty is much weaker.

Loeb and McEwan (chapter 6) find that a variety of education interventions hold promise. While direct dollar transfers to schools show mixed results, there is evidence that reductions in class size can raise test scores. Indeed, evidence from Project STAR showed that investing in smaller class sizes from kindergarten through the third grade resulted in a .15 standard deviation gain in a composite test score. It is important to note, however, that class size reductions are expensive; Project STAR costs reached $12,145 per student. Participants in the "Success for All" reading program scored between .21 and .36 standard deviations higher on a reading test; the program cost $2,789 per student.

Other educational interventions have been found to be successful. Paying teachers higher wages has been found to improve educational performance. One convincing study concludes that increasing teacher pay by 10 percent reduced dropout rates by 3 to 4 percent and increased college enrollment by 1 to 2 percent. The "Teach for America" teacher training program has been found to be successful when the newly placed teachers are replacing teachers of average quality. Teacher training costs of $1,374 have been found to generate increases in math test scores of .07 to .15 standard deviations in these instances.

Studies of other types of educational interventions have yielded mixed results, at best. The evidence does not tend to support the effectiveness of computer-aided instruction programs, professional development programs, and investments in private school vouchers or charter schools.

Shifting to investments targeted mostly at adolescents, chapter 7 by Kilmer and Pacula tackles the topic of adolescent substance abuse. The evidence on these interventions suggests that some programs may be effective in reducing adolescents' consumption of alcohol, drugs, or cigarettes. The evidence is less compelling that these reductions in use persist through high school. It is still the case, however, that short-term program effects could generate significant changes in lifetime consumption—perhaps, for example, by altering a child's peer environment. Further, programs that delay the initiation of substance use can reduce the odds of later dependency. These findings are, however, matched with less compelling evidence on the link between substance use and labor market outcomes. While chronic substance use may impact economic outcomes, modest levels of use may have no effect. As the authors note: "the level of consumption, duration of consumption, and timing of consumption all have important implications in terms of whether we should expect to see an impact on poverty, employment, or earnings." The evidence, as it stands, however, does not suggest a clear and effective policy prescription.

Kearney (chapter 8) reviews programs targeted at reducing teen pregnancy and concludes that these programs are not likely to reduce adult poverty. It is true that several interventions in this area have demonstrated the possibility of delaying the age at which adolescents engage in sexual activity. Some programs, such as the Carrera Program, have successfully increased participants' condom use and reduced rates of teen pregnancy. Unfortunately, however, the literature linking teen pregnancy to adult economic outcomes suggests that teen pregnancy, per se, plays a limited role in causing adult poverty. Thus, from a purely antipoverty perspective, investments in pregnancy prevention are unlikely to deliver a high return.

Educational interventions have also been tried that target students at older ages and are designed to keep them from dropping out of high school or to encourage them to attend college. Long's discussion in chapter 9 concludes that research on dropout prevention programs has not been able to convincingly demonstrate success. This is largely attributable to poor research designs and inadequate data. The one intervention that does seem to have some success is to extend mandatory school laws to require attendance through older ages. A policy of this sort is different than the other types of interventions considered in this volume, which are more apt to provide additional resources rather than impose stricter rules.

College aid programs appear to be more successful in encouraging students to continue with their schooling. Deming and Dynarski (chapter 10) report that providing aid without large administrative burdens is successful in increasing college attendance. They conclude that the best estimates indicate that offering a $1,000 aid award will increase college attendance by about 4 percentage points. They also report that evidence from the Opening Doors intervention raises the possibility that a combination of services and financial incentives also may increase retention among college students.

Programs designed to change the environment in which children (not necessarily just adolescents) live have also been studied, yielding mixed results. Burdick-Will and Ludwig review these programs in chapter 11. These programs attack the claim that a child's neighborhood can affect his or her outcomes through role models, access to resources, and other factors; moving children outside this environment, the argument goes, would improve outcomes in many dimensions, including academic outcomes, that would lead to greater human capital development and higher subsequent wages.

The studies, however, are not overwhelming in their support of the success of these policies. Some bright spots emerge from the literature. Moving certain population subgroups in some studies have been found to successfully improve children's outcomes. Some of these studies do not perfectly address the selection problem regarding who moves and findings of broad-based improvements in children's outcomes are rare.

Job training programs, broadly speaking, also have not been found to have a meaningful impact on the earnings capacity of disadvantaged youths. As Lalonde and Sullivan review in chapter 12, most programs implemented in the past that have been rigorously evaluated are not found to lead to significant earnings gains among program participants. They argue that a likely explanation for this is that the level of intensity of these programs makes success difficult. If a nine-month school year can increase wages by 10 percent, how effective could a training program be that meets for a few hundred hours? Consistent with this point, the exceptions to their findings involve Career Academies and the Job Corps programs. Career Academies provide both basic skills and vocational training within high schools. The Job Corps is a very intensive residential training program that provides a very comprehensive set of services, including counseling, training, work experience, health care, and job placement. The benefits of this program are large, but costs are as well. Career Academies seems to provide greater benefits relative to its costs. It does not target as poor a population as does Job Corps.

13.3   Effectiveness in Reducing Poverty: Methods

The preceding section shows that there are a number of areas in which policy interventions appear to alter children's outcomes in ways that can improve their longer run economic well-being. The question then becomes which types of interventions can best accomplish this task. This is a difficult question because we are rarely able to observe, say, thirty-year program impacts, which would make such an analysis rather straightforward. Even if we could, it is not obvious how to interpret evidence from interventions that took place thirty years ago.

Instead, we are typically only able to observe outcomes that occur at the time of the intervention or perhaps within a few years of its completion. This limitation means that any attempt to estimate the longer term effectiveness of program interventions will require us to simulate the subsequent earnings impact. Once we conduct that simulation, then we can compare that impact to the cost of the intervention to determine which types of programs deliver more "bang for the buck." This section will describe our methodology for conducting this analysis and provide some caveats that are important to consider in interpreting these results. The results themselves will be presented in the subsequent section.

13.3.1 Overview of Our Approach

To estimate the poverty-reducing impact of an intervention, we employ a two-stage empirical approach comparable to that used by Krueger (2003) in his analysis of class size reductions. In the first stage, we find "best estimates" of the impact that spending on a particular type of program has on contemporaneous outcomes. These outcomes, which include things like high school grades and math and reading test scores, represent indicators of the child's level of human capital. This stage was accomplished in the preceding section. The second stage relates these outcomes to subsequent earnings as an adult, a task that will be completed in this section. Combining these results enables us to estimate the impact of the intervention on adult earnings.[2]

Consider, for example, a hypothetical intervention that has been shown to be effective in improving the test scores of program participants by .2 standard deviations. Suppose we augment that finding with additional evidence that for every standard deviation improvement in test scores, students' subsequent earnings rise by 10 percent. One could combine these estimates to indicate that the program increases wages by 2 percent. Combining this estimate with an estimate of baseline lifetime earnings provides a means to determine the program's impact. If a typical program participant would earn $500,000 over his or her worklife (in present discounted value terms), then a 2 percent program impact means that participant's lifetime earnings would be estimated to increase by $10,000. This is the value that we would compare to the cost of the program.

One complication in all of this is the timing of when the program effect occurs. Interventions targeted at young children, for instance, may increase test scores in the near term, but those effects may fade over time. On the one hand, if it is the direct skill linked to the test score that matters, then if the effect fades over time, it should have a limited impact on wages. An alternative perspective is that the test score is just a marker for a wide variety of impacts that the test may measure. Even if the specific skills measured by the test fade over time, the other attributes of the individual that have been altered by the program may linger. It is in this sense that one may prefer to use short-term test score impacts to capture the total impact of the pro-

---

2. More formally, we incorporate evidence from equations of the form:

$$\text{Adult Outcomes}_i = \beta_0 + \beta_1 HC_i + \beta_2 X_i + \varepsilon_i$$

$$HC_i = \gamma_0 + \gamma_1 INV_i + \gamma_2 Z_i + e_i,$$

where adult outcomes are things like earnings or poverty status, HC represents some measure of a child's human capital (e.g., test scores), INV represents investments made in the child (i.e., program participation), X and Z represent other factors that affect adult outcomes and level of human capital, respectively, and i indexes individuals. In this model, β_1 represents the impact of human capital on adult outcomes, and γ_1 represents the impact of the investment on human capital, so that the product of β_1 and γ_1 indicates the impact of the investment on the adult outcome.

gram. In our case, when long-term effects on final educational attainment or direct observations on wages are available, we will use those outcomes as the program impact. Where they are not, we will use the short-term test score impact. This decision is one that we will evaluate subsequently in the one instance (Perry Pre-School) where we have both short-term impacts on test scores and long-term impacts on wages.

The tasks that remain to be completed include evaluating the percentage impact on earnings and estimating baseline lifetime earnings. These steps will be accomplished in the following subsections.

13.3.2   Review of the Literature

Past research has examined the impact of academic outcomes on subsequent earnings; we will heavily rely on that research. In his survey of the evidence, Krueger (2003) concluded that a suitable summary statistic is that a 1 standard deviation increase in math or reading test scores is associated with an earnings gain of around 8 percent. Hanusheck (2006) conducted a similar survey and concluded that a 1 standard deviation increase in test scores is associated with an earnings gain of 12 percent.

Yet none of the surveyed studies informs precisely the question that we have in mind. Past studies tend to focus on test scores obtained in high school; the academic outcomes that are available to us from the interventions previously reviewed tend to be measured at younger ages. Longitudinal studies of sufficient duration to capture both early/mid-childhood academic outcomes and adult earnings are hard to come by. The British National Child Development Survey, used by Currie and Thomas (2001), gets around this problem because it includes math test scores at ages seven and sixteen and wages at age thirty-three. It would be our preference, however, to use American data that would more accurately reflect the labor market realities relevant for the children participating in the programs we consider. The data sets that have been employed are also a bit dated, focusing on educational measures from the early 1980s and examining outcomes just a handful of years after that. We will explore this relationship further in the subsequent section.[3]

We will also rely on prior research to assign a benefit to programs that are shown to increase educational attainment. The impact of educational attainment on wages is an issue that has been extensively studied. Despite the important difficulties in estimating a causal impact, researchers have introduced methods that are sufficiently convincing that a consensus has emerged. It has become commonplace to attribute a 10 percent return to every additional year of education a child receives.

---

3. Another potential problem with these analyses is that the wages measured tend to be from relatively young adults and the impact of greater ability may rise over time. If so, then the estimates from past studies as well as our own investigation reported later will understate the true program impact.

13.3.3   Analysis of NLSY Data

Before proceeding, we report an analysis that we have conducted that updates previous research on the relationship between test scores on subsequent wages. We do so by using data from the children of respondents to the 1979 National Longitudinal Survey of Youth (NLSY79) as well as the newer NLSY cohort, which began in 1997 (NLSY97). The NLSY79 represents a sample of over 12,000 individuals born between 1957 and 1964 who have been surveyed annually through 1994 and biennially since then. Starting in 1986, the children of the female respondents to this survey have also been tracked biennially. To date, over 11,000 children have been born to these women. Children fifteen and over participate in a "young adult" survey. We concentrate on those survey participants who were born in 1987 or earlier, making them age nineteen or older in 2006, the last year for which data are available. There are almost 5,000 individuals that satisfy this condition. We focus on those aged nineteen or over because they have passed the regular point of high school completion, so that many of them will have fully entered the labor market. Most survey respondents in our sample are between the ages of nineteen and twenty-nine.

In addition to this measure of educational attainment, these data also provide several developmental measures, including tests of cognitive ability, which were obtained for each child beginning from about age five and through age fourteen.[4] In our analysis, we take advantage of scores on the Peabody Individual Achievement Test (PIAT), which measures a child's performance in math, reading recognition, and reading comprehension. We have also aggregated across the three components of the PIAT, estimating average scores, and we will use this aggregate measure in our analysis as well. These data are available for about 4,700 of the children born in our sample of those born in 1987 or earlier.

Along with data on test scores, a wealth of other information is available for NLSY respondents and their children. In particular, wage data is obviously necessary for this analysis and it is available in these data. About 1,600 of the remaining sample are still available in the survey, have entered the labor force, and reported earnings in 2006. We also control for characteristics of the individual and his/her mother that may be related to both an individual's wage and his/her test scores. Mother's characteristics include: her age at the time of birth of the child, her completed years of schooling, her score on a test of aptitude/achievement (the Armed Forces Qualifying Test, or AFQT), the number of children she had up until the year 2000, the fraction of the child's life that the mother was married, and her average annual

---

4. We have also investigated whether scores on tests taken between the ages of five and nine have a different impact than scores on tests taken between the ages of ten and fourteen. The results were similar, so we chose to proceed combining the ages at which the tests were taken.

family income in the year since the child was born. We also control for a number of characteristics of the child as well, including: the child's birth order; a variable indicating whether or not the child was the first born to the mother; and whether the child was female, nonwhite, or Hispanic. Missing data on these other explanatory variables reduces the sample to about 1,400.

We use these data to estimate regression models where the dependent variable is the natural log of the wage. The results of our analysis are reported in the top panel of table 13.4. Each row presents the results of a separate regression model that differs depending upon the specific test score included as the key explanatory variable. Here we see that a 1 standard deviation increase in a number of different types of test scores increase adult wages on the order of about 6 to 10 percent. The results are reasonably robust to the specific type of test and to the fact that these tests were given to younger children than those examined in earlier studies.

We further examined this assertion by using a more recent cohort of data, the NLSY97. There are about 9,000 respondents in the NLSY97, all of whom were between the ages of twelve and sixteen as of December 31, 1996. Respondents are surveyed biennially; the most recent data available is from 2006, when they are twenty-two to twenty-six. Wage data for those in the labor market are available in 2006, along with data on an AFQT-type test like that administered in the NLSY79.[5] The NLSY97 is a data set similarly rich like the NLSY79, including information on age, gender, race, ethnicity, household structure and mother's and father's educational background. We include all of these variables as controls and estimate comparable models to those reported earlier using the children of the NLSY79.

The results of this exercise are reported in the middle panel of table 13.4. The results are remarkably similar to those from the NLSY79. In these data, a 1 standard deviation increase in test scores increase wages by 8.9 percent.

Based on this evidence and the simplicity of maintaining a single estimate for the estimated impact of test score effects, we will use a value of 10 percent as the return on a 1 standard deviation increase in test scores in our calculations. We arrived at this conclusion by combining our own evidence with the reviews discussed previously by Krueger (2003) and Hanusheck (2006). They concluded that an estimate of 8 percent and 12 percent, respectively, are appropriate values. Our preferred value of 10 percent is the midpoint of those conclusions and it is generally consistent with our findings as well.

We also conducted one additional analysis using NLSY data to enable us to convert the impact on high school grades to subsequent wages. The data that we use for this exercise is the original NLSY79 cohort (the parents of

---

5. Notes from the NLSY97 indicate this AFQT-type variable is "similar to the AFQT score generated by the Department of Defense, (but it) reflects work done by NLSY program staff and is neither generated nor endorsed by (the Department of Defense)."

Table 13.4   Estimated impact of cognitive test scores and high school grades on wages

Human capital measure and data set	Coefficient/(standard deviation)
NLSY79: Young adults	
Impact of 1 sd increase in aggregate test score	9.23 (1.44)
Impact of 1 sd increase in math	9.35 (1.41)
Impact of 1 sd increase in reading recognition	6.42 (1.07)
Impact of 1 sd increase in reading comprehension	6.03 (1.37)
NLSY97	
Impact of a 1 sd increase in AFQT-type test score	8.91 (1.10)
NLSY79: Original sample	
Impact of 1 point increase in high school GPA	15.87 (1.52)

Notes: Standard deviation in parentheses. Each cell represents estimates from different regression models, which are multiplied by 100 so that they may be interpreted as a percentage effect. These estimates are obtained from regression models that also control for the following characteristics. In the NLSY79 young adult sample: characteristics of the mother (age at birth of the child, educational attainment, aptitude/achievement test score, number of children, the fraction of the child's life the mother was married, and the log of the mother's average family income since the child was born) and of the child (birth order; whether or not the child was firstborn; gender, race, and ethnicity). In the NLSY97: age, gender, race, ethnicity, household structure, and mother's and father's educational attainment. In the NLSY79 original sample: age, gender, race and ethnicity, household structure while growing up, and mother's and father's educational attainment. Standard errors are adjusted to correct for heteroskedasticity.

the respondents used in our earlier exercise). We use wage data available in 2006, when respondents are between the ages of forty-one and forty-seven.

The most important characteristic of these data for the purposes of the analysis conducted here is that usable high school transcript data is available for almost 9,000 NLSY respondents, respectively. Since the courses each respondent took come from their high school transcript and are not self-reported, these data should be quite reliable. Because of sample attrition between 1979 and 2006 and the fact that not all NLSY respondents were employed in 2006, the sample size available for this exercise is about 4,600 respondents.

We use these data to estimate regression models where the dependent variable is the natural log of the hourly wage that the individual received in 2006. The results of our analysis are reported in the bottom panel of table 13.4. Here we see that a one-point increase in a student's GPA is associated with a 15.87 percent increase in adult wages.

13.3.4   Net Present Value Calculations

The last component that we need to simulate the impact on lifetime earnings associated with an intervention is a net present value calculation. Consider a program that increases test scores by 1 standard deviation and we are willing to attribute an 8 percent wage effect associated with that program based on our earlier discussion. To what number do we apply that 8 percent and how does that alter lifetime earnings? In our analysis, we follow the general approach that Krueger (2003) used in taking wage data from the March Current Population Survey, in our case aggregating data from the 2006 through 2008 surveys.[6] We estimate the age-earnings profile, and then calculate the net present value of lifetime earnings, assuming that an individual hitting the labor market today would face the same wage profile as the current age-earnings profile. We assume a discount rate of 3 percent, as Krueger does.

One important difference in our calculations is that we use data from high school graduates only. In Krueger's case, he was dealing with a broad-based class-size intervention that would affect all students, so using the age-earnings profile of the average worker would be appropriate. In our case, we are dealing with interventions that largely target a lower income population, so the average worker's age-earnings profile is likely to be too high a starting point. It is difficult to know what the right education level is to assume for this population in this exercise; we have chosen those who have graduated from high school and not gone on to college. Based on this age-earnings profile and a 3 percent discount rate, we calculate that a typical worker would earn $555,000 over the course of his life (in 2007 dollars).

13.3.5   Caveats

We want to be clear that we recognize the limitations of a simulation of the nature we just described. Without long-term follow-up studies to the program evaluations, we have no other method of estimating earnings impact thirty or more years after the intervention. The approach we are using enables us to simulate that impact, but clearly that approach is not perfect and we want to clarify at least some of the important oversights that we make when we implement it.

The first main problem that we face using our approach is that we overlook standard errors in our estimates. Every estimate that we use comes with a standard error and we ignore all of those. The underlying problem is even worse than that, however. One way to view sample size is to consider the number of observations in a particular evaluation and those sample sizes are often relatively small (100 observations?). Another way to view sample size is to consider the number of interventions studied. One can easily imagine that there is a distribution of impacts associated with any particular type of intervention. Things like the quality of the program administrator and differences in the populations being treated could easily alter the results of any program. In larger multisite evaluations, differences in estimated impacts across sites are commonplace. Yet our simulation process ignores this variability in projecting the earnings impact of each intervention. Without the

---

6. These data provide wage information for 2005 through 2007; we treat them as if the results are in 2006 dollars to adjust for inflation.

ability to implement formal methods of statistical inference, it is important to keep in mind the imprecision that affects all of our estimates. If two estimates are "close," we will do our best to resist the temptation to rank them.

The second main problem is that we ignore the role that noncognitive factors may play in improving children's life outcomes. By focusing exclusively on educational outcomes, we miss the many other important determinants of lifetime earnings. Earnings may just as easily be influenced by "soft skills," like the ability to get along with others, communicate effectively, and to act appropriately in a work environment, as they are influenced by one's cognitive ability. Our approach does not take any of those other factors into account.

It is possible, however, to at least provide a preliminary gauge regarding the role of those other factors based on the results of the long-term follow-ups available from the Perry Pre-School intervention. We can use the short-term impacts on cognitive ability from that intervention, simulate longer term outcomes, and then compare those simulated longer term outcomes with actual longer term outcomes available in the data. Results from Perry Pre-School indicate that the intervention increased students' IQ scores at age four by .87 standard deviations (see the discussion in chapter 2 by Duncan, Ludwig, and Magnuson). Based on the results of our analysis and those of previous studies, we assume that a 1 standard deviation increase in test scores would increase wages by 10 percent. This means that Perry Pre-School would increase wages by about 8.7 percent. From a base lifetime earnings of $555,000 (in 2007 dollars), this wage increase would amount to an additional $48,285 over the working life of each participant.

Duncan, Ludwig, and Magnuson (chapter 2) also report from their review of the evidence that the present discounted value of lifetime earnings of program participants is about $60,000 higher than that of control group members in 2007 dollars. This means that the estimate we obtain by simulating a lifetime increase on the basis of the returns to improved cognitive ability is about 80 percent of the observed lifetime wage increase on the basis of the experimental findings. Although there are implicit standard errors associated with both numbers that are difficult to incorporate into an analysis like this, it suggests that the improvement in cognitive ability accounts for a large share of the overall wage increase.[7]

---

7. We can also conduct a similar exercise, simulating lifetime earnings effects on the basis of the increase in educational attainment. Evidence from the Perry evaluation indicates that the program increased the likelihood of high school graduation by 17 percentage points. Although we do not have access to continuous educational attainment measures, we hypothesize that this means that 17 percent of the participants received two more years of education. Valuing a year of education at 10 percent, this means that lifetime earnings for program participants should have risen, on average, by 21 percent for 17 percent of the participants, for an expected value rise in earnings of 3.57 percent. Again, using a base level of lifetime earnings of $555,000, this amounts to a $19,813 increase in 2007 dollars. Again, this suggests that this standard human capital measure can explain a sizable portion of the observed wage increase ($60,000 in 2007 dollars), but a sizable portion still remains unexplained.

13.4   Effectiveness in Reducing Poverty: Results

The goal of our exercise is to identify the programs that provide the greatest earnings impact relative to the cost of the intervention.[8] To standardize across interventions, we convert all of our results into the earnings impact per $1,000 expenditure. Those that yield the biggest impact on that scale are the ones that should be supported more strongly. But there is another option that must be considered that is not presented in this table or earlier in the report. One possible intervention would be simply to give the $1,000 to the children either directly or in the form of a deposit in a savings account that cannot be used until adulthood. If a programmatic intervention cannot yield greater lifetime earnings than this alternative $1,000 gift, then it is not clear that the program should be supported. But any increase in earnings beyond the $1,000 that a program may generate can be thought of as a return on the investment in the program. In other words, if the $1,000 investment generates $1,200 in higher earnings for the participant, then one could view this as a 20 percent rate of return.

The results of this analysis are presented in table 13.5. This table displays only those programs that are found to have impacts on the types of human capital measures that are likely to be related to higher lifetime incomes, as reported in tables 13.1, 13.2, and 13.3. We report the impact of specific interventions or categories of interventions in those instances where we have summarized the impact of a number of interventions of the same type. The first column of the table reports the impact on human capital. These results are taken directly from tables 13.1, 13.2, and 13.3, which have been taken from the relevant chapters where the program is discussed. The second column converts the impact on human capital to the impact on lifetime earnings, implementing the methodology described earlier. Each human capital measure is converted into a percentage wage effect using the results of prior research and our own analysis and then converted into a lifetime earnings impact by multiplying by our estimate of lifetime net present value of earnings ($555,000 in 2007 dollars). Column (3) reports the cost of the intervention, also measured in 2007 dollars.

Our calculations suggest that almost all of the programs that are estimated to improve a child's human capital result in subsequent lifetime earnings gains that are greater than the costs of the program. One might argue that any of these interventions show enough promise to receive support from those seeking to invest in children in a way that will improve their economic well-being.

---

8. Another present discounted value calculation is required in comparing benefits and costs since there is a significant time lag between the time of the intervention and labor market entry. That time lag also differs for different types of interventions. A $1,000 intervention that takes place at age five is "more expensive" than a $1,000 intervention at age sixteen because more time elapses between the earlier intervention and labor market entry during which that money could have been invested elsewhere.

Table 13.5   Effectiveness of childhood interventions on adult earnings (all 2007 dollars)

Intervention	Impact on human capital (1)	Impact on lifetime earnings (2)	Cost (3)	Earnings impact per $1,000 cost (4)
Early childhood education				
Perry Pre-School	Earnings measured directly	$60,000	$15,700	$3,822
Abecedarian	1 year increase in average educational attainment	$55,500	$90,000	$611
Head Start	.21 pp HS grad	$24,476	$8,000	$3,060
State Programs	.29 sd on math test	$16,095	$6,100	$2,639
Mentoring programs				
Big Brother Big Sister	.08 grade points	$7,046	$1,480	$4,761
Education reforms				
Class size reduction (Project STAR)	.15 sd on test scores	$8,325	$12,145	$685
Curriculum and instruction (Success for All)	.29 sd on reading test	$16,095	$2,789	$5,771
Teacher wages (10% increase)	3.5% reduction in HS dropout and 1.5% increase in college enrollment	$5,775	$4,440	$1,307
Teacher training (Teach for America)	.11 sd increase on math test	$6,105	$1,374	$4,443
College aid				
$1,000 Reduction in Cost	4 pp increase in college attendance	$4,662	$1,000	$4,662
Vocational training				
Job Corps	$1,695 annual earnings increase for men	$40,355	$21,000	$1,922
Career Academies	$2,088 annual earnings increase	$49,712	$2,800	$17,754

Indeed, some of the relative returns are impressive. Evidence from a recent evaluation of Career Academies indicates that those programs provide a very large return on their investment. Eight years following the intervention, treatment group members had an annual earnings gain of $2,088 (Kemple and Wilner 2008). Extrapolating this estimate to a present discounted value of lifetime earnings gains (at a 3 percent discount rate) generates $49,712 in returns. The incremental cost of the program was just $2,800 ($700 per year for four years), leading to a return of over $17,000 per $1,000 investment. This is a very large return on the investment and certainly would require further verification to further solidify the magnitude of this effect. The scale of the evaluation, though, was rather large, enhancing its precision. Perhaps the cost estimates are understated in that they are reported as incremental and program expansion may require greater outlay of upfront costs. Nevertheless, these results are encouraging.

Job Corps presents a different profile. The benefits of the program are very large, but so are the costs. In an absolute sense, Job Corps generates the second largest improvement in lifetime earnings, but at $21,000 in cost per participant, the returns per dollar invested are smaller than some other programs. In reality, it is difficult to imagine a program with costs this large to be offered to more than a relative handful of participants because more widespread implementation would wipe out governmental or private foundation outlays.

The Big Brothers Big Sisters mentoring program is another one of the programs with impressive results. We find that a cost of $1,480 generates almost five times that in terms of higher lifetime wages of program participants. Providing additional college aid also has a large effect, similarly generating about five times more earnings than the additional aid provided. The Teach for America teacher training program and Success for All reforms to curriculum and instruction also have very large effects. Although these returns are quite large, it is important to remember that they are based on a single intervention, suggesting that the standard errors on these estimated returns may be quite large.

Early childhood education programs also appear to be strong performers, if not at the highest level of returns. One favorable interpretation about the impact of these programs is that there is a number of this type of intervention, including some large-scale evaluations (Head Start), and they yield relatively similar returns. This may say something about the implicit standard error being small on programs like these relative to, say, Big Brother Big Sister, which is based on a single, relatively small intervention. Placing your bets on something that is more likely to pay off, even at a smaller rate, may have a higher average level of benefit.

The remaining highlight from this table is college aid. The evidence from this literature suggests that a $1,000 investment in college aid pays off with a return of over 4.6 times that cost in the form of higher lifetime earnings of recipients. This conclusion is based on a number of studies that explore different types of interventions lowering the cost of attending college, strengthening our belief in the reliability of this estimate. As long as these aid programs are not administratively burdensome on families (as the Pell Grant is), they appear to generate large returns in what would appear to be a lower risk investment.

We can categorize these programs, taking into consideration both the magnitude of the estimated return per $1,000 cost and the implicit standard error related to the number and size of the studies generating these estimated returns. Three programs jump out as the ones that show the most promise in terms of poverty reduction. College aid (with a simple interface) appears to be the intervention with one of the largest returns and one of the lower standard errors. We would place this intervention in this category. Similarly, early childhood education also belongs in this group. Although the returns are not estimated to be quite as large as some of the other interventions, there are a number of different types of studies that all support the existence of a sizable impact. Career Academies round out this group. These programs show very large returns and have been evaluated using credible methods and large samples. Our trade-off between risk and return would lean in the direction of supporting programs like these.

Other interventions certainly show promise. The estimated returns from Success for All and Teach for America are certainly impressive and suggest that reforming curriculum and improving teacher training may be very effective ways to proceed. The same may be said of mentoring programs like Big Brother Big Sister. Nevertheless, our risk averse nature suggests that we would be willing to support these programs much more strongly if there were more evidence supporting these findings.

References

Currie, J., and D. Thomas. 2001. Early test scores, socioeconomic status, school quality, and future outcomes. *Research in Labor Economics* 20:103–32.

Hanushek, E. A. 2006. School resources. In *Handbook of the economics of education,* ed. E. Hanushek and F. Welch, 865–908. Amsterdam: Elsevier.

Kemple, J. J., and C. J. Willner. 2008. *Career academies: Long-term impacts on labor market outcomes, educational attainment, and transitions to adulthood.* New York: MDRC.

Krueger, A. B. 2003. Economic considerations and class size. *Economic Journal* 113 (485): F34–F63.

14

Conclusions

Phillip B. Levine and David J. Zimmerman

Our goal in this volume has been to identify the childhood interventions that are most successful at alleviating subsequent poverty. That goal is, in the words of one referee of this volume, "outlandishly ambitious." Ambition, however, seems essential when 13 million children are living below the official poverty line. Each day that passes, money, time, and energy are devoted to reducing child poverty. "Bang for the buck" is likely to be a key factor in policy choice for poverty reduction. Dollars spent on low return interventions are dollars that could have done more to reduce poverty.

Our empirical approach, described in this volume, has been designed to guide an efficient allocation of resources in this endeavor. As a matter of practical necessity, these investment decisions need to be made using the best information currently available. The reality is that decisions need to be made now, not sometime in a utopian future when all of the relevant effects and interactions have been precisely pinned down. Indeed, we suspect that such a fully informed state of affairs will not be arriving anytime soon. That practical reality puts the burden on developing an approach that is no doubt prone to error, but that, hopefully, is reasonable and useful and, importantly, can be put into action now.

In this volume we have attempted to forge such an approach. We have assembled a comprehensive review of the existing base of knowledge on a wide range of interventions targeted at children, with the aim of raising their lifetime economic prospects. We have attempted to provide a rational sifting of the evidence, connecting the dots between interventions and

Phillip B. Levine is the Class of 1919 Professor and chair of department of economics at Wellesley College and a research associate of the National Bureau of Economic Research. David J. Zimmerman is a professor of economics and Orrin Sage Professor of Political Economy at Williams College and a research associate of the National Bureau of Economic Research.

outcomes—often forcing us to extrapolate the effects several years into the future. That indeed is an "ambitious" enterprise. We hope that we have conveyed throughout the volume that this enterprise has been undertaken with a spirit of deep humility. We began this project with our eyes wide open—with excitement about the potential benefits, but also painfully aware of the difficulties the analyses presented. While we may not have inventoried all of the potential pitfalls, we have tried to be as transparent in our choices as possible. That transparency is intended to allow future research to refine and improve on our efforts. Indeed, it is best to think of this first effort as a prototype upon which future efforts can extend and improve. Any refinements that advance our initial goal are zealously encouraged.

What, then, have we learned? First, and not surprisingly, some interventions show more promise than others. Several interventions convincingly show positive impacts on the human capital of children, while others do not. Early childhood education programs, mentoring programs, reductions in class sizes, curricular reforms, improved teacher training and increased teacher pay, increased college aid, and intensive vocational training can all be credibly linked to poverty reduction. On the other hand, parenting programs, school vouchers, after-school programs, dropout prevention programs, substance abuse programs, general jobs programs, and employment/training subsidies either show limited effectiveness in reducing poverty or lack a credible empirical basis from which to draw conclusions. Further, child care programs, child health programs, housing vouchers, or programs targeting teen pregnancy may demonstrate credible treatment effects, but have little impact on the human capital characteristics likely to raise a child's economic outcomes. As we have tried to convey, many of these interventions may make a great deal of sense as a matter of social policy. For example, teen pregnancy prevention programs can generate high benefits by way of reducing subsequent welfare expenditures. These programs, however, appear to have little impact in creating the human capital necessary to keep the program participants out of poverty.

The second conclusion (again, not surprising) is that there is considerable variation in the size of the returns generated by the competing investments. These returns, quantified as the impact on children's lifetime earnings resulting from a $1,000 investment in a given intervention, vary positively with the size of the intervention's effect on lifetime earnings and negatively with the cost of the intervention. Measuring the earnings impact per $1,000 investment across a heterogeneous mix of interventions is one of the signature contributions of this volume. Some interventions show great promise, whereas other investments may have significant impacts on a child's human capital but do not generate positive net benefits due to their cost. Based on our interpretation of the results presented in chapter 13, our view is that intensive early childhood education, college aid, and intensive vocational training appear to be the three interventions that have the largest effect, relative to their cost, in reducing subsequent poverty.

These results, of course, must be interpreted with caution. First and foremost, reducing poverty is only one of many goals in determining which public policies ought to be pursued. Clearly there are other important goals that must be taken into consideration. Our analysis has solely focused on poverty reduction.

Moreover, there are a variety of technical issues that need to be taken into consideration as well. For example, there are no standard errors around the benefit-cost ratios and simply sorting the interventions from high to low on this criterion would suggest a level of precision in the estimates that simply does not exist. Indeed, such a sorting would reflect the various strategic decisions that made this analysis possible. First, the set of interventions being considered is a result of the set of interventions that have been studied. Further, only those interventions that have been subjected to a rigorous evaluation are given consideration. There may be interventions that work, but that have not yet been attempted, have not been subjected to a credible evaluation, or by chance, have not demonstrated their efficacy in the existing evaluations. For some interventions we have the benefit of several well-structured evaluations. For other interventions we may know much less.

Further, there are methodological difficulties that are inherent in testing certain interventions. Universal programs, for example, cannot be randomly assigned. There is also a fundamental problem in that we often face a trade-off between observing a current intervention along with some necessarily short-term outcome versus an old intervention along with a good estimate of the impact on lifetime earnings. For example, we might observe an educational intervention today along with its impacts on the test scores of young children versus an educational intervention that occurred several decades earlier but that allows us to observe the resulting impact on lifetime earnings. Here we must consider the difficulties of extrapolating the effects of the current program versus the possible external invalidity of the older study. All of these considerations impact the set of interventions ultimately being considered.

There are other complications. The production of human capital may be a multiplicative process. For a child to thrive interventions might need to be sustained and not be piecemeal. Integrated programs offered with some continuity may have effects, whereas isolated programs may not. Interventions that are short-lived or of insufficient intensity may deliver only modest and perhaps fleeting effects. We might not be surprised to see the effects of preschool "fade away" if investments in the child end with that program. We might not be surprised to see limited effects from a low-budget training program targeting highly disadvantaged young adults. The returns from one intervention may also hinge on earlier investments. For example, the returns to curricular reforms may be affected by whether the child attended a high quality preschool and is "school-ready." Fortunately, the range of interventions we have considered can shed light on some of these concerns. Some programs are comprehensive. Some persist for several years. We do not know, however, what an optimal mix of programs might be. We are, ultimately, constrained by the interventions that have been constructed and evaluated.

It is also worth noting that just because a program has high net benefits does not mean it can easily be expanded. Expanding a program entails certain risks. Some programs may be difficult to "scale-up." It may be difficult, for example, to reduce class sizes while at the same time holding teacher quality constant. A successful comprehensive program may hinge on the ability to recruit extraordinary program administrators. Furthermore, such administrators may be in short supply.

Beyond these difficulties, our rankings depend on our mapping outcomes that occur early in life to economic outcomes that sometimes occur much later. It is a mildly heroic task to extrapolate improvements in test scores at a young age to improvements in lifetime earnings. There is limited research helping us here and we have attempted to fill the gap by providing estimates of our own. We also provide some evidence suggesting our estimates are sensible. Again, however, there is uncertainty around these estimates and this uncertainty is not reflected in our rankings. If we have overstated the effect of an early improvement on later outcomes then programs that occur earlier might have exaggerated benefits. Similarly, underestimates would provide muted benefits.

Another concern is that the populations served by the various studies differ in how poor they are. Programs like QOP or Job Partnership Training Act (JPTA) are targeted at very disadvantaged populations. They face a challenging task in delivering returns. Other programs such as mentoring have targeted somewhat less disadvantaged populations. The hurdle they face is lower if the returns associated with an intervention vary inversely with the challenges facing the targeted population.

Given these and a myriad of other possible concerns we suggest that the results be interpreted with caution. While there are no doubt flaws in our approach, we do believe that we have used the existing evidence to the best of its ability. One might reasonably approach the results with the aim of deciding where to place their bets in fighting child poverty. Some interventions look like goods bets. Some are risky. Some simply do not look like winners and, given the current state of our knowledge, should not be supported.

We should also note that our approach has been entirely empirical. Our findings have not been guided by any particular model of human development. The connection between intervention and outcome is, in effect, a black box. One fruitful extension would be to synthesize our findings with different models of child development to see which models are most consistent with the empirical evidence. Ultimately, it would be helpful to understand the mechanisms at play. A clearer understanding of how interventions affect the dynamics of family behavior, for example, would be useful. Indeed, an understanding of the mechanisms at play at the house, neighborhood, school, or neural level, for example, would allow better predictions regarding promising future interventions.

Perhaps the strongest conclusion we can draw is that additional evidence is needed. In an ideal world we would know the full range of plausible interventions; the nature of their interactions; their optimal target group, duration, and timing; and a complete understanding of the mechanisms at play, along with information of their long-run impact on economic outcomes. We would then select those programs so as to equate the marginal benefit of poverty reduction to the marginal cost. This ideal certainly suggests the value of panel data on a wide range of experimentally evaluated interventions, along with a theoretical framework for interpreting the findings. We are a long way from that ideal. Indeed, what often confronts us is an abundance of unconvincing research. Careful, systematic, experimental studies are needed to separate the wheat from the chaff. Such a process is incremental and slow. To that end, we hope this volume provides some useful guidance.

Contributors

Patricia M. Anderson
Department of Economics
Dartmouth College
6106 Rockefeller
Hanover, NH 03755-3514

Julia Burdick-Will
Department of Sociology
University of Chicago
1126 East 59th Street
Chicago, IL 60637

David Deming
National Bureau of Economic
  Research
1050 Massachusetts Avenue
Cambridge, MA 02138

Greg J. Duncan
Department of Education
University of California, Irvine
2001 Berkeley Place
Irvine, CA 92697-5500

Susan Dynarski
Ford School of Public Policy and
  School of Education
University of Michigan
735 South State Street
Ann Arbor, MI 48109-3091

Melissa Schettini Kearney
Department of Economics
University of Maryland
3105 Tydings Hall
College Park, MD 20742

Beau Kilmer
RAND
1776 Main Street, PO Box 2138
Santa Monica, CA 90407-2138

Robert LaLonde
The Harris School of Public Policy
The University of Chicago
1155 East 60th Street, Room 145
Chicago, IL 60637

Phillip B. Levine
Department of Economics
Wellesley College
106 Central Street
Wellesley, MA 02481

Susanna Loeb
524 CERAS, 520 Galvez Mall
Stanford University
Stanford, CA 94305

Bridget Terry Long
Harvard University
Graduate School of Education
Gutman Library 465
6 Appian Way
Cambridge, MA 02138

Jens Ludwig
The Harris School of Public Policy
The University of Chicago
1155 East 60th Street
Chicago, IL 60637

Katherine A. Magnuson
School of Social Work
University of Wisconsin-Madison
1350 University Avenue
Madison, WI 53706

Patrick J. McEwan
Department of Economics
Wellesley College
106 Central Street
Wellesley, MA 02481

Rosalie Liccardo Pacula
RAND Corporation
1776 Main Street, PO Box 2138
Santa Monica, CA 90407-2138

Lara Shore-Sheppard
Department of Economics
Williams College
24 Hopkins Hall Drive
Williamstown, MA 01267

Daniel Sullivan
Federal Reserve Bank of Chicago
230 South LaSalle Street
Chicago, IL 60604-1413

David J. Zimmerman
Department of Economics
Williams College
24 Hopkins Hall Drive
Williamstown, MA 01267

Author Index

Subject Index

Page numbers followed by f *or* t *refer to figures or tables, respectively.*